Beyond Methodological Nationalism

Routledge Research in Transnationalism

1 **New Transnational Social Spaces**
International Migration and
Transnational Companies in the
Early 21st Century
Edited by Ludger Pries

2 **Transnational Muslim Politics**
Reimagining the Umma
Peter G. Mandaville

3 **New Approaches to Migration?**
Transnational Communities and
the Transformation of Home
Edited by Nadje Al-Ali and Khalid Koser

4 **Work and Migration:**
Life and Livelihoods in a
Globalizing World
Edited by Ninna Nyberg Sorensen and Karen Fog Olwig

5 **Communities across Borders**
New Immigrants and
Transnational Cultures
Edited by Paul Kennedy and Victor Roudometof

6 **Transnational Spaces**
Edited by Peter Jackson, Phil Crang and Claire Dwyer

7 **The Media of Diaspora**
Edited by Karim H. Karim

8 **Transnational Politics**
Turks and Kurds in Germany
Eva Østergaard-Nielsen

9 **Culture and Economy in the Indian Diaspora**
Edited by Bhikhu Parekh, Gurharpal Singh and Steven Vertovec

10 **International Migration and the Globalization of Domestic Politics**
Edited by Rey Koslowski

11 **Gender in Transnationalism**
Home, Longing and Belonging
among Moroccan Migrant Women
Ruba Salih

12 **State/Nation/Transnation**
Perspectives on Transnationalism
in the Asia-Pacific
Edited by Brenda S. A. Yeoh and Katie Willis

13 **Transnational Activism in Asia**
Problems of Power and Democracy
Edited by Nicola Piper and Anders Uhlin

14 **Diaspora, Identity and Religion**
New Directions in
Theory and Research
Edited by Waltraud Kokot, Khachig Tölölyan and Carolin Alfonso

15 **Cross-Border Governance in the European Union**
Edited by Olivier Thomas Kramsch and Barbara Hooper

16 **Transnational Connections and the Arab Gulf**
Edited by Madawi Al-Rasheed

17 **Central Asia and the Caucasus**
Transnationalism and Diaspora
Edited by Touraj Atabaki and Sanjyot Mehendale

18 **International Migration and Security**
Opportunities and Challenges
Edited by Elspeth Guild and Joanne van Selm

19 **Transnational European Union**
Towards a Common Political Space
Edited by Wolfram Kaiser with Peter Starie

20 **Geopolitics of European Union Enlargement**
The Fortress Empire
Edited by Warwick Armstrong and James Anderson

21 **Rethinking Transnationalism**
The Meso-link of Organisations
Edited by Ludger Pries

22 **Theorising Transnational Migration**
The Status Paradox of Migration
Boris Nieswand

23 **Migration, Nation States, and International Cooperation**
Edited by Randall Hansen, Jobst Koehler and Jeannette Money

24 **Beyond Methodological Nationalism**
Research Methodologies for Cross-Border Studies
Edited by Anna Amelina, Devrimsel D. Nergiz, Thomas Faist and Nina Glick Schiller

Beyond Methodological Nationalism
Research Methodologies
for Cross-Border Studies

Edited by
Anna Amelina, Devrimsel D. Nergiz, Thomas Faist and Nina Glick Schiller

NEW YORK LONDON

First published 2012
by Routledge
711 Third Avenue, New York, NY 10017

Simultaneously published in the UK
by Routledge
2 Park Square, Milton Park, Abingdon, Oxfordshire OX14 4RN

First issued in paperback 2014

Routledge is an imprint of the Taylor and Francis Group, an informa company

© 2012 Taylor & Francis

The right of the editors to be identified as the authors of the editorial material, and of the authors for their individual chapters, has been asserted in accordance with sections 77 and 78 of the Copyright, Designs and Patents Act 1988.

All rights reserved. No part of this book may be reprinted or reproduced or utilised in any form or by any electronic, mechanical, or other means, now known or hereafter invented, including photocopying and recording, or in any information storage or retrieval system, without permission in writing from the publishers.

Trademark Notice: Product or corporate names may be trademarks or registered trademarks, and are used only for identification and explanation without intent to infringe.

Library of Congress Cataloging-in-Publication Data

Beyond methodological nationalism : research methodologies for cross-border studies / edited by Anna Amelina ... [et al.]
  p. cm. — (Routledge research in transnationalism ; 24)
Includes bibliographical references and index.
 1. Emigration and immigration—Social aspects—Research.
 2. Globalization—Social aspects—Research. 3. Nation-state and globalization—Research. 4. Transnationalism—Research. I. Amelina, Anna.
  JV6035.B49 2012
  320.54—dc23
  2011042462

ISBN: 978-0-415-89962-8 (hbk)
ISBN: 978-0-415-75457-6 (pbk)

Typeset in Sabon
by IBT Global.

Contents

List of Figures		xi
List of Tables		xiii
Preface and Acknowledgments		xv
1	Methodological Predicaments of Cross-Border Studies ANNA AMELINA, THOMAS FAIST, NINA GLICK SCHILLER AND DEVRIMSEL D. NERGIZ	1

PART I
Researching International Migration after Redefining Space and Mobility

2	Transnationality, Migrants and Cities: A Comparative Approach NINA GLICK SCHILLER	23
3	Transnational Migration and the Reformulation of Analytical Categories: Unpacking Latin American Refugee Dynamics in Toronto LUIN GOLDRING AND PATRICIA LANDOLT	41
4	Overcoming Methodological Nationalism in Migration Research: Cases and Contexts in Multi-Level Comparisons ANJA WEISS AND ARND-MICHAEL NOHL	65

PART II
Materiality, Culture and Ethnicity: Overcoming Pitfalls in Researching Globalization

5 Global Ethnography 2.0: From Methodological Nationalism to Methodological Materialism 91
ZSUZSA GILLE

6 Uncomfortable Antinomies: Going Beyond Methodological Nationalism in Social and Cultural Anthropology 111
DAVID N. GELLNER

7 Approaching Indigenous Activism from the Ground Up: Experiences from Bangladesh 129
EVA GERHARZ

PART III
Juxtapositions of Historiography after the Hegemony of the National

8 The Global, the Transnational and the Subaltern: The Limits of History beyond the National Paradigm 155
ANGELIKA EPPLE

9 Incorporating Comparisons in the Rift: Making Use of Cross-Place Events and Histories in Moments of World Historical Change 176
SANDRA CURTIS COMSTOCK

10 Interrogating Critiques of Methodological Nationalism: Propositions for New Methodologies 198
RADHIKA MONGIA

PART IV
Conclusions

11 Transnational Social Spaces: Between Methodological Nationalism and Cosmo-Globalism 219
LUDGER PRIES AND MARTIN SEELIGER

12 Concluding Remarks:
   Reconsidering Contexts and Units of Analysis   239
   THOMAS FAIST AND DEVRIMSEL D. NERGIZ

   Contributors   245
   Index   251

Figures

3.1	Nationality as a container.	53
3.2	National, intersectional and pan-ethnic organizing.	54
4.1	Relations between cases and contexts.	79
5.1	The relationship between the national, the social, and the material.	92

Tables

5.1	The Relationship between Geographical Scales and Levels of Abstraction in Different Methodological Traditions	100
11.1	An Integrative Typology of Approaches to Socio-geo-spaces	227
11.2	Three Types of International Research	233

Preface and Acknowledgments

This collected volume is the result of two international conferences that took place in April 2010 at Bielefeld University. Both conferences—"Beyond Methodological Nationalism: Researching Transnational Spaces, Cross-Border Diffusion and Transnational Histories" and "New Methodologies to Research on Transnational Migration: Identifying Problems and Solutions"—brought together scholars from a wide range of academic disciplines to discuss fundamental methodological problems of cross-border studies. To organize these conferences would not have been possible without the financial support of the Bielefeld Graduate School in History and Sociology at Bielefeld University (BGHS) as well as the German Research Foundation (DFG), to whom we are grateful.

As with the two conferences, this volume addresses two particular questions. First, it raises the question of analytical advantages emerging from the criticism of *methodological nationalism*. This question refers to the reliability of new epistemological assumptions about the relationship between space, the social and mobility, which call for a more sophisticated understanding of categories such as nation and space. Second, it addresses the subject of research organization that allows adequate studies on transnational migration, global transformation of culture and material artifacts as well as on cross-border history writing. In sum, the collection of cross-border methods in this volume is apt to stimulate the further development of methodologies beyond the national lens.

Last but not least, we would like to thank our contributors, who made this book possible. It was a great pleasure to read the commissioned chapters. We would also like to thank those whose efforts have helped to finish this book and whose work never gets to be seen: Michael Wittig, Heather Frederick, Jana Schäfer and Peter Lenco. Without them the whole book project would not have been as efficient and speedy. Finally, many thanks to Max Novick at Routledge; with his support this book has become reality.

Anna Amelina
Bielefeld University

Devrimsel D. Nergiz
Bielefeld University

Thomas Faist
Bielefeld University

Nina Glick Schiller
Manchester University

1 Methodological Predicaments of Cross-Border Studies

*Anna Amelina, Thomas Faist,
Nina Glick Schiller and Devrimsel D. Nergiz*

Which research methodologies are adequate for cross-border studies? How can cross-border relations be studied without falling into the trap of methodological nationalism? From which ways of reflection and strategies of contextualization do researchers benefit? Which units of analysis are most useful? To address these and related questions, this volume builds on the existing work in cross-border studies and on its criticism of the nation-centered research lens.

We define cross-border studies as a broad set of concepts addressing issues of cross-border mobility, global institutional restructuring, complex cultural transformations and cross-border histories. This introduction uses the term cross-border studies as an encompassing category to address a variety of cross-border relations. Khagram and Levitt (2008) prefer "transnational studies" to speak of similar concerns. Since this book aims to encourage an interdisciplinary dialogue among sociologists, social anthropologists and historians we view the term *cross-border studies* as the most appropriate common denominator.

The field of cross-border studies has certainly become multidimensional, expanding from an initial focus on international relations and transnational corporations (Nye and Keohane 1971) to discussions of global cities (Sassen 1991), global ethnoscapes (Appadurai 1996) and world society (Meyer et al. 1997). Cross-border studies have subsequently included the debates on transnational migration (Basch, Glick Schiller and Szanton Blanc 1994; Kearney 2000; Smith and Guarnizo 1998), cosmopolitanism (Beck and Sznaider 2006; Darieva, Glick Schiller and Gruner-Domic 2011) and transnational history writing (Bayly et al. 2006).

However, as the field of cross-border studies has grown and become more prominent, scholars engaged in its development have warned of its pitfalls and reflected on their own work as well as on the work of others (Levitt and Glick Schiller 2004; Brenner 2004; Faist 2000; Beck and

Sznaider 2006). The critique from within the field has focused on the continuing use of concepts of nation and the nation-state as the major point of reference, despite an effort to develop a scholarship and topics that were not bounded by these frameworks.

Recently, the criticism of *methodological nationalism* has been rapidly becoming en vogue within different disciplinary fields including sociology, social anthropology and historiography. Those deploying this term use it to question the nation-centered lens that defines nations as natural units of analysis. They also use it to question the nation-state focus that equates nation-states with the social unit of society. In fact they have been concerned with epistemology as well as with methodology. Moreover, the theorists of a transnational approach in migration studies (Basch, Glick Schiller and Szanton Blanc 1994; Kearney 1991, 2004; Rouse 1992) have reflected on the barriers imposed by the nation-bounded concept of society in some detail. In particular, Wimmer and Glick Schiller (2003) introduced the term methodological nationalism into the discussion of migration studies by identifying the three main gaps in social sciences research generally and in migration studies particularly:

1) *Omitting nationalism*, which overlooks the continuous relevance of nationalism in contemporary social life.
2) *Naturalizing nation-states*, which is an implicit strategy to see nation-state institutions as being the main social context when studying all the issues in question.
3) *Imposing territorial limitations*, which binds empirical research strategies to the territory of any selected nation-state (Wimmer and Glick Schiller 2003: 581).

They noted that methodological nationalism becomes particularly apparent in studies on geographical mobility and migration, where research questions are constrained because empirical data collection is confined to the territory of an immigration state. The goal of their critique has not been to negate the significance of the nation-state but to insure that nation-states are not the exclusive framework of study and analysis but one of several possible social contexts within which to empirically analyze social relations, institutions, cultures, spaces, ethnicities and histories.

It is worth remembering that challenges to the conceptual equation of societies and nation-states are not new in the social sciences. Influential historical and contemporary scholars in a lineage that begins with—Karl Marx and Frederick Engels (Marx and Engels 1848) and extends to Immanuel Wallerstein (1989) in sociology; Fernand Braudel (1980) in history; Paul Gilroy (1993) in cultural studies; Henry Lefebvre (1991) in social geography; Eric Wolf (1982), James Clifford and George Marcus (1986), Benedict Anderson (1991) Linda Basch, Nina Glick Schiller and Christina Szanton Blanc (1994) and Akhil Gupta and James Ferguson (1997a, 1997b) in social anthropology, to name only a few—have previously explored the ways social formations extend beyond national arrangements. However, the globalization debate in the 1990s (Appadurai 1996; Giddens 1994; Lash and Urry 1994; Robertson 1998; Swyngedouw 2004) renewed a critique of the theoretical foundations of many social science disciplines, resulting in a more detailed debate on the conceptual relationship between society, the nation-state and space.

In responding to the changing conditions and debates, the critique of methodological nationalism specifically built on already existing concerns voiced by Eric Wolf (1982), who used a billiard ball analogy to scrutinize the ways in which social sciences thought of nation-states as bounded units. In a similar way Martin Albrow (1995) criticized theories of society that assigned social practices in question to a particular national "container." Other contemporary critiques of boundedness use different vocabularies. For example, Neil Smith (2003) analyzed globalization as a complex spatial restructuring, namely the process of rescaling, which includes the national scale as only one of many spatial dimensions. In a similar vein, Neil Brenner reviewed the state-centrism of globalization studies, which defined space in an essentialist way "as timeless and static" (Brenner 2004: 38). Authors in a range of disciplines have been using varying yet intersecting terms to address the same problem.

However, the methodological implications resulting from the reexamination of methodological nationalism have only been partly applied to the empirical research methodologies of cross-border studies. To be more precise, some research strategies, such as cosmopolitan (Beck and Sznaider 2006; Darieva, Glick Schiller and Gruner-Domic 2011) and scale approaches (Brenner 1999), explicitly tried to overcome methodological nationalism in empirical studies, while others, such as global (Burawoy *et al.* 2000) and multi-sited ethnography (Marcus 1995), though implicitly rejecting methodological nationalism, did not manifestly address its underlying premises.

This volume exemplifies various ways through which the criticism of methodological nationalism can be turned into constructive research programs. The contributions shed light on how research methodologies, such as transnational and multi-scalar research programs and global and multi-sited ethnography, as well as the incorporating comparison approach and the entangled history approach address a research agenda beyond methodological nationalism.

Criticizing bounded thinking and conceptualizations of society and units of analysis centered on nations and nation-states, this volume builds on scholars who have worked across an array of disciplines including sociology, anthropology, historiography, geography, cultural studies and political science. All these disciplines, situated within particular national academic traditions, have approached issues of globalization with different theoretical emphases and methodological questions. To move past the disciplinary divides and their national myopia the contributions to this volume suggest transcending disciplinary boundaries in order to focus on particular research methodologies or research problems. Thus, this book combines various disciplinary logics to broaden the debate on methodologies of globalization and transnationalization, to identify domains for methodological challenges and innovations and to suggest some ways to overcome *container* methodology. In doing so, the volume critically reflects on the conceptual relationship between social units, space, nation and nation-state in three thematic areas: migration studies, globalization studies and cross-border historiography. In sum, the volume assesses various research methodologies and discloses how they benefit from overcoming nationally bounded thinking. The next section provides insights into the main methodological challenges of cross-border studies, and the subsequent part highlights particular methodological innovations featured in this volume.

METHODOLOGICAL INNOVATIONS CROSSING DISCIPLINARY BOUNDARIES

Immanuel Wallerstein (1976) argues that occasional review of established methodologies within social sciences is hardly an exceptional event. On the contrary, the revision and redefinition of conventional research strategies usually accompanies scientific transformations.[1] From this point of view, one could say that the globalization debate has engendered a reinterpretation and redefinition of terms paving the way for the current critique of methodological nationalism.

In particular, globalization debates arose in relationship to global economic restructuring of capital production, including the privatization of public resources and the ensuing changes of state-based regulatory regimes. It was in this context that scholars engaged in the critique of methodological nationalism (Beck and Sznaider 2006; Chernilo 2006; Wimmer and Glick Schiller 2003), identifying the epistemological foundations that have guided much of social science research and calling for revisions in both methodologies and paradigms. They took a dialectical approach, noting that it is important to distinguish between the changing objective conditions in the world on the one hand and the subjectivity of researchers and their paradigms on the other hand in order to explore the interrelationship between them. This perspective complements those who critique research that equates territorial and social entities and views their interrelationship as static (Brenner 2004; Pries 2008).

This volume builds from current critical pespectives to demonstrate how the empirical research strategies of cross-border studies profit from the critique of nationally bounded thinking. To achieve this goal researchers of cross-border relations have to deal with two particular questions: First, how can relevant units of analysis be specified while studying processes of transnationalization and globalization? Second, how can the units of analysis in question be contextualized without presuming the nation-state to be the only relevant societal and spatial context? Accordingly, cross-border studies do not seek to define *the* unit of analysis or *the* relevant context; this would be an expression of static thinking. There cannot be only one unit of analysis or one relevant context since cross-border studies focus on the intersection of various scales. Addressing these two subjects in the following subsections, we highlight the relevant methodological strategies.

Defining Units of Analysis after Methodological Nationalism

In sociological globalization studies the challenge to identify adequate units of analysis became explicit as a consequence of the controversy between the network and world polity approaches. The first, the network approach to globalization (Castells 1996; Lash and Urry 1994), indicates mechanisms by which social realities and practices are no longer confined within or defined by territorial limitations in general and from nation-state territories in particular. Society is, therefore, not reduced to the nation-state institutions but defined as built by social networks. The second position, represented by the world polity approach (Meyer 1999), views the globe as encompassed in a single overarching system. Although this theory reflects on nation-building as a historically specific process, theorists working in the frames of this approach predominantly view space and geographic mobility as unchanging physical properties that need not be the concern of social theory.

While the network approach eschews fixed categorizations and stresses the novelty of hybridity and mixity in a world of constant motion, it leaves unchallenged the notions that in the past ethnic and national identities were fixed. Overgeneralizing deterritorialization it overlooks processes of spatialized capital accumulation (Massey 2005; Taylor and Flint 2006) as well as the global, neoliberal restructuring of spatial scales. The world polity approach, despite its focus on global processes, implicitly presupposes state-centric views, taking for granted that the division of populations by national and ethnic categorizations is the main organizing principle. This is because its state-centrism dictates a view that social identities are mutually exclusive, since they are still based on national institutions.

Both lines of argument fail to define units of analysis, which encompass identities, networks, organizations or institutions that are multiple, fluid, spatially constituting and constituted yet span geography and time. Transnational spaces (Faist 2000; Pries 2008), transnational social fields (Basch, Glick Schiller and Szanton Blanc 1994; Glick Schiller 2003), but also postcolonial (Chakrabarty 2000) and cosmopolitan (Beck and Grande 2010) approaches provide alternative definitions of units of analysis general enough to think of social entities as territorialized and deterritorialized as well as nationalized and cosmopolitan at the same time. Consequently, these approaches suggest defining transnational and cosmopolitan relations, transnational networks, organizations and institutions, and postcolonial hierarchies of power as possible units of analysis. Nina Glick Schiller (Chapter 2 in this volume) discusses globe spanning strategies of place-making[2] and the transnational linkages of cities as possible units of analysis. In a similar vein, Luin Goldring and Patricia Landolt (Chapter 3 in this volume) identify transnational migrant organizations as relevant units of analysis. The definition of the units of analysis in these cases is contingent and guided by the research questions.

In a similar examination of units of analysis in studies of global cultural transformations (Appadurai 1996; Bhabha 1994; Hannerz 1996), scholars have refused to view culture as nationally, ethnically or territorially bounded. These scholars define units of analysis as hybrid scapes or creolized or cosmopolitan cultural worlds. At the same time, their theorization has been constrained by an implicit projection of internally homogeneous original cultures that constitute the components of subsequent cultural hybridity. However, these scholars also seek to explore and to denaturalize the interrelation between global and local cultural dynamics. In this volume two contributions by David Gellner and Eva Gerharz address the methodological and theoretical challenges that globalization processes raise for studies of cultural transformations. David Gellner (Chapter 6) highlights the main pitfalls of empirical studies of cultural globalization. In particular, he questions their implicit holist and universalist notions that presume cultures to be coherent and inclusive entities. Eva Gerharz's case study (Chapter 7) offers insights into the intersection between local indigenous activism in Bangladesh and the global cultural repertoire of belonging. In doing so, she analyzes how ethnic belonging is socially produced at global and local socio-spatial scales simultaneously.

These developments complement new approaches to history such as transnational (Conrad 2009; Gabaccia and Iacovetta 2002; Rüger 2010), postcolonial (Chakrabarty 2000), subaltern (Chatterjee 2006) and entangled history (Werner and Zimmermann 2002) that similarly address the need to formulate adequate units of analysis. As Angelika Epple (Chapter 8 in this volume) indicates, these approaches build on the plural and fragmented quality of history itself, of historiographic writing and of relevant historic data (Chakrabarty 2000; Wolf 1982). Breaking with the definition of national history as the main unit of analysis, they focus on the relationship between the processes of nationalization, (de-)territorialization and cross-border linkages (see for example the contribution by Radhika Mongia in Chapter 10 of this volume). In short, after insisting that social boundaries of societies, cultures or civilizations are permeable and mutually constitutive, the scholars of cross-border histories define units of analysis as *interwoven* and *shared* histories.

In sum, cross-border studies offer multiple ways to identify units of analysis and reject a research paradigms that portrays the world as naturally divided into national societies. This volume attempts to deepen the critique of methodological nationalism by indicating the need simultaneously to deconstruct nationalism, nation-states, national cultures and national histories and to avoid essentializing transnational relations, hybrid cultural entities, non-national histories, mobility and networked connections (Bauböck and Faist 2010). As Jansen and Löfving (2009: 5) have noted, it is important to "approach the key concepts of sedentarist and placeless paradigms—including territorialization and deterritorialization, and emplacement and displacement—as empirical issues to be investigated rather than as philosophical assessments about what characterizes our age." Thus, by defining their units of analysis relative to their problem, scholars of cross-border relations are able to avoid the tendency toward bounded, static thinking while not disregarding the processes that actually construct emplacement, territorialization and the construction of ethnic, national and diasporic identities.

Contextualizing Cross-Border Relations after the Diagnosis of Fragmentation of Space, Cultures and History

The debate on units of analysis is strongly connected to the question of how to contextualize empirical studies on transnational and global phenomena. We argue that neither the paradigm of rhizomic, infinite networks nor the world as a system or society provides an adequate framework within which to conduct empirical research. Instead, we think that previously mentioned concepts such as transnational field, transnational spaces, and postcolonial and cosmopolitan arenas are sufficient to contextualize research questions because they encompass cross-border social relations without normatively assigning them a global saliency or universality (Faist 2000: 210–11). Moreover, these concepts situate research within both geographic and cyber-spatiality, even as they encompass the physical mobility of individuals and objects.

However, these concepts should be complemented by explicit steps that contextualize prospective empirical studies. The contribution by Nina Glick Schiller (Chapter 2 in this volume) directly addresses this issue by discussing the processes of city-making and the role of migrants in these processes. This approach to locality views place-making as a product of the multiple simultaneous constitutions of geographic scales (Glick Schiller and Çağlar 2009, 2011). In particular it addresses processes by which migrants build an array of pathways that allow their incorporation into the local social and institutional networks of the specific city, as well as connecting that city to the constituting processes of the nation, the region and the world. According to this methodological approach, the researcher does not assume that a city is a bounded unit but rather as an entry point within which to study unequal networks of power.

Besides the city and place-making approach, multi-sited ethnography (Marcus 1995; Falzon 2009) that traces the mutual constitution of multiple sites of connection and belonging is one of the best candidates for contextualizing empirical research. It prompts scholars to literally *follow* trajectories of geographical mobility of individuals, ideas or artifacts. In the first place, this strategy enables researchers to access those multi-sited social contexts, which are constituted and remade within cross-border networks, organizations or institutions. Moreover, this method encourages researchers to become mobile in order to contextualize cross-border relations.

A different strategy is proposed by the global ethnography approach that addresses the embeddedness of small-scale interactions within the global context. In particular, the early versions of global ethnography (Burawoy *et al.* 2000) sought to study global transformation on the local scale, paying special attention to the three dimensions of globalization: global forces, global connections and global imaginations. Some later attempts incorporated scale and place-making concepts in this research program (Gille and Ó Riain 2002). On the one hand, global ethnography is general enough to contextualize studies on cultural transformations by reconstructing the fragmentation and fluidity of cultural dynamics (Gellner, Chapter 6 in this volume). On the other hand, it is instructive for analyzing how globalization is co-constituted by assemblages of human agencies *and* material artifacts (Zsusza Gille, Chapter 5 in this volume). Building on Bruno Latour's (2005) theoretical framework, the latter version of global ethnography considers the circulation of material artifacts as relevant for contextualizing empirical studies on cross-border relations.

In addition to the previously mentioned strategies, scholars of cross-border histories not only consider socio-spatial and cultural but also time dimensions in their strategies of research contextualization. In particular, a new generation of historiographers criticize understandings of time/history as irreversible and fluid as contrasted with space as static and inflexible (see Epple, Chapter 8 in this volume). Reinterpreting the teleological perspective on time they increasingly identify space as a socially produced entity that is flexible and changeable throughout time (Bayly *et al.* 2006; Tyrell 2007). Instead of defining a spatial container as a context, they analyze historically specific strategies of territorialization and nationalization (Feldman-Bianco 2001; Patel 2007, 2008; Schenk 2002). For example, the contribution by Radhika Mongia (Chapter 10 in this volume) explores the political strategies of nationalization of an empire in the context of labor migration from colonial India to Canada at the beginning of the 20th century.

To conclude, utilizing their empirical studies representatives of different disciplines are joined in questioning container thinking. As possible relevant contexts, emplaced transnational fields of unequal power, transnational spaces, cosmopolitan arenas and cross-border histories are reconstructed by relating to the mobility experiences of actors and objects on the one hand, and by focusing on social strategies of doing space and doing entanglement on the other.

Research Strategies between Positional and Theoretic Reflexivity

Research strategies to define units of analysis as well as to contextualize empirical studies particularly profit from the reflexive turn within social sciences (Clifford 1988; Marcus and Fischer 1986). The contributions in this volume primarily build on two different kinds of reflexivity—the positional and the theoretical. Positional reflexivity (Marcus 1998) reveals how the researcher's subjectivity and positionality shape the research. This type of self-questioning highlights how each author's cultural and historical background frames her or his research on cross-border relations. For example, David Gellner (Chapter 6 in this volume) points to the central determinants of a researcher's positionality, including gender, ethnicity, age and whether the research is done collaboratively.

Other contributors in this volume offer a theory-based reflexivity (Bourdieu and Waquant 1992; Foley 2002) that discloses the disciplinary or interdisciplinary scientific conditions of knowledge production. For example, contributions in this volume by Nina Glick Schiller (Chapter 2), Luin Goldring and Patricia Landolt (Chapter 3), as well as Radhika Mongia (Chapter 10) interrogate the epistemological underpinnings and implications of nationally bounded knowledge production in the social sciences. In addition, Angelika Epple (Chapter 8) reflects on the asymmetries of discursive power in the representations of cross-border histories.

TOWARD A METHODOLOGICAL TOOL FOR CROSS-BORDER STUDIES

By building on a cross-disciplinary outlook, the authors in this volume are able to reinterpret some of the central methodological questions that confront cross-border research. For example, they ask about the relationship betwen theories, methodologies, methods and findings of cross-border studies. Which definitions of contexts and units of analysis are most appropriate for the task at hand? Which new forms of data collection and data interpretation are appropriate? How do social scientists justify new methodological approaches and concepts?

In general, the strategies used attempt to avoid reference to the taken-for-granted concepts of nation and nation-state in studies of international migration and in research on global cultural and material transformations, as well as in the analysis of cross-border histories. In doing so, they combine the logic of concrete empirical field studies with the logic of abstract scientific arguments. Most authors in this volume begin their empirical investigations with *bottom up* ethnography of particular cross-border relations and practices. This grounded approach to theory facilitates unexpected research results whose generalizabilty can then be explored as an aspect of theory building.

Part I, "Researching International Migration after Redefining Space and Mobility," includes contributions by Nina Glick Schiller (Chapter 2), Luin Goldring and Patricia Landolt (Chapter 3) and Anja Weiß and Arnd-Michael Nohl (Chapter 4). Reinterpreting a conceptual relationship between space, the social context and geographic mobility, they introduce research designs and strategies that escape the container thinking that generally confines empirical studies on international migration. The particular question of these chapters is how to contextualize the current empirical studies on international migration without falling into the trap of methodological nationalism.

In her contribution Nina Glick Schiller addresses this issue by focusing on the process of city-making and on the impact of migrants to the transnational embeddedness of cities. However, *city* is not analyzed as a container or a fixed context, but as an entry point for the empirical study (Glick Schiller and Çağlar 2009, 2011). Using the results of her research in Manchester (UK), Dallas-Fort Worth (US), and Halle/Saale (Germany), Glick Schiller outlines a comparative approach to understand how international migration and city-making mutually influence each other. Relating theory and methodology, she argues that in order to be able to encompass the processes of territorialization and deterritorialization, the city can never be reduced to a context. On the contrary, the researcher must ethnographically examine the intersections of hierarchies of different forms of power that both shape and are shaped by migrants as they participate within the emplacement of transnational social fields in specific localities.

In a similar vein, Luin Goldring and Patricia Landolt pay particular attention to contextualization strategies that overcome nation-state-centered research limitations. The authors present a fine-grained reflection about their large-scale comparative project on Latin American migrants' incorporation in Canada and these migrants' respective transnational engagements. The particular project's focus was on the Latin-American migrants' organizational landscape in Canada. In the first step, Goldring and Landolt reformulate their initial definition of the "context of departure", revising their original assumptions about the similarity of places of emigration. In the second step, they illustrate how to overcome the trap of overgeneralizing the context of destination by reflecting on their original spatial-temporal assumptions and by suggesting one view of the "context of reception . . . as both an independent and dependent variable" (Goldring and Landolt, Chapter 3 of this volume). Finally, Goldring and Landolt question the initial study's interest in selecting "groups of migrants" according to their national background using cultural and intersectional approaches.

Methodological Predicaments of Cross-Border Studies 11

The exploration of the relationship between contexts and units of analysis is continued by Anja Weiß and Arnd-Michael Nohl, who suggest a rotational method to extract the relevance of contexts for units of analysis in question. Building on a large-scale and internationally comparative research project on highly skilled migrants, Weiß and Nohl propose a multi-level comparative research design to reconstruct the relevance of the nation-state, the nation-state system and transnational contexts on pathways of migrant integration into the labor market. The authors explore how to design a typology of "case groups" (for example, groups of migrants which serve as units of analysis) without immediate reference to a national context. In order to highlight the relevance of potential contexts they suggest sampling cases according to both a "bottom up (ethnographic)" approach and the "top down (country-comparative)" (Weiß and Nohl, Chapter 4 of this volume) method. The novelty of this approach is a "systematic variation of context relations" (Weiß and Nohl, Chapter 4 of this volume), which allows researchers to empirically reconstruct the impact of the national context, the nation-state system *and* the transnational large-scale social context on the relevant groups of migrants.

Part II, "Materiality, Culture and Ethnicity: Overcoming Pitfalls in Researching Globalization," move from strategies with which to contextualize migration and geographic mobility to methodologies and methods to contextualize cross-border material and cultural transformations. Both Zsuzsa Gille (Chapter 5) and David Gellner (Chapter 6) addresss the initial efforts of Michael Burawoy and his colleagues to create global ethnography that discloses local experiences of global transformations (Burawoy *et al*. 2000). However, while Gille builds on Actor-Network-Theory (Latour 2005) to revise its idealist notions, Gellner interrogates global ethnography from the social and cultural anthropological point of view.

Zsuzsa Gille calls for methodological concreteness in studies of global transformations, arguing that the task of combating methodological nationalism lies not only in unraveling the social from the national but at the same time in "entanglement" of the social with the material. Gille attempts to replace methodological idealism, which only focuses on the social, with methodological materialism, which includes nonhuman actors in the analysis of globalization. Using the example of the Hungarian paprika ban in 2004, Gille argues that the new version of global ethnography—Global Ethnography 2.0—aims "not to switch the levels of analysis (from local to the global or from micro to macro) but rather to switch levels of abstraction, that is shifting from abstract to concrete" (Gille, Chapter 5 of this volume).

While Gille's chapter examines the challenges of contextualizing the research on global material transformations, Gellner combines contextualization with the question of how the research is organized. Addressing the challenges of researching cultural globalization, he points to the paradoxical logic of ethnographic studies on globalization. This resuls from the contradiction between the holistically oriented face-to-face methods of social and cultural anthropologists, which embrace the danger of methodological nationalism as well as methodological tribalism, and the global dynamics that these researchers seek to explore. To address this methodological dilemma, Gellner counterposes the multi-sited and global ethnography approaches. The first is seen as a research method that enables researchers to adjust ethnographical inquiry to "the new connectivity of the wider world" (Gellner, Chapter 6 of this volume), when the choice is no longer to construct the empirical field by clearly defined *sites*. The second is, on the contrary, defined as a broader research program for qualitative methodologies to understand the complex dynamics of globalization. In short, Gellner's contribution argues that the contradiction between the fragmentation of current anthropologists' research fields and the still-present holistic way of doing ethnography is an unavoidable tension that, if it cannot be overcome, must be at least reflected upon.

The question of how to contextualize global dynamics within empirical research is also the subject of Eva Gerharz's contribution in Chapter 7 of this volume. Building on elements of the global ethnography approach previously discussed by David Gellner, she explores the transformation of indigenous activism within both global and local indigenous activities. Gerharz argues that to understand the formation of a global indigenous movement we need research methodologies that conquer the simplistic dichotomization between the local and the global (Goodale and Merry 2007). Building on the results of her empirical study conducted in Bangladesh, Gerharz suggests taking a closer look at how indigenous activism varies across socio-spatial scales such as global, national and local. To reconstruct the intersection between these scales Gerharz analyzes processes of vernacularization within local arenas, the variety of knowledge domains relevant for indigenous activism and the relevant ethnic boundary-making. To conclude, Gerharz deploys empirical techniques that go beyond the understanding of indigenous activism as a local phenomenon.

The search for methodological concreteness is continued in the subsequent contributions of Part III, "Juxtapositions of Historiography after the Hegemony of the National." The chapters by Angelika Epple (Chapter 8), Sandra Comstock (Chapter 9) and Radhika Mongia (Chapter 10) question the exclusive focus of nation-centered history writing by denationalizing the research vocabulary. In particular, they deal with the question of how to legitimate cross-border and cross-place histories as appropriate units of analysis for history writing.

According to Angelika Epple the concept of entangled histories provides a good alternative to define the unit of analysis. To establish her argument she critically compares approaches such as a) world history, b) transnational and entangled history and c) post-colonial and subaltern history. While world history attempts history writing of the world as a coherent unit und includes universalizing notions (for criticism see Therborn 2000), the transnational and entangled history approaches point to the idea of shared history (Bayly *et al.* 2006). On the contrary, post-colonial history approaches highlight the impacts of history writing from the prospective of the colonial powers (Chakrabarty *et al.* 2007). Epple works to combine the entangled and post-colonial history approaches to design the unit of analysis. While the first approach allows researchers to consider the networked quality of history, the latter discloses methodological problems resulting from the definitory power inherent in scientific writing. Finally, Epple introduces micro-history and translocality approaches that enhance productive writing on entangled histories.

In her contribution Sandra Curtis Comstock continues to debate research programs that validate cross-place histories as relevant units of analysis. According to the author the method of incorporating comparisons is productive in reconstructing the meaning of cross-border interactions for changes in world history. Thus, the method is truly relevant even beyond the scope of the world systems theory from which it originates (McMichael 1990). To highlight its benefits Comstock contrasts the incorporating comparisons method with the hermeneutic, the experimental and the encompassing comparisons approaches. While hermeneutic comparisons (Steinmetz 2007) attempt to identify the particularities of different local histories in order to discover their internal peculiarities, experimental comparisons (Mahoney 2001) contrast local histories to understand the corresponding dynamics of historical transformations. Besides that, the encompassing comparisons approach (Tilly 1984) analyzes historical changes occurring within predefined national containers against the background of general historical patterns in the encompassing world system. In contrast to those approaches the incorporating comparison method is able to incorporate both cross-place interactions and general world reconfigurations as equally relevant to the analysis of world historical change "without treating nation-states as fixed, self-perpetuating entities" (Comstock, Chapter 9 of this volume). In short, this method does not only suggest viewing cross-place histories as units of analysis, but also historicizes them.

Finally, this section is complemented by Radhika Mongia's contribution in Chapter 10, which demonstrates how to historicize the process of nationalization in a concrete empirical study. Presenting a study of labor migration from India to Canada at the beginning of the 20th century, Mongia sheds light on how and by which social conditions cross-border migration became nationalized. Addressing this point, Mongia builds on Rogers Brubaker's "eventful approach" to illustrate the contingent emergence of nationhood (1996). Moreover, Mongia calls for a historicization of state formation enabling scholars to abandon nation-centered terms typically deployed in historiography. Noting that the concept of empire-state is supportive to her research, she presents "an anti-teleological, yet spatiotemporal analysis" (see Chapter 10). Finally, the author historicizes not only national but also transnational formations by reflecting on the categorization of cross-border relations and enterprises.

In summary, all three contributions offer ways to avoid teleological and universalizing arguments in studies of cross-border histories. However, these chapters do not simply stress the necessity to historicize comparisons and nationhood, but provide conceptual alternatives, strategies and techniques for achieving this goal. Only by reflexively theory building can scholars who denationalize history writing also prevent cross-border histories from becoming a new taken-for-granted orthodoxy.

Part IV, "Conclusions," includes two contributions providing classifications of cross-border studies that aim to clarify differences between the proposed methodological strategies. Chapter 11 by Ludger Pries and Martin Seeliger suggests a typology of international studies distinguishing between the cross-national comparison, world-systems and transnational studies approaches. They build on two concepts of space dominant in social sciences—the substantial (or essentialist) and the relational (or nonessentialist) approaches—to classifying cross-border research. Pries and Seelger insist that transnationalist manner of research contextualization builds a the relational optic, while the world-systems and cross-national comparison approaches in the main replicate the essentialist understanding of space. The authors conclude that empirical studies on cross-border relations profit from reflecting on spatial concepts, because this encourages researchers to clearly contextualize research questions and units of analysis.

The final remarks by Thomas Faist and Devrimsel D. Nergiz briefly outline a variety of ways by which the collected contributions conceptualize the relationship between units of analysis and contexts of studies. In addition, they state that cross-border studies methodological tools serve as an instrument of critique to "contest" container-bounded thinking. Finally, they conclude by pointing out categorical boundaries not being addressed by the contributors.

CONCLUSION

The point of departure for this volume is that the globalization debate has produced new conceptual challenges in the social sciences. Furthermore we observed that these theoretical innovations require new empirical research strategies. It is useful to conclude by commenting on the epistemological status of the methodological strategies presented.

As various theorist of science have stressed, scientific knowledge as socially produced (Foucault 1966; Kuhn 1962) and theory, methodology and empirical research findings are reciprocally related. To put it in different words, scientific methods and methodologies are not a neutral medium that facilitate the acquisition of objective data from the nonscientific world because all knowledge production reflects the social positioning of the observer. As outlined in the previous sections, the chapters collected in this volume build on reflexive approaches to scientific knowledge production

(Clifford 1988; Marcus and Fischer 1986). Consequently, the contributions consider the contingency of social science research on the one hand and call for positional and theoretic reflexivity in empirical studies on the other.

First, the reflexive position allows reinterpretation of the units of analysis that were formerly seen as fixed, bounded entities such as national or ethnic groups, or cultures or histories that needed to be researched on only one particular—the global, the local, the transnational or the national—scale. Debating on units of analysis from different disciplinary perspectives, this volume sheds light on how research perspectives and research questions change when scholars move beyond nationally bounded thinking. Secondly, because it examines how social scientists produce research contexts and field sites, the reflexive angle encourages a re-examination of the contextualization strategies of migration studies, studies of global cultural and material transformations as well as studies of cross-border histories.

In fact the main thrust of this volume is that, on the basis of the critique of methodological nationalism, it reflexively presents current strategies and methods, including transnational, multi-scalar and cosmopolitan perspecives, as well as global and multi-sited ethnography, the incorporating comparisons approach and the entangled history program. In other words, the contributions do not seek to develop a superior knowledge, but to stimulate new research questions and research outcomes. At the same time, they introduce scientific vocabulary for studies on globalization and transnationalization while being aware of their own limitations.

NOTES

1. For Wallerstein (1976) the scientific transformation results from the long-term competition between two methodological stands, a nomothetic and an ideographic approach. While the former position is characterized by a tendency to generalize phenomena and explore objective regularities and laws, the latter aims at specification of phenomena by interpreting them as contingent and subjectively constructed.
2. The term 'space' highlights the general logic of spatial production, which is constituted by the nexus between social practices and material artefacts. At the same time, the term 'place' points to a particularity or uniqueness of spatial arrangements, which result from how they are lived in and experienced. According to David Harvey (1985) scholars profit from conceptualizing the link between space and place as a dialectical relationship between universal forms of spatial production and a particular distinctiveness of lived places.

REFERENCES

Albrow, M. (1995) *The Global Age: State and Society beyond Modernity*, Cambridge: Polity Press.
Anderson, B.R. (1991) *Imagined Communities: Reflections on the Origin and Spread of Nationalism*, London, New York: Verso.

Appadurai, A. (1996) *Modernity at Large. Cultural Dimensions of Globalization*, Minneapolis: University of Minnesota Press.
Basch, L., Glick Schiller, N. and Szanton Blanc, C. (1994) *Nations Unbound. Transnational Projects, Postcolonial Predicaments and Deterritorialized Nation-States*, Amsterdam: Gordon and Breach Science Publishers.
Bauböck, R. and Faist, T. (2010) *Diaspora and Transnationalism. Concepts, Theories and Methods*, Amsterdam: Amsterdam University Press.
Bayly, C.A., Beckert, S., Connelly, M., Hofmeyr, I., Kozol, W. and Seed, P. (2006) "AHR conversation: On transnational history", *American Historical Review*, 111(5): 1442.
Beck, U. and Grande, E. (2010) "Varieties of second modernity: The cosmopolitan turn in social and political theory and research", *The British Journal of Sociology*, 61(3): 409–43.
Beck, U. and Sznaider, N. (2006) "Unpacking cosmopolitanism for the social sciences: A research agenda", *British Journal of Sociology*, 57: 1–23.
Bhabha, H. (1994) *The Location of Culture*, London, New York: Routledge.
Bourdieu, P. and Waquant, L.D. (1996 [1992]) *Reflexive Anthropologie*, Frankfurt/Main: Suhrkamp.
Braudel, F. (1969) *Ecrits sur l'histoire*, trans. S. Reynolds (1980) *Fernand Braudel: On History*, Chicago: University of Chicago Press.
Brenner, N. (1999) "Beyond state-centrism? Space, territoriality and geographical scale in globalization studies", *Theory and Society*, 28: 39–78.
—— (2004) *New State Spaces: Urban Governance and the Rescaling of Statehood*, Oxford, New York: Oxford University Press.
Brubaker, R. (1996) *Nationalism Reframed: Nationhood and the National Question in the New Europe*, Cambridge: Cambridge University Press.
Burawoy, M., Blum, J.A., Sheba, G., Gille, Z., Gowan, T., Haney, L., Klawiter, M., Lopez, S.H., Ó Riain, S. and Thayer, M. (2000) *Global Ethnography: Forces, Connections, and Imaginations in a Postmodern World*, Berkeley, Los Angeles: University of California Press.
Castells, M. (1996) *The Rise of the Network Society. The Information Age: Economy, Society and Culture*, Vol. I, Cambridge, MA, Oxford, UK: Blackwell.
Chakrabarty, D. (2000) *Provincializing Europe: Postcolonial Thought and Historical Difference*, Princeton, NJ: Princeton University Press.
——, Majumdar, R. and Sartori A. (2007) *From the Colonial to the Postcolonial: India and Pakistan in Transition*, Oxford: Oxford University Press.
Chatterjee, P. (2006) "A brief history of subaltern studies", in G. Budde, S. Conrad and V. Janz (eds) *Transnationale Geschichte: Themen, Tendenzen und Theorien*, Göttingen: Vandenhoeck & Ruprecht.
Chernilo, D. (2006) "Social theory's methodological nationalism. Myth and reality", *European Journal of Social Theory*, 9: 5–22.
Clifford, J. (1988) *The Predicament of Culture: Twentieth Century Ethnography, Literature and Art*, Cambridge, MA: Harvard University Press.
—— and Marcus, G.E. (eds) (1986) *Writing Culture. The Poetics and Politics of Ethnography*, Berkeley: University of California Press.
Conrad, S. (2009) "Double marginalization. A plea for a transnational perspective on german history", in H.G. Haupt and J. Kocka (eds) *Comparative and Transnational History. Central European Approaches and New Perspectives*, New York: Berghahn Books.
Darieva, T., Glick Schiller, N. and Gruner-Domic, S. (2011) *Cosmopolitan Sociability. Locating Transnational Religious and Diasporic Networks*, London: Routledge.
Faist, T. (2000) *The Volume and Dynamics of International Migration and Transnational Social Spaces*, Oxford: Clarendon Press.

Falzon, M. (ed) (2009) *Multi-Sited Ethnography: Theory, Praxis and Locality in Contemporary Research*, Farnham, UK, Burlington, VT: Ashgate Publishing.

Feldman-Bianco, B. (2001) "Brazilians in Portugal, Portuguese in Brazil: Cultural constructions of sameness and difference", *Identities: Global Studies in Culture and Power*, 8(4): 607–50.

Foley, D.E. (2002) "Critical ethnography. The reflexive turn", *International Journal of Qualitative Studies of Education*, 15(4): 469–90.

Foucault, M. (1970 [1966]) *The Order of Things: An Archaeology of the Human Sciences*, New York: Phanteon Books.

Gabaccia, D. and Iacovetta, F (eds) (2002) *Women, Gender, and Transnational Lives: Italian Women around the World*, Buffalo, NY: University of Toronto Press.

Giddens, A. (1994) *Beyond Left and Right. The Future of Radical Politics*, Cambridge: Polity Press.

Gille, Z. and Ó Riain, S. (2002) "Global ethnography", *Annual Review of Sociology*, 28: 271–95.

Gilroy, P. (1993) *The Black Atlantic: Modernity and Double Consciousness*, Cambridge, MA: Harvard University Press.

Glick Schiller, N. (2003) "The centrality of ethnography in the study of transnational migration: Seeing the wetland instead of the swamp", in N. Foner (ed) *American Arrivals*, Santa Fe, NM: School of American Research.

—— and Çağlar, A. (2009) "Towards a comparative theory of locality in migration studies: Migrant incorporation and city scale", *Journal of Ethnic and Migration Studies*, 35(2): 177–202.

—— and Çağlar, A. (eds) (2011) *Locating Migration: Rescaling Cities and Migrants*, Ithaca, NY: Cornell University Press.

Goodale, M. and Merry, S.E. (eds) (2007) *The Practice of Human Rights: Taking Law between the Global and the Local*, Cambridge: Cambridge University Press.

Gupta, A. and Ferguson, J. (eds) (1997a) *Culture, Power, Place: Explorations in Critical Anthropology*, Durham, NC: Duke University Press.

—— (eds) (1997b) *Anthropological Locations: Boundaries and Grounds of a Field Science*, Berkeley: University of California Press.

Harvey, D. (1985) *The Urbanization of Capital*, Oxford: Blackwell.

Hannerz, U. (1996) *Transnational Connections. Culture, People, Places*, London: Routledge.

Jansen, S. and Löfving, S. (2009) "Introduction: Towards an anthropology of violence, hope and the movement of people", in S. Jansen and S. Löfving (eds) *Struggles for Home: Violence, Hope and the Movement of People*, London: Berghahn Press.

Kearney, M. (1991) "Borders and boundaries of the state and self at the end of empire", *Journal of Historical Sociology*, 4(1): 52–74.

—— (2000) "Transnational Oaxacan indigenous identity: The case of Mixtecs and Zapotecs", *Identities*, 7(2): 173–95.

—— (2004) *Changing Fields of Anthropology: From Local to Global*, Lanham, MD: Rowman & Littlefield Publishers.

Khagram, S. and Levitt, P. (2008) *The Transnational Studies Reader: Intersections and Innovations*, New York: Routledge.

Kuhn, T. (1962) *The Structure of Scientific Revolutions*, Chicago: University of Chicago Press.

Lash, S. and Urry, J. (1994) *Economies of Signs and Space*, London, Thousand Oaks, New Delhi: Sage Publications.

Latour, B. (2005) *Reassembling the Social: An Introduction to Actor-Network-Theory*, Oxford: Oxford University Press.

Lefèbvre, H. (1974) *Production de l'espace*, trans. D. Nichold-Smith (1991) *The Production of Space*, Oxford: Basil Blackwell.

Levitt, P. and Glick Schiller, N. (2004) "Transnational perspectives on migration: Conceptualizing simultaneity", *International Migration Review*, 38(3): 1002–40.

McMichael, P. (1990) "Incorporating comparison within a world-historical perspective: An alternative comparative method", *American Sociological Review*, 55: 385–97.

Mahoney, J. (2001) *The Legacies of Liberalism*, Baltimore: Johns Hopkins University Press.

Marcus, G.E. (1995) "Ethnography in/of the world system: The emergence of multi-sited ethnography", *Annual Review of Anthropology*, 24: 95–117.

—— (1998) *Ethnography through Thick and Thin*, Princeton, NJ: Princeton University Press.

—— and Fischer, M. (1986) *Anthropology as Cultural Critique*, Chicago: University of Chicago Press.

Marx, K. and Engels, F. (1848) *Manifesto of the Communist Party*, Malden: Blackwell.

Massey, D.B. (2005) *For Space*, London: Sage Publications.

Meyer, J. (1999) "The changing cultural content of nation-states: A world society perspective", in G. Steinmetz (ed) *State/Culture: The State-Formation after the Cultural Turn*, Ithaca, NY: Cornell University Press.

——, Boli, J., Thomas, G. and Ramirez, F. (1997) "World society and the nation-state", *American Journal of Sociology*, 103(1): 144–81.

Nye, J.S. and Keohane, R.O. (1971) *Transnational Relations and World Politics*, Cambridge, MA: Harvard University Press.

Patel, K.K. (2007) "In search for a transnational historicization. National Socialism and its place in history", in K.H. Jarausch and T. Lindenberger (eds) *Conflicted Memories. Europeanizing Contemporary Histories*, New York: Berghahn Books.

—— (2008) "'Transnations' among 'transnations'? The debate on transnational history in the US and Germany", *Harvard University Center for European Studies Working Paper Series*, No. 159, Cambridge, MA: Harvard University Center for European Studies.

Pries, L. (2008) "Transnational societal spaces. Which units of analysis, reference and measurement?", in L. Pries (ed) *Rethinking Transnationalism. The Meso-Link of Organizations*, London: Routledge.

Robertson, R. (1998) "Time-space and homogeneity-heterogeneity", in M. Featherstone, S. Lash and R. Robertson (eds) *Global Modernities*, London: Sage Publications, pp. 25–35.

Rouse, R. (1992) "Making sense of settlement. Class transformation, cultural struggle, and transnationalism among Mexican migrants in the united states", *Annals of the New York Academy of Sciences*, 645: 25–52.

Rüger, J. (2010) "OXO or: The challenges of transnational history", *European History Quarterly*, 40: 656–68.

Sassen, S. (1991) *The Global City: New York, London, Tokyo*, Princeton, NJ: Princeton University Press.

Schenk, F.B. (2002) "Mental maps. Die Konstruktion von geographischen Räumen in Europa seit der Aufklärung", *Geschichte und Gesellschaft*, 28(3): 493–514.

Smith, M.P. and Guarnizo, L. (eds) (1998) *Transnationalism from Below*, New Brunswick, NJ: Transaction Publishers.

Smith, N. (2003) "Remaking scale: Competition and cooperation in prenational and postnational Europe", in N. Brenner, B. Jessop, M. Jones and G. MacLeod (eds) *State/Spaces: The Reader*, Oxford, Boston: Blackwell, pp. 227–39.

Steinmetz, G. (2007) *The Devil's Handwriting*, Chicago: University of Chicago Press.
Swyngedouw, E. (2004) *Glocalisations*, Philadelphia: Temple University Press.
Taylor, P.J. and Flint, C. (2006) *Political Geography. World-Economy, Nation-State and Locality*, Harlow: Pearson Education Limited.
Therborn, G. (2000) "'Modernization' discourses. Their limitations and their alternatives", in W. Schelke, W. Krauth, M. Kohli and G. Elwert (eds) *Paradigms of Social Change: Modernization, Development, Transformation, Evolution*, Frankfurt: Campus, New York: St. Martin's Press.
Tilly, C. (1984) *Big Structures, Large Processes, Huge Comparisons*, New York: Russell Sage Foundation.
Tyrell, I. (2007) *Transnational Nation: United States History in Global Perspective since 1789*, Basingstoke: Palgrave Macmillan.
Wallerstein, I. (1976) "A world-system perspective on social sciences", *British Journal of Sociology*, 27(3): 343–52.
—— (1989) *The Modern World-System III: The Second Era of Great Expansion of the Capitalist World-Economy, 1730–1840s*, San Diego, CA: Academic Press.
Werner, M. and Zimmermann, B. (2002) "Vergleich, transfer, verflechtung. der ansatz der histoire croisée und die herausforderung des transnationalen", *Geschichte und Gesellschaft*, 28: 607–36.
Wimmer, A. and Glick Schiller, N. (2003) "Methodological nationalism, the social sciences, and the study of migration: An essay in historical epistemology", *International Migration Review*, 37: 576–610.
Wolf, E.R. (1982) *Europe and the People without History*, Berkeley: University of California Press.

Part I
Researching International Migration after Redefining Space and Mobility

2 Transnationality, Migrants and Cities
A Comparative Approach[1]
Nina Glick Schiller

To speak of transnationality and the city is to challenge the paradigms that underlie most urban research and public policy. The term *transnationality* places cities within the synergies and tensions of the mutual construction of the local, national and global. It also situates migrants and their transnational connectivities fully within the forces that are constitutive of *the urban*. Sometimes used as a synonym for what I would call transnational social fields and others call transnationalism, the term *transnationality* can more usefully be employed to signal the simultaneous social-cultural, economic and political processes of local and cross-border participation, sociality, membership, connection and identification. This reading of the term *transnationality* emphasizes the concept of nationality embedded yet problematized by the term. Transnationality invokes both processes of social connection and belonging (Ribeiro 1994). Conceptualized in this way, the term makes reference to a world judicially divided into states that claim legitimacy to power through claims to represent a nation, while also highlighting the border crossing processes that are foundational to all modern nation-state building processes. By theorizing transnationality and the city, this chapter contributes to the growing understanding that scholars need to situate cities and their diverse inhabitants in multiple, interpenetrating scales of relationality. These interpenetrating dimensions of connection and identification are produced and reproduced within both time and space (Amin and Graham 1997; Massey 2005; Mitchell 2003; Smith 2001).

Because transnational migrants have been integral yet only intermittently acknowledged contributors to both the past and present of cities and their transnationalities, the relationship between migration and cities is a central theme in this chapter. Despite the fact that the study of migration and that of urban life have been closely linked since the emergence of the social sciences as organized disciplines of study, we know too little about how the relationships between migrants and cities are both shaped by and shape the specific ways cities are constituted within transnational economic, social, cultural and political processes. The division of labor among academic disciplines, which has divided the topics of cities, migration, internal migration and transnational processes into separate fields of research and theory, has mediated against the comparative study of the transnationality of cities. In this chapter, I will first look at past and current work in urban studies and migration to better understand why the relationship between transnationality and the city has so rarely been addressed. Next I suggest ways in which thinking comparatively about the relationships between migration and cities can contribute to new understandings of both topics and the broader subject of transnationality. This leads me to highlight the methodological implications of the approach I am advocating.

DEFINING TERMS

The term *transnationality* is used far less often than *transnationalism, global/globalization, diaspora* and *translocality*, all of which from the 1990s became prominent in the academic literature, with meanings that are often conflated. The terminological confusion has been amplified by the fact that scholars have used the terms *globalization* and *transnationalism* both to signal the changing nature of the social world and as new analytical paradigms with which to conceptualize social processes (Mittelman 1996; Beck and Sznaider 2006; Glick Schiller 1999). After some intense debate and much confusion, most analysts have agreed that there have been significant changes around the world in how life is organized and experienced and that these changes have made new paradigms prominent. The new paradigms in turn shape how scholars think about the extent and nature of current social transformations and their similarities to and differences from past historical conjunctures.

Currently, most analysts of cross-border processes, whatever terms they favor, make the following points:

1. There are economic and cultural processes that bind localities, regions and nation-states around the world together, and human mobilities have always been part of these processes.
2. These processes are not new but also do not proceed at a constant or uniform pace—there are ebbs, flows and transformations in this global intertwining and interpenetration.
3. During the past four decades, while there has been an interpenetration of geographic scales, nation-states have not lost their significance and national narratives remain potent, although processes of governance have been restructured.
4. Governance has recently been reorganized within and across states so that the legal, financial and military institutions of Europe and North America have become explicitly global, serving corporate and financial interests around the world and reducing even the semblance of sovereignty within many less powerful states.

Transnationality, Migrants and Cities   25

5. The recent period has been shaped by the restructuring of processes of the accumulation and rapid movement of capital and related but increasingly restricted movements of people.
6. The recent restructuring of capital has taken place with a specific rationale and logic that justifies the reorganization of governance, economic and cultural production, distribution and consumption and the constitution of self.
7. This project of transformation and legitimation, often termed *neoliberalism,* has generated various forms of contestation, many of them centered on the city.

For the purpose of the argument I am making here about transnationality and cities, the term *transnationality* indicates cross-border connective processes that are both social and identificational, while the term *transnational* indicates the specific relationalities. These relationalities constitute networks that connect individuals or groups of people located in several specific nation-states. Those who engage in a set of such relations constitute a transnational social field defined as a network of networks of unequal power that link individuals to one or more institutions that organize and regulate the daily economic, political, cultural, social and religious activities of social life. In using the term *social field,* I build on the seminal work on social networks and fields done by the urban anthropologists of the Manchester School (Epstein 1967; Mitchell 1969). The utility of the concept of transnational social field is that researchers can study various social processes that contribute to place-making practices, identities, representations and imaginaries without drawing a sharp binary between natives and foreigners.

People who have migrated are often central actors in building transnational social fields, although some people who migrate and many people who have a family history of migration do not belong to transnational social fields. On the other hand, people who have no such personal or family history and are considered natives of a state often are part of transnational social fields. They enter these fields either through their relationships with people of migrant background who do participate in connections across borders or by establishing ongoing relationships based on various forms of communication and travel that cross borders.

None of these forms of relationality are new or dependent on recent technologies of communication. Regular connections including exchanges of documents and goods across different political regimes preceded the modern nation-state. There have been ebbs and flows in the degree of social connections across the boundaries of states since the rise of states five millennia ago. With the advent of modern nation-states and their border regimes, social fields established through such relationship were made *transnational,* in that they crossed national borders. Within this context, it is useful to use the term *globalization* to indicate the more recent situation of intensified penetration in which the historic forms of networked connections intensify and transnationality—the processes of communication, commodification, identification and shared affect across borders—penetrates into all states (Eitzen and Zinn 2006).

TRANSNATIONALITY AND URBAN STUDIES

The initial social science of the city, such as that developed by members of the Chicago School of Sociology, often linked the nature of cities to their mix of diverse streams of people and ideas. From this perspective processes of migrant incorporation were integral to urban life. Moreover, the founding generation of urban researchers noted that not only were industrial cities built by immigrants but also that these migrants tended to live across borders (Park and Miller 1921; Thomas and Znaniecki 1958). Hence, research on migrant transnationality is as old as modern urban studies.

However, this classic scholarship of the city generally failed to address the historical transborder social processes that have given rise to urban life since the emergence of cities. Instead the past was placed in the realm of static tradition in contrast to the mobility and diversity of modernity. The imposition of this binary opposition precluded adequate theories of the transnationality of the city. Left unaddressed was the archeological and historical record, which documents that the rise of cities and their specific histories is a story of urban places serving as the crossroads of long distance trade routes that linked together states and empires (Wolf 1982). Merchants and traders established transnational kinship, religious and ethnic connectivities as they traveled and settled in response to ruling-class demand for scarce and precious goods—indigo, frankincense, spices, silk, salt and slaves—with which to validate their superior status.

Neither this global urban history nor those social theorists who recognized the relationship between mobilities and urbanity adequately explored the varying ways in which cities were shaped within transnational processes including migration. Instead, theorization of urban life reflected the binary contrast of Western social theory between traditional and modern, which was read through a technological division between "pre-industrial" and "industrial cities" (Sjoberg 1960). Migrants were pictured as part of the urban industrial workforce but not theorized as constitutive of transnational processes within which cities are situated. Alternative efforts to theorize cities did little to address this problem. Neither Lefebvre's (2003) theorization of urban space as generative of social transformation nor Castells's (1977) critique of this position, which emphasized capitalist development, left room for the transnationality of cities and transnational social fields. Similarly, although the urban scholars in the 1970s–1980s who spoke of the "postindustrial" city, the "post-Fordist/post-modern metropolis" and the "capitalist city" acknowledged globe spanning economic or cultural processes, they did not adequately theorize transnational processes as constitutive of cities and paid little attention to processes of migration (Scott and Soja 1996: viii; Smith and Feagin 1987; Waldinger and Bozorgmehr 1996: 4, 14).

This continuing analytic tradition was ruptured by the emergence of a global or world cities literature that reintroduced migrants as significant contributors to the life of certain cities and placed the urban within transnational processes and connections (Friedmann 1986; Sassen 1991). However, global cities research and related work in cultural studies that specifically spoke of the transnationality of cities initially assumed that only a small set of cities was situated within transnational processes (Holston and Appadurai 1996). All other cities were confined within national terrains.

Subsequently, a new perspective on the spatialized restructuring of capitalist accumulation developed that critiqued but built upon the insights of the global cities literature (Brenner 1999; England and Ward 2007; Harvey 2006; Smith 1995). Examining the neoliberal restructuring of cities, these researchers argued that increasingly all cities and states were being rescaled in relationship to new forms of capital accumulation. They used the term *neoliberalism* for an agenda of "reforms" that, while instituted differently in different states and localities, legitimated certain kinds of restructuring in diverse places. This restructuring included the privatization of formerly public resources, spaces and forms of governance, as well as the reduction of state efforts to equalize regional inequalities through public investments and the reliance on increasingly precarious conditions of labor including short-term contracts and migrant labor with few or any rights. Urban scholars of neoliberalism emphasized that cities around the world increasingly competed for flows of international capital. For these scholars, the terms *scale*, *rescaling* and *jumping scale* did not refer to nested territorial geographies but to interpenetrating relational processes within hierarchies of globe spanning power (Brenner 1999; Smith 1995; Swyngedouw 1997).

However, crucial aspects of urban life including the agency of migrants and the role of contestatory social movements in urban transformations were neglected. The descriptions of urban restructuring often failed to highlight the way contradictions within the neoliberal restructuring of self and social relationality can produce aspirations for social justice and new social visions. As a result, some scholars of urban processes have rejected the global perspective on cities and their transnationalities offered by the literature on urban rescaling (Marston *et al.* 2005). Others dismissed efforts to compare cities in terms of their economic, political or cultural power as colonialist European narratives that deny the vitality and viability of the cities of Africa and Asia (Robinson 2006). Instead, a recent urban scholarship, especially in geography, speaks of "spatialities" linked by networks (Leitner *et al.* 2007). Michael Peter Smith (2001) dismissing the critique of neoliberalism offered the phrase "transnational urbanism" more as a metaphors than a topic amenable to comparative research methods. Some scholars have gone further and argued that each city is unique with its own history and forms of sociality and comparison is ultimately not possible or desirable. More recently new calls for a comparative urbanism have developed among geographers accompanied by provocative but underdeveloped reference to "experiential methodologies" (Robinson 2011; Ward 2008).

Not specifically addressing cities but arguing against a "flattened ontology" that rejects concepts of scale and rescaling, Hoefle (2006) notes that ultimately such a perspective normalizes, naturalizes and privileges the local. Researchers are left without an analytical lens with which to study the multiple ways in which the local and global are mutually constituting. Despite its intentions, the new localism, which can only approach the transnationality of the city in its local manifestations and struggles, is ultimately disempowering. Without a global perspective, it is difficult to build social movements across time and space.

Yet clearly place and time needs to be theorized within discussions of the transnationality of cities. Researchers not only need to constantly situate their theorization of urban life in place and time but also develop a comparative analysis of cities. Inhabitants of specific cities must be understood not only as constantly repositioning their city within fields of power that are transnational in their scope but also as actors who are shaped by and shape the variations of transnationality produced within such repositioning.

This dialectic of place is not unique to cities. However, cities are good places to study these transnational processes and their outcomes comparatively. From a transnationality of cities perspective cities serve not as bounded units of analysis but as analytical entry points from which to examine transnational processes. This is because cities usually are territorially based administrative units, and as such have various powers—regulatory, policing, taxation and representational. These powers contribute to a commonality of experience that is generative of identity and loyalty. Analyzing cities through a comparative and global lens defines migrants and people of migrant background who live in a city as local actors rather than within binaries of native/foreign or citizen/outsider or legal/illegal. People of migrant background live within configurations of wealth, power, education, family and forms of cosmopolitan sociabilities that are part and parcel of the varying transnationality of cities (Jeffery and McFarlane 2008).

MIGRATION AND URBAN TRANSNATIONALITIES

Migration scholars also have been hindered by the inability to examine the relationship between migrants' transnational social fields and their relationship to specific cities and ongoing urban transformations. One might expect that since migration is about movement across space, the transnationality of cities would be obvious within migration studies. This has not been the case. There is a vast scholarship of migration that describes the ways in which migrants live *in* cities. Increasingly this work has examined the social relations and identities that migrants maintain and construct as they live across borders and "simultaneously" settle into a new life and become reterritorialized (Levitt and Glick Schiller 2004). However, there has been too little comparative work done to examine the migrants' *varying relationships* to the positioning of cities. This is because migration scholars have been hindered by their methodological nationalism and ethnic lens (Glick Schiller and Çağlar 2009).

Methodological nationalism is an intellectual orientation that approaches the study of social and historical processes as if they were contained within the borders of individual nation-states (Beck 2000; Smith 1983; Wimmer and Glick Schiller 2002). The term *ethnic lens* refers to the propensity of migration researchers to rely on ethnic boundaries to define the unit of study and analysis in research on immigrant settlement and transnational connection (Glick Schiller, Çağlar and Guldbrandsen 2006).

As a result of methodological nationalism and the ethnic lens, researchers often approach the terrain of the nation-state as a single homogenous national culture, while defining a migrant population as a community of culture, interest and identity. This mode of study and analysis sets aside acknowledged internal ,regional and cultural differences within each nation-state and ignores differences within national and ethnic populations along the lines of region, class, region of origin, gender, sexual orientation and identity, as well as linguistic, religious, and political differentiation.

Members of a migrating population settling in a specific neighborhood that is identified as an ethnic enclave and spoken of as a community stand in for the totality of the ways in which migrants and people of migrant background live not only in that city but in an entire country. In addition, the transnationality of an "ethnic group" is reduced to ties to and identification with a homeland. Sometimes it is the researcher herself who makes these discursive moves; in other cases the significance of the local data is disregarded within more general discussions about parallel lives, ghettoization, cultural values, religious moralities, racism or different national immigration policies and integrative strategies. Much is lost from this perspective including the multiple forms of sociability that migrants may have that connect them to persons locally, nationally and transnationally, even when not bound by shared ancestral identity. Also precluded are analyses of migrants' agency as it reshapes and is shaped by the transnational processes that construct neighborhood and urban life.

Cities are not themselves homogenous spaces. Neighborhood differences highlight, reflect and reproduce the uneven transnational processes of place-making within which cities are constantly rebuilt and reimagined. For the past several hundred years the ongoing globe spanning constitution and destruction of capital has constantly revalued and restructured not only various cities but also their particular neighborhoods. Migrants and people of migrant backgrounds are part and parcel of the processes of the reconstitution of capital and of localities as urban places are differentially evaluated within transnational social fields that link together cities and their various quarters. In turn urban developers, planners, boosters and investors construct urban imaginaries of difference in relationship to specific areas of migrant settlement and commerce. It is in relationship to the projection of migrant sociability, vulnerability and affect that various localities within a city come to be seen as desirable, exotic, enticing, diverse, cosmopolitan, dangerous or criminal.

Even social theorists and public intellectuals who decry the pernicious political and moral effects of the national/foreign divide as it is used to structure concerns about national well-being and social cohesion within and across city neighborhoods perpetuate the problem when they confine themselves to critiquing national binaries of difference.. Moreover they have offered too few alternatives (Agamben 1995; Delgado Wise 2006). A theorization of transnationality and the city may not only contribute new perspectives on the constitution of urban life and the emerging differentiation and transformation of specific urban spaces and neighborhoods, as well as local public policy, but also offer wider horizons for social movements built around the right to the city.

Recently, in an effort to address urban variation, migration scholars who have done ethnographic work in specific cities have begun to write about the city as context (Brettell 2003). This approach resonates with seminal work that highlights the role of differential urban opportunity structures in fostering differential migrant pathways of incorporation (Collins 1980; Garbaye 2005; Rath and Kloosterman 2000; Waldinger 1986). There has also been an increasing number of studies that highlight migrant incorporations and transnational connectivities in a variety of cities (Çağlar 2006, 2007; Itzigsohn and Saucedo 2002; Smith and Eade 2008). Some of these contribute important insights into the varying relationships between cities and migrants' transnational social fields by exploring ways cities differ in their political, economic and cultural barriers and opportunities (Brettell 2003; Landolt 2007). The task still remains to delineate the variation in city positioning as well as variations in particular localities within different cities that foster cosmopolitan sociability. The tendency has been for researchers to work in cities labeled global because of their concentrations of wealth as well as political and cultural power and then assume that this form of globality produces cosmopolitanism. There has been little effort to explore variations in the transnationality of cities and the possible relationships between the differential outcomes of urban structuring and the ways in which cosmopolitan sociability is constructed, facilitated, maintained, impeded or challenged (Iverson 2006).

The challenge at hand is one of "variation finding," a method that would compare cities in terms of their positionality and transnationality in relationship to regional, national and global hierarchies of power (Tilly 1984: 83; Glick Schiller and Çağlar 2011b). The goal of variation finding is not to establish absolute comparisons but rather to discover relative similarities and differences within the parameters being compared. In urban studies, variation finding is a method of comparison that delineates several factors that can be systematically examined between cities without positing that the cities being compared are similar in all respects. In the study of the transnationality of cities, analysts examine the ways in which migrants and a specific city shape the relative global positioning of that city as migrants settle and form transnational connections. Building on both the world and global cities comparative literature and its critique, Ayse Çağlar and I have advocated examining both empirical factors such as employment opportunities or barriers, local tax revenues, investment levels in the city, wage levels, opportunities for education and social mobility, decent housing, rights to local settlement, legal protection, degrees of global connectivity and openness to migrants and also more subjectively assessed aspects of city positioning such as reputation and the political and cultural capital concentrated in a city (Brenner 2001; Çağlar and Glick Schiller 2011; Glick Schiller and Çağlar 2011a, 2011b; King 2004; Robinson 2011; Ward 2008). The cultural capital of a city as a whole and its specific neighborhoods is a product not only of the efforts of urban branders but also of its construction within migrant transnational social fields. The method of variation finding I have summarized here will be explicated in the following section.

A COMPARATIVE PERSPECTIVE OF THE VARYING TRANSNATIONALITY OF CITIES

To move beyond an acknowledgement of context and toward the comparative study of the transnationality of cities, I sketch an approach to the relationship between migrants' transnational social fields and the relative positionality of cities (Glick Schiller and Çağlar 2009, 2011a, 2011b; Çağlar and Glick Schiller 2011). The comparative material I briefly present develops the concept of the *relative positionality and rescaling of cities* and demonstrates the utility of this approach. Much of the current research on migrant settlement and transnational fields in specific cities can be rethought from this vantage point. Of particular use is the work on cities that are not global centers of power (Goode 2011). Such work illuminates what is in fact specific to cities that have been dubbed global or world cities and how other cities have different forms of transnationality. Migrants contribute to, settle and build transnational social fields within this range of contingencies, possibilities and limitations.

Manchester, UK, and the US metroplex of Dallas-Fort Worth are two upscaling cities where migrant transnationalities are contributing to efforts to reposition each city, although they are specifically not thought of as central to each city's urban marketing rebranding. After experiencing radical restructuring, the Manchester leadership chose to redevelop their city as a vibrant center of knowledge and design that could attract high tech workers into a youthful urban, chic lifestyle. Craig Young, Martina Diap, and Stephanie Drabble's research on the reinvention of Manchester as a cosmopolitan urban center, as well as my own current research on the topic in 2011, indicated that the contributions of migrants were seen as peripheral to city making processes. At best in the early stages of redevelopment. migrants were seen as local color, attracting tourists to Manchester's Chinatown and "curry mile". However, migrant transnational networks and business interests produce more than multicultural sites and colorful neighborhoods. Transnational social fields built by people of migrant background have been playing a significant role, one not acknowledged by Manchester developers.

An event in 2007 illustrates the significant relationship between migrants and the transnationality of Manchester. A private Pakistani airline, Airblue, initiated flights to Manchester International Airport from Islamabad. As reported in Pakistan (*Pakistani Times* 2007), Airblue executives chose to make the Manchester-Islamabad route their first direct connection between Pakistan and the UK because of the large population in the Manchester area originating from Mirpur, Pakistan, who continue to maintain dense family, economic and cultural networks with this region. However, the new air route was also of interest to travel agents and airport officials, as well as business and travel entrepreneurs in both cities. And it was welcomed by city leaders in Manchester, who understood that their efforts to improve the competitive position of Manchester are linked to the success of the city's international airport, a development initiative threatened by cutbacks in the airline business. It is important to note that Manchester urban developers and political leaders found they needed the Pakistani migrants' transnational connections at the same time that national authorities were defining these links as threatening to national security.

The efforts of corporate leaderships in the metroplex of Dallas-Fort Worth to welcome and utilize transnational ethnic networks of a highly skilled Indian workforce offers a parallel case of the synergies between migrant and urban transnationality and local urban transformation in an upscaling city (Brettell 2011). Websites tht market Dallas make no mention of multiculturalism and the city makes no cosmopolitan claims. However, as Caroline Brettell (2011) has demonstrated, highly skilled migrants are vital to the region's competitive position as a center of computer and electronic industries. The corporate leaders in these industries have looked to Indian transnational organizations to recruit high tech professionals who otherwise would have chosen to settle in a more globally prominent city. Such recruitment has contribute to the success of the region corporations within a highly competitive global industry. Corporate support of Indian organizations has enable migrant groups to invest in institutions of higher education in India, shaping the uneven terrain of development there. Migrants transnationality has helped the efforts of Dallas to become a global financial and manufacturing center. In 2011, the Dallas Regional Chamber of Commerce (City of Dallas, 2011 p.6) noted that "Dallas-Fort Worth (D-FW) is one of the spikes in the global economy, claiming the 12th largest metro economy in the world." City promoters mentioned Asian migrants as contributing to Dallas' global reach.

In contrast, Halle/ Saale in eastern Germany provides insights into the relationships between a city and its migrants that emerge when a city has been dramatically disempowered.[2] Although the city leaders spoke of rebuilding the city as a center of knowledge and technology, the city had insufficient infrastructural, corporate, public resources or cultural capital to attract and retain highly skilled migrant professionals. Nonetheless research I conducted in the downsized city of Halle/Salle from 2000–2007 demostrated that migrants were important to the city's reputation and played a role in the city's urban regeneration and the daily life. Historically and within the German Democratic, Halle had been a center of science and of petroleum and chemical industries. After German unification in 1989, Halle experienced dramatic de-industrialization, massive unemployment and out migration. Efforts on the part of the European Union and German state to revitalize the city contributed to a refurbishment of its historic center but did not lead to a revitalization of the city's economy. With stiff competition even for low paying undesirable and illegal work, both migrants and non-migrants struggled to find employment. Yet some people of migrant background sought to settle in the city including refugees, students, and migrant business people.

The 26 city leaders I interviewed spoke about migrants through the lens of the city's disempowered position and desire to reinvent and regenerate their city. To do this they had to change the public image of the city, not only in Germany, but worldwide. In this task they faced numerous obstacles, including the fact that the city had gained a reputation as racist following several attacks on migrants by an angry, neo-Nazi youth, a small fraction of the population. Publicity surrounding these attacks proved detrimental to efforts to attract investment, industry, and "global talent." In point of fact, the city also had a vibrant anti-racist music scene and a coalition of mainstream organizations committed to standing up to racism but these were unable to change the city's negative image.

In this context, city leaders declared that migrants including asylum seekers were welcome in Halle. Halle's inclusive stance was not only rhetorical and not primarily multicultural. Despite a shrinking tax base and public resources, in their efforts to be migrant friendly, impoverished Halle defied national policies and provided various services to migrants including asylum seekers. Many migrants did in fact find ways to claim the city and become "social citizens" through an array of local and transnational networks including marriage and family, born-again Christianity, international scouting, Esperanto club, employment found despite barriers, and various entrepreneurial activities (Glick Schiller and Çağlar 2008b;

Glick Schiller, Çağlar and Guldbrandsen 2006). Migrants transnational networks and family ties played a role in the synergy between the development of a commercial sector and the recruitment of migrants into a city generally seen as unwelcoming to foreigners. However, these various forms of migrant transnationality and the positive stance taken toward migrant entrepreneurs by city leaders did not effect the positioning and relative disempowerment of the city

The examples from Manchester, Dallas, and Halle/Saale point to the importance of people of migrant background—sometimes acknowledged and sometimes not–for efforts to redevelop and rescale non-"global cities". The short sketches I have presented of the restructuring and rescaling projects of various cities indicate several different ways in which migrants are active agents in the neoliberal transformation of cities and their current transnationality. Migrants constitute not only part of the labor force but also contribute to the recruitment of workers, entrepreneurs, and the establishment or maintainence of infrastructure transportation and communication links. They are actors within networks that provide and constrain the various economic and social opportunities available to urban residents. In addition, migrants in the past and present have linked residents of cities to alternative social, religious, political and moral visions. The differing positionality of cities indicates that the degree and kinds of transnationality of migrants and of cities is integrally part of the same process and must be analyzed together.

CONCLUSION

Scholars need to do more than acknowledge the past and present transnationality of cities. A comparative analytical framework is needed that can highlight the varying ways in which the transnationality of cities is constituted and experienced. Such an approach to cities will allow both researchers and policy makers to set aside the migrant/foreign divide and see migrants as actors contributing to and reshaping their urban environments and the transnational processes that constitute cities. In this scholarship of the relationship between cities and migration, a concept of the relative and changing positionality of cities is useful. This concept depicts residents of cities as engaged in rescaling processes that place cities within the simultaneous and ongoing construction of local, national, regional and global scales.

Migrants enter into urban life in different ways and have a differential impact in the restructuring trajectories of cities, depending on the city's comparative positioning. The urban developers and corporate and political leaders of upscaling cities such as Manchester or Dallas may find that the transnationalities of migrants of various classes are crucial components of their efforts to reposition their city within global fields of power. They may at the same time take these connections for granted as part and parcel of "global cities" rather than something they need to organize or market. Cities that are downscaled such as Halle are often unable to provide public or corporate support for ethnically based community organization. Nor do such cities offer opportunities for economic mobility to migrants or support for a strata of migrant professionals, who are usually the key actors in local ethnic politics and successful diasporic organizations found in global cities such as New York or London.

Researchers concerned to analyze the relationships between city-making and migrants need theory and methods that facilitate the tracing of transnational social fields connecting persons of migrant background and those categorized as 'natives' both to each other and to the social, economic, cultural, religious and political process that extend into other localities and locally situated institutions in various states around the world. To carry out such research a combined and multi-scalar set of research methods is required. Interviews with city leaderships including developers, promoters, politicians and representatives of national and multinational institutions are necessary, as are the analysis of local statistics and other descriptive indicators of the economic, cultural and political structures of neighborhoods, city and region. These interviews allow the researcher to assess the local configurations that assist or impede residents—migrants and natives of various levels of skill, education and access to capital including the social capital of local and transnational networks—to form social networks that link local residents to local, national and transnational institutions. Participant observation in the daily convivialities of a range of social activities within urban settings that bring people of multiple backgrounds together is a necessary complement to this assessment. By tracing networks and the daily socialities that actuate and maintain them, researchers can identify and highlight the processes of transnational city-making as it takes place within fields of uneven power. Researchers can also identify those social settings and places that facilitate or impede the interactions of openness to shared human experiences and aspirations, that is to say the possibilities of and the variations of cosmopolitan urbanism.

I close by noting that there is a politics to the approach to transnationality of cities offered here. Increasingly, there has been an effort to turn both highly skilled and unskilled workers into a contractual workforce who have few rights and protections and are seen as outside the body politic of the state to which they contribute their talents and labor. Although they are integrally part of cities, the nation-states in which migrants work increasingly deny new arrivals the right to settle permanently, offering them at best only temporary legal status. Circular labor and remittances sent to "homelands" are celebrated while migrants' contributions to the transnationality of cities in which they are laboring is denied (World Bank 2006; Portes 2007).

In this conjuncture cities can provide base areas for broader struggles not only for migrants' rights but also against all forms of social and economic inequalities. Increasingly city leaderships where migrants play central roles in urban restructuring and competitiveness see that their cities have different interests than those articulated in national anti-immigrant legislation. Through policies and narratives local urban leaderships acknowledge that migrants have rights in a city, whatever their official legal status. At the same time, in ways that vary with the positionalities of the city, people of migrant background and natives are able to join in common struggles, aspirations and forms of conviviality and diasporic cosmopolitanism (Gilroy 2004; Salzbrunn 2011; Mitchell 2007). If the transnationality of cities is acknowledged, then demands for the "right to the city" from those being swept aside by urban restructuring can contribute to global struggles for social justice. These struggles will be both site-specific and able to critique a world of global disparities in wealth and power. Solidarities and alliances can be built that are simultaneously spatial and global.

NOTES

1. This chapter is an expanded version of "Transnationality and the City," originally published in Gary Bridge and Sophie Watson (eds), *The New Blackwell Companion to the City* (Oxford: Wiley-Blackwell, 2011). It builds on an analysis of the relationship between locality and migration developed collaboratively with Ayse Çağlar, Professor of Anthropology at the University of Vienna, and published in Glick Schiller and Çağlar (2009, 2011a, 2011b).
2. The view of Halle provided here emerged from research I conducted between 2001–2007, with assistance of ethnographic research teams of students and scholars. We interviewed a representative sample of 21 officials, service providers, and religious officials and a snowball sample of 81 migrants of all legal statuses. Our ethnography included attendance at public meetings, religious services, and events that concerned migrants, as well as informal visiting with some of our respondents. For two years of this period, the ethnographic team in Halle was managed by Evangelos Karagiannis and co-lead by Ayse Caglar. Migrants interviewed including citizens, permanent residents, refugees, asylum seekers, students, and professionals with most of the respondents coming from the Congo, Nigeria, Russia, Bosnia, Vietnam, Iraq, and Syria.

REFERENCES

Agamben, G. (1995) *Homo Sacer: Il potere sovrano e la nuda vita*, trans. D. Heller-Roazen (1998) *Homo Sacer: Sovereign Power and Bare Life* (Stanford, CA: Stanford University Press).
Amin, A. and Graham, S. (1997) "The ordinary city", *Transactions of the Institute of British Geographers*, 22(4): 411–29.
Beck, U. (2000) "The cosmopolitan perspective: Sociology of the second age of modernity", *British Journal of Sociology*, 51(1): 79–105.
——— and Sznaider, N. (2006) "Unpacking cosmopolitanism for the social sciences: A research agenda", *British Journal of Sociology*, 57(1): 1–23.

Brenner, N. (1999) "Beyond state-centrism? Space, territoriality and geographical scale in globalization studies", *Theory and Society*, 28(1): 39–78.

—— (2001) "World city theory, globalization and the comparative-historical method: Reflections on Janet Abu-Lughod's interpretation of contemporary urban restructuring", *Urban Affairs Review*, September, 124–47.

Brettell, C.B. (2003) "Bringing the city back: Cities as contexts for immigrant incorporation", in N. Foner (ed) *American Arrivals: Anthropology Engages the New Immigration*, Santa Fe, NM: School of American Research Press, pp. 163–95.

—— (2011) "Scalar positioning and immigrant organizations: Asian Indians and the dynamics of place", in N. Glick Schiller and A. Çağlar (eds) *Locating Migration: Rescaling Cities and Migrants*, Ithaca, NY: Cornell University Press, pp. 85–103.

Çağlar, A. (2006) "Hometown associations, the rescaling of state spatiality and migrant grassroots transnationalism", *Global Networks*, 6(1): 1–22.

—— (2007) "Rescaling cities, cultural diversity and transnationalism: Migrants of Mardin and Essen", *Ethnic and Racial Studies*, 30(6): 1070–95.

—— and Glick Schiller, N. (2011) "Introduction: Cities and migration", in N. Glick Schiller and A. Çağlar (eds) *Locating Migration: Rescaling Cities and Migrants*, Ithaca, NY: Cornell University Press, pp. 1–22.

Castells, M. (1977) *The Urban Question*, Cambridge, MA: MIT Press.

City of Dallas. 2011 *Municipal government of Dallas, Texas, USA*. http://www.linkedin.com/company/city-of-dallas

Collins, T.W. (ed) (1980) *Cities in a Larger Context*, Athens: University of Georgia Press.

Delgado Wise, R. (2006) "Migration and imperialism: The Mexican workforce in the context of NAFTA", *Latin American Perspectives*, 33(2): 33–45.

Eitzen, D.S. and Zinn, M.B. (2006) "Globalization: An introduction", in D.S Eitzen and M.B. Zinn (eds) *Globalization: The Transformation of Social Worlds*, Belmont, CA: Thompson Wadsworth, pp. 1–11.

England, K. and Ward, K. (eds) (2007) *Neo-Liberalization: States, Networks, People*, Oxford: Blackwell.

Epstein, A.L. (ed) (1967) *The Craft of Social Anthropology*, London: Tavistock.

Friedmann, J. (1986) "The world city hypothesis", *Development and Change*, 17(1): 69–84.

Garbaye, R. (2005) *Getting into Local Power*, Oxford: Blackwell.

Gilroy, P. (2004) *After Empire: Melancholia or Convivial Culture?*, London: Routledge.

Glick Schiller, N. (1999) "Transmigrants and nation states: Something old and something new in the US immigrant experience", in C. Hirshman, P. Kasinitz and J. DeWind (eds) *The Handbook of International Migration: The American Experience*, New York: Russell Sage Foundation, pp. 94–119.

—— (2005) "Transborder citizenship: Legal pluralism within a transnational social field", in F. von Benda-Beckmann, K. von Benda-Beckmann and A. Griffiths (eds) *Mobile People, Mobile Law: Expanding Legal Relations in a Contracting World*, London: Ashgate, pp. 27–50.

—— (2009a) "A global perspective on migration and development", *Social Analysis*, 53(3): 14–37.

—— (2009b) "'There is no power except for God': Locality, global Christianity, and immigrant transnational incorporation", in B. Turner and T. Kirsch (eds) *Permutations of Order*, Farnham: Ashgate Press, pp. 125–47.

—— and Çağlar, A. (2008) "Beyond methodological ethnicity and towards the city scale: An alternative approach to local and transnational pathways of migrant incorporation", in L. Pries (ed) *Rethinking Transnationalism: The Meso-Link of Organisations*, London: Routledge, pp. 40–61.

—— and Çağlar, A. (2009) "Towards a comparative theory of locality in migration studies: Migrant incorporation and city scale", *Journal of Ethnic and Migration Studies*, 35(2): 177–202.

—— and Çağlar, A. (2011a) "Locality and globality: Building a comparative analytical framework in migration and urban studies", in N. Glick Schiller and A. Çağlar (eds) *Locating Migration: Rescaling Cities and Migrants*, Ithaca, NY: Cornell University Press, pp. 60–84.

—— and Çağlar, A. (2011b) "Down-scaled cities and migrant pathways: Locality and agency without an ethnic lens", in N. Glick Schiller and A. Çağlar (eds) *Locating Migration: Rescaling Cities and Migrants*, Ithaca, NY: Cornell University Press, 190–202.

Glick Schiller, N., Çağlar, A. and Guldbrandsen, T. (2006) "Beyond the ethnic lens: Locality, globality, and born-again incorporation", *American Ethnologist*, 33(4): 612–33.

Goode, J. (2011) "The campaign for new immigrants in Philadelphia: Imagining possibilities and confronting realities", in N. Glick Schiller and A. Çağlar (eds) *Locating Migration: Rescaling Cities and Migrants*, Ithaca, NY: Cornell University Press, pp. 143–65.

Harvey, D. (2006) *Spaces of Global Capitalism: Towards a Theory of Uneven Geographical Development*, London: Verso.

Hiebert, D. (2002) "Cosmopolitanism on the local level", in S. Vertovec and R. Cohen (eds) *Conceiving Cosmopolitanism: Theory, Context and Practice*, Oxford, New York: Oxford University Press, pp. 209–223.

Hoefle, S.W. (2006) "Eliminating scale and killing the goose that laid the golden egg?", *Transactions of the Institute of British Geographers*, 31(2): 238–43.

Holston, J. and Appadurai, A. (1996) "Cities and citizenship", *Public Culture*, 8(2): 187–204.

Itzigsohn, J. and Saucedo, S.G. (2002) "Immigrant incorporation and sociocultural transnationalism", *International Migration Review*, 36(3): 766–99.

Iverson, K. (2006) "Strangers in the cosmopolis", in J. Binnie, J. Holloway, S. Millington and X. Young (eds) *Cosmopolitan Urbanism*, New York: Routledge, pp. 70–86.

Jeffrey, C. and McFarlane, C. (2008) "Performing cosmopolitanism", *Environment and Planning D: Society and Space*, 26(3): 420–7.

King, A. (ed) (2004) *Spaces of Global Cultures: Architecture, Urbanism, Identity*, London: Routledge.

Landolt, P. (2007) "The institutional landscapes of Salvadorean refugee migration: Transnational and local views from Los Angeles and Toronto", in L. Goldring and S. Krishmamurti (eds) *Organizing the Transnational: Labour, Politics and Social Change*, Vancouver: University of British Columbia Press, pp. 191–205.

Lefebvre, H. (1970) *La révolution urbaine*, trans. N. Smith (2003) *The Urban Revolution*, Minneapolis: University of Minnesota Press.

Leitner, H., Sheppard, E.S., Sziarto, K. and Maringanti, A. (2007) "Contesting urban futures: Decentering neo-liberalism", in H. Leitner, J. Peck and E. Shepperd (eds) *Contesting Neo-Liberalism: Urban Frontiers*, New York: Guilford, pp. 1–25.

Levitt, P. and Glick Schiller, N. (2004) "Transnational perspectives on migration: Conceptualizing simultaneity", *International Migration Review*, 38(3):1002–39.

Lofland, L. (1998) *The Public Realm: Exploring the City's Quintessential Social Territory*, New York: Aldine de Gruyter.

Marston, S.A., Jones III, J.P. and Woodward, K. (2005) "Human geography without scale", *Transactions of the Institute of British Geographers*, 30(4): 416–32.
Massey, D. (2005) *For Space*, Los Angeles: Sage.
Mitchell, J.C. (1969) *Social Networks in Urban Situations: Analyses of Personal Relationships in Central African Towns*, Manchester: Manchester University Press.
Mitchell, K. (2003) *Crossing the Neo-Liberal Line: Pacific Rim Migration and the Metropolis*, Philadelphia: Temple University Press.
—— (2007) "Geographies of identity: The intimate cosmopolitan", *Progress in Human Geography*, 31(5): 706–20.
Mittelman, J. (ed) (1996) *Globalization: Critical Reflections*, Boulder, CO: Lynne Rienner.
Pakistani Times (May 31, 2007) "AirBlue flights to build Pakistan, UK stronger bonds". Online: http://pakistantimes.net/2007/05/31/business1.htm (accessed April 2008).
Park, R. and Miller, H.A. (1921) *Old World Traits Transplanted*, New York: Harper.
Portes, A. (2007) "Migration, development, and segmented assimilation: A conceptual review of the evidence", *Annals of the American Academy of Political and Social Sciences Quick Read Synoposis*, 610: 270–2. Online: http://ann.sagepub.com/cgi/reprint/610/1/266.pdf (accessed October 2009).
Rath, J. and Kloosterman, R. (2000) "Outsiders' business: A critical review of research on immigrant entrepreneurship", *International Migration Review*, 34(3): 657–81.
Ribeiro, G.L. (1994) "The condition of transnationality", paper delivered at meeting of the American Anthropological Association, Atlanta, GA, December 1, 1994.
Robinson, J. (2006) *Ordinary Cities: Between Modernity and Development*, New York: Routledge.
—— (2011) "Cities in a world of cities: The comparative gesture", *International Journal of Urban and Regional Research*, 35(1): 1–23. Online: http://dx.doi.org/10.1111/j.1468-2427.2010.00982.x (accessed July 3, 2011).
Salzbrunn, M. (2011) "Rescaling processes in two 'global' cities: Festive events as pathways of migrant incorporation", in N. Glick Schiller and A. Çağlar (eds) *Locating Migration: Rescaling Cities and Migrants*, Ithaca, NY: Cornell University Press, pp. 166–189.
Sassen, S. (1991) *The Global City: New York, London, Tokyo*, Princeton, NJ: Princeton University Press.
Scott, A.J. and Soja, E. (1996) *The City: Los Angeles and Urban Theory at the End of the Twentieth Century*, Berkeley: University of California Press.
Sinatti, G. (2006) "Diasporic cosmopolitanism and conservative translocalism: Narratives of nation among Senegalese migrants in Italy", *Studies in Ethnicity and Nationalism*, 6(3):30–50.
Sjoberg, G. (1960) *The Preindustrial City, Past and Present*, Glencoe, IL: Free Press.
Smith, A. (1983) "Nationalism and social theory", *British Journal of Sociology*, 34: 19–38.
Smith, M.P. (2001) *Transnational Urbanism: Locating Globalization*, Oxford: Blackwell.
—— and Eade, J. (2008) *Transnational Ties: Cities, Migrations and Identities*, New Brunswick, NJ: Transaction Publishers.
—— and Feagin, J. (1987) *The Capitalist City: Global Restructuring and Community Politics*, Oxford: Basil Blackwell.

Smith, N. (1995) "Remaking scale: Competition and cooperation in pre-national and post-national Europe", in H. Eskelinen and S. Folke (eds) *Competitive European Peripheries*, Berlin: Springer Verlag, pp. 59–74.

Swyngedouw, E. (1997) "Neither global nor local: 'Glocalization' and the politics of scale", in K.R. Cox (ed) *Spaces of Globalization*, New York: Guilford Press, pp. 137–66.

Tilly, C. (1984) *Big Structures, Large Processes, Huge Comparisons*, New York: Russell Sage Foundation.

Thomas, W.I. and Znaniecki, F. (1958 [1909]) *The Polish Peasant in Europe and America*, New York: Dover Publishing.

Vertovec S. and Cohen, R. (2002) *Conceiving Cosmopolitanism: Theory, Context, and Practice*, Oxford: Oxford University Press.

Waldinger, R. (1986) *Through the Eye of a Needle. Immigrants and Enterprise in New York's Garment Trade*, New York: City University Press.

—— and Bozorgmehr, M. (1996) "The making of a multicultural metropolis", in R. Waldinger and M. Bozorgmehr (eds) *Ethnic Los Angeles*, New York: Russell Sage Foundation, pp. 3–28.

Ward, K. (2008) "Commentary—Towards a comparative (re)turn in urban studies? Some reflections", *Urban Geography*, 29(4): 405–10. Online: http://dx.doi.org/10.2747/0272-3638.29.5.405 (accessed July 1, 2011).

Wimmer, A. and Glick Schiller, N. (2002) "Methodological nationalism and beyond: Nation state building, migration and the social sciences", *Global Networks*, 2(4): 301–44.

Wolf, E. (1982) *Europe and the People without History*, Berkeley: University of California Press.

World Bank (2006) *Global Economic Prospects: Economic Implications of Remittances and Migration*, Washington, DC: World Bank.

Young, C., Diap, M. and Drabble, S. (2006) "Living with difference? The 'cosmopolitan city' and urban reimagining in Manchester, UK", *Urban Studies*, 43(10): 1687–714.

3 Transnational Migration and the Reformulation of Analytical Categories
Unpacking Latin American Refugee Dynamics in Toronto[1]

Luin Goldring and Patricia Landolt

Comparative research offers the promise of enhancing transnational migration studies. Typical research designs build on the comparison of two or more *groups* in a given *destination* or one or more *groups* in more than one place of settlement and expand this to include their transnational social fields. Comparative research highlights the role of contexts of departure and destination in shaping distinct modes of incorporation and variation in the types, scope and sustainability of transnational engagements (Ostergaard-Nielsen 2001; Portes and Böröcz 1989; Portes, Escobar and Walton Radford 2007). North American–based comparative research has theorized processes of immigrant integration, segmented assimilation and transnational engagements as multipath processes with potentially distinct group-level trajectories (Guarnizo, Portes and Haller 2003; Itzigsohn and Saucedo 2002; Portes, Fernandez-Kelly and Haller 2005) and/or location-specific experiences (Landolt 2007). Recognizing the significance of these contributions does not preclude questioning the methodological limitations of the *experimental* paradigm on which much of this research is based or critiquing the application of methodological nationalism to immigrant experiences of incorporation and transnationalism (Wimmer and Glick Schiller 2003). In fact, we challenge researchers to *not* take for granted the role of nation-states as containers and fundamental organizers of social life, to interrogate the practice of using *given* populations, such as national or ethnic, as well as other categories associated with different groups, and not take the constitution of contexts of departure and destination as self-evident.

Immigration scholarship has been anchored in a positivist epistemology, guided by a Cartesian concept of time-space and centered on experimental or quasi-experimental research methods (Bloemraad 2007; Smelser 2003), whether using quantitative, institutional, qualitative or mixed approaches to research design and data collection (Koopmans *et al.* 2001; Ostergaard-Nielsen 2001). The bulk of migration research seeks to explain social processes over time. Linear, forward change over time is privileged (integration, assimilation), and geographic spaces (for example, the home country, host society, immigrant neighborhood) are defined as discrete points on a two-dimensional social landscape (Harvey 1989; Kivisto 2003).

In comparative migration research, similar assumptions are reflected in how places and the people who inhabit them are conceptualized. Contexts of departure and reception are operationalized as geographic locations (home and host countries) and treated as independent analytical units within which the relevant contingencies remain the same over time and space (Portes and Rumbaut 1996). The analytical category of *contexts* is used to construct *de facto* units with which to compare two or more social groups from specified contexts of departure in a single context of reception, or one or more groups across multiple locations or contexts. The definition of *groups* is thus critical. Seen as containers of social life, national boundaries and nation-states are used to organize processes and define analytical categories in ways that are taken for granted. Data collection practices, such as a *national* census or the classification of immigrants and racialized minorities based on nationality, ethnicity, "race" or culturalized region (for example, Latin American or South Asian) illustrate these processes. In sum, the analysis of people and places begins with preconceived analytical categories whose composition and boundaries are taken to be self-evident rather than open to investigation (Ragin 2006).

Contemporary scholars of transnationalism and globalization focus on processes occurring in redrawn spaces and on multiple scales. They make explicit the assumptions about time-space and categories of analysis that are normalized in most immigration scholarship. Wimmer and Glick Schiller (2003) advanced the concept of methodological nationalism to critique how the social sciences work with container models of society; analytically, the bounded nation-state (or village, neighborhood and so on) approach to the *social* severs webs of social life that occur across borders or containers. Living lives across borders suggests a simultaneity of engagement with *here* and *there* that breaks assumptions of linear assimilation associated with mainstream theories of immigrant incorporation. Transnational social fields and related analytical categories—networks, practices and identities that span nation-state borders—are the conceptual starting point for studying social relations, formations and processes that are constituted without propinquity and not necessarily bound by place or national containers (Glick Schiller, Çağlar and Guldbrandsen 2006; Levitt and Jaworsky 2007; Pries 2008). While scholars of transnational engagements have alerted us to the pitfalls of national container models of social life, practical and theoretically informed "solutions," particularly for *comparative* transnational migration studies, are only emergent (Glick Schiller 2010). Glick Schiller and colleagues call on us to recognize non-national bases for collective action in locally situated spaces as well as transnational social fields, while paying attention to global hierarchies of power. Pries (2008) offers a model for specifying units of analysis in transnational studies. Both offer valuable pointers for addressing methodological nationalism from different epistemological orientations. Accordingly, we interrogate the constitution of analytical categories and add that this can be extended beyond those based on nationality and ethnicity.

The tensions between national and transnational ways of framing scholarship noted in this chapter emerged in our work as part of a larger collaborative and comparative project, Social Cohesion and International Migration in a Globalizing Era: Transnational Solidarities and Newcomer's Incorporation in Canada.[2] We designed a Latin American Research Group to examine transnational practices among four Latin American groups and their relationship to trajectories of incorporation. Given the dearth of research on Latin Americans in Canada at the time, we wanted to map out general patterns, paying particular attention to the relationship between Latin American organizations and Canadian civil society organizations, and to the relationship between incorporation and transnational engagements. Our interest in gathering data on immigrant organizations rested on the assumption that identities rooted in nationality would shape collective organizing and institution building in Toronto and in transnational social fields, including the countries of origin. A key objective was to compare patterns across the selected groups: Chileans, Salvadorans, Guatemalans and Colombians.

Our original formulation did not question mainstream methodological assumptions about how to construct the social and geographic spaces of contexts of departure and reception, or about place and time and their interrelationships. Guided by the tenets of comparative experimental methods, we planned to compare groups with ostensibly similar contexts of departure marked by forced movement in one settlement location, Toronto. Nationality organized our definition of *groups*. While their context of departure was considered similar, we distinguished three contexts of reception: Toronto in the 1970s when Chileans arrived, the 1980s when Central Americans appeared, and the 1990s and early 2000s when Colombians began showing up. Variation in patterns of incorporation would be attributable to the different contexts of reception encountered by broadly similar groups at different times, with Canadian civil society groups understood as an important social aspect of the context of reception. Explaining variable transnational engagements was left open because of the exploratory quality of the research, but we hypothesized they would relate to factors such as time in Canada, home country policies and patterns of incorporation in Canada, including interaction with Canadian organizations. We expected group-level variations without fully considering the implications of this assumption.

During the course of the research, we found it necessary to reformulate our analytical categories by unpacking contexts, interrogating given populations and related categories, and drawing on the sociology of culture. Our reformulations draw on comparative historical sociology, particularly

McMichael's incorporated comparison approach, which "views all objects of inquiry as historical and historically connected" (McMichael 2000: 672). From this perspective, cases cannot be abstracted from their time-space location, and "[c]omparison is incorporated into the very process of defining the object of analysis" (2000: 672). McMichael developed this approach in the context of world systems theory, but it is relevant to other comparative projects, including studies of transnational migration (see Comstock in Chapter 9 of this volume). It has implications for our work, including our acknowledgment of the temporal and social interdependence of contexts of arrival—more specifically, how earlier migrants shape the contexts of reception for subsequent arrivals.

We reformulated conceptual categories and analytical strategies in response to three limitations we discovered in quasi-experimental comparative approaches. The first involved treating the four countries of origin as a single *type* of context of departure marked by forced migration which, together with Canadian policy, produced the category of *refugee*. This homogenizing framework erased relevant differences and contributed to methodological nationalism by making nationality a key marker of difference among migrants who shared a forced migration context of departure.

A second limitation was the use of cases and linear forward-directed notions of temporality to define *contexts of reception*. Typically, independent social and geographic categories are naturalized as discrete and thus rendered comparable. Comparative migration studies generally hold time constant by conducting synchronic studies (for example, Koopmans and Statham 2003; Ostergaard-Nielsen 2001). If time is considered, it is usually in terms of individuals' length of time in the country, or a group's peak period of arrival. Different periods of arrival become translated into potential differences in the context of reception. Alternatively, different cases are compared at various times, but time is not explicitly theorized (Itzigsohn 2000). Yet we discovered that a single context of reception is continually modified by *earlier arrivals* as they become part of and modify the local landscape for subsequent arrivals; thus, contexts as containers are generally not independent. In addition, there is often slippage between contexts as conceptual categories and units of analysis, with contexts taken as *de facto* comparable containers of units of analysis. Finally, local contexts are globally embedded and transnationally connected with consequent implications for understanding pathways of incorporation.

Third, using *Chilean, Salvadoran, Guatemalan*, or *Colombian* organizations as units of analysis assumed both the primacy of nationality and the ongoing importance of nationality over time. Our reformulation shifts from using "given populations" to considering how changing times transform elements of collective identities. This historically situated approach to populations and contexts of departure and reception draws on an understanding of political culture (and culture more generally) as a shared but not necessarily uniformly distributed tool-kit or repertoire of meanings and practices (Grimson 2011; Swidler 1986).

The next section situates the research and outlines our initial questions, data collection methods and analytical strategies. The third section identifies methodological problems and the subsequent adjustment of our research strategy and analysis. The closing section discusses implications of our conceptual reformulations.

SITUATING THE PROJECT

This section introduces the original research question of our project, the research context and methods, as well as the project's original ways to define populations.

Research Questions and Context

Our research questions[3] concerning Latin American incorporation and transnational engagements were formulated in a specific context of knowledge production. At the start of the 2000s, Canada celebrated ethnic and cultural diversity but lacked breadth in immigration research. There was a dearth of studies comparing immigrant incorporation across groups, limited research on Latin Americans[4] and minimal scholarship on migrant transnationalism.[5] There was little research on forced migrants' transnational engagements; at the same time, work on refugee transnationalism (Al-Ali, Black and Koser 2001) was just emerging in Europe. With a few exceptions (Hamilton and Stolz Chinchilla 2001; Manz 1988; Menjívar 2000; Zolberg, Suhrke and Aguayo 1989), US-based immigration research failed to theorize the specificity of Latin Americans as refugees, and the topic was absent from the literature on migrant transnationalism.

Data Collection, Methods, and Comparability

In keeping with the larger project, our work was to be qualitative and institutional. To generate data comparable with those of other project researchers, we planned to do the following:

1) Collect primary data through focus groups and interviews with key members of selected Latin American and Canadian organizations.
2) Compile available secondary quantitative data (for example, government sources).
3) Review existing literature.

Defining Study Populations

Our mandate was to select Latin American refugee groups. As noted, we chose Chileans, Salvadorans, Guatemalans and Colombians to capture variation in the temporal context of arrival (1970s, 1980s, late 1990s and

2000s). We unreflectively defined our populations as *given* in two ways, assuming that each population of "forced migrants" constituted a refugee-like movement and using national origin to define *groups*. The latter assumes the centrality of country of origin–based identities and forms of organization and turns nationality into an analytical category informing the composition of the units to be compared.

Composing Categories for Comparison

We initially conceptualized our *units of analysis* as Latin American country of origin–based organizations and related Canadian civil society organizations. Latin American migrant organizations and their activities were proxies for other analytical categories of comparison:

1) Nationality-based patterns of organizing around transnational and settlement agendas (for example, Chilean versus Colombian organizing around homeland and Canadian-based agendas).
2) Contexts of departure (for example, Chile under Pinochet or Colombia in the 1990s).
3) Contexts of reception (for example, Toronto in the 1970s and 1990s).

Similarly, Canadian civil society organizations were conceptualized as part of the context of reception and as units of analysis. We posed questions to individual migrant and non-migrant "activists" about the organizations in which they participated. We sought to map out patterns at the national group level rather than at the individual level because of the larger project's design.

We set out to conduct group interviews with Chileans, Salvadorans, Guatemalans and Colombians active in organizations framed around country of origin identifications. We assumed we would collect information on sports and cultural associations as well as locality or hometown and other types of organizations. As our previous research[6] had alerted us to the importance of both pan-ethnic umbrella groups (Latin American organizations) and gender (San Martin 1998), we planned to conduct group interviews with activists from the four national origin groups, women's groups and umbrella organizations. We soon recognized that these did not capture a broad enough spectrum, so we expanded the range of organizations.

The research topic was the relationship between Canadian civil society organizations and immigrant groups. The operationalization of the groups was left open but began with faith-based groups. In Canada, as in the US, religious congregations have a history of active participation in refugee resettlement and advocacy (Anderson 2003; Bibler Coutin 1993; Chute 2002). We conducted group interviews with faith-based, solidarity and refugee rights organizations.

Focus Groups

Between October 2004 and June 2005, we conducted 18 group interviews with just over 100 Latin American and Canadian participants. While we asked participants for basic sociodemographic information about themselves, our focus was on them as participants in the collective life of their communities and organizations. As part of a "mapping" exercise, we asked them to name organizations they had participated in or knew about; to provide information on the organizations' longevity, temporality, agendas, membership, organizational structure, interlocutors, and geographic and institutional orientation; and to address key internal debates and reasons for organizational change.

To summarize, we began with *given* populations and units of analysis rooted in the country of origin and refugeeness, or, for Canadians, in a particular political position and area of practice in civil society. As shown below, we reconceptualized our analytical categories based on what we learned in the early part of the research. We reformulated our approach to contexts of departure and destination, with implications for addressing the practical challenges of methodological nationalism.

REFORMULATING CATEGORIES *ON THE GO*

This section presents three moments when we reformulated conceptual categories and analytical themes. It highlights the need to work through challenges rooted in methodological nationalism and illustrates solutions developed *on the go*.

Unpacking Contexts of Departure: Refugeeship, Violence, and Politics

We initially framed the project as a study of four Latin American refugee groups, based on an assumption that their contexts of *departure* were similar and also distinct from others with less violence and forced movement. The term *refugee* is a state and supranational designation fraught with political, international relations, legal and budgetary considerations that does not necessarily respond to humanitarian crises (Hein 1993; Malkki 1995). Nonetheless, seeing commonality among the four groups made sense. People leaving Chile in the 1970s, El Salvador and Guatemala in the 1980s, and Colombia in the late 1990s and early part of this century were generally not "economic" migrants but people fleeing polarized conflict and danger.

State policies in the national context of *reception* are also recognized as a crucial element shaping incorporation and transnational engagements

48 *Luin Goldring and Patricia Landolt*

(Hein 1993; Koopmans *et al.* 2001; Ostergaard-Nielsen 2001; Portes and Boröcz 1989). Applying the term *refugee* to the selected groups seemed straightforward in formal terms, not only because of their contexts of departure, but also because the Canadian state has admitted Chileans, Salvadorans, Guatemalans and Colombians as refugees. While there are differences in how it has admitted people from the four countries, Canada has provided a relatively welcoming context of reception and refugee status. Thus, applying the refugee category to Chileans, Salvadorans, Guatemalans and Colombians should have been unproblematic.

Inhabiting the Refugee Category: Violence and Migration Narratives

Being a refugee does not have a constant meaning across groups or over time. There is variation in the experience of refugeeness and people's willingness to inhabit the category, regardless of formal or state-designated status. If one views community organizations as an expression of collective identities, Chilean, Salvadoran and Guatemalan groups have identified themselves more closely with categories of exile and refugee than Colombians. For the former, these categories convey the initial impossibility of return and the hope of returning in the long term when conflict is resolved. They are tied to a narrative that represents their departure from Chile, El Salvador or Guatemala in terms of their position in the political conflict. In contrast, for Colombians, the refugee category is ambivalent. It has negative connotations related to political affiliation or class, leading to an avoidance of the term or a reconstruction of refugee status as an "accident" of conjunctural events (for example, kidnapping threats) and fortuitous policies (for example, Canadian policy recognizes Colombia as a refugee-producing country).

Thus, in addition to being a state-imposed category, refugeeness is a variably inhabited social category. It may be inhabited in ways that provide a basis for organizing and creating community, or it may be inhabited uncomfortably, a stigmatizing category to be avoided or hidden. While nationality becomes a shorthand for particular political experiences and processes of departure, it is not nationality or national culture *per se* that holds explanatory power as an analytical category. Thus, not all Chileans, by virtue of being from Chile or sharing "Chilean culture," inhabit the refugee category in a particular way; rather, a social cohort of Chileans with a specific political experience identified with the refugee and exile categories.

The consequences of this finding go beyond recognizing the politics and power behind state and multinational institutions in designating refugees. It questions assumptions based on the experimental comparative approach—specifically, about the taken-for-granted dimension of defining *refugee* and the degree to which the meaning of the category is constant. It questions the assumptions that contexts of departure produce refugees in a relatively uniform manner and that the reception of groups formally recognized as refugees is similar and hence comparable in a quasi-experimental sense.

This finding also has implications for understanding variable forms of community organizing and transnational engagement. The actual experience of refugeeness is intimately tied to forms of violence and has a strong impact on migrant narratives that address "who we are," "why we came" and "what we are doing here." As we proceeded with the research and national group level comparative analysis, we began to see connections between different forms and experiences of pre-migration violence, socially expected durations (*SEDs*),[7] sources of social capital[8] and nationally based differences in ways of doing politics in Canada—both transnational politics and locally oriented community organizing.[9]

Different approaches to refugeeness, narratives of departure and SEDs shape community organizing. Study participants from the selected countries formed organizations ostensibly based on national origin identities. However, we found that bases for organizing and identifications were complex and not static (see next section). For people from Chile, El Salvador and Guatemala, early forms of organizing centered on partisan affiliations and identities: political parties and social movements. Exile identity was central to Chilean organizations, and the initial assumption was that they would return. Salvadorans and Guatemalans did not articulate return as clearly (Nolin 2006), but they oriented much of their institutional activity around solidarity and support for movements and family in Central America. In the case of Colombia, transnational engagements look very different. Most organizations focus on settlement issues (family reunification, business and professional organizations), while a small network addresses the political situation in Colombia.

Our approach recognizes the state's power to designate and the strategic use of personal narratives to negotiate borders and bureaucracies. Analyzing how organizations and social groups with specific experiences of violence, narratives of migration and SEDs relate to the refugee category highlights problems of population construction and specification that complement and go beyond current critiques of methodological nationalism. Potential variation in how groups inhabit the category means that the *a priori* assumption of uniform refugeeness as an invariant attribute of these populations is problematic, partly because of the arbitrariness of the state's application of the category and partly because differences in experiences of violence, political organization and so on, and the ways these are interpreted by Canadians, lead to variations in forms of organization both in Canada and transnationally, and to differences in people's use of the category. Again, it is not nationality *per se* that shapes variable identification with refugeeness. National history intersects with individual and collective political experience to produce patterns that appear to be "national" but do not necessarily apply to everyone from a particular country nor are they limited to a single nationality. Changes in the context(s) of destination also contribute to variation in how the refugee category is inhabited, thereby raising questions about the uncritical use of the "given population" of refugees. In spite of similarities, refugeeness and the definition of the refugee category need to be explained in the contexts of departure and reception.

Unpacking Contexts of Reception: Local Specificity, Transnational Connections and Path Dependence

When the context of immigrant reception is an important explanatory factor, conceptualizing place and the *local* becomes critical. Global hierarchies of power and transnational flows and circuits disrupt the assumption that locations—places of settlement or contexts of reception (and origin or departure)—can be analyzed as nationally framed and clearly bounded units suitable for comparison (Glick Schiller 2010; Rivera-Sánchez and Lozano-Ascencio 2009b). Multi-sited research that traces people as well as flows of ideas, goods and symbols offers a potential solution to this problem (Fitzgerald 2006; Marcus 1995). The challenge is capturing the *situated-specificity* of the local as it is embedded within global processes, transnational flows and social fields (Brettell 2003; Ley 2004). This has implications for constructing categories such as contexts of reception, trajectories of immigrant incorporation, and transnational engagement (Glick Schiller, Çağlar and Guldbrandsen 2006).

Three analytical challenges forced us to reconsider the spatial-temporal assumptions of the experimental comparative method. The first was our effort to come to terms with the non-independence and multivalence of territorial locations. Focus group participants mapped relevant organizations in time and space, creating a visual record of when organizations were established, how membership and agendas overlapped or competed and when they ended, as well as showing the networks between organizations and key interlocutors at various levels of geography and jurisdiction. Although conducted in one site, this mapping exercise responded to the methodological call to follow the webs of social life (Marcus 1995) rather than bounding social relations and formations according to preconceived notions about their spatial parameters.

The mapping exercise and corresponding discussions brought to light tensions between situated-specificity and transnational social fields. The organizational trajectories of the four "groups" reflect the situated-specificity of the settlement city. An urban center's immigration history, political culture, traditions of civic participation, labor market structures, array of faith-based groups and ethno-racial composition and concentration constitute part of the context of reception and hence shape pathways of immigrant incorporation (Brettell 2003; Glick Schiller, Çağlar and Guldbrandsen 2006). A global immigrant gateway city, Toronto has received over 40 percent of Canada's annual total of newcomers since the mid-1990s. Its labor markets reflect a decline in manufacturing and an increase in low-end service work characteristic of the new economy (Preston, Lo and Wang 2003). There is a trend toward the deregulation of the labor process and an erosion of working conditions and workers' rights (Cranford, Vosko and Zukewich 2003). These features contour Latin American social and economic incorporation as a whole. (Further discussion is beyond the scope of this chapter.)

Our findings indicate that each study "group" is embedded in a distinct transnational social field in which home country politics play a key role (Landolt and Goldring 2010). In the Chilean transnational social field, which includes Chilean and related solidarity organizations in Mexico, Venezuela, Cuba and multiple European locations, Toronto represents an important center in terms of decision making and fundraising for regime change. In contrast, Salvadoran and Guatemalan transnational politics revolve around Los Angeles and Chicago, respectively. Toronto Salvadorans or Guatemalans are minor political players to whom party orders are dictated; Toronto's social and political location as a city of minor import within the transnational social field affects their tenor and organizational dynamics (Landolt 2008).

Our second challenge was comparing multiple groups arriving at different times in a single location or *context of reception,* as this makes the requirement for independent cases difficult to uphold. We set out to compare place-making and modes of political incorporation (assimilative and transnational), with each population entering what we originally conceptualized as three discrete contexts of reception marked by different settlement landscapes and institutional opportunity structures. As noted above, Chileans arrived in Toronto at time one, Salvadorans and Guatemalans at time two and Columbians at time three. We found that the three contexts of reception were not discrete. Rather, the contexts changed over time in a path-dependent fashion so that the lessons and organizational outcomes of first-wave Latin American refugee migration (Chilean) informed subsequent interactions between Latin American refugees and previously arrived migrants as well as non-migrant populations and institutions. Political learning, demonstration effects and path dependencies constitute "Latin American Toronto" as a single evolving context of reception. Within this single, fairly stable context, new groups encounter the organizations created by previous arrivals and migrant/non-migrant interactions as part of the emergent landscape. The context of reception can be understood as both an independent and a dependent variable, complicating causal ordering (McMichael 1990; Pero 2007).

The third challenge was the need to unpack the broad and homogenizing notion of a *welcoming context of reception* for refugees. In general terms, the four groups entered a *welcoming* context of reception; recognizing each country as refugee producing, the federal government established categories and programs to facilitate entry and settlement. In addition, the refugee rights lobby mobilized on behalf of each group. Nevertheless, certain institutional and discursive differences in the context of reception organized the four processes of incorporation and place-making. Our longitudinal analysis of Canadian refugee rights and solidarity advocates' engagement with Latin American refugee flows captures how contexts of reception constitute moments of discursive and organizational engagement. Broadly similar *welcoming* contexts of reception are rewritten as distinct political landscapes for refugee and migrant populations.

First, the settlement landscape varies over time. Chilean refugees faced a sparse settlement and social service landscape that was ill-equipped to deal with the needs and customs of a militant and well-organized Spanish speaking population. In the 1980s, Central Americans accessed a variety of settlement and social services through ethno-specific Spanish-speaking agencies and frontline workers as well as faith-based organizations (Mennonites, Quakers) with growing expertise in the settlement of refugee populations. When Colombians arrived, settlement services had become highly bureaucratized. Today, local agencies are no longer as involved in setting settlement priorities, and the sector is underfunded.

Second, Canadian activist mobilization for the regulated entry of Chilean refugees and the political learning that occurred in the encounter between Chileans and Canadians helped to shape the subsequent production of the context of reception for Central Americans and Colombians. Each migrant/non-migrant encounter influences expectations about and the character of subsequent encounters. Similarly, Canadian state policy on Colombia and the mechanisms of policy delivery are influenced by the government's policy on Chilean and Central American refugees, which, in turn, is a product of the refugee rights lobby's ongoing work.

Thus, our longitudinal analysis led us to unpack the notion of a "welcoming" context of reception in terms of its dynamic organizational and discursive elements (Landolt and Goldring 2010).

Unbounding Nationality: From Nationality to Tool-Kits of Political Culture

In our original formulation, national origin was an analytical category informing our comparative analysis and the construction of organizations as units of analysis. Two moments in our research process prompted us to reformulate the significance and role of nationality:

- First, during early fieldwork, focus groups with country of origin–based activists revealed the importance of *non*-national origin organizations for the Latin American process of political incorporation in Toronto.
- Second, the comparative analysis of institutional relations between each of the study populations and Canadian civil society organizations showed important differences.

Transnational Migration 53

We were uncomfortable explaining these simply as a product of *national cultures*, with taken-for-granted containers of identity and organizers of political practice and institution building. We had already established the relationship between modalities of violence, migration narratives (SEDs, social capital), approaches to the refugee category and ways of doing politics. We drew on the sociology of culture to extend this argument.

Organizational Polysemy[10]

As we began to conduct group interviews using nationality as the starting point to identify organizations, we became aware of two patterns. First, we discovered certain non-nationality-based identities and forms of organizing (artists, educational groups, church groups, mental health professionals) that we had not included in our original analytical categories or list of types of organizations (for example, Chilean refugees, Colombian refugees). Second, certain cleavages, divisions and forms of exclusionary and racialized classification threw into relief non-nationality-based identities (for example, indigenous Latin American identities) and affiliations (for example, political divisions). Figure 3.1 delineates our original conception of nationality as a container of immigrant organizing and organizations. It shows how pan-ethnic umbrella and women's intersectional pan-ethnic organizations overlap with certain nationality-based organizations.

Recognizing the limits of our original formulation, we conducted additional focus groups organized around emergent themes (religious congregations, mental health professionals, artists) to add relevant categories of collective identity and organizing. Figure 3.2 offers an alternative formulation of identity categories around which Latin Americans in Toronto have organized. It identifies the organizational forms that emerged among particular national origin groups, situates them outside or on the borders of the national circles and presents boundaries with broken lines to indicate porosity. Figure 3.2 summarizes but does not convey the temporal dynamics at play. Nationality is more important at first, but it clearly does not sufficiently

Figure 3.1 Nationality as a container.

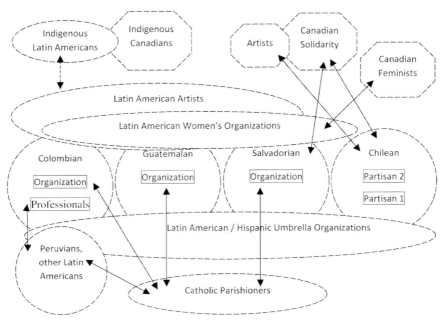

Figure 3.2 National, intersectional and pan-ethnic organizing.

capture the identities and forms of organization that we identified through the above-mentioned mapping exercise and group discussions.

Elsewhere (Landolt and Goldring 2009), we trace the political trajectories of Latin American pan-ethnic sectoral and intersectional organizing (artists, women's organizations) to show that such organizations open up possibilities for cross-sectoral dialogue and alliance-building among Latin Americans while expanding the meanings of Latin American grassroots politics and generating forms of institutional mainstreaming and alliances with non–Latin American organizations and institutions. Despite having significant policy impacts, however, they have failed to generate electoral gains or spark the interest of political parties.

From National Cultures to Cultural Tool-Kit

Levitt notes that immigration scholarship either ignores culture or takes it as an underlying set of shared, discrete and coherent unitary values (Portes, Escobar and Walton Radford 2007) that explain human behavior (Levitt 2005: 52). As noted, we used nationality as an organizing category but were uncomfortable with the chauvinistic use of national cultures to explain difference. How then could we make sense of the Chilean case?

Chileans are an impressive presence in Latin American and Canadian organizations. Their leadership in a range of sectors (schools, unions), the mythologies generated about them and the genuine political camaraderie between progressive Canadians and Chileans all suggested there was something different about Chileans migrants. Time in Canada was not enough to explain this specificity, so we turned to Chilean exile politics and culture.

Some work in the sociology of culture has recast national culture as a cultural tool-kit, developing a notion of political culture that takes a dynamic approach to understanding ways of doing politics (Levitt 2005; Swidler 1986). Swidler notes that culture operates as a framework for explaining continuity, as in the case of immigrants following cultural traditions in a new setting, but argues that culture is also involved in developing "new strategies of action" (1986: 278), particularly during periods of what she calls "unsettled lives," which occur both at the individual and macro levels in periods of heightened social transformation. She uses the metaphor of tool-kit to refer to elements of continuity and to the ability to integrate new strategies into an evolving repertoire of culturally informed action. Grimson's (2011) approach to culture and interculturality is similar; he argues against the extremes of either essentialist or constructivist approaches, insisting that cultural meanings and practices are not uniformly distributed among ethnic, national or cultural groups and that the boundaries around groups and their meaning-making practices are porous.

Drawing on these insights, we use *political culture* to refer to political repertoires that include values and actions manifested in particular strategies and repertoires of action (Landolt and Goldring 2010). This allows us to understand forms of organizing as building on political repertoires that migrants and refugees bring with them. To explain variations in ways of doing politics among people from Chile, El Salvador, Guatemala and Colombia, as well as the variable types of institutional alliances and relationships that develop between each group and Canadian social justice and solidarity organizations, we conceptualize community organizing and politics (including those of Canadian organizations) as informed by a tool-kit of political culture that people bring or have, but which is modified socially. Recognizing that cultural tool-kits and repertoires are rooted in but variably distributed among people from a particular ethnic or nationally constructed group (Grimson 2011) helps us interpret the variable group-level patterns of migrant activism, as well as the interaction between each group and "Canadians."

From this perspective, exile activists from Chile came with certain values, dispositions and strategies shaped by their previous socialization and history, political and otherwise. These strategies may be rooted in Chilean "national culture" in the sense that they are historically, socially, symbolically and politically situated. However, Chileans do not have a uniform political culture; some organize along partisan lines, others organize sports teams and still others stay home (do not organize). Post-coup migration consisted largely of opponents of the Pinochet regime who sustained various partisan affiliations and formed a variety of political and other organizations rooted in their political and cultural experiences in Chile. In the case of people leaving Colombia, we know from Riaño-Alcalá and Villa Martinez's work (2009) and our own that Colombians in Canada (as elsewhere; see Guarnizo, Sanchez and Roach 1999) mistrust other Colombians when it comes to stating political positions and organizing politically. Nevertheless, Colombians in Canada *have* organized in various ways, as for example, business and professional organizations, as well as groups advocating family reunification (Landolt, Goldring and Bernhard 2011; Riaño-Alcalá and Goldring 2006). The conflict in Colombia has generated ways of doing politics that produce variable political cultures of anti-politics as well as solidarity. This approach to political culture also informs our conceptualization of Canadian social justice activists' ways of doing politics (Landolt and Goldring 2010). More generally, it allows us to reformulate analytical categories, going from nationally framed categories (for example, Chilean or Colombian refugees, or Canadian solidarity) to categories (re)constructed on conceptual grounds and data pointing to dynamic configurations of strategies, identifications and alliances.

Our work thus shifts from cataloguing discrete individual or organizational practices (national organizing cultures) toward analyzing patterned interactions between migrants and non-migrant political actors. Chilean and Colombian activists sustain very different types of relations with Canadian activists. Chilean-Canadian activist dialogues reflect a convergence of political agendas and strategies of action grounded in a high degree of mutual intelligibility and an easy translatability of concerns. Meanwhile, Colombian-Canadian activist dialogues show a divergence of strategies of action that result in a deepening lack of respect, intelligibility and translatability. In temporal terms, the two types of dialogues are associated with long-term and sustained versus sporadic and *ad hoc* collaboration. Community activists from Colombia not only arrive with their own political culture tool-kit, they encounter arenas of political activity conditioned by preceding political dialogues between Chileans and Canadians and between Canadians and Central Americans. The "dialogues" developed through earlier interactions have laid the basis for expectations for political practice that are sometimes at odds with Colombian activists' approaches. Thus, activists' political repertoires are shaped, albeit indirectly, by the political repertoire of earlier immigrant/refugee activists.

The character of activist dialogues helps us explain different pathways of political incorporation and transnational engagements (Landolt and Goldring 2010). The analytical category of activist dialogues replaces nationally framed culturalized approaches to organizing while recognizing porosity in ethno-culturalized boundaries and opening up the possibility of identifying and comparing patterns of interaction and social learning. In other words, the notion of exile political culture provides a basis for examining the interaction between selected Chilean activists and Canadian activists and the later interaction between Colombian activists and various Latin American and Canadian activists.

IMPLICATIONS FOR COMPARATIVE STUDIES OF MIGRATION AND TRANSNATIONAL ENGAGEMENT

Comparative studies of immigrant incorporation and transnational engagements enhance our understanding of both specific "cases" and broader processes and patterns. What we derive from comparisons, however, depends on how we conduct them and whether we are willing to reformulate our categories and questions during analysis. Most comparative migration research is based on an experimental or quasi-experimental approach; it defines populations, categories, units and geographic contexts in ways shaped to varying degrees by methodological nationalism. Our questioning of this approach led to the reformulation of our categories and lines of inquiry in a bid to generate solutions and offer emergent methodological alternatives.

Briefly stated, we reframed three assumptions resting on the quasi-experimental approach to comparative research and implicitly informed by methodological nationalism. First, we initially treated the four contexts of departure as a single "type" characterized by forced movement. This, together with our initial understanding of Canadian refugee policy, meant that we assumed the *refugee* category would be applicable across the four groups. The understanding was rooted in a methodological nationalism that privileged the state's power to classify and our analytical power to group "contexts of departure." We found that the comparability of the refugee-producing contexts and state category was problematic. This allowed us to question the classification of refugees based not only on the state's power to designate or recognize but also on the variable ways individuals and groups experience violence and movement and how they inhabit the category of *refugee*.

A second assumption involved the independence of the categories being compared and an approach to temporality that sees contexts of reception as discreet and independent. This aspect of the experimental comparative method gives the geographic container approach both temporal and territorial boundary-making power. We originally framed the temporal periods of arrival for each group as separate contexts and did not adequately theorize the effects of previous arrivals in shaping the context for later arrivals. We discovered, however, that the contexts were not independent, with consequent implications for understanding pathways and path dependency for incorporation and transnational engagements. In our reformulation, we understand the context of reception as continually modified by successive arrivals through a variety of mechanisms, including their interaction with Canadian civil society groups (Landolt and Goldring 2010) and their structuring of the policy and institutional landscape. Temporally, events in time one shape events in time two; thus, "outcomes" in the former become part of the array of independent variables in the latter. At a macro level, this underscores the importance of viewing local processes as embedded in transnational spaces and contexts (McMichael 1990).

A third assumption led us to define *groups* on the basis of shared nationality. This form of methodological nationalism produces two tendencies. The first is to consider nationality as a valid "container" and primary basis for defining and generating identities, practices and organizations. The second is to take for granted the durability of this primacy over time. Our reformulation rested on a mapping exercise that revealed a complex web of interactions; more specifically, intersectional and sectoral identities, practices and organizations changed over time and were conducted at variable geographic scales (Landolt and Goldring 2009). It should be noted that while we examine networks of action based on "ways of doing politics," other concepts may be equally useful.

Our process of reformulation has implications for comparative transnational studies. Rather than a quasi-experimental design, we argue for a strategy based on critical reflection on the composition of boundaries of social categories (cf. Lamont and Molnár 2002). This is not a call for a postmodern critique of epistemological foundations or a rejection of relevant categories but a call for critical and ongoing reflection on the relationship between conceptual categories—namely, the theoretical assumptions that guide their construction and boundaries—and the evidence gathered. Our methodology builds on McMichael's institutional and comparative-historical approach and contributes to recent innovations in migration scholarship. For example, Levitt (2005) calls for attention to culture in migration research; Bloemraad (2006) combines migration scholarship and social movement research; Others, including Glick Schiller and colleagues, address challenges of methodological nationalism.

Our reformulations allow us to *unpack* the contexts of departure and reception by paying close attention to units of analysis and measurement, identity, culture and temporality. First, as analysts of mixed migration now argue, forced migration contexts of exit are rarely uniform, nor are they necessarily distinguishable from those of "voluntary" migrants. Together with a dynamic understanding of culture, this perspective on violence and migration establishes the importance of variable political cultures that make up the tool-kit that people bring with them as immigrants/refugees. The repertoire of culturally framed strategies has a national dimension, but national culture is neither the sole nor the primary determinant of political culture. In many contexts, experiences of violence, movement and political partisanship intersect with class, gender and racialization to generate variation in the political culture and dispositions that groups of people from a given country bring to a new context. National-level variation may have more to do with the specific experiences of a particular group defined by partisan affiliations or experiences of persecution in a particular temporal context than nationality *per se* and the experiences of particular social groups in the social and geographic context of reception. Receiving country state policies may classify refugees in terms of nationality, but in reality, they may select or facilitate the entry of more narrowly defined social groups.

Second, considering the temporal interdependence of contexts can shed light on key social processes. In Canada, successive arrivals from Latin America encountered civil society organizations with whom they set up patterns of interlocution based on political culture. These "dialogues" varied due to differences in political culture and the way earlier dialogues conditioned expectations and subsequent dialogues. The context of reception is dynamic; it changes with policy shifts and with migrant and civil society agency. The contours of this agency are shaped, in part, by the political culture tool-kits that Latin American and Canadian activists bring to bear on their dialogues, but the process and quality of the dialogues modifies subsequent engagements and dialogues. However, it is not enough to add *types of violence* or *types of dialogues* to the analysis. We must consider a broader set of questions, including how populations and units of analysis are defined; whether certain bases of organization and identification are privileged while others are obscured; the changing importance of intersectional, sectoral and pan-ethnic identities and organizations; the ways in which contexts may be temporally and socially interdependent and so forth (Landolt and Goldring 2009, 2010; Landolt, Goldring and Bernhard 2011).

Research on migrant political engagements needs to consider a wider range of identities and bases for organizing. There is a disconnect between scholarship that recognizes the importance of faith-based groups, community-based organizations and other non-national grassroots activism and work that emphasizes nationality as a basis for organizing. We question whether nationality is as important in organizing identities and community organizations as is generally assumed. We call for a nuanced, reflective approach to understanding "given" populations, categories and units, including *refugee, nationality* and *context*. We also ask colleagues to consider the role of narratives in constructing powerful metaphors and identities that help to structure practice and to examine the role of interactions with other collectivities, including non-migrant associational forms and institutions. When the latter are considered in more fluid forms, we will develop a better understanding of social organization and social change in and across transnational social fields.

NOTES

1. We are grateful to Anna Amelina, Devrimsel Nergiz, Thomas Faist and Nina Glick Schiller for inviting us to contribute to this volume, and to Anna Amelina for her thoughtful comments. An earlier version of this chapter was published in Spanish in a collection edited by Liliana Rivera-Sánchez and

Fernando Lozano-Ascencio (2009a). Participants in the workshops leading to that publication offered valuable comments; we are particularly grateful to Liliana Rivera-Sánchez, Marie Laure Cubés, Ninna Nyberg-Sørensen and Luis Guarnizo.
2. Michael Lanphier (York University) was the principal investigator of the Social Cohesion project, funded by the Social Sciences and Humanities Research Council of Canada (2003–2006). The project gathered 12 scholars from various disciplines to study 12 ethno-national groups in Canada (online at www.yorku.ca/cohesion). We formed the Latin American Research Group (*LARG*) together with Judith Bernhard to study four Latin American groups in Toronto. For more on LARG, see online at www.yorku.ca/cohesion/LARG/html/largindex2.htm.
3. For information on the research questions and methods see Goldring and Landolt (2009) and Landolt and Goldring (various).
4. Unlike the US, where Latin Americans dominate the foreign-born population and research on immigration, in Canada, Latin Americans are less significant on both counts. When we began, research consisted largely of case studies and work on refugee adaptation and related issues (Basok 1986; Diaz 1999; Kendall 1992; Kowalchuk 1999a, 1999b; Kulig 1998; Simmons 1993). Research on their economic incorporation was limited, partly because of limitations in data construction, disaggregation and access (Barragan 2001; Garay 2000; Mata 1985); work on their political incorporation was nonexistent. Researchers have since begun to address these gaps. On the political participation of Latin Americans, see Schugurensky and Giginiewicz (2006), Goldring *et al.* (2006), Veronis (2007) and Landolt and Goldring (2009, 2010).
5. Exceptions include Kobayashi (2002) and Hiebert and Ley (2003). Collections edited by Satzewich and Wong (2006) and Goldring and Krishnamurti (2007) indicate the increasing research on migrant transnationalism in Canada.
6. Goldring conducted exploratory research on the civic engagement of Latin Americans in Toronto with support from CERIS (CELAT project); Landolt studied Salvadorans in Los Angeles and Toronto.
7. Socially expected durations (*SEDs*) are collectively patterned expectations about temporal durations embedded in social structures of various kinds (Merton 1984).
8. Social capital is defined as the ability to secure resources by virtue of membership in social networks or larger social structures. Sources of social capital are distinguished by the presence/absence of overarching structures defining the character of the transaction and include both altruistic and instrumental sources (Portes 1998).
9. A detailed discussion of these differences is not possible here, but see Goldring and Landolt (2009) and Landolt and Goldring (2010).
10. We draw on Morawska (2001), whose work on ethnicization emphasizes the multiplicity and polysemy of actors' practices and identities.

REFERENCES

Al-Ali, N., Black, R. and Koser, K. (2001) "Refugees and transnationalism: The experience of Bosnians and Eritreans in Europe", *Journal of Ethnic and Migration Studies*, 27: 615–34.

Anderson, K. (2003) *Weaving Relationships: Canada Guatemala Solidarity*, Waterloo, ON: Wilfrid Laurier University Press.

Barragan, J. (2001) *Hispanic Immigrant Women in Toronto's Labour Market*, Toronto: University of Toronto.
Basok, T. (1986) "Central American refugees: Resettlement needs and solutions", *Refuge (Canada's Periodical on Refugees)*, 5(4): 7–9.
Bibler Coutin, S. (1993) *The Culture of Protest: Religious Activism and the U.S Sanctuary Movement*, San Francisco: Westview Press.
Bloemraad, I. (2006) "Becoming a citizen in the United States and Canada: Structured mobilization and immigrant political incorporation", *Social Forces*, 85: 667–95.
—— (2007) "Of puzzles and serendipity: Doing research with cross-national comparisons and mixed methods", in L. DeSipio, S. Kossoudji and M. Garcia y Griego (eds) *Researching Migration: Stories from the Field*, New York: Social Science Research Council.
Brettell, C.B. (2003) "Bringing the city back in: Cities as context for immigrant incorporation", in N. Foner (ed) *American Arrivals: Anthropology Engages the New Immigration*, Santa Fe, NM: School of American Research.
Chute, T. (2002) "New El Salvador directors know about taking risks", *Canadian Mennonite*, 6: 32.
Cranford, C., Vosko, L.F. and Zukewich, N. (2003) "Precarious employment in the Canadian labour market: A statistical portrait", *Just Labour: A Canadian Journal of Work and Society*, 3: 6–23.
Diaz, H. (1999) *Chileans*, Toronto: University of Toronto Press.
Fitzgerald, D. (2006) "Towards a theoretical ethnography of migration", *Qualitative Sociology*, 29: 1–24.
Garay, E. (2000) *Integrated Settlement Planning Project: Social, Economic and Demographic Profile Hispanic Community*, Toronto: Hispanic Development Council.
Glick Schiller, N. (2010) "A global perspective on transnational migration: Theorising migration without methodological nationalism", in R. Baubock and T. Faist (eds) *Diaspora and Transnationalism: Concepts, Theories and Methods*, Amsterdam: Amsterdam University Press, pp. 109–29.
——, Çağlar, A. and Guldbrandsen, T.C. (2006) "Beyond the ethnic lens: Locality, globality, and born-again incorporation", *American Ethnologist*, 33: 612–33.
Goldring, L. and Krishnamurti, S.V. (eds) (2007) *Organizing the Transnational: The Experience of Asian and Latin American Migrants in Canada*, Vancouver: University of British Columbia Press.
Goldring, L. and Landolt, P. (2009) "Reformulación de las unidades, identidades, temporalidad, cultura y contextos: Reflexiones sobre la investigación de los movimientos migratorios", in L. Rivera Sánchez and F. Lozano-Ascencio (eds) *Encuentros disciplinarios y debates metodológicos: La práctica de la investigación sobre migraciones y movilidades*, Mexico City: Miguel Angel Porrúa and CRIM-UNAM, pp. 125–61.
Goldring, L., Landolt, P., Bernhard, J. and Barriga, M. (2006) "Toronto Hispano, Toronto Latino: Latin American institutional community development in the greater Toronto area (1973–2005)", in D. Schugurensky and J. Giginiewicz, (eds) *Ruptures, Continuities and Re-Learning: The Political Participation of Latin Americans in Canada*, Toronto: OISE, Transformative Learning Centre, pp. 58–71.
Grimson, A. (2011) *Los límites de la cultura: Crítica de las teorías de la identidad*, Buenos Aires: Siglo Veintiuno.
Guarnizo, L.E., Portes, A. and Haller, W. (2003) "Assimilation and transnationalism: Determinants of transnational political action among contemporary migrants", *American Journal of Sociology*, 108: 1211–48.

Guarnizo, L.E., Sanchez, A.I. and Roach, E. (1999) "Mistrust, fragmented solidarity, and transnational migration: Colombians in New York City and Los Angeles", *Ethnic and Racial Studies*, 22: 367–96.
Hamilton, N. and Stolz Chinchilla, N. (2001) *Seeking Community in a Global City: Guatemalans and Salvadorans in Los Angeles*, Philadelphia: Temple University Press.
Harvey, D. (1989) *The Condition of Postmodernity: An Enquiry into the Origins of Cultural Change*, Cambridge: Blackwell.
Hein, J. (1993) "Refugees, immigrants, and the state", *Annual Review of Sociology*, 19: 43–59.
Hiebert, D. and Ley, D. (2003) "Characteristics of immigrant transnationalism in Vancouver", Working Paper 03-15, Vancouver: Vancouver Center of Excellence, Research on Immigration and Integration in the Metropolis.
Itzigsohn, J. (2000) "Immigration and the boundaries of citizenship: The institutions of immigrants' political transnationalism", *International Migration Review*, 34: 1126–54.
—— and Saucedo, S.G. (2002) "Immigrant incorporation and sociocultural transnationalism", *International Migration Review*, 36(3): 766–98.
Kendall, P.R.W. (1992) "The Spanish-speaking community in Toronto. Ethnocultural and health profiles of communities in Toronto", Vol. 7, Toronto: Department of Public Health, Health Promotion and Advocacy Section.
Kivisto, P. (2003) "Social spaces, transnational immigrant communities, and the politics of incorporation", *Ethnicities*, 3: 5–28.
Kobayashi, A. (2002) *Transnationalism, Citizenship and Social Cohesion: Changing Concepts of Citizenship among Recent Immigrants from Hong Kong*, Kingston, ON: Queen's University.
Koopmans, R. and Statham, P. (2003) *How National Citizenship Shapes Transnationalism: Migrant and Minority Claims-Making in Germany, Great Britain and the Netherlands*, New York: Palgrave Macmillan.
Koopmans, R., Statham, P., Costa-Lascoux, J. and Hily, M.-A. (2001) "How national citizenship shapes transnationalism. A comparative analysis of migrant claims-making in Germany, Great Britain and the Netherlands", *Débats contemporains* [Current debates], 17: 63–100.
Kowalchuk, L. (1999a) "Guatemalans", in R.P. Magocsi (ed) *Encyclopaedia of Canada's Peoples*, Toronto: University of Toronto Press, pp. 626–30.
—— (1999b) "Salvadorans", in R.P. Magocsi (ed) *Encyclopaedia of Canada's Peoples*, Toronto: University of Toronto Press, pp. 1109–15.
Kulig, J.C. (1998) "Family life among Salvadorans, Guatemalans, and Nicaraguans: A comparative study", *Journal of Comparative Family Studies*, 29(3): 469–79.
Lamont, M. and Molnár, V. (2002) "The study of boundaries in the Social Sciences", *Annual Review of Sociology*, 28: 167–95.
Landolt, P. (2007) "The institutional landscapes of Salvadoran refugee migration: Transnational and local views from Los Angeles and Toronto", in L. Goldring and S. Krishnamurti (eds) *Organizing the Transnational: Labour, Politics and Social Change*, Vancouver: UBC Press, pp. 191–205.
—— (2008) "The transnational geographies of immigrant politics: Insights from a comparative study of migrant grassroots organizing", *The Sociological Quarterly*, 49: 53–77.
—— and Goldring, L. (2009) "Immigrant political socialization as bridging and boundary work: Mapping the multi-layered incorporation of Latin American immigrants in Toronto", *Ethnic and Racial Studies*, 37: 1226–47.
—— and Goldring, L. (2010) "Political cultures, activist dialogues and the constitution of transnational social fields: Chilean, Colombian and Canadian organizing in Toronto", *Global Networks*, 10: 443–66.

—— , Goldring, L. and Bernhard, J. (2011 forthcoming) "Latin American immigrant political incorporation in Toronto: A dynamic and multi-layered social field", *American Behavioral Scientist*, 55: 1235–1266.

Levitt, P. (2005) "Building bridges: What migration scholarship and cultural sociology have to say to each other", *Poetics*, 33: 49–62.

—— and Jaworsky, N.B. (2007) "Transnational migration studies: Past developments and future trends", *Annual Review of Sociology*, 33: 129–56.

Ley, D. (2004) "Transnational spaces and everyday lives", *Transactions of the Institute of British Geographers*, 29: 151–64.

Magaly San Martin, R. (1998) *Picking up the Thread: An Oral History of the Latin American Women's Collective in Toronto 1983–1990*, Toronto: University of Toronto.

Malkki, L.H. (1995) "Refugees and exile: From "refugee studies" to the national order of things", *Annual Review of Anthropology*, 24: 495–523.

Manz, B. (1988) *Refugees of a Hidden War: The Aftermath of Counter Insurgency in Guatemala*, Albany: State University of New York Press.

Marcus, G.E. (1995) "Ethnography in/of the world system: The emergence of multi-sited ethnography", *Annual Review of Anthropology*, 24: 95–117.

Mata, F. (1985) "Latin American immigration to Canada: Some reflections on the immigration statistics", *Canadian Journal of Latin American and Caribbean Studies*, 10: 35–40.

McMichael, P. (2000) "World-Systems Analysis, Globalization, and Incorporated Comparison", *Journal of World-Systems Research*, 6 (3): 668–690

Menjívar, C. (2000) *Fragmented Ties: Salvadoran Immigrant Networks in America*, Berkeley: University of California Press.

Merton, R.K. (1984) "Socially expected durations: A case study of concept formation in sociology", in W.W. Powell and R. Robbins (eds) *Conflict and Consensus: A Festschrift for Lewis A. Coser*, New York: The Free Press.

Morawska, E. (2001) "Immigrants, transnationalism, and ethnicization: A comparison of this great wave and the last", in G. Gerstle and J. Mollenkopf (eds) *E Pluribus Unum? Contemporary and Historical Perspectives on Immigrant Political Incorporation*, New York: Russell Sage Foundation, pp. 175–212.

Nolin, C. (2006) *Transnational Ruptures: Gender and Forced Migration*, Aldershot, UK, Burlington, VT: Ashgate.

Ostergaard-Nielsen, E. (2001) "Transnational political practices and the receiving state: Turks and Kurds in Germany and the Netherlands", *Global Networks*, 1: 261–82.

Pero, D. (2007) "Anthropological perspectives on migrants' political engagements", Working Paper No. 20, Oxford: Center on Migration Policy and Society (COMPAS).

Portes, A. (1998) "Social capital: Its origins and applications in modern sociology", *Annual Review of Sociology*, 24: 1–24.

—— and Böröcz, J. (1989) "Contemporary immigration: Theoretical perspectives on its determinants and modes of incorporation", *International Migration Review*, 23: 606–30.

—— , Escobar, C. and Walton Radford, A. (2007) "Immigrant transnational organizations and development: A comparative study", *International Migration Review*, 41: 242–81.

—— , Fernandez-Kelly, P. and Haller, W. (2005) "Segmented assimilation on the ground: The second generation in early adulthood", *Ethnic and Racial Studies* 28(6): 1000–40.

—— and Rumbaut, R.G. (1996) *Immigrant America: A Portrait*, Berkeley: University of California Press.

Preston, V., Lo, L. and Wang, S. (2003) "Immigrants' economic status in Toronto: Stories of triumph and disappointment", in P. Anisef and M. Lanphier (eds) *The World in a City*, Toronto: University of Toronto Press, pp. 192–262.

Pries, L. (2008) "Transnational societal spaces: Which units of analysis, reference, and measurement?", in L. Pries (ed) *Rethinking Transnationalism: The Meso-Link of Organisations*, Oxon, UK; New York: Routledge, pp. 1–20.

Ragin, C.C. (2006) "How to lure analytic social science out of the doldrums", *International Sociology*, 21: 633–46.

Riaño-Alcalá, P. and Goldring, L. (2006) "A Colombian diaspora? Characteristics, tensions and challenges in transnational engagements", in International Centre for Knowledge for Peace (ed) *Expert Forum on Capacity Building for Peace and Development: Roles of Diaspora*, Toronto: University for Peace.

Riaño-Alcalá, P. and Villa Martínez, M.I. (2009) "Migración forzada de colombianos: Una mirada relacional" in L. Rivera-Sánchez and F. Lozano-Ascencio (eds) *Encuentros disciplinarios y debates metodológicos: La práctica de la investigación sobre migraciones y movilidades*, Mexico City: Miguel Angel Porrúa and CRIM-UNAM.

Rivera-Sánchez, L. and Lozano-Ascencio, F. (eds) (2009a) *Encuentros disciplinarios y debates metodológicos: La práctica de la investigación sobre migraciones y movilidades*, Mexico City: Miguel Angel Porrúa and CRIM-UNAM.

—— (2009b) "Entre los contextos de salida y las modalidades de la organización social de la migración: Una radiografía del proceso de investigación", in L. Rivera-Sánchez and F. Lozano-Ascencio (eds) *Encuentros disciplinarios y debates metodológicos: La práctica de la investigación sobre migraciones y movilidades*, Mexico City: Miguel Angel Porrúa and CRIM-UNAM, pp. 189–232.

Satzewich, V. and Wong L.(eds) (2006) *Transnational Identities and Practices in Canada*, Vancouver: University of British Columbia Press.

Schugurensky, D. and Giginiewicz, J. (2006) *Ruptures, Continuities And Re-Learning: The Political Participation of Latin Americans in Canada*, Toronto: OISE, Transformative Learning Centre.

Simmons, A. (1993) "Latin American migration to Canada: New linkages in the hemispheric migration and refugee flow system", *International Journal*, 48: 282–309.

Smelser, N.J. (2003) "On comparative analysis, interdisciplinarity and internationalization in sociology", *International Sociology*, 18: 643–57.

Swidler, A. (1986) "Culture in action: Symbols and strategies", *American Sociological Review*, 51: 273–86.

Veronis, L. (2007) "Strategic spatial essentialism: Latin Americans' real and imagined geographies of belonging in Toronto", *Social and Cultural Geography*, 8: 455–73.

Wimmer, A. and Glick Schiller, N. (2003) "Methodological nationalism, the social sciences, and the study of migration: An essay in historical epistemology", *International Migration Review*, 37: 576–610.

Zolberg, A.R., Suhrke, A. and Aguayo, S. (1989) *Escape from Violence: Conflict and the Refugee Crisis in the Developing World*, New York: Oxford University Press.

4 Overcoming Methodological Nationalism in Migration Research
Cases and Contexts in Multi-Level Comparisons

Anja Weiß and Arnd-Michael Nohl

In contemporary societies, migration is often discussed as an anomaly with respect to the nation-state system and migration research has been prone to methodological nationalism in two of its most explicit forms. First, sociology places migrants inside a nation-state, even though they are empirically situated in more than one nation-state. This is especially true for circular migrants, but also for migrants who settle in the country of destination and who have spent part of their lives abroad. Their educational titles may be from abroad and they will compare their economic situation with that of former compatriots and other migrants. The second generation, too, may have ties with the country of their parents' origin or may be viewed by others as really belonging to the origin country. Research on globalization has suggested that even sedentary people are not only situated in nation-states, but also, for example, in global consumer markets, and that international trends and developments have an impact on their lifestyles (Albrow 1996; Kennedy 2010; Pries 1999; Robertson 1995).

A second form of methodological nationalism is in evidence when migrants are reduced to their national and/or ethnic origin, with little regard to other defining criteria. For example, it is widely acceptable in the social sciences to average the educational achievements of "the Turks" (as compared to "the Italians" or "the Greeks") in a country, without much attention being paid to the (self-)selection of migrants and the socioeconomic status of the ethnically defined groups (see Woellert *et al.* 2009). This means, for example, that the educational achievements of a group of people whose (grand-)parents decided to emigrate from Turkey, who chose Germany (and not the UK, for instance) as a final destination, who then spent many years in Germany (where educational institutions vary significantly in terms of the opportunities they offer to migrant children), during which time they neither returned to Turkey nor moved on to another country nor became naturalized, are characterized as "Turkish'. This corresponds to public discourse (Billig 1995) in Germany which generously applies the label "Turkish" to a heterogeneous population of migrants and their children. It is questionable, however, whether this application of methodological nationalism can be justified using more scientific reasoning.

The prevailing practice of explaining social phenomena by using the proper name of the nation-state in which the phenomenon is situated met with early criticism in macro-sociological comparative research (Przeworski and Teune 1970). Notwithstanding this inspired self-critique, country comparative research in the quantitative research tradition continues to treat countries as "container spaces" (Pries 1999) that can be characterized by mutually exclusive territories to which individuals and other social phenomena can be clearly assigned. Today, the relation between social spaces and their territorial extension is understood in many different ways. We are using the term *context* in this chapter to encompass large-scale frameworks that need not be territorially fixed nor mutually exclusive. Civilization scholars, for example, think of civilizations as large historically path-dependent cultural contexts that are unbounded and internally heterogeneous, and that affect each other, even though this view also tends to define *civilization* as similar to *state* in empirical research (Brenner 1999). Postcolonial studies literature shows that postcolonial spaces are not only large and unbounded but also dominated by centers that may be a long distance away. This has a profound effect for the analysis of migration. For example, in our empirical research to which this chapter will refer, some Iraqi graduates were placed in both the Iraqi and the British educational systems. This dual placement proved beneficial for their labor market integration when they left Iraq, and it is inaccurate to treat their educational degrees as strictly "Iraqi." As an extreme, Luhmannian systems theory argues that the functional subsystems of world society should be viewed neither as anchored in a territory nor as territorially bounded (Luhmann 1995, 1997). Contexts that are mainly characterized by specific *rules of the game* and not by their territorial extension have also been suggested by field theories in the Bourdieuian tradition (Rehbein 2006) and by Walby (2009), who, in contrast to Luhmann, argues for seeing systems as spatially extended.

With the aim of pursuing a deeper understanding of the relation between social spaces and territorial formations, the critique of methodological nationalism has questioned whether the nation-state frame is an adequate model for analyzing social phenomena (Beck 1997; Wimmer and Glick Schiller 2002; Beck and Grande 2010; Weiß 2010a). Today this critique is well developed, and it suggests that the nation-state cannot completely contain the social phenomena that are situated (partially) within its territory, and that some social phenomena should be seen as situated in plurilocal, transnational spaces or fields (Faist 2000; Levitt and Glick Schiller 2004; Pries 2008b). This suggests another, more abstract methodological question: How can we situate cases in macro-social contexts? The real difficulty today lies not in challenging methodological nationalism. Instead, we must consider how best to overcome methodological nationalism in empirical research.

In this chapter we introduce a research strategy that was developed in an internationally comparative research project on the cultural capital of highly skilled migrants.[1] The chapter's purpose is methodological, but it uses material and results from the research project in order to illustrate procedures and potential outcomes. By comparing what we call "typologically situated case groups" (Nohl 2009: 101), we are able to empirically reconstruct how macro-social contexts shape cases. We combine bottom-up (ethnographic) and top-down (country comparative) sampling strategies in order to avoid problems associated with both research paradigms. After this introduction we take a closer look at the relationship between cases and contexts in empirical research and how the effects of contexts can be reconstructed in (comparative) case analyses in the second section of the chapter. Note that throughout this chapter we use *context* and *case* as relational categories. Whereas *case* refers to the social phenomenon (individual actors, for example) for which empirical data are directly collected, *contexts* constitute the background in which the social phenomenon is studied. As shown above, definitions of large-scale contexts vary significantly. The theoretical implications of specific context definitions cannot be discussed extensively in this methodological chapter, however.

The third section of the chapter introduces the cultural capital research project and then elaborates on the ways in which the structuring impact of contexts on cases can be reconstructed with the help of the documentary method. In the fourth section, we introduce the research strategy of comparing typologically situated case groups across theoretically predefined context categories. A comparison of typologically situated case groups sheds light on the heterogeneity of cases within a given context prior to cross-context comparison. In this way, we avoid attributing causality to nation-state contexts solely on the basis of a case being found there. Given well-chosen contrasts in the sample, a comparison of typologically situated case groups in different nation-state contexts enables us to take empirically grounded decisions about how best to understand a specific case, whether in the context of a specific nation-state, the context of the nation-state system or in other, non-national contexts. The proposed research strategy can thereby overcome some of the pitfalls of methodological nationalism and enable us to better understand the impact of the nation-state on cases in an empirically valid manner. We do not claim, however, to have solved the problem of methodological nationalism once and for all and the final section of the chapter presents several problems that deserve further consideration.

THE RELATIONSHIP OF CASES AND CONTEXTS IN EMPIRICAL RESEARCH

Empirical research in the social sciences depends on observation. Researchers therefore must determine what constitutes the unit of analysis that is the case. Since observations in the social sciences cannot be organized as true experiments—as in some of the natural sciences—the social sciences are also challenged to determine the best comparative method. Traditionally this leads to the question of which case is best compared with another case (Mill 1973). Ideally, a well-chosen comparative design should be able to shed light on causal relations by varying conditions or outcomes between cases. While the advantages of comparison are universally recognized in the social sciences, how comparative designs should be structured is a subject of intense debate (see for example Yin 2009: 46–55). This debate has obscured an important question: In which contexts are comparisons possible and sociologically meaningful? This question is central for any attempt to overcome methodological nationalism.

Implicit Choice of Contexts

Because social phenomena are situated in contexts,[2] some knowledge of context is necessary in order to understand a particular case, and we cannot compare anything or any person with everything else, irrespective of context. For example, a German national who earns Euros and spends them in the European Union (*EU*) clearly occupies a context different from that of an informal migrant worker in Croatia who does not earn Euros but often has to pay EU prices.[3] The resilience of methodological nationalism is due in part to its apparent capacity to solve exactly this problem of contextualization: It treats the territory of the nation-state as a clearly delimited context, characterized by a unified set of institutional arrangements and a relatively high degree of social, cultural, political and economic homogeneity. As discussed above, social formations often transcend national borders. Nevertheless, when the social sciences need a context in which to place cases, most of the time they fall back on situating cases in nation-states in lieu of a better solution.[4]

For some research questions, the placement of cases in a nation-state context is convincing. If we are interested in the impact of social policies on the welfare of single parents, we can assume that the institutional context of interest is clearly identified with the (subunit of the) nation-state and will have some causal impact on the welfare of single parents. Most social phenomena, however, are *somewhat* connected to national contexts, but not in a clear manner and not exclusively. The welfare of single parents may also be related to values of family life, which may be influenced by the media and religion, for example. Cultural trends like these cross national borders in a diffuse way, not only in their territorial reach but also in their social content. This means that organizational networks or cultural communities may be better suited as contexts for the analysis of particular discourses and their impact on the welfare of single parents. By habitually situating cases in only one context—the nation-state—we may lose our ability to recognize alternative contextualizations. This is a problem for every social phenomenon that potentially extends across national borders.

It is especially important in migration research because migration must always be placed in more than one nation-state.

The context in which a case is placed is important not only because it enables researchers to understand the case and because it delimits potential options for comparison. The definition of a context also implies theoretical assumptions. Research on social inequality, for example, is placed in nation-states not only for pragmatic reasons, but also because general concepts about justice are closely connected with the nation-state frame (Beck 2007; Fraser 2007). Here the context offers the conceptual frame in which social structures are understood, and it helps to shape the ways in which social phenomena are measured. For example, the ratio of job vacancies to persons in search of employment within a nation may differ significantly from the same ratio within a region, a profession or the internal labor market of a global corporation. Note that we have not talked of unemployment: The concept of unemployment as a status is institutionalized by nation-states and would be meaningless in the context of a corporation. Thus, the choice of context is significant both for understanding the case and for understanding the ways in which institutions and other social structures influence the case.

Ways in Which Cases Can Be Related to Contexts

Empirical researchers who want to avoid the pitfalls of methodological nationalism therefore must ask themselves whether they have a good reason to place their case in the nation-state frame, and if not, which other context or contexts would be better suited to frame their case. This question can be solved theoretically, and the debate about methodological nationalism so far has been mostly concerned with *theoretical* concepts beyond the nation-state. We want to suggest options for avoiding methodological nationalism in *empirical* research through methodological strategies. With respect to empirical material, there are three ways in which cases can be related to contexts. First, actors can refer explicitly to a context and place themselves in it. They may attribute causality to a larger context or assume an identity related to it. For instance, a highly skilled migrant physician may explain her decision to work as a nurse with the argument that the labor market is flooded with doctors educated in the country. Note that this argument is not a scientific one, and even though social scientists will be attentive to lay theories, such theories cannot simply be taken as true in terms of social science. From a social scientific perspective we may have other evidence that shows, for example, that the region in which the doctor resides actually suffers from a shortage of doctors. This may lead social scientists to conclude that the informant is unaware of the regional context and that her decision to work as a nurse can be causally linked to discrimination; that is, the doctors working in the region are neither interested in reducing the physician shortage nor in hiring foreign doctors.

A second way in which researchers can relate cases to contexts is emphasized in the reconstructive tradition in the social sciences (Bohnsack, Pfaff and Weller 2010; Oevermann et al. 1976; Schütze 2003). This tradition typically argues that a predominant part of social practice is habitualized, so that actors may not be consciously aware of complying with the unwritten rules of the field or situation. The physician in the example above might claim that she has never experienced discrimination in her life. She may prove this by emphasizing that potential employers were friendly and wanted to hire her. Later in the narration we may learn that the exacting legal restrictions stipulated by governing bodies and professional medical organizations make hiring foreign-trained physicians nearly impossible. Researchers may deduce from narratives of this kind that her inability to gain employment is not a result of interpersonal hostility but, rather, of legal and professional restrictions that are implicitly hinted at in her narration and that researchers may term *institutional discrimination*.

A reconstruction of contexts can yield results that go beyond the perspective of the individual actor. Nevertheless, this kind of approach has one significant disadvantage. Relevant contexts can be reconstructed from practice and narrations only if they have become visible to the actor. For example, another physician in a similar situation may find it impossible to continue in her profession any longer, retire from medicine and choose to focus on personal life goals instead. In an interview she may talk primarily about her children and mention the legal situation only in passing. When we reconstruct contexts from practice or narrations in individual cases, a high degree of hidden contingency is involved. This underscores the importance of comparison—as a third way of relating cases to contexts—for understanding a diversity of contexts.

Understanding the Relevance of Contexts through Comparison

The social sciences have developed two very different paradigms for understanding contexts through comparison. Researchers in one of these paradigms, the ethnographic tradition, adopt a complex definition of *the case* that clearly goes beyond sociology's interest in individual actors. By following various and diverse informants and comparing manifold traces, these researchers determine the context of their case bottom up, and have been remarkably successful in reconstructing large-scale contexts from clues found in the field. For example, Glick Schiller, Çağlar and Guldbrandsen (2006) use small cities as entry points into transnational social fields. Their study includes reflections about the scalar position of their case in the field research. One result of their research shows that small towns offer specific opportunities to migrants because they try to market the cultural diversity of their population in an attempt to place themselves in global circuits. In the course of their fieldwork, when Glick Schiller *et al.* (2006) approached churches with mostly migrant members, they became wary of what they termed the *ethnic lens* in migration research. Just because these churches were often founded by migrants did not mean that they were ethnic or migrant churches. Instead, the authors found good reason to see these churches as universalist, in this case, born-again Christian communities that offer significant roles and connectivities to both migrant and local members.

From early on, ethnographic approaches have attempted to respond to the challenges posed by the processes of globalization and transnationalization. By following "the people," "the thing," "the metaphor," "the story," "the biography," and "the conflict" (Marcus 1995: 106), researchers situate their cases in a variety of contexts and/or place them in a transnational social field. Proposals for a "global ethnography" (Gille and Ó Riain 2002) suggest a multi-sited approach, which includes different scales and degrees of abstraction as well as historical material. The ethnographic approach is clearly elaborate, especially with respect to the challenge posed by cases situated in more than one (local) context. Nevertheless, it remains restricted to context relations that can be found in the case somehow: "What ties together fieldwork locations is the ethnographer's discovery of traces and clues, her logic of association" (Gille and Ó Riain 2002: 286). Ethnographic research is at its best when contexts for the case are visible in actors' identities and discourses or through the researcher's imagination. This approach can lead scholars to overlook another way in which contextual effects can be deduced from empirical material through comparison.

Cases can also be situated in contexts without obvious signs in practice, narration or even documents. This kind of relation between contexts and cases typically is analyzed by another social scientific paradigm, the macro-sociological approach, which differs radically from the ethnographic approach, but also uses comparison in order to reveal the impact of contexts on cases. In an approach that could be called top down, macro-sociological researchers look at a large number of cases that are most of the time defined as actors. Macro-sociological research has little interest in the multiplicity of contexts, but places the cases in one abstract context, usually the nation-state, or it compares several national contexts with each other. The Globalife Project, for example, compares life trajectories in several Organization for Economic Co-operation and Development (*OECD*) countries and finds that short-term work contracts tend to increase insecurity and therefore delay marriage decisions (Blossfeld *et al.* 2005). This is only true, however, in insider–outsider labor markets in which a portion of the population holds stable jobs, making it very difficult for outsiders to gain access. In flexible labor markets, such as that of the US, the correlation between job contract and marriage age cannot be found, as many job contracts are short term and new positions are found easily if the old ones are terminated. This research can well identify contexts in which institutions work as invisible hands, when their impact is neither seen nor elaborated upon by actors.

72 *Anja Weiß and Arnd-Michael Nohl*

The problem with the macro-sociological approach is in predefining a context and in identifying this context with the nation-state. This research is therefore as prone to methodological nationalism as ethnographic migration research that takes the *ethnic lens* as a given case definition. Comparative research has taken a different turn in some case study approaches to macro-social historical comparison (Ragin 1987). Here, contexts are predefined on the basis of theory, much as in the macro-sociological approach, but contexts are understood as "big structures" in general and also "large processes" (quoting the title of Tilly 1984). One strategy for understanding the specifics of larger contexts is in elucidating them more thoroughly through a reconstruction of internal heterogeneity (Mahoney 2003). Typically, these approaches propose a circular relation between theory formation and empirical research, much as it has been suggested in the tradition of building a "grounded theory" (Glaser and Strauss 1967; Kelle 2007). They elucidate contexts both bottom up from an in-depth empirical understanding of carefully selected cases (Schittenhelm 2009) and top down by testing the relevance of a theoretically predefined contextualization. In situations where we cannot assume a clear-cut relation between a case and a given nation-state context, but in which several contexts could be relevant and in which the potentially relevant contexts may not be fully institutionalized but may intermix somewhat and have fuzzy borders, an alternation between preconceived theoretical context definitions and empirically reconstructed context definitions is especially helpful in order to overcome methodological nationalism. We will now describe in more detail how this can be achieved with the help of the documentary method in internationally comparative migration research.

BUILDING RECONSTRUCTIVE TYPOLOGIES: THE EXAMPLE OF AN INTERNATIONAL PROJECT IN MIGRATION RESEARCH

A circular relation between theoretical considerations and empirical research has been essential for the international project *Cultural Capital during Migration*, on the basis of which we have developed the methodological argument for this chapter. The project was intended to deepen our understanding of how cultural capital (Bourdieu 1986) can be transported across national borders, and the kinds of barriers encountered by highly skilled migrants when they attempt to enter national labor markets. We assumed that the recognition of cultural capital is structured by meso- as well as macro-social contexts (Nohl *et al.* 2006), but both the concept of labor market integration and our initial approach to macro-social contexts were informed by country comparative research and therefore envisioned nation-states as container spaces. Nevertheless, transnational phenomena showed up clearly in our empirical results, which were based primarily on

206 narrative interviews (Schütze 2003) conducted in Germany, Canada, Great Britain and Turkey, capturing the biographies of migrants in personal retrospectives. The interviews were analyzed comparatively using the documentary method and were supplemented by the analysis of existing statistical material, documents and expert interviews.

Founded on Karl Mannheim's (1952) sociology of knowledge, the documentary method has been developed as a modern reconstructive approach by Ralf Bohnsack (Bohnsack 2007; Bohnsack, Pfaff and Weller 2010) and adapted to the interpretation of interviews by Nohl (2010a). Its main features are the explication of the implicit and practical knowledge of the research subjects, the comparison of cases and the development of reconstructive typologies. Since this method emphasizes comparison, which is guided both by theoretical concepts and empirical contrasts, it offers a good starting point for attempts to overcome methodological nationalism.

In our research project, the usefulness of the documentary method to overcome methodological nationalism became obvious when the documentary interpretation of the narrative interviews revealed the existence of contexts that we had not expected to find using the country comparative approach with which we had begun our study. We also found that some contexts that we had anticipated were not relevant for our cases. In this and the following section we describe how we reconstructed (un)expected contexts in the cases and, from these reconstructions, developed typologies. In doing so, we introduce the reader to the documentary method as well as to a systematic alternation between theoretically preconceived and empirically grounded contextualizations, an approach that was not only pivotal for our research but should be seen as a major tool to overcoming methodological nationalism.

Steps of Documentary Analysis

In documentary interpretation, the contexts of cases are deciphered in a series of steps. In the first step, the transcribed interview text is reformulated and summarized by the researcher, who thereby captures the thematic content of the interviewee's experiences. This "formulating interpretation" (Bohnsack 2007: 34) focuses on experiences and contexts *explicitly* mentioned by the interviewee. In other words, the researcher works out *what* a text or action is about. For example, this interpretive step should tease out whether a foreign doctor felt she could not find a job due to the large number of competitors with native degrees.

The main focus of the documentary method is on the *implicit* and tacit connections between cases and contexts. Mannheim (1952: 57) defines the "documentary meaning" of an action as a meaning that the actor may not be aware of, but which is documented in her actions. In the second step, then, the "reflective interpretation" (Bohnsack 2007: 34), the researcher asks *how* a topic is elaborated. Researchers reconstruct the implicit assumptions and the tacit knowledge that is the "orientation framework" (Bohnsack 2007: 135) in which a practice is meaningful and becomes possible. During reflective interpretation we are able to detect contexts of the case that are mentioned in passing by the interviewee, who does not pay explicit attention to them. For example, several doctors among our interviewees described their job applications in detail, including those through which they finally succeeded in securing a position in the German labor market. Although they did not explicitly point to this, their narrations were implicitly structured by the fact that the medical practices in which they finally secured employment catered primarily to migrants. The reconstruction of the interview texts showed the significance of ethnic labor market segregation.

Building Typologies through Comparison

If reflective interpretation were based on a singular interview, the only contexts that could be detected would be those contexts that are mentioned, however obliquely or indirectly, by the interviewee. It is only through the third step in documentary analysis, the comparison of cases, that the researcher may become aware of contexts that structure the orientation framework despite the lack of direct mention in a specific interview. For example, migrants who had married natives and received spouses' visas easily did not even bring up the issue of getting a visa in their biographical narration. This omitted legal context became visible only when these cases were contrasted with the narrations of asylum seekers who faced many legal barriers and talked about them extensively. Hence, case comparisons help to reveal contexts that are otherwise hidden within the narrative of an unproblematic experience.

There are several ways in which relevant contexts can be identified through comparison. The bottom-up strategy in the documentary method looks for maximal contrasts between cases—first, for example, by comparing the experience of a spouse of a citizen with that of an asylum seeker. Maximal contrasts are very helpful for the identification of hidden contexts. Once the maximal contrasts have revealed hidden (as well as implicit) contexts, researchers can compare more similar cases with each other in order to determine whether a context that has been reconstructed from a maximal contrast is evident across several interviews that appear more similar to each other in that respect.

Building upon the use of multiple comparisons, the documentary method's fourth step is the construction of types and typologies (cf. Bohnsack 2007: 141–54; Nohl 2010a: 211–14). When orientation frameworks are identified across several cases, they can be abstracted from their respective cases and formulated as a type. For example, the simple way by which spouses of citizens obtain residence permits may be formulated as a type as soon as we have empirically shown that this pattern pertains not only to one individual but to other persons who had married a citizen of another country. The precision and validity of this type depends on the construction of contrasting types—for example, the difficult visa application procedures experienced by asylum seekers.

As long as such types are constructed in only one dimension, such as how some migration motives can be turned into residence permits, they describe a range of variations rather than explicate how several aspects of a context are connected to several typical features of a case or cases. Hence, as a further step, we need to understand how the respective context is systematically linked to typical patterns that have been discovered in other dimensions of the cases compared. To be able to talk of a typical link, the connection between several dimensions must be observed across several cases. For example, in our research project we discovered that a relatively swift inclusion into very restricted labor markets, like the medical profession in Germany (a type in the first dimension), is empirically connected with legal privileges enjoyed by spouses of German citizens (a type in the second dimension).[5] The validity of such *multidimensional typologies* depends on the researchers' ability to understand and empirically define one typical link vis-à-vis other typical links, such as the problems faced by asylum seekers who want to work as doctors. The typology used as an example here focuses on the systematic connections between several patterns of labor market inclusion and several ways in which migration motives are turned into residence permits.

By viewing only multidimensional typologies as true typologies, the documentary method, notwithstanding methodological differences, concurs with other approaches in sociology (Kelle and Kluge 2010; Weber 1968). True typologies accomplish a systematic analysis of links between typical patterns in different dimensions. In contrast to statistical approaches, which aspire to the same goal, reconstructive typologies do not reveal probabilistic connections but instead reconstruct such links as the meaningful connections between different experiential dimensions.

The documentary method includes several steps through which contexts are reconstructed *bottom up* from narrations. Especially in the construction of multi-level typologies, comparison is also based on theoretically induced sample construction. It then can be seen as a *top-down* contextualization similar to elements of macro-sociological research. The advantage of the documentary method lies in the combination of building typologies from the bottom up and of theoretically induced sampling strategies. The discussion that follows expands upon this advantage and enables us to suggest one way in which migration research can be designed in order to both discover different contexts of migration (including national contexts) and avoid the pitfalls of methodological nationalism.

Comparing Typologically Situated Case Groups

Whether it is possible to reconstruct contexts from case comparisons depends very much on the sample drawn. Contrasts in the sample can in part be defined on the basis of "sensitizing concepts" (Glaser and Strauss 1967) based on a combination of theoretical and field knowledge. For example, in our research we expected the labor market trajectories of the highly skilled to be influenced by the kind and quality of their cultural capital. Therefore, the sample considered diverse levels of degrees and professions (Nohl *et al.* 2006). Since the project focused on migrants, the sampling also varied the ways in which cultural capital can be connected to specific nation-states. Our project therefore started with four theoretically constructed migrant status groups:

1) Migrants who had obtained their latest academic degree abroad and had full legal access to the labor market.
2) Those whose labor market access was restricted.
3) People who, as the descendants of migrants, had received their academic education in the country.
4) Descendants of migrants who received vocational education in the country.

Note that the status groups reflect relations to the nation-state system that are not simply ethnic or national. Instead, they vary the legal status of the migrant and the local or foreign nature of the educational degree. Legal status and location of degree both offer a clear-cut causal relation to our topic of interest, labor market integration. We have thereby replaced proper names with variables—in order to quote country comparative research once more.

As discussed above, the connection of many social phenomena to the nation-state system is diffuse, and sociology has not given enough attention to the question as to whether the nation-state is in fact the best context in which to understand these social phenomena. We can try to resolve this problem by looking for a clear causal link between a phenomenon and a nation-state context. However, we also must acknowledge that some important contexts may not be identical with specific countries nor confined within their borders. For example, the symbolic status of an ethnic group may be quite different in Europe and the Middle East, but not as a result of differing legislation in Germany and Israel. At the same time, we may expect important variations between large-scale contexts that were not foreseen by the sensitizing concepts that we used when designing our research project.

For this reason our project tried to vary contexts in order to maximize contrasts and shed light on context characteristics not anticipated by our initial theorizing. We did so by incorporating an unusual kind of country comparison: All status groups were studied intensively in Germany, and then each status group was compared to a similar status group in another country. The country of comparison was chosen with the expectation of a strong contrast for the respective status group: Canada for status groups 1 and 3, the United Kingdom for status groups 3 and 4 and Turkey for status group 2. This theoretically defined sampling strategy served to illuminate the German national context by maximizing contrasts and opening our eyes to other large-scale contexts.

The initial focus on one nation-state was inspired by country comparative research, and we tried to avoid methodological nationalism by using two strategies:

1) We focused on diverse, analytically differentiable ways in which migrants could be placed in the nation-state system (place of educational title, legal status, and so on).
2) We compared migrants with a similar relationship to the nation-state in at least two maximally contrasting nation-state settings.

Dealing with Previously Unknown Contexts

Despite the elaborate theorizing reflected in our initial research strategy (Nohl *et al.* 2006), this strategy turned out to be much too simplistic. This is to be expected in theoretically defined "qualitative sample plans" (Kelle and Kluge 2010: 52), but should be noted nonetheless. While interpreting the numerous interviews conducted within the different status groups and countries, we came to understand that the contexts in which the cases were embedded were far more complex than we had assumed. We discovered relations to unforeseen contexts while looking for (expected) contexts in vain and had to redefine contexts as new information was acquired.

The reconstruction of cases within each status group pointed to a variety of relevant experiences and contexts in addition to the location of educational title and legal status, which had been considered in the first theoretically founded sample plan. We could manage this unexpected variety only by postponing the comparison *among* status groups in Germany and *between* status groups in two maximally contrasting state contexts in favor of a comparative analysis *within* each status group. Comparative analysis inside the status groups revealed different dimensions of migrant experience and contexts (see in detail Nohl and Ofner 2010). We could not elaborate on all of these dimensions but focused further fieldwork on those that seemed most relevant for our research interest.

In order to construct typologies within each status group we had to redesign and refine our sampling strategies (as proposed in "theoretical sampling" by Glaser and Strauss 1967) and search for (maximally and minimally) contrasting cases within each status group. For example, we looked not only for successful managers but also for persons who were relegated to nonacademic positions. The reconstructive typologies discussed above (Nohl and Ofner 2010) pointed to contexts that had been less overt and were not theoretically anticipated in our initial research design. To a certain degree, these typologies also pertained to social structures less established and visible than the place and level of academic education or the legal restrictions to labor market access (Nohl 2012).

Given the internal heterogeneity within each status group, it would have been problematic to compare a complete status group inside Germany with an entire status group in a contrasting country, as we had originally intended to do. This would have been meaningful only if we could have assumed that the nation-state frame is so central that it structures and contains every other social relation—the fallacy of methodological nationalism. Instead we sought a research strategy that could elucidate contexts from the bottom up, yet at the same time compare cases across diverse (partly theoretically defined) contexts. Put differently, we needed a research strategy that enabled us to contrast the differing contexts in which status groups are placed, without neglecting their individual, internal heterogeneity (cf. Schittenhelm 2009).

It was at this point that we developed the strategy of comparing "typologically situated case groups" (Nohl 2009). Rather than comparing *any* case of status group 1 to *any other* case of status group 2, we juxtaposed only those cases that were similarly situated in the typologies of each status group. We use the term "typologically situated case groups" only for case groups located in multidimensional typologies (see above).

We then used these typologically situated case groups for cross-status and cross-country group comparison. For example, in order to make a comparison between those who had full legal access to the labor market and those who did not, we focused only on cases of physicians who had been educated abroad, who catered to fellow migrants and whose migration motives (spouses versus asylum seekers, for example) had supplied them with different residence permits. This strategy can, of course, be applied to several typologically situated case groups (Nohl and Weiß 2009). We thus avoided assigning similarities to cases simply because they were all placed in a particular country, and we made sure that our cross-country comparisons used cases that occupied comparative positions in each context.

Understanding the Relevance of National and Other Contexts

The results of a comparison of typologically situated case groups can shed some light on whether and how specific national contexts or the nation-state system become relevant for our cases. We can show that some typologically situated case groups are singular, meaning specific to a certain nation-state (see Figure 4.1, Option 1). For example, a case group of highly skilled migrants who are excluded from the labor market and who do not work even informally could be found only among German asylum seekers who are confined to camps, receive substandard welfare and hope to be legalized after a long waiting period if they are not caught exhibiting illegal behavior such as taking an informal job (see Weiß *et al.* 2010). In this example, our analysis of nation-state specific institutional structures clarifies why this typologically situated case group is found only in one of the four countries in our study.

Overcoming Methodological Nationalism in Migration Research 79

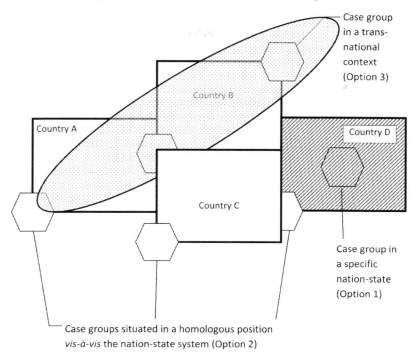

Figure 4.1 Relations between cases and contexts.

Note that we cannot be certain that a type is specific to a nation-state just because it was found only there. Since we could not explore the full variation of cases inside a state, and we did not include more than four states in the analysis, the preliminary finding that a phenomenon is specific to one national context is a result of institutional analysis and theoretical work, as well as typology building on the basis of narrative interviews.

We can show that other typologically situated case groups are found in various contexts. Minor characteristics may vary, but the main pattern is the same. This can be interpreted as evidence for three more ways in which cases relate to larger contexts and nation-state contexts in particular. We have identified a second relation between cases and contexts in which some issues appear to be specific to a nation-state, but are in fact structurally homologous across states (see Figure 4.1, Option 2). This is the case with marriage migration, for example, which is generally accepted in international practice and law (Cornelius *et al.* 2004; Hollifield 2000). We found that migrant spouses of citizens technically occupy differing legal positions in Germany and Turkey. In Germany they receive full labor market access right away, whereas in Turkey they are allowed only to settle (Pusch 2008a). However, since the Turkish labor market accepts informal employment even in skilled positions, the labor market position of the spouses is *de facto* very similar in Germany and Turkey. We interpret this as reflecting the migrant spouses' structurally homologous positions in both countries with respect to the nation-state system. Even states whose migration policies are as different from each other as those of Turkey and Germany avoid a *de facto* exclusion of spouses of citizens from the labor market (Weiß *et al.* 2010). Again, this finding should not be generalized without further research. It serves to show that case groups can also be structurally homologous with respect to nation-states; they may differ in detail but remain bound by the logic of the nation-state system and its international regimes.

Third, migrants can be placed in a truly non-national context (see Figure 4.1, Option 3). Natural scientists and medical researchers, for example, work in a field in which rules and expectations transcend national borders and even employing organizations may be linked through transnational networks. As we have shown elsewhere (Nohl 2010b), the career of a migrant natural scientist or medical researcher may start with a degree in biochemistry in China, for example, and then lead to PhD and post-doctoral positions in laboratories in Germany, the US, and then back in Germany. Although in our sample there were only a few migrants who were able to find qualified positions without a personal connection to the respective country, these cases confirmed that there are labor markets, especially in the natural sciences, that exist largely independent from a nation-state-specific context level.

Finally, case groups can be independent from a specific national context but also show signs of structural homologies across national contexts. Findings of this kind are a combination of the three other possibilities. They are introduced as a fourth relation between cases and (non-)national contexts because they are empirically more likely than complete transnationalization. For example, Nohl's analysis of migrant managers has shown that managers always have to achieve a high degree of local language skill and that they must learn the local codes of labor. The content of the codes differs, as does the way in which the local codes of labor are learned. Nevertheless, we can conclude that for this case group the professional field results in structurally homologous demands across national contexts (Nohl 2010b).[6]

By combining the process of building a typology with a comparison of typologically situated case groups across contexts in different nation-states, our research can elucidate contexts to some extent from the bottom up, much like ethnographic strategies that start from a single, albeit complex case definition and elucidate its multiple context relations. The difference lies in a sampling strategy that is aimed at a systematic variation of context relations. Much like in macro-sociological research, our sampling strategy is theoretically guided. However, it is amended in the course of empirical research both by further sampling and by identifying typologically situated case groups and comparing them across contexts. As a result, we are able to judge the validity of a preconceived, theoretically induced contextualization on the basis of empirical results, and we are able to discover new contexts.

CONCLUSIONS AND FURTHER CONSIDERATIONS

Starting from a critique of the epistemic constraints entailed by methodological nationalism we have suggested a multi-level comparative research design that can shed light on the ways in which specific nation-states, the nation-state system itself and other large-scale—mostly non- or transnational—contexts structure social phenomena. Overcoming methodological nationalism in empirical research is especially important for studies of migration, because scholars of globalization and transnationalism have shown the complexity in the relationship between cases and contexts unless reduced to nation-states and singular membership in the first place.

In this chapter, we argued that contexts can be reconstructed in two ways. On the one hand, a context may be structured from the bottom up, either through direct references of actors to a context or through an *orientation framework* of actors that clearly shows the impact of a context on the case. Failing this, a reiterative strategy becomes necessary—one that on the one hand constructs multidimensional typologies through multiple case comparisons. On the other hand, sampling is theory guided and top down, but is adapted to the results of fieldwork and the building of typologies in the course of the research. A salient example of this strategy is the comparison of typologically situated case groups, as discussed earlier. In such a comparison, only those cases whose structure and context relations have already been analyzed in a specific context are then compared across contrasting contexts.

We have shown how focusing on typologically situated case groups reduces complexity and offers opportunities for a comparison of context relations. Case groups found only in one nation-state are likely to be specific to this nation-state context. Case groups found in more than one macro-social setting can reflect homologies in the nation-state system but may also be independent from that system and better understood in a transnational context.

Our research strategy does not completely resolve the problem of methodological nationalism, however, and some issues deserve further consideration. First, we have suggested that contexts might be predefined in a top-down manner and that context definitions of this kind should not be restricted to the nation-state context. This brings up the following question: Which other contexts might be interesting for comparative strategies besides the nation-state frame? This question is difficult to answer because very few contexts are institutionalized like the nation-state. Exactly what constitutes another context tends to be difficult to discern as it is unclear which cases belong in such a context, and in any case, their borders may be transient.

This issue is quite obvious in theories on transnational social fields and spaces, which are continuously becoming and enacted in practice, but are not institutionalized in a very clear-cut manner. There seems to be some agreement in migration studies literature that transnational social fields develop around concrete social networks, but include symbolic ties and social institutions. This means that a person may be part of transnational social network without symbolically belonging to it or manifestly moving in it (Levitt and Glick Schiller 2004). Some authors state that transnational social fields are more stable than networks, meaning they comprise some transnational institutions in the broadest sense of the word (Faist 2000; Pries 2008a).

A second problem with our research is common for all empirical research but aggravated by studies that work with large-scale contexts. We have shown how focusing on the context in which a case is placed can serve to highlight relevant contexts empirically through reconstructive interpretation, typologies and multiple comparisons. However, the answers revealed by such strategies are rarely conclusive because the sampling can never reflect the complexity of large-scale contexts entirely. If we consider migrant physicians in Germany, for example, we do not really have a problem as long as Germany is used as a geographical restriction. But if we want to elaborate on how physicians are related to Germany as a nation-state, it will be very difficult to fully understand the complex causal relations in which a nation-state context has an impact on cases. This is due to several interconnected reasons: Research in the reconstructive traditions can handle only a limited number of cases as long as it continues to focus on the individual case (see for a discussion Ragin 1987, 1997). Our project compared 206 cases. To our knowledge, it is numerically among the largest projects using reconstructive methods of analysis, and our design was barely sufficient to understand the relevance of one nation-state context, Germany, for a specific topic involving the labor market integration of highly skilled migrants.

Our conclusion that some types are specific to one nation-state and especially to the German nation-state is relatively well founded in empirical work; a specific connection between one type and one country can be supported by institutional analysis. Our conclusion that other types are transnational is more difficult to prove; a type that has been found in two to four countries could also be specific to a supranational or other regionally specific context. This uncertainty could be amended by research designs that focus on transnational social entities in the first place (see for example Weiß 2005, 2006). But the types that are partially specific to and partially structurally homologous across nation-states would need further sampling in more nation-states before we could think of this finding as empirically founded.

This of course is a problem common to much empirical research.[7] Still, in an analysis focusing on the relevance of large-scale contexts, the problem of partially substantiated findings is aggravated by the fact that large-scale contexts are vague, both in content and in their geographical extension. It is difficult to determine which context or contexts are best suited for a specific case. When looking at the labor market integration of migrant physicians, for example, it is initially unclear whether a particular individual is best placed in a professional community of physicians, a family and ethnic network of Turkish people or the country (Germany) in which she is found.

Even if we reduce this initial complexity to a theoretically presumed causal connection between migrant physicians and integration into the labor market in the country in which they are found, several options come to mind. A physician's position in a presumably national labor market could suffer from the lack of demand that results from the demographic composition in a specific territory. It could also suffer from legal restrictions that can be linked with the political system. And it could suffer from symbolic exclusion, the result of a predominantly racist discourse in a country or region. Countries are complex composites of geographical territory overlapped by both political institutions and social entities at the same time (Weiß 2010b).

Empirical research that attempts to tackle this complexity and to overcome methodological nationalism at the same time will have to be focused on and subsequently examine specific issues individually. Research strategies that accept the plurality and heterogeneity of contexts and which vary these contexts in a systematic manner will enable us to gain a better understanding of the relevance of trans- and non-national contexts for specific cases. Even then, the results of such a variation must be seen as a first step that will inform further research, which will gradually shed more light on the empirical relevance of diverse contexts.

NOTES

1. Part of this article represents collaborative work in the study group Cultural Capital during Migration (funded by the VW Foundation 2005–2009), which the authors led together with K. Schittenhelm and O. Schmidtke. We are grateful to our collaborators for the lively debate about earlier versions of this article. We accept sole responsibility for any mistakes we may have made, however. The empirical results for Turkey are based on Barbara Pusch's published (Pusch 2010; Weiß, Ofner and Pusch 2010) and unpublished (Pusch 2008b) contributions to our project.
2. One of the basic themes of social theory concerns the relationship between agency and structure, between micro and macro, between interaction and institution. We need not delve deeply into these substantial themes in order to highlight the methodological problems involved.

3. We intentionally chose an economically relevant example. With cultural phenomena, the importance of context is more obvious and more generally accepted.
4. For a similar and inspiring critique, see Pries (2008b).
5. This and the following empirical examples of multidimensional typologies are described at length in Nohl and Ofner (2010).
6. See Iredale (2001) for a debate about transnationalizing professions.
7. In the macro-sociological approach, an entire debate focuses on a *small n* problem of a different kind (Ebbinghaus 2005).

REFERENCES

Albrow, M. (1996) *The Global Age*, Cambridge: Polity Press.
Beck, U. (1997) *Was ist Globalisierung?* Frankfurt/Main: Suhrkamp.
────── (2007). "Beyond class and nation: Reframing social inequalities in a globalizing world", *British Journal of Sociology*, 58: 679–706.
────── and Grande, E. (2010) "Varieties of second modernity: The cosmopolitan turn in social and political theory and research", *British Journal of Sociology*, 61: 409–43.
Billig, M. (1995) *Banal Nationalism*, London: Sage.
Blossfeld, H.-P., Klijzing, E., Kurz, K. and Mills, M. (eds) (2005) *Globalization, Uncertainty and Youth in Society*, London: Routledge.
Bohnsack, R. (2007) *Rekonstruktive Sozialforschung*, Opladen: UTB/Uni Taschenbücher.
──────, Pfaff, N. and Weller, W. (eds) (2010) *Qualitative Research and Documentary Method in International Educational Science*, Opladen: Budrich.
Bourdieu, P. (1986) "The (three) forms of capital", in J.G. Richardson (ed.) *Handbook of Theory and Research in the Sociology of Education*, New York, London: Greenwood Press, pp. 241–58.
Brenner, N. (1999) "Beyond state-centrism? Space, territoriality, and geographical scale in globalization studies", *Theory and Society*, 28: 39–78.
Cornelius, W.A., Tsuda, T., Martin, P.L. and Hollifield, J.F. (eds) (2004) *Controlling Immigration: A Global Perspective*, Stanford, CA: Stanford University Press.
Ebbinghaus, B. (2005) "When less is more: Selection problems in large-N and small-N cross-national comparisons", *International Sociology*, 20: 133–52.
Faist, T. (2000) *The Volume and Dynamics of International Migration and Transnational Social Spaces*, Oxford: Clarendon Press.
Fraser, N. (2007) "Reframing justice in a globalizing world", in D. Held and A. Kaya (eds) *Global Inequality*, Cambridge: Polity Press, pp. 252–72.
Gille, Z. and Ó Riain, S. (2002) "Global ethnography", *American Review of Sociology*, 28: 271–95.
Glaser, B.G. and Strauss, A.L. (1967) *The Discovery of Grounded Theory: Strategies for Qualitative Research*, Chicago: Aldine.
Glick Schiller, N., Çağlar, A. and Guldbrandsen, T.C. (2006) "Beyond the ethnic lens: Locality, globality, and born-again incorporation", *American Ethnologist*, 33: 612–33.
Hollifield, J.F. (2000) "Migration and the 'new' international order: The missing regime", in B. Gosh (ed.) *Managing Migration: Time for a New International Regime*, Oxford: Oxford University Press, pp. 95–109.
Iredale, R. (2001) "The migration of professionals: Theories and typologies", *International Migration*, 39: 7–26.

Kelle, U. (2007) "'Emergence' vs. 'forcing' of empirical data? A crucial problem of 'grounded theory' reconsidered", *Historical Social Research*, Supplement 19: 133–56.

────── and Kluge, A. (2010) *Vom Einzelfall zum Typus*, Wiesbaden: VS Verlag für Sozialwissenschaften.

Kennedy, P. (2010) *Local lives and global transformations*, Houndmills, Basingstoke, New York: Palgrave Macmillan.

Levitt, P. and Glick Schiller, N. (2004) "Conceptualizing simultaneity: A transnational social field perspective on society", *International Migration Review*, 38: 1002–39.

Luhmann, N. (1995) *Social Systems*, Stanford, CA: Stanford University Press.

────── (1997) *Die Gesellschaft der Gesellschaft*, Frankfurt/Main: Suhrkamp.

Mahoney, J. (2003) "Strategies of causal assessment in comparative historical analysis", in J. Mahoney and D. Rueschemeyer (eds) *Comparative Historical Analysis in the Social Sciences*, New York: Cambridge University Press, pp. 337–72.

Mannheim, K. (1952) "On the Interpretation of Weltanschauung", in K. Mannheim *Essays on the Sociology of Knowledge*, New York: Oxford University Press, pp. 33–83.

Marcus, G.E. (1995) "Ethnography in/of the world system: The emergence of multi-sited ethnography", *Annual Review of Anthropology*, 24: 95–117.

Mill, J.S. (1973 [1843]) *A System of Logic Ratiocinative and Inductive*. Book 3: *On Induction*, Toronto: University of Toronto Press, and London: Routledge & Kegan Paul.

Nohl, A.-M. (2009) "Der Mehrebenenvergleich als Weg zum kontextuierten Ländervergleich", in S. Hornberg, I. Dirim, G. Lang-Wojtasik and P. Mecheril (eds) *Beschreiben—Verstehen—Interpretieren*, Münster: Waxmann, pp. 95–110.

────── (2010a) "Narrative interview and documentary method", in R. Bohnsack, N. Pfaff and W. Weller (eds) *Qualitative Analysis and Documentary Method in International Educational Research*, Opladen: Budrich, pp. 195–217.

────── (2010b) "Von der Bildung zum kulturellen Kapital: Die Akkreditierung ausländischer Hochschulabschlüsse auf deutschen und kanadischen Arbeitsmärkten", in A.-M. Nohl, K. Schittenhelm, O. Schmidtke and A. Weiß (eds) *Kulturelles Kapital in der Migration*, Wiesbaden: VS Verlag Sozialwissenschaften, pp. 153–65.

────── (2012, forthcoming) Relationale Typenbildung und Mehrebenenvergleich. Wiesbaden: VS Verlag Sozialwissbrschaflen.

────── and Ofner, U. (2010) "Migration and ethnicity in documentary interpretation—perspectives from a project on highly qualified migrants", in R. Bohnsack, N. Pfaff and W. Weller (eds) *Qualitative Research and Documentary Method in International Educational Research*, Opladen: Budrich, pp. 237–64.

────── and Weiß, A. (2009) "Jenseits der Greencard: Ungesteuerte Migration Hochqualifizierter", *Aus Politik und Zeitgeschichte*, 44: 12–18.

──────, Schittenhelm, K., Schmidtke, O. and Weiß, A. (2006) "Cultural capital during migration—A multi-level approach for the empirical analysis of the labor market integration of highly skilled migrants", *Forum Qualitative Sozialforschung*, 7(3) Art. 14. Online: www.qualitative-research.net/index.php/fqs/article/view/142/313 (accessed June 3, 2011).

Oevermann, U., Allert, T., Konau, E. and Krambeck, J. (1976) "Structures of meaning and objective hermeneutics", in V. Meja, D. Misgeld and N. Stehr (eds) *Modern German Sociology*, New York: Columbia University Press, pp. 436–47.

Pries, L. (ed) (1999) *Migration and Transnational Social Spaces*, Aldershot: Ashgate.

────── (2008a) *Die Transnationalisierung der sozialen Welt*, Frankfurt/Main: Suhrkamp.

—— (2008b) "Transnational societal spaces. Which units of analysis, reference and measurement?" in L. Pries (ed) *Rethinking Transnationalism. The Meso-Link of Organisations*, London: Routledge, pp. 1–20.

Przeworski, A. and Teune, H. (1970) *The Logic of Comparative Social Inquiry*, London: Wiley.

Pusch, B. (2008a) "Gefragte und ungefragte Gäste in der Türkei. Zur arbeitsrechtlichen Situation von Ausländern in der Türkei", in B. Pusch and T. Wilkovszewski (eds) *Facetten der internationalen Migration in die Türkei*, Würzburg: Ergon, pp. 55–67.

—— (2008b) *Legaler Status von ausländischen Arbeitskräften in der Türkei*, unpublished manuscript.

—— (2010) "Familiäre Orientierungen und Arbeitsmarktintegration von hochqualifizierten MigrantInnen in Deutschland, Kanada und der Türkei", in A.-M. Nohl, K. Schittenhelm, O. Schmidtke and A. Weiß (eds) *Kulturelles Kapital in der Migration*, Wiesbaden: VS Verlag Sozialwissenschaften, pp. 285–300.

Ragin, C.C. (1987) *The Comparative Method. Moving beyond Qualitative and Quantitative Strategies*, Berkeley: University of California Press.

—— (1997) "Turning the tables: How case-oriented research challenges variable-oriented research", *Comparative Social Research*, 16: 27–42.

Rehbein, B. (2006) "Sozialstruktur und Arbeitsteilung. Eine historische Skizze am Beispiel Festlandsüdostasiens", *Asien*, 101: 23–45.

Robertson, R. (1995) "Glocalization: Time-space and homogeneity–heterogeneity", in M. Featherstone, S. Lash and R. Robertson (eds) *Global Modernities*, London: Sage, pp. 25–44.

Schittenhelm, K. (2009) "Qualitatives Sampling. Strategien und Kriterien der Fallauswahl", in S. Maschke and L. Stecher (eds) *Enzyklopädie Erziehungswissenschaft Online. Fachgebiet Methoden der empirischen erziehungswissenschaftlichen Forschung*, Weinheim, München: Juventa. Online encyclopedia: www.erzwissonline.de (accessed June 3, 2011).

—— (forthcoming) "Pathways to qualified labour. Career trajectories of the second generation", in M. Windzio and M. Wingens (eds) *Migration in a Life Course Perspective*, Dordrecht: Springer.

Schütze, F. (2003) "Hülya's migration to Germany as self-sacrifice undergone and suffered in love for her parents, and her later biographical individualisation. Biographical problems and biographical work of marginalisation and individualisation of a young Turkish woman", *Forum Qualitative Sozialforschung*, 4(3). Online: www.qualitative-research.net/fqs-texte/3-03/3-03schuetze-e.htm (accessed December 1, 2003).

Tilly, C. (1984) *Big Structures, Large Processes, Huge Comparisons*, New York: Russell Sage Foundation.

Walby, S. (2009) *Globalization and Inequalities. Complexity and Contested Modernities*, Thousand Oaks, CA: Sage.

Weber, M. (1968) *Economy and Society: An Outline of Interpretive Sociology*, G. Roth and C. Wittich (eds) New York: Bedminster Press.

Weiß, A. (2005) "The transnationalization of social inequality. Conceptualizing social positions on a world scale", *Current Sociology*, 53(4): 707–28.

—— (2006) "Comparative research on highly skilled migrants. Or: (In what way) can qualitative interviews be used in order to reconstruct a class position?", *Forum Qualitative Sozialforschung*, 7(3) Art. 2. Online: www.qualitative-research.net/index.php/fqs/article/view/136/297 (accessed June 3, 2011).

—— (2010a) "Vergleiche jenseits des Nationalstaats. Methodologischer Kosmopolitismus in der soziologischen Forschung über hochqualifizierte Migration", *Soziale Welt*, 61(3/4): 295–311.

―― (2010b) "Contextualizing capabilities in a world of territorial containers, political closure, and social functionings", paper presented at the *Inaugural Conference of the Research Network on Interdependent Inequalities in Latin America* (desiguALdades.net), Berlin, December 2010.

――, Ofner, U.S. and Pusch, B. (2010) "Migrationsbezogene biographische Orientierungen und ihre ausländerrechtliche Institutionalisierung", in A.-M. Nohl, K. Schittenhelm, O. Schmidtke and A. Weiß (eds) *Kulturelles Kapital in der Migration*, Wiesbaden: VS Verlag Sozialwissenschaften, pp. 197–210.

Wimmer, A. and Glick Schiller, N. (2002) "Methodological nationalism and the study of migration", *Archives Europeennes de Sociologie*, 43(2): 217–40.

Woellert, F., Kröhnert, S., Sippel, L. and Klingholz, R. (2009) *Ungenutzte Potenziale*, Berlin: Berlin Institut für Bevölkerung und Entwicklung.

Yin, R.K. (2009) *Case Study Research. Design and Methods*, Thousand Oaks, CA: Sage.

Part II
Materiality, Culture and Ethnicity
Overcoming Pitfalls in Researching Globalization

5 Global Ethnography 2.0
From Methodological Nationalism to Methodological Materialism
Zsuzsa Gille

The purpose of this chapter is to provide a model for incorporating materiality into the ethnographic study of globalization. Such a theoretical and methodological task is necessary for two reasons. First, it provides a corrective to the depiction of globalization as transcending material constraints or, allegedly having homogenized the world, as neutralizing place-based, concrete conditions of production.[1] Second, such an incorporation is a useful tool in transcending methodological nationalism.

Methodological nationalism, in my reading, stems from the assumption of classic social science research that the social is co-extensive with the national. Marx, Weber and Durkheim, to remain with the classics, imagined society fully within the boundaries of the nation-state. It is not that they—especially Marx and Weber—ignored inter-state, meaning international, social relations but that first, such links tended to form among well-bounded nations, as a whole, and second, the national tended to ontologically precede the international. So the social was not only co-extensive with the national, but this nationally bounded social was also the origin and the cause of the international. This framework becomes a built-in obstacle to the discovery that the international may in fact precede and even affect the social space of the nation.

While there are many successful models for transcending methodological nationalism, such models tend to remain in what I call methodological idealism. This stance evacuates the nonhuman content from social institutions, social relations and change processes—a practice Bruno Latour (1993) has called *purification*. In contrast, scholars in science and technology or consumption studies, and those associated with the *practice turn*, argue that our *social* is best described as hybrid—that is, co-produced by humans and nonhumans. I call this approach *methodological materialism*. I use the terms methodological *idealism* and *materialism* to distinguish the ontological assumptions of scholarship that ignores nonhuman agency even when such entities matter, and scholarship that is open to the possibility that nonhuman actors co-constitute the social. Note that this is a weaker version of the hybrid ontology Latour has in mind, to the extent that he assumes that nonhuman actors always matter. In my mind, whether that is the case is an empirical

92 *Zsuzsa Gille*

question and an issue of clearly demonstrating *what it matters for*. Nevertheless, if our conceptual framework and methodology *a priori* exclude the role materials, objects or nature play in the production of the social, we will not only misrepresent reality but will also draw faulty political conclusions from our studies. Therefore it is more prudent to assume a hybrid ontology.

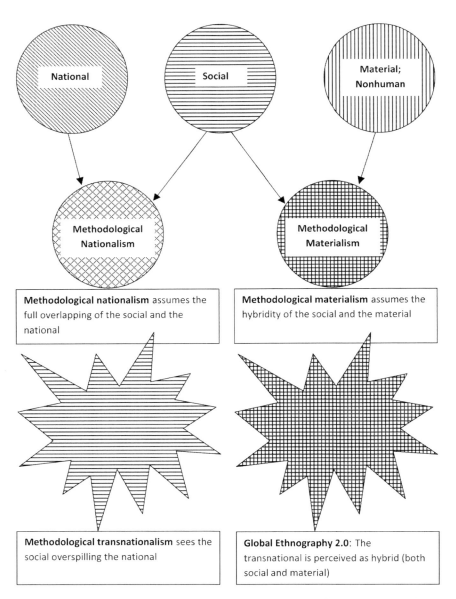

Figure 5.1 The relationship between the national, the social and the material.

In our journey beyond methodological nationalism, we do not simply have to make the move of *disentangling* the social from the national but also *entangling* the social with the material. Furthermore, while such disentangling and entangling have both been achieved in various studies, they were done so in isolation from each other, leading to ignorance of the relationship between these two moves. In what follows, therefore, I will provide a critical review of both perspectives and evaluate how their shortcomings can be transcended by a new, methodologically materialist version of Global Ethnography that I will call, rather cheekily, Global Ethnography 2.0.

PREVIOUS MODELS OF DISENTANGLING THE SOCIAL FROM THE NATIONAL

We have come a long way in disentangling the social from the national, especially in the last 20 years—though some argue that Immanuel Wallerstein's world systems theory, in the early 1970s, was the first systematic break with methodological nationalism. As Neil Brenner (1999) and others have pointed out, however, in world systems theory the primary connectivity is still among nation-states, and only with what we call transnational studies have we seen attention shifting to other types of linkages both above and below the scale of the national, such as Mato (1997) distinguishes it:

1) Local–local relations (in which the locals connected are within different nation-states).
2) Local–national relations (in which the relationship between a nation-state and a local in another country is occurring without the mediation of the state of that local).
3) Local–global relations (in which the local is connected to actors at the supranational level, again without the mediation of its own nation-state.[2]

Many have also called attention to the multidirectionality, and thus the declining predictability, of relations between core and periphery, such as the Global Commodity Chain scholars (Gereffi and Korzeniewicz 1994), and several anthropologists, among whom the most influential has been Arjun Appadurai (1990), with his concept of *scapes*. Others, such as Saskia Sassen (1995), have argued that while the power of the nation-state has indeed weakened relative to global economic actors—whether multinational companies (*MNCs*) or supranational organizations, such as the World Trade Organization (*WTO*) or the World Bank—the state, both at the national, local and subnational regional levels still plays a very important role in facilitating and thus politically, economically and materially grounding seemingly free-floating economic activities. Others too have started paying more attention to the increasing role of the subnational or local scales, including scholars of a more classically Marxist kind, such as David Harvey, who emphasizes the strategic uses of local conditions (urban space, infrastructure, tax laws, labor force and so on) for attracting capital. While quite divergent theoretically and politically, all of these perspectives point not just to a social that is overspilling the national container, but also to a newly positioned and newly emancipated local.

Different scholars however have drawn different conclusions from this emancipation of the local. For Harvey (1990), a methodological concentration on the local is a postmodernist move in ignoring that capitalism is primarily a macro-level and global social order. For this reason he considers locality-based empirical studies as necessarily restricted to the local, meaning parochial, for which Doreen Massey (1994) has criticized him. Other social scientists instead have called for new concepts of space, including the reconceptualization of place and locality (Massey 1994). Yet another group of scholars, the *Global Ethnography* collective I was a part of, teased out the methodological implications of globalization and argued that ethnography based on place-based fieldwork is still relevant for full understanding. Anna Tsing (2000) explicitly critiques the assumption that globalization can and should only be studied at the scale of the global, calling that assumption *globalism*.

In *Global Ethnography*, my colleagues and I, under the guidance of Michael Burawoy, demonstrate how and why globalization and its associated processes and institutions should be studied at the local scale. We argue that people in different parts of the world and differently positioned in their respective societies experience globalization in radically different ways (Burawoy *et al.* 2000). We group these experiences into what we call the three slices of globalization: global forces, global connections and global imaginations. In the first instance, people experience globalization as an external force impinging on the locality and changing their lives in ways over which they have no control, restricting their choices to defensive reactions and/or adaptations. These changes in general are rather negative, such as factories closing or welfare being cut as a result of pressures by supranational agencies committed to a neoliberal economic agenda.

People in other positions, however, may find that globalization and transnationalization, or the deterritorialization of the nation-state, also offer opportunities. For them, whether they are migrants finding employment in countries that are better off or political activists maintaining transnational contacts with movements abroad, globalization opens up a space in which they can build connections to improve their lives and better represent their interests. They actively participate in building these links which, in turn, sustain them economically, socially and culturally, and which allow them to maneuver around the global forces that otherwise might be more constraining than enabling.

Finally, there are social groups that are not only able to take some control over the processes of globalization that affect their lives, but that actively engage in defining, contesting and redefining discourses of globalization. They wage their battles much less with a localist and defensive agenda, and rather enter political struggles with alternative views of what globalization should mean and how it could work in their favor. Here the emphasis is on the material power of global imaginations. Below I will revisit this theoretical and methodological model to demonstrate how Global Ethnography may be "hybridized" into Global Ethnography 2.0.

PREVIOUS ATTEMPTS AT ENTANGLING THE SOCIAL WITH THE MATERIAL

Besides Actor-Network-Theory (*ANT*), there have been other attempts at theoretical and methodological models that allow for the agency of nonhumans. While most of these attempts have not explicitly theorized the transnationality of the social, they have demonstrated how particular socio-material assemblages can get lifted out of their original national milieu and transported into a new social, cultural and natural environment with which of course they dialectically interact. Two such implicitly transnational hybrid ontologies can be found in environmental history and in the legacy of the Annales School.

Environmental History

Environmental historians have long been trailblazers in incorporating natural and material agency into our understanding of seemingly purely social transformations. Donald Worster (1985), for example, argues that historically large-scale irrigation networks have always given rise to what Karl Wittfogel calls *hydraulic societies* (Worster 1985), with extremely centralized state power, which demands labor and/or taxes in return for building waterworks and distributing water. Such societies tend to develop despotism rather than guaranteeing freedom, and they do so quite independently of the nature or level of technological development and the dominant form of ownership. In a similar vein but with more attention to knowledge and imagination, William Cronon (1991) in *Nature's Metropolis*, an environmental history of Chicago, explodes the city-country divide to illuminate urban-rural interdependence, a purpose, according to him, best served by a variety of stories about the paths that lead from Chicago to its hinterland. He describes how nature (geography, climate and natural resources), taken for granted as the ecological conditions of Chicago's birth and development, has been in fact a construction informed by the social interests of Chicago's boosters and other social actors. He implies that their concepts of ecological givens were not endogenous to the society in which they lived but were derived from knowledges of different kind of environments. Here too we see the effort to get away from deriving the spatial and ecological changes of the emergent Chicago from an overall logic of capitalism, as is evident in Cronon's refusal to trace concrete historical processes to any kind of metalogic of capitalist growth, urbanization or the conquering of the frontiers.

Actor-Network-Theory

Actor-Network-Theory, as mentioned above, hypothesizes a hybrid ontology in which humans and nonhumans constantly co-create each other. Latour uses the metaphor of network to decenter human agency. While in recent iterations of ANT, Latour (2005) and John Law (2007) have both reflected self-critically on the network metaphor, this concept has been foundational and rather consequential for their empirical studies and the further elaboration of their theoretical arguments against traditional social science. The best empirical demonstration of the concept's utility is Latour's *Pasteurizing France*. In it, Latour (1993) rewrites the story of Pasteur's role in developing modern medical science. He *decenters* the human actor, Pasteur himself, by demonstrating how it was not Pasteur but the network he built of doctors, hygienists, bacteria, farms, animals, state bureaucrats, laboratories and colonial authorities that instigated the progress usually credited to the sole scientist. At the same time, he also *recenters* Pasteur and his network in the sense that he argues that what Pasteur's web reformed was not only medical practice but society itself. By institutionalizing new scientific knowledge, practices in a whole slew of arenas of social life radically changed, and these practices also shifted the balance of power by empowering some actors (doctors, the colonial army) while disempowering others (indigenous Africans). In fact, these social actors were no longer identical with their pre-Pasteur selves. France as a colonial power, for example, no longer consisted only of settlers, the church, a colonial bureaucracy and an occupying army but also of bacteriological science and practices such as laboratory tests and immunization. In sum, this view of France is not one of classes, parties, ethnicities, institutions or other forces, but of a network in which nodes can be human as well as nonhuman. The agency of the nodes, just as in Manuel Castells (1989)—whose understanding of the global social also makes use of the network metaphor—is not primordial but rather derives from the connections among the nodes.

Entangling Nonhumans with Colonialism

Fernand Braudel's (1981) magnum opus, *The Structures of Everyday Life*, presents social reality between the 15th and 18th centuries as a tripartite structure:

1) The uppermost sphere of wealth concentration and foreign exchange.
2) The market economy—this most familiar sphere of production and exchange in their most visible forms (small shops, banks, markets).
3) And below all this, the zone of material life, "the world of self-sufficiency and barter of goods and services within a very small radius"

(Braudel 1981: 24), the sphere where transformation was the slowest, but on which the upper two layers depended.

Braudel of course does not use language characteristic of ANT, such as "nonhuman agency"; nevertheless his actual case studies focusing on specific material, biological objects and processes do demonstrate that each age has its limits and possibilities determined by this *shadowy* zone of everyday practices. Braudel also does not draw the conclusion implicit in some environmental history (see above) that precapitalist and capitalist social relations gained their key features from the materiality of means and conditions of production. Rather this micro level is presented as the particular of the universal macro, as local(ized) and rather static, especially in relation to the networked, transnational (1981: 24) and dynamic upper zone. In sum, materiality is to be captured at the local or micro level, and this micro level is occupied by *place*, conceptualized as in stasis.[3]

Syndey Mintz (1986) was much inspired by the Annales School, and his classic study demonstrates the role sugar—or as he prefers, sweetness—played in the formation not just of colonial empires but also of capitalism in Europe. He pays particular attention to the material qualities of sugar cane—such as its need for speedy harvesting and processing and the difficulty of smuggling it in preprocessed form, thus rendering it a good tax commodity—and its ability to quickly infuse a large dose of calories into the human body, a quality which made it an ideal "fast food" for the growing industrial working class newly subjected to machine time.

Timothy Mitchell's (2002) work on the role of science, statistics, maps and nonhuman agents, like mosquitoes and paper, in colonizing and modernizing Egypt is in many respects a continuation of the kind of historiography developed by Braudel and Mintz, but it owes more to Latour. In *The Rule of Experts* Mitchell (2002) demonstrates how nonhuman agents were enrolled in the colonizing project, but also how some of them produced distinct economic and political outcomes quite independent of and often contradictory to a modernizing, capitalist or colonialist logic. Mitchell, cognizant of ANT's relative blindness to power or power's endurance, builds his historiography on the synthesis of ANT with poststructuralism (especially Foucault) and postcolonial studies. Finally, it must be remembered that Braudel, Mintz and Mitchell all engage with and critically appropriate Marxism.[4]

Global Assemblages and Technological Zones

The model of entangling the social with the material that engages with globalization studies and multiple scales most self-consciously is provided by the volume *Global Assemblages*, edited by Aihwa Ong and Stephen Collier (2005). Like Mitchell, the authors also follow ANT, poststructuralism, convention theory and other, primarily European, contemporary theories of late capitalism and neoliberal governmentality. The case studies examine specific phenomena—"technoscience, circuits of licit and illicit exchange, systems of administration or governance, and regimes of ethics or values" (Ong and Collier 2005: 4)—that articulate the kinds of shifts previously only captured at the global scale by universal concepts. Ong and Collier's concept of assemblage, taken from ANT, is the product of multiple determinations that are not reducible to a single logic—that is, assemblage refers to the level of the concrete. They also emphasize that the temporality of the assemblage is emergent. "It does not always involve new forms, but forms that are shifting, in formation or at stake" (Ong and Collier 2005: 12). Some of the authors in this rich volume rely on Andrew Barry's (2001) concept of the technological zone, "a space of circulation within which technologies take more or less standardized forms" (Barry 2001: 122). This too is a fluid concept. These are spaces formed when technical devices, practices, artifacts and experimental materials are made more or less comparable and connectable, but they are not fixed structures; "they demand regeneration, adjustment and reconfiguration: frequent maintenance work" (Barry 2001: 40). Barry acknowledges that Europe as a technological zone is not one that is smooth and perfectly well connected, where capital and labor circulate without impediments, but argues that they are full of "fractures and discontinuities" (Barry 2001: 40). Yet the concept does refer to comparability and connectability, and thus, in my mind, to compatibility, and as such, it still does not make space for from-below constructions of alternative compatibilities or even the lack of compatibility. In general, neither the concept of global assemblages nor that of technological zones recognize that micro or macro logics are qualitatively different nor do they deal sufficiently with the autonomy of the macro or the global scales. This is quite understandable given that both major theoretical inspirations for the volume (as well as for Barry's work), ANT and poststructuralism, hope to transcend the micro-macro divide.

THE CONFLATION OF SCALE WITH LEVEL OF ANALYSIS

As argued above, studies within or following Actor-Network-Theory have tended to valorize the micro level. ANT proponents argue that factors sociology tends to attribute to macro-level institutions and relations, such as power or the economy, are always emergent, and since the task is to demonstrate how that happens at the level of *concrete* actors and *specific* situations, the only empirically important scale is the *micro* level. Their theoretical and epistemological ambition is to transcend the macro-micro dichotomy; nevertheless, in empirical research associated with ANT, the micro is never hooked back up to the macro level, and thus the macro does not actually make an appearance. As Ben Fine (2005) and Laurier and Philo (1999) argue, the macro ceases to exist. This unwillingness to distinguish between micro and macro explains Latour's insistence that the topography of the social is flat.

This preference for the micro is animated by what Massey (1994) calls the conflation of social scale with level of abstraction.[5] Social scientists, she argues, have for too long assumed that different social scales, such as macro and micro, or global and local, represent different levels of abstraction, so that studies done at the level of the micro or the local are descriptive of concrete manifestations of larger macro- or global-level forces, institutions or phenomena. In fact, it has been argued that since theory is about producing general claims and since the general can only be captured at the macro or the global scales, studies focusing on the local or the micro levels are limited in terms of their contribution to theory-building. In a way, ANT's move to the micro can be seen as a rebellion against this state of affairs. However, as shown above, in their attempt to fight such reifications with concrete analyses, ANT rushes headlong to the other extreme, namely denying the existence of the macro scale altogether. That is, ANT has bought wholesale into the identification of the macro level with abstraction and the micro level with concreteness.

Law (2004), in his analysis of airplane design, on the surface seems to get around this problem when he identifies varying degrees of complexity as one travels down or up the rungs of social scale. He does not so much deny that the macro or the global exist as argue that the latter can be contained within the local. It is in the local where things attain a desirably baroque complexity. However, to the extent that complexity is a state of many determinations, lining up the complexity-simplicity dichotomy with the micro/local–macro/global dichotomy is just another way of saying that the local and the micro are the true locus of the concrete. So, despite the reordering of social scales—placing the global in the local—he too conflates social scale with level of abstraction.

Massey's critique is not directed at ANT but at Harvey and others wedded to classical Marxist epistemology; however, it is useful to revisit her argument and imagine how she would see ANT's reaction to that type of Marxism. She suggests that if by *concrete* we mean the product of many determinations, then the market, for example, whose existence is constantly called into question by ANT scholars because it is macro and as such too abstract, is not less concrete than certain economic and material practices at the level of the individual, the household or the village. Economists and sociologists can certainly distill abstract laws or logics of the market, but that doesn't mean either of the following:

1) That the logic in question acts alone or is the single cause of a range of phenomena.
2) Nor that those "abstract" laws don't change in certain circumstances under the pressure of concrete actors—human or nonhuman.

In sum, the market too can be the product of many determinations. This however doesn't mean that it doesn't exist or that some actors cannot use it and even mold it to their advantage more than others. Economic sociologists and institutionalist economists have long demonstrated the social construction of the market, and Mitchell (2002) also shows how it is produced both in colonial and in neoliberalized Egypt. The conclusion to draw from these studies is not that there is no such thing as a market—not in the sense of the physical meeting place of seller and buyer at the micro level but in the sense of a macro-level mechanism—but that once it is in place as a mechanism of power it can get entrenched, can extend and can "govern at a distance" (Mitchell 2002), relatively independently from those who set it in motion. An important aspect of power is exactly how it manages to traverse scales and reproduce itself in different concrete situations. ANT makes gestures toward such an understanding when it coins phrases such as *centers of calculation, immutable mobiles* or *translation*, but its analysis always remains at the micro level. That is, it does not recognize that once macro dynamics or macro actors emerge from micro-level exchanges, they can become relatively autonomous from their micro foundations and temporally enduring. As Noel Castree correctly puts it, they may develop an ability to "collect power and condense it" and thereby compel other actors to act as "intermediaries" or act on their behalf (Castree 2002: 141). Their endurance and ability to act as intermediaries is made possible exactly by being embroiled in new macro configurations.

To conclude: If we were to abandon the macro level we would not only leave unanswered this crucial question about how (macro-level) power emerges—that ANT implies is of paramount social significance—but we would also reduce the importance of the micro level, which would be in direct opposition to ANT's principles and methodological ambitions. Latour's insistence on flatness and the denial that macro- and micro-level

Table 5.1 The Relationship between Geographical Scales and Levels of Abstraction in Different Methodological Traditions (source: author)

	Micro/Local	*Macro/Global*
Concrete	ANT Marxist and sociological case studies	Global Ethnography 1.0 (social concrete) "Global Ethnography 2.0" (material and hybrid concrete)
Abstract	Chicago School Grounded theory*	Classical Marxism Environmental flows

*The Chicago School and Grounded Theory in general sought to generate universal social laws by comparing, aggregating or synthesizing empirical findings from micro-level ethnographic work. The point was to ignore the specificities of the local site in order to discover general societal features and dynamics. See this type of characterization in Burawoy (1991).

dynamics are qualitatively different is therefore rooted in the confusion of the social scale with the level of abstraction, the same mistaken assumption many sociological case studies are based on. Therefore, the way to avoid reified social analysis, whether methodological nationalism or methodological idealism, lies not in switching levels of analysis (from local to global or from micro to macro) but rather in switching levels of abstraction—that is, shifting from abstract to concrete.

In what follows, I will demonstrate how global ethnography occupies this preferred cell of combining the study of the global with an attention to the concrete. I will then show through a case study how it can disentangle the social from the national while also entangling the social and the material. I will call this version therefore Global Ethnography 2.0.

GLOBAL ETHNOGRAPHY 2.0

Many in the field of global ethnography wanted to avoid a certain reified social analysis and along with Sassen (1995, 2000), Tsing (2000) or Marcus (1998), aimed at *grounding* globalization by exploring globalization and transnational social relations from below—that is, from the perspective of people whose everyday lives have been touched by processes associated with globalization.

Global ethnography, as in the extended case method (see Burawoy 1991), focuses on the concrete at the level of macro or global. The difference between 1.0 and 2.0 is that the concrete now explicitly includes materiality.

Though global ethnography has allowed for a variety of linkages between local and global, while also retaining the methodological significance of locality-based fieldwork, it has not specifically attended to materiality or the agency of nonhuman agents. In general, until the appearance of the volume *Global Assemblages*,[6] materiality has remained elusive in studies of globalization. To the extent that the study of nonhuman agents and practices is necessarily a study of the concrete, and to the extent that many early studies of globalization assumed that globalization is best studied at the global level, which in turn was assumed to be the proper level of abstract analysis, this silence is understandable. But there has also been an assumption, especially in network approaches, that since locality no longer matters, and since place is where the effects of materiality—natural resources, landscapes, characteristic economic activities, particular proximities and distances—tend to be felt, the material is also transcended, along with the local. At the time of writing *Global Ethnography,* therefore, we were content to demonstrate the significance of place and felt little need or pressure to explore the material.[7]

Social science scholarship now has started to reflect on the increasing mobilization of bodies, genes, molecules and natural resources in new modalities of power, sometimes referred to as *neoliberal governmentality,* sometimes as *biopolitics* (Barry, Osborne and Rose 1996; Foucault 2003; Brown 2003; Clarke 2004; Hay 2003; Ong 2006; Osborne and Rose 1999; Power 1997). While much of this literature is still concerned with the human, having descended to the level of genes and molecules, it has created a new opening toward the consideration of practices wrestling with nonhuman agency. Furthermore, for those of us studying environmental and food issues, the need to find a way to incorporate material flows into the flows and networks aimed at capturing the global social appears rather pressing.

To demonstrate how to bring down even seemingly "big" concepts such as state socialism or neoliberal globalization to the level of the concrete while not denying the specificity of "big" dynamics, let me provide an example. I will use a case study of a food scandal in Hungary to shed light on a material agent—the European Union—and its unique version of capitalism mobilized. This is not a case study in the classical sense, demonstrating the micro-level particularities of macro- or global-level forces or transformations. Rather, it concentrates on concrete materialities and practices that determine the nature of seemingly abstract and pre-given supranational institutions such as the European Union and global economic dynamics such as the neoliberal race to the bottom.

THE EMPIRICAL CASE: THE HUNGARIAN PAPRIKA BAN[8]

On October 27, 2004, the Hungarian government shocked the public by banning the sale of paprika powder and its use in restaurants, issuing a warning against household use until further notice. The chief Hungarian public health authority (*ÁNTSZ*) found that out of the 72 examined commodities containing paprika regularly sold in Hungary, 13 contained aflatoxin B1, a carcinogenic mycotoxin produced by mold. The concentration was as much as 16 times larger than the threshold permitted by the European Union (5 mg per kg). To extend the testing to all products containing paprika, their sale was banned. The testing and thus the ban lasted three days, during which ÁNTSZ gradually released the list of products found to be safe. Ultimately, 48 products tested positive for contamination, though it is not clear how many of these were legally seen as being toxic as well, above the European Union (*EU*) limits, the sale of which would thus constitute a criminal act. Aflatoxin, which in public discourse had been primarily linked to repeated EU bans on African or Brazilian nuts, can only grow in peppers that are produced in Mediterranean or tropical climates. As Hungarian consumers were astounded to find out, the famous Szeged and Kalocsa paprika, sold all over the world as a *Hungaricum,*[9] contained peppers imported from Brazil and Spain. As for food safety experts, they were dumbfounded that contaminated products could find their way to the grocery shelves undetected despite the elaborate food safety standards recently adopted to meet EU accession requirements.

How did this happen? I will argue that the insertion of Hungary into EU networks of commerce and safety monitoring made rational new modes of paprika production and opened up new channels by which this microtoxin, this fungus, could enter the country, which entry then excluded Hungarian paprika as an export product exactly from those Western European markets whose accessibility was the rationale for opening up Hungarian markets.

While trade between Hungary and the EU member countries had been gradually liberalized by the time of formal accession, some pockets of "protectionism" stayed in place until May 1, 2004. One of them was the high import duty levied on paprika. Overnight this was reduced from 44.2 percent to 5 per cent, radically increasing the appeal of cheap Latin American imports. Peppers grown in tropical and Mediterranean climates are generally more vivid in color as well as cheaper than Hungarian varieties, rendering the mixing of peppers grown in different countries an irresistible practice for processors and retailers. Processors and retailers in other countries with no import duties on spice peppers had already been mixing paprika but still marketing it as Hungarian, a designation that fetches a premium price. Hungarian processors simply wanted to reap the same economic benefits after EU accession.

There were two major sources of imports immediately prior to the scandal. Hungary "imported" 22 tons from Spain in September 2004. While the same trade event would have been considered an import just a few months before, after May 1, 2004, that is, after Hungary's formal accession to EU membership, it no longer counted as an import because Spain and Hungary, as EU members, now shared the same customs borders. This has great significance for food safety, as I will show below. The other "real" exporter was Brazil, from where Hungary had imported 88 tons since December 2003. Eight tons of this tested positive for aflatoxin B1.

While it is commonly assumed that with EU membership, candidate countries' food safety regulation would improve, in fact in some cases the opposite came to be true. While member countries are, on the whole, free to enforce standards—whether food safety or environmental standards—that are stricter than those required by the EU, I know of no new member country that retained its standards when those were stricter than the EU's. (In Hungary this was certainly the case with the legal definition of fresh milk, with certain emission standards or with nature protection laws.) This obviously has a lot to do with these countries' hunger for capital and with their poor bargaining positions. It is in this sense that the replacement of national with EU standards in effect resulted in a relaxation of norms.

First of all, in the case of the Spanish peppers, since they were not "real" imports, they were no longer checked when they entered Hungary. This ended up being a problem in August 2004, when through random testing—the only kind of test done since EU accession—one of the Hungarian paprika processors found ochratoxin, another microtoxin produced by molds. In order to avoid a scandal, they silently took back the affected products from grocery stores. Note that what allowed this discovery was that Hungarians traditionally tested for this liver- and kidney-damaging toxin in paprika, even though the EU had no limits for ochratoxin in peppers and spices (*EU Food Law News* 1999).

Second, as trade experts argued, when peppers are imported to Hungary from Spain, there is no certain way of knowing whether they were really grown and dried in Spain or whether Spain itself has imported them from elsewhere (Index.hu 2004).

Third, after accession, even the peppers constituting real imports were removed from the jurisprudence of national authorities, because it is the authorities at the entry port, in this case Rotterdam, that carry out the prescribed controls. However, spice peppers are not on the list of imported goods that must be tested. Furthermore, the amount of required information on peppers has decreased. As the director of the Hungarian Food Safety Bureau (*MÉBH*) said, "Before EU accession we tested the peppers for 20–30 things; now, however, we don't, because the EU does not prescribe such tests" (Show 2004). As he pointed out, the certificates accompanying the import peppers from Latin America "are useless, because they only indicate whether there are any additives in them. Since the EU does not test for mold toxins [in peppers], the certificates obviously don't address them" (Show 2004). After the investigation was complete, the Hungarian government proposed to the Food Safety Committee of the European Union requiring aflatoxin tests on import peppers at EU entry ports. The Committee denied this request.

The paprika scandal had three key consequences. First, several countries, wanting to take charge of protecting their consumers, reacted to the contamination scandal by no longer accepting the safety tests performed by Hungarian laboratories for paprika, even though it was Hungarian authorities using Hungarian laboratories that discovered the contamination. Paying for foreign lab tests is an added expense now for Hungarian exporters, and it is not clear whether they can raise prices to maintain their profit rates. Second, the Hungarian government implemented a stricter labeling requirement so that now the national origin of all paprika has to be explicitly marked on its packaging. Third, the image of Hungarian paprika has suffered greatly, which has not only cheapened the product but lowered the value of the two dominant Hungarian paprika processing firms. In the end, one of them, Szeged Paprika, was no longer able to resist buyout attempts, and now it is in the hands of a new private owner that, according to industry representatives I interviewed, acts on behalf of a large foreign food-retailing corporation.

How would methodological nationalism analyze this case? While methodological nationalism can characterize multiple methodologies, what they would share is the view of paprika as endogenous, fully within the

Hungarian nation-state, a default condition that doesn't change by mixing peppers grown in different countries. Hungarian processors import peppers from other nation-states, mix them with Hungarian peppers and then export the mixed product to other nation-states. This view would fail to see how paprika is a transnational product already: Retailers in other countries have been mixing peppers from different sources and then selling the powdered product as Hungarian. This practice and the resulting expectation it has created about the color of Hungarian paprika (which, as mentioned above, is never as red as that from warmer, sunnier climates) is now part and parcel of what Hungarian paprika is. Even when Hungarian peppers aren't mixed, they already stand in a particular relation with the world market, better or worse, cheaper or more expensive, than the mixed spice, and Hungarianness now expresses a certain transnational or extra-Hungarian element. Furthermore, from the methodological nationalist perspective, the EU would seem to exist outside the nation-states, rather than as a supranational entity whose imposed practices have transformed what the national is to begin with—that is, what a national regulatory system is and what makes Hungarian paprika Hungarian.

Global Ethnography 1.0 would ask which experience of globalization best describes this case. From the perspective of Hungarian paprika growers, the EU appears as a global force; it imposes free trade and its standards, or better said, it selectively imposes standards in a way that they—the local—have no way of objecting to. The combination of free trade and a lack of EU monitoring of aflatoxin has thus resulted in a greater exposure for these actors not just to external competition but also to a fall in sales due to the tarnished image of Hungarian paprika. At the same time, from the perspective of Hungarian paprika processors, entrance to the EU actually meant greater connections with Brazilian and Spanish pepper producers and exporters and an ability to mix paprika of multiple origins that was already being done by non-Hungarian wholesalers. Depending on what the primary focus was—producers or processors—the experience of globalization—that is, EU membership—could be either that of global forces impinging on the local or global connections that provide some new, though not unlimited, opportunities. For the former, the space of maneuver shrinks; for the latter, it expands. Although, since these processors eventually had to use foreign laboratories to certify the safety of their product and since one of them could no longer resist buyout attempts, they too eventually ended up being crushed by this global force.

Actor Network Theorists would primarily see the building of networks composed of paprika producers, processors, laboratories, peppers, pathogens and EU officials. Since they would not see, let alone start with, a macro or global actor such as the EU, most likely they would start with the processors because they seem to be the ones taking initiative to build new connections in an effort to make themselves more independent of domestic producers and their expensive peppers, and to take the economic power arising from mixing peppers away from non-Hungarian wholesalers. Indeed, ANT tends to focus on the time period when networks emerge, rather than on the smooth operation of already existing and well-oiled circuits, to prove again and again that power is emergent and fragile. While it certainly proved to be so for the processors after the ban, after the discrediting of Hungarian laboratories, and after the EU's rejection of the proposal to inspect imported peppers at EU borders for the presence of microtoxins, ANT would fail to notice that it is the presence and the power of an already existing global-level actor, the EU, that resulted in this outcome for the processors.

Unlike ANT, Global Ethnography 2.0 acknowledges the existence of macro- and global-level actors, such as the EU; but, like ANT, it would not reduce it to a purely social institution. The European Union, from this perspective, is not simply an institutional network—it is not purely social. The EU exists and thrives through its material practices, including safety standards and the institutions that design and implement them, the embodied knowledge by which such standards are justified and the plethora of actual commodities produced according to such standards. The EU, however, is not only a network unto itself, it is also a node in the network built by economic actors such as transnational food processing and retailing corporations, who routinely use the EU's network for their own benefit.

Finally, Global Ethnography 2.0 would also emphasize that what creates a particular experience of Europeanization—whether global forces, connections or imaginations—is in part due to the nonhuman things that are brought into circulation and which therefore co-produce the *social* relations that connect local with local and local with global. If it hadn't been for the aflatoxin, the processors would still happily mix imported bright red peppers with the paler though better-tasting Hungarian ones, they would finally start to reap the benefits of mixing, they would increase their independence from domestic producers; in sum, they would experience EU membership as a vast extension of their space of maneuver and would revel in their newly built connections. As for the Hungarian growers, without the aflatoxin, they would have lost much of their bargaining power in negotiations with the processors, but now the new labeling requirements give them new leverage.

CONCLUSION: CAN A FUNGUS SPEAK?[10]

The paprika case is not about a pre-existing abstract macro-level logic of capitalism playing itself out on the Hungarian *puszta*. After all, neither the race to the bottom—the neoliberal version—nor the EU's protectionist race-to-the-top[11] version seems to explain what has happened (Gille 2009). Rather, becoming a member in a supranational organization such as the EU, ANT would remind us, inserts humans and nonhumans into particular networks. Nevertheless, in that process the nature and meaning of those connectivities also change. It is therefore not the case, as ANT would have it, that the macro emerges from the micro, but rather that concrete practices at the micro interact with already existing macro actors and processes, producing new macro- and global-level dynamics. It is not just that EU membership brought a new microscopic agent, aflatoxin, to Hungary, but that by doing so new practices emerged—import restrictions, the discrediting of Hungarian laboratories, the purchase of undervalued Hungarian assets, new labeling requirements—that radically transformed the meaning of the EU's presence in the Hungarian agriculture and food industry.[12]

Studying practices at the level of the concrete but both at the local and at the global scales sheds new light on the workings of supranational actors and transnational capital. Rather than treating the local as simply putting a local flavor on the global and seemingly universal logic of neoliberal capitalism, an "upgraded" global ethnography can demonstrate the role of materials and nature in producing not simply unintended consequences of global social and economic transformations but in modifying the very dynamics and the resulting concrete experiences of new local–global connections.

NOTES

1. I am using conditions of production in Karl Polanyi's (1944) and James O'Connor's (1988) sense. O'Connor borrows the notion of fictitious commodities from Polanyi, and rephrases two of the three, labor and land, as conditions of production, which then include human beings and their labor power, natural resources and the environment in general, as well as urban and rural space. O'Connor argues that there is a contradiction in capitalism not just between the forces and the relations of production but also between the forces and relations of production on the one hand and the conditions of production on the other.
2. The local here will be treated as a necessarily relative designation of geographical scale: *Local* most generally can refer to a village, town or city, or even a natural place, but occasionally if the place is too large, local can refer to a neighborhood, district or other subdivision of that place. With that logic, a very small nation-state, such as Luxembourg for example, can qualify to be designated as local as well as national. *Global* is also a heuristic device, also necessarily relative depending on the empirical context; however, most generally it refers to the geographical scale above the nation-state. In that sense, it can be used synonymously with the term *supranational*. In my usage an entity doesn't have to be present everywhere on Earth to warrant the designation *global*. A corporation or a nongovernmental organization (*NGO*) can be local, national or global, depending on the primary geographical scale at which it engages in most of its activities (Mato 1997). In theory it can be equally active at all of those scales simultaneously. In my usage supranational organizations, such as the World Bank, the World Trade Organization (*WTO*), the International Monetary Fund (*IMF*), NATO or the European Union, are global institutions, because they exert most of their influence at the global level or because what effects they have at the national and local levels are made possible by their global constitution. *Local* here does not

mean particular or specific, and *global* doesn't mean general or universal—more about this in the last section of the paper. While some nation-states may wield global power, I would only use the designation *global* for a state such as the US, for example, if the actual relationship or effect one is studying indeed takes place at the global or supranational scale.
3 See the critique of this view of place in Massey (1994).
4 I cannot incorporate Marxism into this essay, but others have analyzed how his kind of materialism (historical and dialectical) can be rearticulated to leave room for the agency of nature and, in some cases, of materials (Foster 2000; Castree 2002; Fine 2005); I also attempted a synthesis of Marxism with ANT in an article (Gille 2010).
5 Massey (1994) actually calls attention to the common erroneous assumption that phenomena at lower geographical scales (the local) can only be particular, specific and concrete, while the universal, general and abstract can only be found at higher geographical scales (the global). It is consistent with her argument to transpose this critique to the macro–micro dichotomy.
6 Though the volume *Global Governmentality: Governing International Spaces*, edited by William Walters and Wendy Larner (2004), came out a year before *Global Assemblages* and engaged with some of the same empirical issues and theoretical influences.
7 Rather, what we were constructively criticized for at the time was the avoidance of the national scale in conceptualizing our three slices and ignoring the social production of space, and as such, of the local (Hart 2002), instead of treating it as a taken-for-granted scale of action. Soon, two of the co-authors in fact demonstrated how global ethnography could incorporate the production of place and of scales (Gille and Ó Riain 2002).
8 I have analyzed this case in greater detail in Gille (2009).
9 *Hungaricums* are Hungary's signature products, primarily food and drink manifesting long-standing national traditions, local knowledge and identity. Besides paprika, Tokaj wine, Téli salami and the foie gras of Orosháza are among the better known *Hungaricums*.
10 This is a tongue-in-cheek reference to Gayatri Spivak's *Can the Subaltern Speak?* (1988) and Mitchell's chapter title *Can a Mosquito Speak?* (2002).
11 The term was actually coined in direct reference to, in fact in a bitter critique of, the EU's seemingly unfair and protectionist exclusion of African peanuts from European markets because African producers could not meet the EU's aflatoxin norms (Wilson and Otsuki 2001; Otsuki, Wilson and Sewadeh 2001).
12 It also, I might add, negatively impacted people's views of the EU, not an insignificant factor given the recent explosion in the popularity of anti-globalization (and anti-EU) extreme right-wing politics.

REFERENCES

Appadurai, A. (1990) "Disjuncture and difference in the global cultural economy", *Public Culture*, 2(2): 1–24.
Barry, A. (2001) *Political Machines: Governing a Technological Society*, London, New York: Continuum.
———, Osborne, T. and Rose, N. (eds) (1996) *Foucault and Political Reason: Liberalism, Neo-Liberalism and Rationalities of Government*, Chicago: University of Chicago Press.
Braudel, F. (1981) *The Structures of Everyday Life: Civilization and Capitalism 15th–18th Century*, Vol. 1, New York: Harper and Row.

Brenner, N. (1999) "Beyond state-centrism? Space, territoriality and geographical scale in globalization studies", *Theory and Society*, 28: 39–78.
Brown, W. (2003) "Neoliberalism and the end of liberal democracy", *Theory and Event*, 7(1): 1–43.
Burawoy, M. (1991) "Reconstructing social theories", in M. Burawoy (ed) *Ethnography Unbound: Power and Resistance in the Modern Metropolis*, Berkeley: University of California Press, pp. 8–27.
——, Blum, J.A., Sheba, G., Gille, Z., Gowan, T., Haney, L., Klawiter, M., Lopez, S.H., Ó Riain, S. and Thayer, M. (2000) *Global Ethnography: Forces, Connections, and Imaginations in a Postmodern World*, Berkeley and Los Angeles: University of California Press.
Castells, M. (1989) "Conclusion: The reconstruction of social meaning in the space of flows", in M. Castells (ed) *The Informational City*, Oxford: Basil Blackwell, pp. 348–353.
—— (1997) *The Information Age*, 3 Vols., Oxford: Blackwell.
Castree, N. (2002) "False antitheses? Marxism, nature and actor-networks", *Antipode*, 34: 119–48.
Clarke, J. (2004) "Dissolving the public realm? The logics and limits of neo-liberalism", *Journal of Social Policy*, 33(1): 27–48.
Cronon, W. (1991) *Nature's Metropolis: Chicago and the Great West*, New York: W.W. Norton.
EU Food Law News (February 8, 1999) "Contaminants—Mycotoxins—EC Permitted Levels", *Food Law News—EU—1999*. Online: www.reading.ac.uk/foodlaw/news/eu-99-17.htm (accessed April 17, 2011).
Fine, B. (2005) "From Actor-Network Theory to political economy", *Capitalism, Nature, Socialism*, 16: 91–108, 149.
Foster, J.B. (2000) *Marx's Ecology: Materialism and Nature*, New York: Monthly Review Press.
Foucault, M. (2003) *'Society Must Be Defended': Lectures at the Collège de France 1975–1976*, New York: Picador.
Gereffi, G. and Korzeniewicz, M. (eds) (1994) *Commodity Chains and Global Capitalism*, Westport, CT: Prager Press.
Gille, Z. (2009) "Globalizing paprika: Food governmentalities in the postsocialist European Union", in M. Caldwell (ed) *Food and Everyday Life in Postsocialist Eurasia*, Bloomington: Indiana University Press, pp. 97–128.
—— (2010) "Reassembling the macrosocial: Modes of production, actor networks and waste regimes", *Environment and Planning*, A42: 1049–64.
—— and Ó Riain, S. (2002) "Global ethnography", *Annual Review of Sociology*, 28: 271–95.
Hart, G. (2002) *Disabling Globalization: Places of Power in Post-Apartheid South Africa*, Berkeley: University of California Press.
Harvey, D. (1990) *The Condition of Postmodernity: An Inquiry into the Origins of Cultural Change*, Oxford: Blackwell.
Hay, J. (2003) "Unaided virtues: The (neo-)liberalization of the domestic sphere and the new architecture of community", in J.Z. Bratich, J. Packer and C. McCarthy (eds) *Foucault, Cultural Studies, and Governmentality*, Albany: State University of New York Press, pp. 165–206.
Index.hu (October 28, 2004) "Egy éve parlamenti téma volt az import paprika" [Parliament debated Paprika imports one year ago], *Index.hu*. Online: index.hu/gazdasag/magyar/papparl04102 (accessed April 17, 2011).
Latour, B. (1993) *The Pasteurization of France*, Cambridge, MA: Harvard University Press.
—— (2005) *Reassembling the Social: An Introduction to Actor-Network-Theory*, Oxford: Oxford University Press.

Laurier, E. and Philo, C. (1999) "X-morphising: A review essay of Bruno Latour's *Aramis, or the Love of Technology*", *Environment and Planning*, A31: 1047–71.
Law, J. (2004) "And if the global were small and noncoherent? Method, complexity, and the baroque", *Environment and Planning—D: Society and Space*, 22: 13–26.
—— (2007) "Actor network theory and material semiotics", *Heterogeneities DOT net*. Online: www.heterogeneities.net/publications/Law-ANTandMaterialSemiotics.pdf (accessed May 18, 2007).
Marcus, G.E. (1998) *Ethnography through Thick and Thin*, Princeton, NJ: Princeton University Press.
Massey, D. (1994) *Space, Place and Gender*, Minneapolis: University of Minnesota Press.
Mato, D. (1997) "On global and local agents and the social making of transnational identities and related agendas in 'Latin' America", *Identities*, 4(2): 167–212.
Mintz, S. (1986) *Sweetness and Power*, New York: Penguin Books.
Mitchell, T. (2002) *Rule of Experts: Egypt, Techno-Politics, Modernity*, Berkeley: University of California Press.
O'Connor, J. (1988) "Capitalism, nature, socialism: A theoretical introduction", *Capitalism, Nature, Socialism*, 1(1): 11–38.
Ong, A. (2006) *Neoliberalism as Exception: Mutations in Citizenship and Sovereignty*, Durham, NC: Duke University Press.
—— and Collier, S.J. (eds) (2005) *Global Assemblages: Technology, Politics, and Ethics as Anthropological Problems*, Malden, MA: Blackwell.
Osborne, T. and Rose, N. (1999) "Governing cities: Notes on the spatialisation of virtue", *Environment and Planning—D: Society and Space*, 17(6): 737–60.
Otsuki, T., Wilson, J.S. and Sewadeh, M. (2001) "A race to the top? A case study of food safety standards and African exports", in Development Research Group "Trade" (DECRG) (ed) Policy Research Working Paper, WPS2563, Washington, DC: The World Bank. Online: go.worldbank.org/HAS92S2EU0 (accessed June 27, 2011).
Polanyi, K. (1944) *The Great Transformation: The Political and Economic Origins of Our Time*, Beacon Hill, MA: Beacon Hill Press.
Power, M. (1997) *The Audit Society: Rituals of Verification*, Oxford: Oxford University Press.
Sassen, S. (1995) "The state and the global city: Notes towards a conception of place-centered governance", *Competition and Change*, 1: 31–50.
—— (2000) "Spatialities and temporalities of the global: Elements for a theorization", *Public Culture*, 12(1): 215–32.
Show, M. (2004) "Malomparádé" (November 6, 2004) HVG, 45: 97. Online: hvg.hu/hvgfriss/2004.45/200445HVGFriss379 (accessed April 17, 2011).
Spivak, G. (1988) "Can the subaltern speak?", in C. Nelson and L. Grossberg (eds) *Marxism and the Interpretation of Culture*, Urbana, Chicago: University of Illinois Press, pp. 271–313.
Tsing, A. (2000) "The Global Situation", *Cultural Anthropology*, 15(3): 327–60.
Walters, W.P. and Larner, W. (eds) (2004) *Global Governmentality: Governing International Spaces*, London: Routledge.
Wilson, J.S. and Otsuki, T. (2001) "Global trade and food safety: Winners and losers in a fragmented system", in Development Research Group "Trade" (DECRG), Policy Research Working Paper, WPS2689, Washington, DC: The World Bank. Online: go.worldbank.org/491H1G8060 (accessed June 27, 2011).
Worster, D. (1985) *Rivers of Empire: Water, Aridity and the Growth of the American West*, New York: Pantheon.

6 Uncomfortable Antinomies
Going Beyond Methodological Nationalism in Social and Cultural Anthropology

David N. Gellner

> How can ethnography be global? How can ethnography be anything but micro and ahistorical? . . . It was designed to elucidate social processes in bounded communities or negotiated orders in institutions. . . . By convention global ethnography can only be an oxymoron. (Burawoy 2000: 1)

This chapter considers some of the ways in which social and cultural anthropology has changed since its heyday in the immediate post–World War II period.[1] In particular, it focuses on the challenges to anthropological fieldwork methodology, with its stress on long-term stays in specific places, arising from the increasing mobility of people, ideas and things—the process normally labeled *globalization*. Just as practice theorists have argued for an irresolvable antinomy between structure and agency, both sides of which must be embraced (Ortner 1990), I argue here that anthropologists must learn to live with uncomfortable but necessary antinomies (in the Kantian sense) between their face-to-face methods and the global issues they wish to address, and between their commitment to holism (with its associated dangers of methodological nationalism and/or ethnic groupism) on the one side and the necessity of encompassing within their purview flux, movement and change on the other. Whether anthropologists couch their response to globalization in terms of multi-sited ethnography (a methodological stance), global ethnography (a research program) or in some other way, these antinomies cannot be avoided and should be embraced. Ethnographic exemplars are taken largely from the Asian contexts with which I am most familiar, but I hope that nothing advanced here depends on the particular cases considered.

BY GOING GLOBAL, ANTHROPOLOGY REJECTS METHODOLOGICAL NATIONALISM

In 2001 Raman Roy, chief executive at a call center in Delhi, was quoted as saying that geography is history.[2] What he was referring to was the fact that vast quantities of information (and money) can be moved around the world at the click of a mouse, so there is no reason that UK householders should not talk to someone in Delhi (or wherever it is cheap to employ phone operators) in order to answer queries about their utility bills, renew their insurance or get help with a malfunctioning computer.[3] Physical distance is no longer a barrier to communication and consociality. Urban and suburban places that have airports and the internet have moved ever closer to each other; other places—those excluded from this instant connectivity—have moved, relatively, further apart. In this sense, Tokyo is much closer to London than it is to Siberia.[4]

Anthropologists have responded to this salience of "the global"—the loss of "the primitive"—by studying people anywhere, not just in villages or nomad encampments. They now study up (Shore and Nugent 2002), sideways (Hannerz 2004) and in all different directions. They study Japanese business families (Hamabata 1990), the interlinked stories of countercultural mountaineers climbing Mt Everest and Sherpa social and religious change (Ortner 1999), British asylum courts (Good 2007), the interrelationships and mutual influence of Japanese and Western films (Martinez 2009) and many more. Anthropologists study social movements, nongovernmental organizations (NGOs), activist networks and their interactions with the state (cf. Riles 2000; Gellner 2009a, 2010b). They study development practitioners (Mosse and Lewis 2005; Lewis and Mosse 2006) and policy makers (Shore and Wright 1997). They are now beginning to study the key economic institutions that both drive and constitute globalization (cf. Sridhar 2008; Tett 2009; Ho 2009).

Anthropologists also move around more (or at least more openly) than they did in the past, following their subjects. Invoking George Marcus (1995), they frequently do "multi-sited ethnography." Transnationalism, process and flow are in; what Malkki (1997: 61) has dubbed "sedentarist metaphysics" are out. If the ethnographer encounters continuity, rootedness or cohesive communities, these are not to be taken for granted but rather need to be explained as masks for powerful interests. Cohesion and consensus are assumed to be imposed and, if they are accepted, are presumed to be temporary.

Whether they are aware of it or not, what contemporary anthropologists are doing when they subject the notions of system, order, consensus and bounded communities to sustained interrogation and suspicion is to reject methodological nationalism (sometimes they are also and consciously rejecting nationalism *tout court*). Since anthropologists are specialists in the small scale and the local, what they now reject has been called "my tribe-ism," and might equally be called *methodological ethnicism* or *tribalism* (many anthropologists were in fact directly accused of "tribalism," that is, of encouraging tribalist feelings and undermining "nation-building" by nationalists in the immediate postcolonial period). In other words, the besetting sin of anthropology in its classical and formative period was a kind of methodological nationalism writ small. Sociologists took national units for granted; anthropologists did the same for tribal groups.[5] The usual "emic" terms within the anthropological community for such old-fashioned views, now believed to have been superseded, are *essentialism* and *functionalism*.

Indeed, classic, mainstream social anthropology, as introduced by Malinowski in Britain, and cultural anthropology as founded by Boas in the US did depend on the idea, derived ultimately from Herder, that each people had a particular "genius" or ethos, expressed in unique language, customs and traditions—in short a *culture*—that set it off from other peoples. Many (such as Radcliffe-Brown) would have seen the distinctiveness more in terms of a particular social structure, rather than distinctive culture, but the effect was the same: to populate the map with discrete "primitive" peoples, much as the map of Europe was divided up between nation-states. In that sense, 20th century anthropology (along with much of the rest of the social sciences) shared an intellectual inheritance with romantic nationalism, thus leading to what Richard Handler calls "the interpenetration of nationalist and social-scientific discourse" (1988: 8).[6]

Even today there are some anthropologists (perhaps particularly cultural anthropologists) who become specialists in one group, learn one language and identify strongly with it, to the extent of becoming its lexicographer and/or political spokesperson. But, more commonly, contemporary anthropologists find themselves studying the whole process of the politicization of ethnic identity, including the links of local activists to the capital city and with indigeneity movements worldwide (Warren 1998; Shah 2010). Anthropologists, particularly those who study groups claiming indigenous status, are faced with a moral quandary: whether to endorse those claims (and buy into the anthropologically unfashionable methodologically nationalist assumptions that underlie them) or rather to question and deconstruct the claims. Many try to ride both horses at once, supporting indigeneity claims, but in a lukewarm way, as a form of "strategic essentialism."[7]

MULTI-SITED VERSUS GLOBAL ETHNOGRAPHY

George Marcus's (1995) call for multi-sited ethnography has been justifiably influential both within anthropology and well beyond it. There has been considerable discussion of Marcus's paper. Worries focus on whether constant movement on the part of the ethnographer will not make the resulting ethnography superficial, more like sociology, more concerned with bureaucracies and less with grasping and conveying alternative ways of viewing the world (Falzon 2009; Candea 2009; Marcus 2009).

Some have also pointed out that much of what is now called for was in fact done by classic anthropologists (Hannerz 2009). Indeed, anthropologists did not need the impact of globalization, transnationalism and postmodernism to legitimate traveling with their research subjects: Anyone working on nomadic or semi-nomadic peoples (think of classics like Evans-Pritchard's *The Nuer*) will perforce have had to move around. Ethnography may be multi-sited even without the ethnographer moving around, if it takes place in a multicultural location (Baumann 1996). Vice versa, the ethnographer may move around without ever leaving a single cultural bubble. Such movement would be unlikely to satisfy Marcus's criterion of multi-sited ethnography—to engage with more than one place, i.e. with more than one set of contested cultural processes.

Marcus drew attention to more than just movement, which has always existed; his paper argued that old senses of community and place had evaporated, or had at least been seriously attenuated by a new connectivity with the wider world. Thanks to this new connectivity, everywhere being connected to everywhere else, there are no longer clearly defined *sites*. "The field is no longer objectively 'out there'. Rather one networks oneself into a concept of the field through relations of ethnographic research all the way along" (Marcus 2009: 193)—though, as Marcus himself immediately recognizes, there is in fact a dialectic between the ethnographer's choices and the people, networks and institutions studied.

Since it is no longer possible to pretend that the world is made up of discrete cultures, it is no longer enough for the ethnographer to stay put within a given culture, or even to move around within the confines of that culture. The only alternative is to follow people, things, metaphors or plots as they move around *between* cultures. Thus, in recent years there have been many interesting examples of just such multi-sited ethnography following people (Levitt 2001), things (for example, pharmaceuticals: Ecks and Basu 2009) or plots (for example, remade cinema narratives: Martinez 2009).

Implicit in Marcus's paper is a distinction between *places* and *spaces*, a distinction often identified with Massey (1994) and theorized in Augé's book *Non-Places* (1995). Places are spaces with meaning; non-places lack cultural meaning (sometimes the terminology is the other way around, but the distinction is the same). Similar distinctions between gender and sex, social and biological kinship, are well known to anthropologists—and often mistrusted and critiqued. Such distinctions will remain as long as anthropologists wish both to treat all humans as sharing certain universal capabilities and, on the other hand, as creatively producing different ways of interacting (cultures, in brief). Ethnographers try to tease out how that meaning is made and by whom.

Competing with Marcus's idea of *multi-sited* ethnography is the notion of *global* ethnography, particularly associated with the name of Michael Burawoy, an influential ethnographically inclined sociologist who has theorized the predicament in which anthropologists and qualitative sociologists find themselves. He has called specifically for a *global ethnography* that builds on the case study method of the Manchester School (Burawoy 2000, 2009). He argues that ethnography, carried out in full awareness of various kinds of power and global forces, can overcome this oxymoronic dead end.

Gille and Ó Riain (2002) defend global ethnography with this same claim that it necessarily includes notions of power and history, whereas the rather flattening multi-site methodological injunction does not. The same virtues—incorporating history and power into ethnography against the Malinowskian vision—have also been claimed for practice theory and its attempt to combine bottom-up person- and meaning-centered ethnography with analyses of global economic and political processes (Ortner 1984, 1990).[8]

The discussion of multi-sited ethnography begins from the methodological choices facing fieldworking anthropologists under conditions of globalization, whereas that on global ethnography starts from a subtly different place, namely, the question of what qualitative researchers can contribute to understanding a rapidly changing and very unequal world. Reflecting these different starting points, the call for multi-sited ethnography is a methodological imperative, whereas *global ethnography* is the name for a research program. But, as with practice theory, there are many who sail under the flag of global ethnography and the diversity of approaches adopted means that it is perhaps best understood as an aspiration rather than a theoretical school.

PRACTISING ETHNOGRAPHY IN A GLOBALIZED WORLD

As modernization proceeds, most societies experience the institutionalization of some form of public-private dichotomy. The first task of the fieldworker who wants to be really embedded is to gain access to private households, ideally by living in one of them. But this is often problematic in modern societies. When my friend Rajendra Pradhan wished to study a Dutch village, he failed to find anyone willing to have a Nepali anthropologist living in their house (Pradhan 1990).

There are other considerations that may prevent the researcher from sharing everyday life with the people being studied. For example, when the aim is to study slum-dwellers, conditions may just be too deprived for a fieldworker to share them and stay healthy, and a sick or depressed fieldworker is not an effective fieldworker.[9] There are limits to the participant observation mantra—and not just in this connection.

More and more anthropologists are studying organizations and networks, rather than self-defined cultural units, and having to adapt their methods accordingly (Gellner and Hirsch 2001). A practical way of considering the question of scale is to note that there are limits to the number of people one researcher can interact with. My colleague Robin Dunbar argues that, for evolutionary reasons, *homo sapiens* is capable of having meaningful relationships with around 150 people, and that the ability to handle that many is what distinguishes *homo sapiens* from apes and other species of *homo* (Dunbar 2008).

The fieldworker, then, must make complex trade-offs and choices in the field, where there are almost bound to be more than 150 people, and determine which groups and which people to spend time with. The problem multiplies when one is obliged also to pursue global links. Why privilege one set of connections over another? Sometimes the field site provides a fairly obvious answer—when the aid agency that is so salient is connected to a particular place elsewhere—but in other cases it will not be so clear. One person can only be in one place at a time, and can only carry on a limited number of relationships. Candea notes that the overwhelming choice of where to go and what to do during fieldwork meant that "13 months went by with a constant sense of incompleteness and arbitrariness, the obsessive feeling of missing out, of vagueness and unjustifiable indeterminacy, of never being in the right place at the right time" (Candea 2009: 33). Even having studied a village in central Gujerat for three years and in team with two other co-workers, A.M. Shah (2002: 35) reflects: "We left the village with a sense of inadequacy at what we had accomplished, and humility when we realized how little we knew in relation to how much there was to be known."

Edmund Leach clearly concurred with the idea that a fieldworker can only handle a relatively small number of people:

> Fieldwork in this [anthropological] style is a very small-scale, private affair. The research 'team' is usually just a single individual, or perhaps a married couple, with maybe a local assistant. The field of study is a local community; perhaps just a hundred or so individuals, seldom many more than 2000. Initially the principal researchers must be strangers to the community; hopefully, before they depart, they will be just the reverse. (Leach 1982: 129)

Leach argued that the nature of the work reinforces this approach:

> The first essential of intensive fieldwork is that the fieldworker should be able to recognize everyone in his vicinity. . . . The second essential is that he should be able to gain most of his information by direct observation of how these people organize their day-to-day affairs both in space and time. (Leach 1982: 145)

If Leach is right, the attempt to increase the scale of ethnography—to study, for example, in a city of 80,000, as I did in my doctoral work (Gellner 1992)—is doomed to failure. But in fact, as the examples given above show, fieldwork has been done in situations Leach or Malinowski would not have recognized as anthropological, and the monographs that have resulted are often excellent. Collaborative work—teams of ethnographers working separately but on a shared research agenda (very different from working together in the field)—is one way to tackle such social complexity (for example, Gellner and Quigley 1995).

Like Levitt's (2001) transnational villagers, then, anthropologists engaging with the global need to be able to live in two places at once. But can being in two places at once enable the kind of immersion the seeker after "thick description" wants? Bob Simpson has described vividly how strange and different it is to do fieldwork while constantly being within Skyping range of one's family back home. "Part of the attraction of fieldwork for me," he writes, "is that it is a kind of experiment with selfhood—wiping the slate as clean as possible in order that others might write afresh on it" (Simpson 2009: 2). The more "in touch" one is with home, the less likely one is to have the total immersion in another way of life that is necessary for truly holistic fieldwork. That distance, that difference, that ability to go somewhere really far away and wholly cut off seems to be disappearing.

Globalization brings the limits of holism into stark relief: Even the most heroic fieldworker obviously cannot study the whole globe in a face-to-face way. Multi-sited fieldwork does not make this problem go away. Holism, as I have tried to indicate, is not a realistic practice for any but the smallest social units; it is, rather, a regulative ideal, a metaphor for methodological and disciplinary inclusiveness. It therefore needs to be recognized as an ideal, rather than a practice, and the role of the fieldworker's choices—arbitrary, from one point of view, but informed—in constructing the field must be consciously and explicitly recognized.

STILL HOLISTIC AFTER ALL THESE YEARS—AS A REGULATIVE IDEAL

A student in an ethnographic methods class at Brunel University in the early 1990s finally saw the light and blurted out: "So you mean: Doing ethnography is just hanging around and talking to people?!" To which the answer was yes, hanging around and talking to people is necessary, but not sufficient, for ethnographic fieldwork. It is a commonplace of such classes that social anthropologists cannot *just* go and hang around somewhere—they must go with a question and a focus (implying a grasp of theory, some kind of framework for their research, and a background in works on the region and topic). At the same time they should remain open to unexpected and unanticipated connections beyond their immediate focus. In other words, they must always retain a commitment to viewing the environment in which they find themselves holistically. That environment includes the geographical region, the history of that region and the micro-locality, and—today, increasingly important to keep on board—transnational links, whether from below or above. World Bank decisions in Washington, DC, or those of a United Nations subcommittee in Geneva, may have just as much of an impact on the "reality on the ground" as more local state effects (Pfaff-Czarnecka 2007; Sridhar 2008).

In the wider social science marketplace, social and cultural anthropologists have achieved a grudging acceptance as experts in the face-to-face, micro levels of analysis. Anthropologists, however, are not content to focus exclusively on certain aspects or slices of small-scale interaction (small sections of verbal interaction, particular kinds of physical behavior), as some sociologists and psychologists do. Instead they seek always to embed their detailed accounts of local practice in a wider context. The fact that the wider context now frequently includes unmediated connections all over the world is what lies behind the rise of global ethnography. Anthropologists have always sought *both* to be obsessive and complete about some particular order of social facts *and* at the same time to give an account of the whole or at least of the links to some wider whole. This means—as I put it in another context—that anthropological fieldworkers are necessarily cross-eyed, one eye focusing obsessively and systematically on the particular area of research concern, the other roving restlessly around looking for links, contrasts and enlightenment in the wider environment (Hirsch and Gellner 2001: 7).[10]

And yet there is something in the social anthropological method that does indeed require a certain amount of apparently aimless hanging around. The very fact that social anthropologists are supposed to be interested in everything means that there is a commitment to allowing questions to arise from the material, and to follow the questions. This is opposed to the more common social scientific procedure of imposing a framework from the start and never reflecting on whether the concepts and methods with which the enquiry began are indeed fit for purpose. Sometimes it is necessary to hang around long enough for people to feel comfortable articulating what really concerns them. Geertz (1998) tried to dignify this slow, wait-and-see anthropological anti-method with the moniker "deep hanging out."

All this means that, from the point of view of other social sciences, ethnography can seem like the no-method method. *Participant observation*, like *global ethnography*, has always been something of an oxymoron: For most activities, either one participates or one observes, but doing both at once is humanly impossible. The term remains valuable for its indication that one should observe *while participating in the way of life of those observed*. It remains true that, with its openness and aspiration to completeness, ethnography is an impossible task, a grasping after completeness that can never be achieved. At least when studying small groups, the aim may not be quite so hubristic. In the face of great social complexity and in the light of globalization, it may seem positively foolhardy.[11]

In spite of the criticisms that are frequently and justifiably leveled at ethnographic monographs, we know that they do sometimes succeed, so it is worth considering how this is achieved. If we accept that knowledge is sometimes attained, what are the conditions of possibility of that knowledge?[12] I consider three factors—youth, gender and persistent individualism—that help in the anthropological endeavor and the corresponding factors—age, gender again and the tyranny of scientific models—that hinder it. Globalization itself, by removing even the illusion of small and self-contained communities, is also making the holistic ideal harder to live up to. Indeed some anthropologists argue that we should abandon the holistic ideal altogether (Cook *et al.* 2009).

ANTHROPOLOGICAL FIELDWORK: A YOUNG PERSON'S GAME, PERHAPS EVEN A YOUNG WOMAN'S GAME

The time and emotional commitments required mean that participant observation is very difficult to put into practice, and it has been argued that multi-sited ethnography is so antithetical to the method as actually to undermine it (Candea 2009). Many people are temperamentally unsuited to it at any time of life, for others it is appropriate when young. There are a few heroic fieldworkers who manage to continue intense, long-term fieldwork well into old age. Margaret Mead is a debatable hero to hold up in this regard. Johnny Parry of the London School of Economics is someone who has certainly managed it in three radically different kinds of field site spread right across very different parts of northern India ("traditional" village ethnography, premier pilgrimage center and Nehruvian steel town)—though I observe that even his production of ethnographic monographs has slowed with age (compare Parry 1979, 1994, 2001). For most of us, later fieldwork is less intense, less long term, less personally transformative, and more collaborative, more reliant on accumulated experience and more built on second-hand knowledge as opposed to first-hand experience.

In short, the claim advanced here is that first fieldwork is the most participatory, the most detailed, perhaps the most mistake-ridden, but in many ways the best, in the sense that it generally produces the most impressive, detailed and lasting ethnographic monographs (in many cases the author's only ethnographic monograph). In passing, let me note that ethnography may not just be age-related in this way, but possibly gender-related also. In the field of the ethnography of Nepal and South Asia, I have often been struck by the fact that a very large number of the best and most sensitive ethnographies are written by women. In the Nepal case, it is noticeable that many of the best ethnographies are also written by ex–Peace Corps volunteers, who have lived for years in Nepali villages, speak the languages very well and then return for doctoral fieldwork. I am *not* saying here what one can imagine might have been said in Malinowski's day, that women are good at ethnography but men are better at theory. To remain within the South Asian field, one can think of no more theoretically challenging, original and significant detailed ethnography in the post-Dumontian era than Gloria Goodwin Raheja's *Poison in the Gift* (1988), for example. However, I do assert that the bar is continually being raised in terms of high-quality, theoretically sophisticated ethnography, and it is noticeable that a very large proportion of these new ethnographies are by women.

Fieldwork requires a kind of total immersion that, as noted, comes easier for the young, because they are encumbered neither by personal responsibilities nor by job duties that pull them away. The young have another advantage: They fit much more readily into the student role. In most societies hanging out, learning, apprenticing oneself, picking things up as one goes along—all these are activities expected of young people. It is a comfortable position for the young ethnographer to inhabit—both for the ethnographer and for her hosts. As one gets older it is harder and harder to fit into the inconspicuous role of "junior person needing to be instructed." The older you are, the more you are expected to be authoritative, to teach, *to know*. I have frequently had the experience of being pushed into the role of the "one who knows," a *vidvan* ("scholar") in the north Indian vernaculars. In fact, so often did I go to meetings, trying to sit unobtrusively at the side and take notes, only to find myself ushered to the front and on to the stage and then requested to give a speech, that I thought I had better make a virtue out of a necessity and actually formally start to study activists and meetings.[13]

THE TYRANNY OF COLLECTIVE RESEARCH AND SCIENTIFIC MODELS

Anthropologists are familiar with the criticism from other social sciences: They collect anecdotal evidence, stories, small *n* samples; therefore their results are amusing but not widely applicable—appropriate subject matter for after-dinner speeches perhaps, but hardly serious scholarship. The tension between the personalistic interaction that is the bedrock of sociocultural data gathering and the big, widely applicable conclusions that anthropologists would like to draw amounts to one of several uncomfortable antinomies with which anthropologists must live.

Methodologically, this antinomy can push anthropologists in an overly scientific direction. One way in which this happens is through the dominance of a model of research activity that overvalues teamwork. Some big funding councils give the impression that they are no longer interested in giving small amounts of money to send a lone researcher off for two years. They want collaborative team efforts (preferably international and interdisciplinary). But doing fieldwork in a big group, or even a small group of two or three people, prevents the complete immersion and identification (not to mention linguistic adaptation) that the lone researcher is forced to make. There is a tradition of whole classes of anthropology students descending on "traditional" villages in Japan, for example, as occurred with Navaho reservations in the past. Apparently, the inhabitants of the shanty town outside the gates of Jawaharlal Nehru University (JNU) in New Delhi are equally used to being studied by master's students appearing with clipboards. Such frequent or high-density surveying, where those being studied perform their expected roles for short periods in front of the researcher or graduate seminar, cannot produce the kind of ethnography that social and cultural anthropologists are after. For that, loneliness and identification on the part of the researcher are essential.

Allied to the pressure for teamwork is the emphasis on quick results. This has led to numerous adaptations of anthropological methods for use in development—Rapid Rural Appraisal, and so on. Such methods may be valuable for limited purposes and in the hands of experienced professionals, but they have never been known to produce rich ethnography—except ethnography of the aid world itself. The virtues of studies such as David Mosse's *Cultivating Development* (2005) or Celayne Heaton Shrestha's work on NGOs in Nepal (2002, 2006) depend rather more on traditional participant observation carried out in the NGO and international nongovernmental organizations office contexts than they do on any methods of participatory appraisal.

Another very important tendency that undermines and interferes with ethnography is the drive to achieve scientific and quantifiable results. This is closely linked to the preference for teamwork, but it is a deeper tendency and is wider and more pervasive in its effects. The more one seeks to control and quantify the data, the more one's methods get in the way of listening, following and falling in with what people themselves wish to talk about and do. The most essential qualities for good fieldwork are time, patience and a willingness to go with the flow, abandoning preconceived plans. One can hardly imagine a methodological approach more inimical to the puritan drive for testing, results and the accumulation of data. There is, therefore, a vital and inherent contradiction between the search for replicable results and the ability to engage in an ongoing human way, person to person, with "research subjects." This is not to suggest that there is no place for quantification in ethnographic research, nor does it imply that the ethnographer should abandon all concern to demonstrate how representative her findings are. Rather, it is to suggest that the best ethnography combines multiple frames of reference and that the humanistic, person-centered frame is not an optional extra or a mere tool for gaining access, but is at the very heart of the enterprise. The advocates both of multi-sited ethnography and of global ethnography recognize this primacy of the person-centered approach.

ETHNOGRAPHY AND BORDERS

Anthropology has long been interested in those who cross boundaries and in marginal populations. More recently, geographers, sociologists and anthropologists have all participated in the transnationalist vogue that has brought trans-border movement to the center of attention and given it an important place in sociological theorizing. But, in much of the world, it is only rather recently that those who actually live at political borders (as opposed to migrants) have been studied in conjunction with a focus on the state (for example, Wilson and Donnan 1998; van Schendel 2005).

If indeed methodological nationalism is the besetting sin of contemporary social science, where better to make visible the action of the state, and the fact that it is carefully orchestrated, than at borders where two or more sets of state effects come into contact and/or conflict? In fact, it is likely to be at borders also that various forms of resistance are also encountered (Abraham and van Schendel 2005) as well as sheer indifference to and ignorance of the state, not to mention exaggerated loyalty (Aggarwal 2004), depending on the kind of border we are talking about. For those interested in global connections, border locations are an attractive place to start.

Borderlanders often confound the expectations both of states and of methodological nationalists. Ethnic groups merge into one another or undergo kaleidoscopic shifts at unnerving speed. Populations move around and cannot be fixed (Scott 2009). Some states maintain enclaves, tiny pockets of land surrounded by the territory of the neighboring state, where people are either left stateless or with citizenship but unable to access it. For example, van Schendel has documented the extraordinary case of the India–Bangladesh border with its 123 pockets of Indian land inside Bangladesh and 74 Bangladeshi enclaves surrounded by Indian territory (van Schendel 2002, 2005).

Some ethnographic work has been done at borders,[14] but far more remains to be done, and the complexity of the work probably does require teams of researchers working separately but in tandem at different sites. For obvious reasons, many states limit access to their border areas, which accounts for the relatively paucity of ethnographies in frontier zones. But if they can be accessed, such sites offer the possibility of observing global and national processes distilled. What needs to be avoided is the assumption that all borderlands are the same—defined by their distance from the metropolis. Attempts to seek a single "borderland theory" risk reproducing nationalist and "sedentarist" assumptions; border situations are multiple (internal borders may equally be highly significant) and can only be interpreted in relation to diverse state-making strategies. Borders are also a reminder to anthropologists that the world is not one seamless network: Some people can access both sides, others cannot, and issues of power and history are never far away.

CONCLUSION: UNCOMFORTABLE BUT NECESSARY ANTINOMIES

Many have noticed that the contemporary interest in and emphasis on flow and global movement (Hannerz 1997) has effectively taken anthropologists back to the position of the 19th century diffusionists. As Falzon (2009: 5) remarks, "One can only hope that history will judge us to have been less speculative." Yet the reasons why diffusionism was so firmly rejected in the postwar period need to be remembered. Treating culture as a thing of shreds and patches, not animated by any internal coherence and not worthy of being comprehended as a whole, simply did not produce good ethnographies: It led neither to the empathy necessary to understand local worldviews, nor to any rigorous way of analyzing how a local culture fits together. At the same time, we have come to see the attempt to view cultures as isolated and autonomous as wrong-headed, ideologically motivated and worse. In short, there is a structural antinomy between structuralist and functionalist holism on the one side and diffusionism on the other: Both are necessary to good fieldwork. They pull in different directions, requiring our attention to be focused alternately on local meanings and transnational links. Neither can be ignored and the global ethnographer must live with such uncomfortable antinomies, ceding to the exclusivist claims of neither side, but learning to combine both in a creative tension.

Realistically, a single individual can only do rich fieldwork in one, two or, if talented and possessed of superhuman energy, three sites. (Even a single site, where that site is a meeting place of numerous languages, is going to be beyond the competence of a single researcher to grasp in its entirety.) Comparison between them is likely to use the simple method of difference and similarity. Anything more sophisticated requires new kinds of joint projects where ethnographers design their questions and problems together, then work separately in the field, but share their results and publish together.

Global ethnography comprises two competing aspirations. On the one hand, there is an ongoing commitment to the virtues of structural-functionalist, holistic fieldwork, built on an individual really getting to know a new environment, speak the language and come to feel at home. On the other hand, there is the hard-won consciousness that culture is not in fact a coherent and seamless web; the diffusionists of the 19th century and the world systems and transnational theorists of the 20th were right to put flux, flow and movement across boundaries at the center of their analyses. Thus, *global ethnography* is indeed an oxymoron, but a necessary one; the phrase encapsulates the tension between grasping particular lived everyday worlds as they are experienced and, on the other hand, the knowledge and awareness that such local worlds are but a small part of multiple global processes. Living with that tension is, I have argued, a productive and necessary antinomy, however uncomfortable it sometimes makes us. Ethnographers must combine a data-collection tool—participant observation—that has an inbuilt bias towards methodological nationalism and/or methodological ethnicism with a constant awareness of, and constant struggle to overcome, that inbuilt bias.

NOTES

1. Thanks are due to D.P. Martinez, J. Pfaff-Czarnecka and the editors of this collection for detailed comments on earlier versions.
2. "Geography is history. Distance is irrelevant. Where you are physically located is unimportant. I can log on anywhere in the world" (Raman Roy

in Harding, March 9, 2001). The first three paragraphs of this section are reproduced with permission from Gellner (2010a), the afterword to Acosta *et al.* (2010), and are published with the permission of Cambridge Scholars Publishing.
3. Thomas Friedman's *The World Is Flat* was a best-selling journalistic examination of the new connectivity.
4. Cf. Giddens (1990) on space-time compression and the warnings of Favell (2001) and Brubaker (2005) against being carried away by metaphors of flux and change.
5. André Gingrich (2010: 555) argues that anthropology has proved itself better at overcoming methodological nationalism than some neighboring disciplines, such as sociology and philosophy.
6. Thornton (1988) argues that there was also a very strong rhetorical commitment to writing ethnographic monographs in a holistic way.
7. See Barnard (2006) and other articles in the same journal issue discussing Kuper (2003).
8. For a discussion of how Ortner, following Geertz, misconstrued Weber in this connection, see Gellner (2009c).
9. Moffatt (1979: xxiii–xliii) is a moving account of the impossibility of fieldwork under very deprived conditions.
10. For more on anthropology's distinctiveness as a social science, deriving from this openness to what research participants or informants tell us, see Gellner (2009b).
11. In light of this, Gille and Ó Riain's (2002: 273) claim that "[e]thnography is uniquely well placed to deal with the challenges of studying social life under globalization," because it enables the researcher to jump scales of analysis, is particularly bold.
12. I leave to one side the by now well-trodden argument that "success" is entirely constructed through persuasive rhetoric.
13. See Gellner and Karki (2007, 2008), Gellner (2009a, 2010b) and the MIDEA project on democratization. Online: www.uni-bielefeld.de/midea.
14. See Martínez (1994); Wilson and Donnan (1998). For a useful overview, see Baud and van Schendel (1997).

REFERENCES

Abraham, I. and van Schendel, W. (eds) (2005) *Illicit Flows and Criminal Things*, Bloomington: Indiana University Press.
Acosta, R., Rizvi, S. and Santos, A. (eds) (2010) *Making Sense of the Global: Anthropological Perspectives on Interconnections and Processes*, Cambridge: Cambridge Scholars Publishing.
Aggarwal, R. (2004) *Beyond Lines of Control: Performing Borders in Ladakh, India*, Durham, NC: Duke University Press.
Augé, M. (1995) *Non-Places: Introduction to an Anthropology of Supermodernity*, London: Verso.
Barnard, A. (2006) "Kalahari revisionism, Vienna, and the 'indigenous peoples' debate", *Social Anthropology*, 14(1): 1–16.
Baud, M. and van Schendel, W. (1997) "Toward a comparative history of borderlands", *Journal of World History*, 8(2): 211–42.
Baumann, G. (1996) *Contesting Culture: Discourses of Identity in Multi-Ethnic London*, Cambridge: Cambridge University Press.

Brubaker, R. (2005) "The 'diaspora' diaspora", *Ethnic and Racial Studies,* 28(1): 1–19.
Burawoy, M. (2000) "Introduction: Reaching for the global", in M. Burawoy, J.A. Blum, G. Sheba, Z. Gille, T. Gowan, L. Haney, M. Klawiter, S.H. Lopez, S. Ó Riain, M. Thayer (eds) *Global Ethnography: Forces, Connections, and Imaginations in a Postmodern World*, Berkeley, Los Angeles: University of California Press, pp. 1–40.
—— (2009) *The Extended Case Method: Four Countries, Four Decades, Four Great Transformations, and One Theoretical Tradition*, Berkeley: University of California Press.
Candea, M. (2009) "Arbitrary locations: In defence of the bounded field-site", in M.-A. Falzon (ed) *Multi-Sited Ethnography: Theory, Praxis and Locality in Contemporary Research*, Farnham: Ashgate, pp. 25–45.
Cook, J., Laidlaw, J. and Mair, J. (2009) "What if there is no elephant? Towards a conception of an un-sited field", in M.-A. Falzon (ed) *Multi-Sited Ethnography: Theory, Praxis and Locality in Contemporary Research*, Farnham: Ashgate, pp. 47–72.
Dunbar, R. (2008) "Mind the gap: or why humans aren't just great apes", *Proceedings of the British Academy*, 154: 403–23.
Ecks, S. and Basu, S. (2009) "The unlicensed lives of antidepressants in India: Generic drugs, unqualified practitioners, and floating prescriptions", *Transcultural Psychiatry*, 46(1): 86–106.
Evans-Pritchard, E.E. (1940) *The Nuer: A Description of the Modes of Livelihood and Political Institutions of a Nilotic People*, Oxford: Clarendon Press.
Falzon, M.-A. (2009) "Introduction. Multi-sited ethnography: Theory, praxis and locality in contemporary research", in M.-A. Falzon (ed) *Multi-Sited Ethnography: Theory, Praxis and Locality in Contemporary Research*, Farnham: Ashgate, pp. 1–24.
Favell, A. (2001) "Migration, mobility and globaloney: Metaphors and rhetoric in the sociology of globalization", *Global Networks*, 1(4): 389–98.
Friedman, T. (2006) *The World Is Flat: The Globalized World in the Twenty-First Century*, London: Penguin.
Geertz, C. (1998) "Deep hanging out", *The New York Review of Books*, 45(16). Reissued in C. Geertz (2000) *Available Light: Anthropological Reflections on Philosophical Topics*, Princeton, NJ: Princeton University Press. Online: www.nybooks.com/articles/archives/1998/oct/22/deep-hanging-out (accessed May 1, 2011).
Gellner, D.N. (1992) *Monk, Householder, and Tantric Priest: Newar Buddhism and Its Hierarchy of Ritual*, Cambridge: Cambridge University Press.
—— (ed) (2009a) *Ethnic Activism and Civil Society in South Asia*, Delhi: Sage.
—— (2009b) "The awkward social science? Anthropology on schools, elections, and revolution in Nepal", *JASO-online* (NS), 1(2): 115–40. Online: www.isca.ox.ac.uk/fileadmin/ISCA/JASO/1%202_115-140_Gellner.pdf (accessed October 2, 2010).
—— (2009c) "The uses of Max Weber: Legitimation and amnesia in Buddhology, South Asian history, and anthropological practice theory", in P. Clarke (ed) *The Oxford Handbook of the Sociology of Religion*, Oxford: Oxford University Press, pp. 48–62.
—— (2010a) "Geography as history is also now history: Some comments on anthropology's role in making sense of the global", in R. Acosta, S. Rizvi and A. Santos (eds) *Making Sense of the Global: Anthropological Perspectives on Interconnections and Processes*, Cambridge: Cambridge Scholars Press, pp. 195–205.

—— (ed) (2010b) *Varieties of Activist Experience: Civil Society in South Asia*, Delhi: Sage.

—— and Hirsch, E. (eds) (2001) *Inside Organizations: Anthropologists at Work*, Oxford: Berg.

—— and Karki, M.B. (2007) "The sociology of activism in Nepal: Some preliminary considerations", in H. Ishii, D.N. Gellner and K. Nawa (eds), *Political and Social Transformations in North India and Nepal: Social Dynamics in Northern South Asia*, Vol. 2, Delhi: Manohar, pp. 361–97.

—— and Karki, M.B. (2008) "Democracy and ethnic organizations in Nepal", in D.N. Gellner and K. Hachhethu (eds) *Local Democracy in South Asia: The Micropolitics of Democratization in Nepal and Its Neighbours*, Delhi: Sage, pp. 105–27.

—— and Quigley, D. (1995) *Contested Hierarchies: A Collaborative Ethnography of Caste among the Newars of the Kathmandu Valley, Nepal*, Oxford: Clarendon.

Giddens, A. (1990) *The Consequences of Modernity*, Cambridge: Polity.

Gille, Z. and Ó Riain, S. (2002) "Global ethnography", *Annual Review of Sociology*, 28: 271–95.

Gingrich, A. (2010) "Transitions: Notes on sociocultural anthropology's present and its transnational potential", *American Anthropologist*, 112(4): 552–62.

Good, A. (2007) *Anthropology and Expertise in the Asylum Courts*, Abingdon: Routledge Cavendish.

Hamabata, M.M. (1990) *Crested Kimono: Power and Love in the Japanese Business Family*, Ithaca, NY: Cornell University Press.

Handler, R. (1988) *Nationalism and the Politics of Culture in Quebec*, Madison: University of Wisconsin Press.

Hannerz, U. (1997) "Flows, boundaries, and hybrids: Keywords in transnational anthropology", in A. Rogers (ed) *Working Paper Series*, WPTC-2K-02, Oxford: Institute of Social and Cultural Anthropology at the University of Oxford. Online: www.transcomm.ox.ac.uk/working%20papers/hannerz.pdf (accessed May 1, 2011).

—— (2004) *Foreign News: Exploring the World of Foreign Correspondents*, Chicago: University of Chicago Press.

—— (2009) "Afterword: The long march of anthropology", in M.-A. Falzon (ed) *Multi-Sited Ethnography: Theory, Praxis and Locality in Contemporary Research*, Farnham: Ashgate, pp. 271–82.

Harding, L. (March 9, 2001) "Delhi calling", *The Guardian*, Online: www.guardian.co.uk/g2/story/0,3604,448955,00.html (accessed August 23, 2009).

Heaton Shrestha, C. (2002) "NGOs as thekadar or sevak: Identity crisis in Nepal's non-governmental sector", *European Bulletin of Himalayan Research*, 22: 5–36.

—— (2006) "'They can't mix like we can': Bracketing differences and the professionalization of NGOs in Nepal", in D. Lewis and D. Mosse (eds) *Development Brokers and Translators: The Ethnography of Aid and Agencies*, Bloomfield, CT: Kumarian, pp. 195–216.

Hirsch, E. and Gellner, D.N. (2001) "Introduction: Ethnography of organizations and organizations of ethnography", in D.N. Gellner and E. Hirsch (eds) *Inside Organizations: Anthropologists at Work*, Oxford: Berg, pp. 1–15.

Ho, K.Z. (2009) *Liquidated: An Ethnography of Wall Street*, Durham, NC, London: Duke University Press.

Kuper, A. (2003) "The return of the native", *Current Anthropology*, 44(3): 389–95.

Leach, E. (1982) *Social Anthropology*, London: Fontana Paperbacks.

Levitt, P. (2001) *The Transnational Villagers*, Berkeley: University of California Press.
Lewis, D. and Mosse, D. (eds) (2006) *Development Brokers and Translators: The Ethnography of Aid and Agencies*, Bloomfield, CT: Kumarian.
Malkki, L. (1997) "National geographic: The rooting of peoples and the territorialization of national identity among scholars and refugees", in A. Gupta and J. Ferguson (eds) *Culture, Power, Place: Explorations in Critical Anthropology*, Durham, NC: Duke University Press, pp. 52–74.
Marcus, G.E. (1995) "Ethnography in/of the world system: The emergence of multi-sited ethnography", *Annual Review of Anthropology*, 24: 95–117. Republished in G.E. Marcus (1998) *Ethnography through Thick and Thin*, Princeton, NJ: Princeton University Press, pp. 79–104.
—— (2009) "Multi-sited ethnography: Notes and queries", in M.-A. Falzon (ed) *Multi-Sited Ethnography: Theory, Praxis and Locality in Contemporary Research*, Farnham: Ashgate, pp. 181–96.
Martinez, D.P. (2009) *Remaking Kurosawa: Translations and Permutations in Global Cinema*, New York: Palgrave Macmillan.
Martínez, O.J. (1994) *Border People: Life and Society in the U.S.-Mexico Borderlands*, Tucson: University of Arizona Press.
Massey, D. (1994) "Global sense of place", in D. Massey (ed) *Space, Place, and Gender*, Cambridge: Polity.
Moffatt, M. (1979) *An Untouchable Community in South India: Structure and Consensus*, Princeton, NJ: Princeton University Press.
Mosse, D. (2005) *Cultivating Development: An Ethnography of Aid Policy and Practice*, London: Pluto.
—— and Lewis, D. (eds) (2005) *The Aid Effect: Giving and Governing in International Development*, London: Pluto.
Ortner, S.B. (1984) "Theory in anthropology since the sixties", *Comparative Studies in Society and History*, 26: 126–66. Reissued in N.B. Dirks, G. Eley and S.B. Ortner (eds) (1994) *A Reader in Contemporary Social Theory*, Princeton, NJ: Princeton University Press, pp. 372–411.
—— (1990) *High Religion: A Cultural and Political History of Sherpa Buddhism*, Princeton, NJ: Princeton University Press.
—— (1999) *Life and Death on Mt Everest: Sherpas and Himalayan Mountaineering*, Princeton, NJ: Princeton University Press.
Parry, J. (1979) *Caste and Kinship in Kangra*, London: Routledge.
—— (1994) *Death in Banaras*, Cambridge: Cambridge University Press.
—— (2001) "Ankalu's errant wife: Sex, marriage and industry in contemporary Chhattisgarh", *Modern Asian Studies*, 35(2): 783–820.
Pfaff-Czarnecka, J. (2007) "Challenging Goliath: People, dams, and the paradoxes of transnational critical movements", in H. Ishii, D.N. Gellner and K. Nawa (eds) *Political and Social Transformations in North India and Nepal*, Delhi: Manohar, pp. 421–57.
Pradhan, R. (1990) "Much ado about food and drinks: Notes towards an ethnography of social exchange in the Netherlands", *Ethnofoor*, 3(2): 48–68.
Raheja, G.G. (1988) *The Poison in the Gift: Ritual, Prestation, and the Dominant Caste in a North Indian Village*, Chicago: The University of Chicago Press.
Riles, A. (2000) *The Network Inside Out*, Ann Arbor: University of Michigan Press.
Scott, J.C. (2009) *The Art of Not Being Governed: An Anarchist History of Upland Southeast Asia*, New Haven, CT, London: Yale University Press.
Shah, A.M. (2002) "Studying the present and the past: A village in Gujerat", in M.N. Srinivas, A.M. Shah and E.A. Ramaswamy (eds) *The Fieldworker and*

the Field: Problems and Challenges in Sociological Investigation, Delhi: OUP, pp. 29–37.
—— (2010) In the Shadow of the State: Indigenous Politics, Environmentalism, and Insurgency in Jharkand, India, Durham, NC: Duke University Press.
Shore, C. and Nugent, S. (eds) (2002) *Elite Cultures: Anthropological Perspectives* (Association of Social Anthropologists Monographs No. 38), London: Routledge.
—— and Wright, S. (eds) (1997) *Anthropology of Policy: Critical Perspectives on Governance and Power*, London: Routledge.
Simpson, B. (2009) "Messages from the field", *Anthropology Today*, 25(5): 1–3.
Sridhar, D. (2008) *The Battle against Hunger: Choice, Circumstance, and the World Bank*, Oxford: Oxford University Press.
Tett, G. (2009) *Fool's Gold: How Unrestrained Greed Corrupted a Dream, Shattered Global Markets and Unleashed a Catastrophe*, London: Little, Brown.
Thornton, R.J. (1988) "The rhetoric of ethnographic holism", *Cultural Anthropology*, 3(3): 285–303.
van Schendel, W. (2002) "Stateless in South Asia: The making of the India-Bangladesh enclaves", *Journal of Asian Studies*, 61(1): 115–47.
—— (2005) *The Bengal Borderland: Beyond State and Nation in South Asia*, London: Anthem.
Warren, K.B. (1998) *Indigenous Movements and Their Critics: Pan-Maya Activism in Guatemala*, Princeton, NJ: Princeton University Press.
Wilson, T. and Donnan, H. (eds) (1998) *Border Identities: Nation and State at International Frontiers*, Cambridge: Cambridge University Press.

7 Approaching Indigenous Activism from the Ground Up
Experiences from Bangladesh[1]

Eva Gerharz

The activist movements for the rights of indigenous people have, in recent years, established themselves in global representative bodies, and, through frequently being able to address global institutions, they have ensured the inclusion of their issues in development agendas. Moreover, collectives advocating the rights of indigenous people have managed to gain space for articulation and representation with regard to global issues such as climate change and resource management. Seen from this angle, they constitute a transnational movement *par excellence*. At the same time, indigenous populations are often constructed and represent themselves as confined to remote localities. The movements' positioning as localized and the relating of their claims to their special relationship with the land on which they live turns their local space into an important resource (Pfaff-Czarnecka 2005) when they are negotiating for indigenous rights in global forums. They therefore constitute a case that exemplifies the dynamics of activism stretching across scales of spatiality from localization to globalization.

By investigating the emergence of indigenous activism in contemporary Bangladesh, I attempt to explore activism for indigenous people's rights as a complex, multifaceted social process in translocal space. Revealing the broad range of negotiations and the ways in which the indigenous movement positions itself in local, national and global contexts; how it makes use of local and global repertoires and what kind of cultural processes determine the negotiations between the actors involved, I wish to transcend the limits set by methodological nationalism and ethnic groupism (Brubaker 2002), which have long set the agenda for the social sciences. This requires a perspective that enables the researcher to move between and beyond the various dimensions and levels, for example, an open process that is flexible enough to catch a glimpse into sites located at and connecting different scales and societal levels.

After discussing methodological nationalism and ethnicity in relation to indigenous activism, the notion of *translocality* (Freitag and von Oppen 2010; Lachenmann 2010) will be introduced. This concept addresses the social construction of various scales and, at the same time, stresses social interaction at and between different societal levels (individual and collective). With the help of the notion of *translocality* it is possible to unravel the myriad connections, coalitions, formal and informal networks and power constellations. Emphasis lies on the activists' own perspectives and positionings: How do they assess the potentials of their position and the organizations and networks they are taking part in? A systematic analysis of interaction and actor-constellations, their contextualization and supplementary analysis of the existing networks and coalitions reveal how activists are involved in the global stage of indigenous activism. Analysis at this level, first, takes into account how the different actors construct spatiality on different scales and how they refer to these as spaces for representation. Second, it looks at horizons of varying reach,[2] because depicting such constructions and representations necessitates analyzing these as embedded into settings located at different levels of analysis.

With the help of this perspective on the processes of translocalization it is possible to understand how global and local dimensions of activism intersect and how new horizons of action emerge for the activists, their allies and their opponents. Therefore, after the field of indigenousness in Bangladesh has been introduced, three methodological strategies will be applied to the empirical material collected over the preceding years.

- The first strategy to investigate indigenous activism beyond methodological nationalism is to analyze processes of vernacularization and adaption of globalized terminologies within specific local arenas.
- The second aims at unraveling the ways that different knowledge domains are interrelated and constitute translocal spaces.
- The third focuses on analyzing dynamics of ethnic boundary-drawing as embedded into complex constellations of belonging.

The conclusion summarizes the methodological strategy and points at the challenges still lying ahead.

CHALLENGING METHODOLOGICAL NATIONALISM

Three different forms of methodological nationalism and ethnic groupism, which are relevant when researching the translocalization of indigenous activism, can be distinguished. The crudest form has been addressed by a critique targeting the tradition that takes the nation-state as the unit of study, and therefore equates society with the nation-state This has been well criticized by, for example, Wimmer and Glick Schiller (2003). The related assumption that national borders define identity can be challenged by taking indigenous movements as one's focus. In this particular case it is illustrative that despite recent successes in defending their demands, indigenous populations tend to be pushed to the margins of nation-states and are collectively excluded from access to rights and privileges that are designed to fulfill the demands of the majority within a national society.

At the same time, activists promoting the equality of indigenous people have joined global forums within the United Nations (UN) (Muehlebach 2001; Oldham and Frank 2008) or networks bringing them together with counterparts from different regions of the world. Local and global activism are related to each other through knowledge flows and interaction, leading to the creation of translocal spaces beyond and beneath the national realm. Investigating the dynamics of negotiation in the *translocal space* constituted by interaction and knowledge flows between specific locations or in global debates (Lachenmann 2010), and taking the local, national and global as mutually constituting each other therefore helps to overcome methodological nationalism.

Since the *transnational turn* in social sciences there has been another tendency that takes the boundaries of nation-states as the primary entities under investigation, so that although these do not demarcate the "field" any longer, they themselves constitute the primary objects of investigation. Taking, for example, for one's object of study a putatively homogeneous group of citizens moving from one nation-state to another implies continuing a form of the binary thinking criticized by Nina Glick Schiller in this volume (Chapter 2). She argues that the emphasis on differences between "us" and "them" or on "confronting the other" reproduces methodological nationalism, because it does not take the relational dimensions of sociality into account. Following these suggestions, indigenous activism can be studied from a perspective that highlights the constitution of *transnational social fields*, comprising heterogeneous social formations. This can be shown with regard to recent debates about transnational activism in which a growing scholarship has shown that transnational movements can be successful in pressing for the reformulation of national policies (see, among many others, Keck and Sikkink 1998; Tarrow 2005; della Porta and Tarrow 2005). The case of the indigenous movement, which has been successful in convincing at least some national governments to ratify international conventions protecting the rights of indigenous people, confirms this assumption. These approaches, however, fall short of explaining the various contradictions and modes of negotiation taking place at a number of different levels and interfaces, which may result in a lack of concessions. Recent research findings reveal that the actor-constellations shaping the process of recognizing indigenous people's rights, agendas and policies are much more complex than a perspective that focuses on transnational networking can reveal: Stewart's investigations, for example, have shown that the focus on the transnational dimensions glosses over the divergent interests and conflicts within the movement and fails to reveal internal power hierarchies (Stewart 2004). It has also been argued that transnationalized movements may operate at different levels of spatial and social order simultaneously, which entails contradictions and complexities instead of unified action on behalf of uncontested political interests (Pfaff-Czarnecka 2007).

The complexity of divergent interests characterizing the movements themselves and the social spaces in which they operate calls for a thorough contextualization that allows us to take various, quite often divergent, rationalities and interests into account (see also Ghosh 2006; Gandhi 2003). It is therefore important not only to focus on transnational activism and its potential impact on national policy making, but also to scale that focus down to local levels in order to depict the dynamics of negotiation between different ethnic groups as well as between the activists and those that they seek to represent. This leads to a methodological perspective that goes beyond processes anchored in though transcending states, but which takes the mutual constitution of a deterritorialized global space and the local into account (see Gupta and Ferguson 1997; Pfaff-Czarnecka 2005; Fisher 2010; Lachenmann 2010).

The question of representation leads to a third trap that may arise in the process of choosing the unit of analysis, apart from methodological nationalism. Investigating an indigenous movement as a given, homogeneous group may produce ethnic groupism—which is, in fact, of no more analytical value than methodological nationalism. Although indigenousness can nowadays be regarded as a "universal," globally unifying category that brings together members of various linguistically and culturally diverse groups, and although there is great awareness about the constructed character of ethnicity, ethnic boundaries still tend to be naturalized in public discourses and scientific research alike; an *ethnic lens* has continued to determine different research areas (Glick Schiller and Çağlar 2010b: 65). Moreover, the study of ethnicity has often been based on groupism, a methodological point of view that implicates the concept of the group rather than analyzing it. Brubaker (2002) argues that taking groups for granted in the study of ethnicity naturalizes and reifies them. In order to overcome this methodological problem it is important to trace how ethnicity is constituted within a relevant context and how it is negotiated within particular social fields. Brubaker calls for thinking of ethnicity not in terms of groups, but of processes of ethnicization (Brubaker 2002: 167). Moreover, how activists make use of ethnicity as a resource in political struggles should be analyzed (Pfaff-Czarnecka 2010), even when the collective constructed by them is highly diverse. The movement for the rights of indigenous people, for example, not only comprises members of diverse origins, but also activists who would be labeled as non-indigenous. They can be regarded as advocates for the promotion of the rights of a conglomerate of people constructed as a particular category based on specific criteria, to which they themselves do not belong. Rather than focusing on ethnic differences and relations it may be more fruitful to investigate (translocal) *spaces of belonging* (Pfaff-Czarnecka and Toffin 2011).

RESEARCHING TRANSLOCALIZATION

To approach the field of indigenous activism, a methodological perspective that allows us to look beyond the structural relations overcomes the images of harmonious and productive cooperation within and among existing networks and institutions within and across local and national boundaries. Such a methodological framework needs to enable the researcher to trace and depict interactions across predefined spatial entities and beyond ethnic boundaries. It helps us to show how spatial and symbolic boundaries are constituted within specific situations at different scales and societal levels.

The methodology I am using in my analysis enables me to unravel the translocal constitution of social spaces and is based on three presumptions. The first emphasizes processes and connections at different socio-spatial scales (see also Nina Glick Schiller, Chapter 2 of this volume). The concept of scaling, which "refers to the ordering of socio-spatial units within multiple hierarchies of power," helps to grasp the ways different levels of spatial order are related to each other and how the "relationships of power between specific socio-spatial units of governance" are reorganized (Glick Schiller and Çağlar 2010a: 7). Allowing one to trace the mutual constitution of the local, national and the global, the scalar perspective enables one to show how localities are constructed not only in a geographical sense, but as a space that serves people for identification and representation as well (see Pfaff-Czarnecka 2005). At the same time, the focus on scales underlines the changing relationship between localities and the state within a global framework; for example, it serves as a methodological tool to understand the ways in which indigenous movements make use of global repertoires to articulate their locally specific concerns in national arenas and how they make use of their transnational networks in order to lobby for acknowledgment of their rights in the national sphere.

The translocality approach addresses, secondly, the interrelations among and between different levels of society that are constituted through negotiation of knowledge and meaning. Tracing the ways in which individuals negotiate[3] among themselves within different societal fields reflects their rationalities and knowledge repertoires, as well as power structures shaping these fields. The focus on negotiations also highlights the ways in which different societal levels relate to each other—for example, how individual agency shapes and is shaped by society and institutions, including the state (see Gille, Chapter 5 of this volume). In this regard, the concept of knowledge interface[4] (Long and Long 1992; Long 2001) is a central methodological tool, because this is where actors with different knowledge repertoires confront each other and constitute (translocal) spaces where meaning is negotiated. If social space is conceptualized as constituted through interaction, it represents the interlocking mechanisms relating an individual actor's agency with institutionalization and structuration at the societal level (Lachenmann 2010: 342). Transcending geographical boundaries, these processes are more or less global in scale. Tracing how knowledge interfaces at different scalar positions in actors' restructuring of society constitutes one elementary way of understanding processes of translocalization.

The third aspect concerns the level of representation, which can be but is not necessarily located beyond the concrete situations of interaction. Of particular interest here are the divergences between activists and those whom they seek to represent. Moreover, the cross-ethnic constellations of belonging that emerge from ethnic boundary-making processes are a relevant dimension. This concerns the ways in which activists represent indigenous concerns and what kind of strategies they employ at different levels; it is particularly interesting to analyze the ability of locally based activists to reach beyond local boundaries (see also Fisher 2010: 251). This will help to assess the consequences of these activities for local social change, which is becoming particularly important in the context of the recognition of minority rights and the negotiation of democratization and development, which is a central issue in Bangladesh amid considerations of developing countries' political cultures and institutions as potentially problematic with regard to good governance. For example, with respect to structural inequalities, ethnic exclusions and human rights violations, investigating the patterns of and thereby the potentials of indigenous activism and its border-crossing dimensions remain an important exercise for ensuring equality and developmental benefits for all citizens. Research on indigenous movements is thus also related to activism itself: The moment the researcher elaborates upon the ways in which activism is actualized, she becomes complicit with the field (Marcus 1998; Gerharz 2009). The way the unit of analysis is chosen decisively determines the ways in which the character of a movement like that for indigenous rights is recognized in public and political debates.

Studying translocalization thus goes beyond investigating transnational spaces, because it does the following:

- First, it takes the different scales and rescaling projects into account.
- Second, it emphasizes the ways different societal levels are constituted by each other through interaction and knowledge interfaces.

In contrast to the transnational space approach, perspectives on translocality highlight the complexity of global–local relations beyond those crossing the borders of nation-states. In the subsequent analysis this will be shown in a number of ways, for example with regard to ethnic boundary-making for which translocal processes within the nation-state are constitutive.

First, building on the translocality approach, the methodological strategy focuses on processes of negotiation at selected knowledge interfaces, which are investigated on the basis of data collected during a number of field visits over the last 12 years. The program of researching indigenous activism rests on a set of methods that are open, flexible and oriented toward ethnography (see Gellner, Chapter 6 of this volume). The emphasis lies on following the circular logic of the research process and constantly generating theoretical assumptions out of the material collected. The aim is to develop categories of analysis that help to structure the data in order to adjust the way forward. Consequently, understanding processes of translocalization requires multiperspective approaches such as multi-sitedness and multi-level analysis. The data used in the analysis presented in this chapter derive from in-depth research I conducted between 1999 and 2010 and collected with the help of expert interviews, participant observation and conversations in local everyday life and on ethnic identity-formation.

Second, to move between the different local sites and translocal scales at or on which activism manifests itself, I have applied a multi-sited strategy and performed "participant observation" on activism for Bangladesh in Germany and Europe. This opened new vistas for a long-term perspective, enabling me to remain immersed in the circular process of (re)working "(hypo)theses within the framework of (repetitive) interpretation of empirical data" (Lachenmann 2010: 341) in the sense of *grounded theory*. Consequently, the method of data collection is based on the analysis of events. The opportunity to participate in and observe the celebrations of the World Indigenous People's Day in Dhaka (2008, 2010) offered a perspective on translocal dimensions, because these events were centered on the articulation of globally circulating concepts of indigenousness and their local adaptation (Spiegel 2008). Likewise, lobby work for Bangladeshi indigenous people in other parts of the world, and conferences on these issues that were held in Berlin and Brussels, helped in clarifying the ways indigenousness is translated into the Bangladeshi policy context.

The following sections concentrate on the presentation and analysis of selected data generated from the strategies of field research beyond methodological nationalism. The material presented has been selected on the basis of theoretical sampling, for example, according to its relevance for the three analytical approaches:

- Processes of vernacularization
- Interplay of different knowledge domains
- Dynamics of ethnic boundary-making

Before delving more deeply into these issues, the field and its translocal dimensions are presented.

BANGLADESHI INDIGENOUS ACTIVISM

Bangladesh officially counts more than 45 so-called tribal groups, who, however, constitute less than 4 percent of the population. The largest concentration is the *Jumma* people[5] in the mountainous Chittagong Hill Tracts (CHT) in the southeast. Other groups labeled as "plainland *adivasi*" live on the plains, mainly in northern Bangladesh. Especially in the CHT, indigenous activism is not a recent phenomenon. From 1975 until 1997, political and militant activists, the Shanti Bahini, were engaged in an armed conflict for the autonomy of the area, which had enjoyed special status during

British colonialism. The struggle was recognized worldwide and opened access to and spaces for articulating the *Jumma* grievances in international groups and forums (van Schendel 1992a). A peace accord signed by the *Jumma* political leadership and the government of Bangladesh in December 1997 enabled activists to transform the movement from one stereotyped as "terrorist" to a nationally more accepted political movement.[6] Although the peace accord has not been fully implemented yet, and frequent outbreaks of ethnic violence reveal that those regarded as belonging to the indigenous populations still face numerous challenges, the new conditions set by the accord have opened new vistas for networking with activists representing the plainland *adivasis* in the north.

Most indigenous populations living in the plains look back at a history of enduring marginalization (Bleie 2005; Hassan and Ali 2009; Barkat *et al*. 2009). Despite a tendency to categorize indigenous people as marginalized *per se*, there is great diversity in their experiences. Many Garo, for example, a predominantly Christianized group that is dominant in numerical terms, have managed to acquire a good average level of education as a result of missionary efforts, and they have benefited from the special status of the Garo Hills in neighboring Meghalaya (India) under British colonialism (Bal 2007). Thanks to comparatively good access to education based on their collective background as Christians, many Garo have managed to get access to the white-collar job market in Dhaka. Garo women in particular have established themselves as beauty workers in Bangladesh's urban centers, although this includes being stereotyped in a depreciative way (Gulrukh 2004). Others, like the Santals living in the northwest, are regarded as more disadvantaged in terms of standard development indicators, but also in terms of legal rights (Bleie 2005). At the same time, there is a tendency among plainland *adivasi* to express feelings of being dominated by those living in the CHT, whose representatives have been more eloquent in raising their voices in the past. The armed conflict and the subsequent peace accord have dominated national politics and public discourses for a long time, tending to silence indigenous people's more general concerns.

The formation of a national Indigenous People's Forum and a variety of other new institutions and platforms promoting the recognition of indigenous rights in Bangladesh in a more inclusive way has considerably changed indigenous people's access to the national public and political decision making processes. Its emergence is related to the global initiative that came about after 1993, which was the International Year of the World's Indigenous People. This has been followed by two International Decades of the World's Indigenous People (1995–2004 and 2005–2015). Celebrating global events such as World Indigenous People's Day has gained much popularity in Bangladesh, because it is regarded as an opportunity to express indigenous concerns under the protection of the power of global institutions.

The forum's leadership has gained recognition in global forums such as the Working Group on Indigenous Populations (*WGIP*), and the global discourse on indigenous people has considerably strengthened the activists' motivation for adapting and lobbying for the concept. A great opportunity may arise from the selection of a Bangladeshi representative as a member in the United Nations Permanent Forum on Indigenous Issues (*UNPFII*) in 2010. The activism that has been institutionalized at the national level seeks to unify the indigenous populations living in the plains and hills and addresses the great number of shortcomings and limitations to guaranteeing indigenous people's equality. It therefore constitutes one point of entry for the analysis of the translocal negotiations of indigenous activism.

Utilizing the unifying category and constructing "unity" at a national level is essential to frame grievances and demands in a globally acceptable manner. *Indigenousness*, a denomination officially acknowledged by the United Nations, has been adapted in order to fit into global discourses and regulations such as the UN Declaration of the Rights of Indigenous People and International Labour Organization (*ILO*) Convention 169.[7] The new indigenous activism has thus emerged in response to the global initiative of creating a category beyond that of national ethnicity and with universal validity. However, indigenousness by itself tends to be an essentialist concept that is based on ethnic demarcations and boundary-drawing mechanisms. From the methodological point of view, these dynamics of demarcation take place at different levels and on different scales and are central to the negotiations of indigenous activism at interfaces in translocal space. Understanding the emergence of the new institutions and networks addressing the grievances of indigenous people requires tracing the demarcations across symbolic and territorial boundaries to depict the shifting nature of their coalitions. For example, ethnic boundary-drawing constitutes one central mechanism shaping indigenous activism, quite apart from other power differentials and hierarchies that are based on the socioeconomic status of individuals and that have led to conflicts between leaders and their constituencies. We also need to consider the various forms of negotiating indigenous people's representation that become central in different terrains. Whereas activists may feel the necessity to apply a certain strategy in the regional context, it may be possible that the global arena where indigenous claims are debated and negotiated is ruled by completely different rationalities. In order to understand the dynamics of translocal negotiations of indigenous activists' claims, it is therefore essential to investigate how different forms of knowledge are adapted, translated or vernacularized by whom, for which audience and under what conditions. These processes are often shaped by internal power hierarchies and shifting constellations of belonging within the movement, but also in demarcation from others, particularly the ethnic majority within the state and the national government.

PROCESSES OF VERNACULARIZATION AND ADAPTATION

The concept of *vernacularization* serves the purpose of analyzing the ways that "transnational ideas" such as human rights are adapted in local social settings (Merry 2006). It particularly concentrates on the space "in-between" and looks at how intermediaries[8] translate between the different levels structuring the translocalized world. Recognizing that indigenous rights are, in a similar manner to human rights, taken as a potentially universal legal framework, it is particularly interesting how the globally standardized language of indigenous activism has been adapted. However, questions such as the following arise: How do different actors make use of the globally generated ideas and concepts, in which contexts, and what do they expect from their efforts? How do they translate them into local concepts, and how are they appropriated? How do they go together with local or regional notions? What challenges do activists face when adapting the new concepts, and what strategies do they choose to negotiate their claims, particularly on problematic terrains?

Successive governments have refused to recognize the notion of *indigenous people,* arguing that all people living in Bangladesh are indigenous to the land. This argument, which marches in line with India's policy (Bleie 2005: 60), is deeply rooted in the founding principles of the Bangladeshi state as the nation of the Bengalis, which is based on the relationship between people and territory (see for example Mohsin 2003; van Schendel 2009). Since Bangla*desh*'s independence, the concept of *desh* is defined as "the land of the Bengalis (the Bangla-speaking people)" and the Bengalis in terms of the *desh,* as "the people ancient to this land" (Gardner 1993: 15). A representative of the Bangladesh Embassy in Germany even claimed that there are no minorities in Bangladesh at a meeting which I attended in Berlin in 2008. This has also been one of the reasons international conventions that address the rights of indigenous people directly (ILO Convention 169, UN Declaration on the Rights of Indigenous Peoples) have not been ratified and why most provisions set by others, like ILO Convention 107 for Indigenous and Tribal Populations, ratified in 1972, remain mostly unimplemented (Asia Indigenous People's Pact 2009). In Bangladesh's public sphere, however, intense debates on the notion of indigenousness as it has been defined and adapted in the UN context have been going on during the last couple of years, and civil society representatives are making use of it more frequently.

The debate about the notion of indigenousness shows that policy makers and activists have applied different interpretations based on their rationalities and on their aims in following a particular political strategy. Whereas national policy makers follow an argumentative logic that is based on the ideal of national integration and unity and therefore denies the allocation of a special status and minority rights, the activists draw on globalized notions of indigenousness to secure a special status protecting their

Approaching Indigenous Activism from the Ground Up

distinctiveness. These opposing interpretations take place in a situation in which the local indigenous movement is subject to oppression by the more powerful national forces. Especially in the Chittagong Hill Tracts, activists are under close surveillance. Consequently, the activists have developed strategies of circumvention and apply modified versions of earlier strategies that assert the distinctiveness testified in their application of the globalized notion of indigenousness. The data presented in the following sections show that the activists draw on the globalized notion, but activate genuinely local arguments and terminologies to produce and maintain difference.

In the Chittagong Hill Tracts (*CHT*), the period of guerrilla warfare (1975–1997) has led to a militarization of the region that has continued until today. Although the peace accord of 1997 included the withdrawal of all temporary army camps, large numbers of troops remain stationed in the Hills. The military frequently interferes in civilian life and influences decision making processes in local administrative institutions. The repressive mode of governance in the CHT was aggravated when the last caretaker government, which ruled between January 2007 and December 2008, imposed a state of emergency in the country. Apart from a campaign against corruption that was accompanied by numerous arrests and charges against high-level politicians and businesspeople, the space for civil society action was severely curtailed. This particularly affected the CHT, because the military used the state of emergency to "suppress the voice of indigenous *Jumma* people of CHT" (Asia Indigenous People's Pact 2009: 44). Arrests on the basis of false charges against local leaders such as the environmentalist and land rights activist Ranglai Mro became more frequent. After the change in government in early 2009, the military's control over civilian affairs persisted.[9]

In addition, activism for human rights issues and indigenous people's rights has been under the control of the national NGO Affairs Bureau, which oversees nongovernmental organization (*NGO*) registration and the allocation of funds from abroad. Some local NGOs concerned with human rights issues and indigenous approaches to development have faced severe pressure for the past couple of years. During my fieldwork in 2009, NGO representatives I interviewed reported that they refrained from using the notion of "human rights" or "indigenous people" locally, although they had become used to their frequency in international contexts as well as in communication with foreign development partners, whose agenda was at times focused on strengthening local awareness of human rights in line with rights-based approaches in development cooperation. The local representatives reported that the NGO Affairs Bureau would not only reject funding proposals but freeze all funds and even cancel the organization's registration as an NGO, as had already happened in some cases. This applied to the use of the sensitive terms in documents such as project proposals, but also in interaction with the local population and project beneficiaries, because the massive military (intelligence) presence created a sense of being observed in everyday life.

The NGO activists described how they developed different strategies to convey their messages on human rights to the people. A prevalent strategy of localizing the idea of indigenous people's rights is the celebration of international days, which constitute occasions to raise the awareness of civil rights. The celebrations of Indigenous People's Day on August 9 not only take place in urban areas, but are popular even in remote villages. In addition, the activists report that they make use of other codes in their people-centered programs. For example, they place emphasis on what they describe as indigenous tradition and culture: They would encourage the people to wear ethnic dress and to observe local customs with regard to food preparation, cultivation methods and handicrafts. At the same time, they report that the national media and civil society representatives at the national level have strengthened their position recently by using the "forbidden terms" more freely in public. However, even large international organizations like the United Nations Development Programme (*UNDP*) reportedly faced some pressure from governmental authorities when they did not comply with the norms set.

Adapting the logic sustained by global discourses on indigenousness and translating them in the way promoted by the activists, on the basis of local tradition and heritage,[10] has brought about interesting ambivalences in the context of modernization. This became apparent in the case of a young couple, a lawyer and a researcher, whom I interviewed in the CHT. They stressed their identity as belonging to the Chakma group based on the traditional shifting cultivation (*jhum*), traditional customs and customary laws, and traditional culture. Regarding developmental issues, they also argued in a strongly traditionalist way by claiming that supporting local modes of cultivation and encouraging people to follow their ancestral customs should be emphasized. Both of them, however, spent more time in Dhaka than in their little hometown in the CHT and were attracted to modern lifestyles and educational progress. The woman in particular had an increased interest in career opportunities abroad and revealed her enthusiasm about the Western lifestyles she had experienced when she had traveled abroad to attend seminars and workshops. At this point, the contradictions in the indigenous discourse, as entrenched between claims based on traditionalist views on the one hand and the attractiveness of modernized lifestyles on the other hand, become evident. The empirical example shows how strategies of vernacularizing a globalized activist language can become quite antagonistic to practices in everyday life as well as to personal visions of the future. It will be illuminating to look deeper into the adaptation of semantics as well as related concepts in order to depict the future vision of society that emerges out of this ambivalent positioning. This raises questions concerning the manifestation of social inequalities: They hint at internal power differentials with regard to accessing not only resources but also knowledge.

INTERPLAY OF DIFFERENT KNOWLEDGE DOMAINS

Activism for indigenous people's rights and recognition takes place within a variety of domains and sectors. Especially in developing countries like Bangladesh, civil society members' activism is mostly related to development cooperation in different ways. Indigenous activism in Asian Muslim countries, especially, has attracted international support in opposition to the dominant national societies (Tsing 2007). This case shows that indigenous interests and national developmental goals have often been contradictory in the past. Which contrasting logics of action guide developers, activists and the local population? How do indigenous pressure groups address such discrepancies? What strategic concessions are made by the state and donors? What strategies do activists aspire to at the various levels of decision making within the political and administrative realm? These questions are relevant with regard to the power relations within translocal space constituted by development cooperation.

Shortly after the CHT peace agreement was signed, international development organizations had great interest in planning and implementing development projects in the CHT. The missions and assessments dealing with possible projects were plentiful and, quite often, related to the overarching goal of promoting peace through development (Gerharz 2002). This process of opening up was accompanied by large-scale transformations within the local pool of development experts. Several NGO representatives in the CHT complained that the bigger organizations, such as UNDP and others, tie up the scarce local knowledge resources. Local development experts who had gained some experience in local NGOs or in government service were hired and employed for disproportionate wages on a *per diem* basis. Emphasizing that "development should not be a business," one activist voiced the trenchant criticism that "they," the international organizations, "are taking away our brains" and "stealing our ideas" (Chittagong Hill Tracts Commission, September 2009: 20). The international development organizations instead emphasized the view that development NGOs lacked know-how and implementation capacities, complaining how difficult it was to find qualified personnel. This exemplifies one of the crucial differences that are particularly noticeable in contexts where development cooperation has just begun. Whereas large parts of the developing world have adapted to the requirements of international agencies and have developed structural prerequisites and a labor force catering to them, areas that have been isolated in the course of armed conflict lack such an infrastructure. Consequently, local indigenous representatives have drawn on knowledge repertoires that do not comply with those of development cooperation but are more in line with indigenous discourses stressing distinctiveness and local knowledge.

This case shows how two global institutional contexts have produced conflicting knowledge repertoires that are negotiated with reference to one particular locality between actors situated differently in translocal space. People also complained that the approaches applied by international and national development organizations "do not fit with the local culture". The criticism has been made that NGOs act in technocratic ways, without much awareness of the social and political circumstances determining indigenous people's everyday life. This phenomenon is not uncommon in aid-receiving countries where NGOs primarily function as service providers rather than as civil society actors (Neubert 1995; White 1999). It was also argued by activists that some international organizations acted rather apolitically and, seemingly unaware of local power struggles, co-opted the "wrong" NGOs. With regard to NGOs originating from Bangladesh's mainstream development scene, the major critique was directed against so-called micro-credit schemes. Apart from criticizing the technocratic logic of micro-credits, indigenous activists mainly employed traditionalist arguments, rejecting micro-credit schemes as locally inappropriate. Representatives of local NGOs argued that their market-oriented logic did not fit with the indigenous subsistence-based modes of production and the resulting logics of economic action based on exchange (Gerharz 2002). The divergent concepts of economic action promoted by local and national NGOs thus represent one of the ways in which knowledge domains clash with each other.

In the plains, where indigenous people have been subject to Christianization efforts since colonial times and where interlinkages between development and Christianity have been a persistent feature, missionaries have pursued education along with other standards of Western development for a long time.[11] Two interrelated aspects may be highlighted here. On the one hand, the attempts of Christian missions to convert indigenous believers in animism have contributed to images of indigenous "backwardness" ever since the colonial period. The interrelation of Christianity and development (in the sense of conventional modernization following Western ideals) has certainly contributed to the popularization of such images and to the depreciation of ancient beliefs and lifestyles. A local informant disclosed for example that some missionaries prohibited the consumption of the local liquor and demonized local cultural practices and rituals.[12] Analyzing these interrelations reveals how different knowledge domains intersect and how they impinge on each other. On the other hand, while acknowledging development in this way, Christianity has also turned into a means to liberation and emancipation locally, because it has implied a chance to overcome backwardness. That this image is prevalent today can be observed in the northern district of Mymensingh, where Christian Garo and Muslim Bengali live side by side. Due to a lack of governmental educational services, the institutions of religious education are very popular. Whereas many Muslim boys and girls receive education in the *madrasha*, most Garo attend Christian (boarding) schools where education is oriented toward Western standards and includes English as the medium of instruction. However, the boundaries become blurred when Bengali Christians (of whom there are few) merge with the indigenous populations.

The intersections between religion and development as two knowledge domains thus relate the different socio-spatial scales to each other. The interreligious interaction in local everyday life increasingly resembles global confrontations between Islam and Western Christianity. At the same time, Christian missions have discouraged indigenous activists from raising their voices at the national level: The disputed and fragile position of Christian churches in this Muslim country has been problematic for many years, and church representatives have been very conscious of the need not to provoke opposition, fearing any possible outbreak of violence. This puts indigenous activism in the context of religion and development as it is negotiated at the national level, at which the emphasis on Islam in Bangladeshi nationalism has determined the national political culture since independence. Being a marginal minority, Christians have, in response, developed strategies to avoid confrontations. The indigenous movement challenges these practices and provokes the formation of different factions within the movement that distance themselves from the religious institutions. This reinforces the development of new strategies for negotiating indigenousness stretching across local and national scales and thus perpetuates the formation of translocal spaces.

DYNAMICS OF ETHNIC BOUNDARY-MAKING

More recent approaches in the study of ethnicity are based on a perspective that emphasizes the significance of individual agency in everyday life or political movements in designing ethnic groups and the boundaries between them (Barth 1969; Wimmer 1995; Schlee and Werner 1996). The concept of boundary-making specifies these dynamics by highlighting the different ways in which boundaries are "made," through expansion, transvaluation, contraction, boundary-crossing and repositioning, or blurring (Wimmer 2008). The construction of ethnicity thus takes place not only between groups with fixed boundaries, but is subject to highly dynamic processes of reaffirmation, transcendence and rejection. In Bangladesh, many of the indigenous groups and a handful of Bengalis (academics, development organizations, state representatives) seek to represent the indigenous people. While these allies are considered as resources bringing with them a great deal of power and bargaining potential within the national context as well as beyond, there is also opposition to their participation in the movement, because ethnic boundary-drawing leads to the construction of difference and the maintenance of "us" versus "them" in everyday life.[13] The multiethnic constellations also represent translocal social spaces because they are constituted by actors located on different spatial scales, for example, activists in particular localities inside and outside Bangladesh.

The dynamics of boundary-drawing have their roots in colonial constructions, but the politics of nationalism have also been impinging upon ethnic cleavages since independence (Mohsin 1997). Do translocal networks have the potential to connect and represent diverse and disparate indigenous groups? How do such networks reproduce historical power hierarchies and patterns of domination? Under what conditions do indigenous activists co-opt ethnic "others"?

The indigenous population in Bangladesh is small but highly diverse and marked by numerous fractions and frictions. It has been shown above that one line of differentiation cutting through the movement relates to geographical concentrations, for example in the plains and in the CHT. This difference is of crucial importance for identity formation for a variety of reasons. One reason is the history of the country's regions and the way the British colonialists' categorization of them gave way to a politics of inclusion and exclusion during the nation-building process under Pakistan's rule and after Bangladesh's independence in 1971. Another is the way that indigenous populations have been dealt with in ethnographic writing during the last 120 years. Whereas the *Jumma* of the CHT and the Garo enjoyed a comparatively comfortable status of having been confined to so called tribal areas, other groups have been subject to attempts to incorporate them into mainstream Bengali society. Notably, the way that ethnographers have depicted certain groups in the CHT, an area that has attracted attention because of its extreme diversity (among others, Bernot 1964; Brauns and Löffler 1996; Mey 1984), has considerably influenced their elites' bargaining power within and beyond the nation-state. Although historical narratives (for example, Francis Buchanan's account compiled by van Schendel 1992b) have highlighted the variability and flexibility of ethnic boundaries in the CHT, colonial categorizations (Lewin 1884; Hutchinson 1978) also defined ethnic identities in terms of clear-cut characteristics in essentialist ways. These categorizations have been the product of theoretical assumptions originating from other parts of the world. They have been applied by colonizers and researchers entering the local arena, and as a result of negotiating them at translocal knowledge interfaces they have been adapted yet modified in national discourses about ethnicity and nationalism. This has certainly contributed to a process of hardening and naturalizing ethnic boundaries.

What can be witnessed today is that the ways those seeking to represent indigenous people relate to each other are characterized by these essentialist notions, sometimes glossing over differences. Ethnic categories, thus, serve as a resource in the negotiations with the state for special provisions. These categorizations are often related to social inequalities in terms of developmental categories, such as access to health care, education and infrastructure. At the same time, language, religion and "culture" determine ethnic differences and contribute to boundary-drawing mechanisms, preventing the formation of a unified movement. The Chakma, for example, who form the majority of the *Jumma* living in the CHT and constitute the most powerful group in terms of access to land, education and other resources, have been dominating the movement for self-determination, partly as militants during the war, but also as activists who have entered the global terrain. This has antagonized others and resulted in conflicts that have been fought out along ethnic as well as religious lines. Accordingly, local interviewees have reported on the emergence of cleavages between the majority Buddhists, to whom the Chakma but also the Marma and some other smaller groups belong, and the Christians, who have incorporated most of the minor groups and seek to represent their interests within regional decision making bodies. However, these different coalitions are again shaped by internal differences that limit their potentials to form a unified indigenous movement. Ethnic and religious boundaries, but also gender, socioeconomic status and access to national and global institutions produce conflicts within the movement.

One particular challenge consists of access to national and global decision making processes and the individual's power over the channels that are needed to communicate indigenous grievances. In a Santal village in Rajshahi, local leaders complained strongly about the indigenous representatives in national decision making bodies. Also in other local settings, interviewees expressed their dissatisfaction with those allegedly representing them in globalized institutions such as the meetings of the UN bodies, who were regarded as having distanced themselves from the "community" in favor of a cosmopolitan lifestyle in urban Dhaka. Moreover, the recognition of indigenous leaders who have entered the terrain of global activism has perpetuated ethnic and socioeconomic differences and tended to create even deeper cleavages.[14] This shows the boundary-drawing mechanisms crisscrossing the movement and the ethnic categorizations therein, though it has at times been regarded as unified. Differences between the linguistic and religious groups cannot be glossed over by the adoption of any unifying category, but erupt in disputes about access to resources and power hierarchies. Boundaries, however, are also drawn between group members of different socioeconomic or educational backgrounds. Differences in lifestyle relate to spatial categories such as rural and urban contexts, where the latter represent more sophisticated and comfortable opportunities than village life, which lacks access to social services and consumption. These differences thus enable individuals to access social worlds beyond everyday life in a rural context not only in their imaginations, but through co-presence and produces dynamics of boundary-drawing that are located beyond the relevance of ethnicity.

A number of Bengali activists and intellectuals have been engaged in representing indigenous lifestyles but also political claims. In recent years, Dhaka-based intellectuals, including artists and academicians, have sought to create networks and form coalitions on behalf of indigenous groups. This kind of engagement has been interpreted in very ambivalent ways.

On the one hand, it has been regarded as an act of solidarity. Some of the Bengali intellectuals who have supported the movement are well connected among the national political and military elites and therefore have the potential to mediate between the activists and the state. On the other hand, indigenous interviewees have said that they felt these attempts were exoticizing and paternalist.

The historical accounts of the CHT clearly highlight the fact that the different groups originated in various regions in South and Southeast Asia and have always been connected to other national contexts (see Löffler 1968; van Schendel 1992a). Neighboring northeast India in particular is inhabited by collectives who share a number of cultural similarities and religious affiliations with the minorities of Bangladesh. These similarities have attracted some activists, forcing the movement to look beyond Bangladesh's boundaries and to intensify contacts. One activist from the Chittagong Hill Tracts reported that he and his colleagues invited a group of people from neighboring Tripura to celebrate the Buddhist festival in April together and to exchange ideas about cultural similarities and differences. Likewise, indigenous Buddhist monks network with monasteries in Myanmar, and Christian missionaries have maintained cross-border networks for a long time. Borders created during decolonization have cut through the territories inhabited by members of several linguistic groups. Garo, Tripura, Santal and others live on both sides of the border but maintain contact with each other through informal trade and (temporary) migration (Bal 2007).

Constructions of ethnicity are thus taking place the nation-state and in relation minority–majority constellations (Pfaff-Czarnecka and Rajasingham-Senanayake 1999). The dynamics at the national level, however, are related to colonial and global discourses and paradigms on ethnicity, incorporating their rationalities into the local knowledge repertoire. Although the rise of indigenous activism represents an attempt to create a category of belonging that glosses over ethnic differences, these distinctions nevertheless become relevant in particular situations. At the same time, indigenousness has created new space for incorporating the ethnic "other" and creating cross-ethnic alliances within and across the borders of the nation-state in order to improve the chances of negotiating more successfully for indigenous rights within the national realm. The formation of this translocal space thus connects different scales and levels.

BEYOND NATIONAL BORDERS

Researching the indigenous movement in Bangladesh "from the ground up" has revealed new perspectives on how activists operate in a globalized world. The approach presented in this chapter aims at overcoming methodological nationalism and ethnic groupism by showing how the Bangladeshi movement is engaged in struggles at different scales and societal levels constituting translocal space. This concept offers a perspective that goes beyond the focus on transnational space itself, because it highlights the diverse and complex dimensions of interaction across symbolic and geographical boundaries. The Bangladeshi indigenous movement, a social phenomenon that has not received much attention as yet, serves as an exemplary case to reveal how the negotiations of indigenous activism take place at different levels and in different sites of negotiation. The complexity of negotiations creates the necessity to bring together a number of methodological strategies, such as the analysis of knowledge interfaces and interactions, as well as multi-level analysis from a perspective focusing on everyday life in which activism is embedded. This chapter highlights three selected ways of investigating the multiplicity of actors' perspectives, aims and rationalities within different actor constellations.

First, it has been shown how global concepts are vernacularized and adapted under locally specific conditions that are, in the empirical cases described in this paper, shaped by political processes and discourses featuring nationalism and the creation of a homogeneous community therein.

Second, investigating how different knowledge domains, for example, indigeneity and development, intersect reveals how global and national development ideas shape the positioning of indigenous activism within the local and national realms, but also beyond.

Third, dynamics of ethnic boundary-making, which which have also seen the product of the representations of "foreign" ethnographers, reinforce the emergence of new coalitions that cross local and national boundaries.

The mechanisms within the national space may increase the significance of outside allies who are regarded as more trustworthy. But quite often, these allies are involved in complex situations in which different negotiations and processes take place rather simultaneously. This point throws particular emphasis on the fact that the hierarchical logic of the local-national-(transnational)-global order does not count. It may be the case that indigenous activists address potential allies, such as Bengali or foreign activists, who are situated differently within the space concerned without following a clear-cut agenda reflecting any kind of spatial order. The demands of the specific issue they are lobbying for, the partners negotiated with or the context of a specific event (for example, international days) determines how actors construct the local *vis-à-vis* the global. Taking into account the fact that antagonistic relationships between those citizens claiming special rights as indigenous people and the state may lead to a lack of identification with the national space, it makes sense to question the national as a primary reference for border-crossing dimensions. In many cases, there is empirical evidence that the notion of homeland, for example, does not apply to the country of origin but to the specific locality.[15] Space, thus, is constructed always in relation to the actors' individual (or collective) rationalities, with horizons sometimes being confined to, and sometimes extending, local boundaries and national borders.

NOTES

1. I wish to thank especially Joanna Pfaff-Czarnecka, Gudrun Lachenmann, Sandrine Gukelberger and the editors of this volume for inspiring and constructive comments on earlier versions of this paper.
2. Schütz and Luckmann (1978: 36–40) distinguish two different kinds of spatial stratification of the life-world. "Actual reach" refers to the part of the world that is accessible to our immediate experience and characterized by face-to-face relationships. "Potential reach" instead refers to restorable or attainable reaches that are more distant and beyond the immediate life-worldly experience. In a globalizing world, the latter are increasingly relevant in social analysis, because interaction across long distances structures a significant part of people's everyday life and thus contributes to its translocalization.
3. For the notion of *negotiation* see Strauss (1978).
4. The notion of *interface* is central to an actor-oriented approach based on the premises of a sociology of knowledge as it is applied in the analysis presented in this paper. Interfaces are the sites of struggle, where different knowledge systems clash and are negotiated between collective and/or individual actors. As a methodological tool, the notion of interface helps to analyze dynamics of interaction in specific situations and brings into focus the negotiation of meaning in translocal space.
5. The descriptive term *jumma* derives from the traditional slash and burn cultivation (*jhum*). It is one attempt to find a concept that includes the eleven indigenous groups living in the CHT. Others prefer to call this collectivity *pahari* ("hill people").
6. Although the movement managed to gain some recognition as representing the *Jumma* people, the leadership has recently been heavily criticized for its non-democratic decision making. The various internal disputes that have dominated the movement for several months now will not be discussed in this paper.
7. The term *indigenousness* in the way it is used in the United Nations is of local origin as well, but has been subject to negotiation in the global forum (see Oldham and Frank 2008). Constructions that address the connection with other national or regional contexts are also illustrated by the term *adivasi*, which has become a common way of denominating the indigenous people living on the plains. The term itself is an invention originating in India in the 1930s (Bates 1995) and has been recently promoted by activists from Jharkand, India (Ghosh 2006).
8. Classical examples have been originally described and theorized by Max Gluckman, a later conceptualization is that of "the broker" in development (Bierschenk, Chauveau and Olivier de Sardan 2009; Mosse and Lewis 2006).
9. See report of the Chittagong Hill Tracts Commission (CHTC) (February 16–22, 2009).
10. What is termed as local tradition by many actors in the field should not be taken for some set of cultural practices that have persisted throughout the centuries without having been changed. Tradition is rather constituted by an enduring process of social and cultural change that has always been embedded in translocal exchange.
11. The impact of Christian missionaries on development work is a well-known phenomenon in contexts where conversion has taken place.
12. This is a much more complex relationship, of course. The literature showing the ways that Christianization has been adapted to local contexts and how ancient rituals were incorporated into Christian practice is vast. Very interesting in this regard is David Mosse's work on the reproduction of existing power relations in *dalit* Christian activism in Tamil Nadu (Mosse 2009).

13. For the mechanisms of ethnic boundary-drawing among the Garo, see Bal (2007), and in the Chittagong Hill Tracts, van Schendel (1992a, 2002) and Gerharz (2000). Both empirical works are based on constructivist approaches as elaborated by Barth (1969), Schlee and Werner (1996) and others.
14. See Ghosh (2006) for similar findings from Jharkand, India.
15. I have discussed in Gerharz (2011) the ways notions of homeland are negotiated in the context of northern Sri Lanka and how these lead to (re-)negotiations of belonging between migrants and "locals."

REFERENCES

Asia Indigenous People's Pact (2009) *Indigenous People's Human Rights Report in Asia 2008*, Chiang Mai: Human Rights Campaign, Policy and Advocacy Committee.

Bal, E. (2007) "Becoming the Garos of Bangladesh: Policies of exclusion and the ethnicisation of a 'tribal' minority", *Journal of South Asian Studies*, 30(3): 439–55.

Barkat, A., Hoque, M., Halim, S. and Osman, A. (2009) *Life and Land of Adibashis: Land Dispossession and Alienation of Adibashis in the Plain Districts of Bangladesh*, Dhaka: Pathak Shamabesh Books.

Barth, F. (1969) *Ethnic Groups and Boundaries. The Social Organization of Difference*, Long Grove, IL: Waveland Press.

Bates, C. (1995) "'Lost innocents and the loss of innocence': Interpreting Adivasi movements in South Asia", in H.B. Robert, A. Gray and B. Kingsbury (eds) *Indigenous Peoples of Asia*, Ann Arbor: University of Michigan Press, pp. 103–20.

Bernot, L. (1964) "Ethnic groups of the Chittagong Hill Tracts", in P. Bessaignet (ed) *Social Research in East Pakistan*, Dacca: Asiatic Society of Pakistan, pp. 137–71.

Bierschenk, T., Chauveau, J.-P. and Olivier de Sardan, J.-P. (2009) "Local development brokers in Africa. The rise of a new social category", *Working Papers*, No. 13, Mainz: Institut für Ethnologie und Afrikastudien, Johannes Gutenberg-Universität. Online: www.ifeas.uni-mainz.de/workingpapers/Local.pdf (accessed June 28, 2011).

Bleie, T. (2005) *Tribal Peoples, Nationalism and the Human Rights Challenge. The Adivasis of Bangladesh*, Dhaka: University Press Limited.

Brauns, C.-D. and Löffler, L.G. (1996) *Mru. Bergbewohner im Grenzgebiet von Bangladesch*, Basel/Boston/Stuttgart: Birkhäuser Verlag.

Brubaker, R. (2002) "Ethnicity without groups", *Archives Européennes de Sociologie*, XLIII(2): 163–89.

Chittagong Hill Tracts Commission (CHTC) (February 16–22, 2009) *Report of the Chittagong Hill Tracts Commission's Mission in Bangladesh*. Online: www.internal-displacement.org/8025708F004CE90B/(httpDocuments)/9A639 17651BD79B0C12575CC003EE564/$file/CHTC+MissionFebruary+2009.pdf (accessed June 27, 2011).

della Porta, D. and Tarrow, S. (eds) (2005) *Transnational Protest and Global Activism. People, Passions, and Power*, Lanham, MD: Rowman and Littlefield.

Fisher, W. (2010) "Civil society and its fragments", in D. Gellner (ed) *Varieties of Activist Experience: Civil Society in South Asia*, New Delhi, Thousand Oaks, CA, London: Sage, pp. 250–68.

Freitag, U. and von Oppen, A. (2010) "Introduction. 'Translocality': An approach to connection and transfer in area studies", in U. Freitag and A. von Oppen (eds)

Translocality. The Study of Globalising Processes from a Southern Perspective, Leiden, Boston: Koninklijke Brill, pp. 1–21.

Gandhi, A. (2003) "Developing compliance and resistance: The state, transnational social movements and the tribal peoples contesting India's Narmada Project", *Global Networks*, 3(4): 481–95.

Gardner, K. (1993) "Desh-Bidesh: Sylheti images of home and away", *Man, New Series*, 28(1): 1–15.

Gerharz, E. (2000) *The Construction of Identities. The Case of the Chittagong Hill Tracts in Bangladesh*, Bielefeld: Transnationalisation and Development Research Centre (TDRC), Bielefeld University. Online: www.uni-bielefeld.de/tdrc/downloads/lefo_gerharz.pdf (accessed June 27, 2011).

—— (2002) "Dilemmas in planning crisis prevention: NGOs in the Chittagong Hill Tracts of Bangladesh", *The Journal of Social Studies*, 97: 19–36.

—— (2009) "Ambivalent positioning. Reflections on ethnographic research in Sri Lanka during the ceasefire of 2002", *Working Papers in Development Sociology and Social Anthropology*, No. 361, Bielefeld: Bielefeld University. Online: www.uni-bielefeld.de/%28de%29/tdrc/ag_sozanth/publications/working_papers/Wp361.pdf (accessed June 27, 2011).

—— (2011) "Mobility after war: Re-negotiating belonging in Jaffna, Sri Lanka", in G. Pellegrino (ed) *The Politics of Proximity. Mobility and Immobility in Practice*, Aldershot: Ashgate, pp. 83–104.

Ghosh, K. (2006) "Between global flows and local dams: Indigenousness, locality and the transnational sphere in Jahrkand, India", *Cultural Anthropology*, 21(4): 501–34.

Glick Schiller, N. and Çağlar, A. (2010a) "Introduction. Migrants and cities", in N. Glick Schiller and A. Çağlar (eds) *Locating Migration. Rescaling Cities and Migrants*, Ithaca, NY, London: Cornell University Press, pp. 1–19.

—— (2010b) "Locality and globality. Building a comparative analytical framework in migration and urban studies", in N. Glick Schiller and A. Çağlar (eds) *Locating Migration. Rescaling Cities and Migrants*, Ithaca, NY, London: Cornell University Press, pp. 60–81.

Gluckman, M. (1961) "Ethnographic data in British social anthropology", *Sociological Review*, 9(1): 5–17.

Gulrukh, A. (2004) *Ethnicity and Migration: The Case of Mandi Beauty Workers*, Dhaka: Department of Women and Gender Studies, University of Dhaka.

Gupta, A. and Ferguson, J. (1997) "Discipline and practice: The 'field' as site, method and location in anthropology", in A. Gupta and J. Ferguson (eds) *Anthropological Locations. Boundaries and Grounds of a Field Science*, Berkeley, Los Angeles: University of California Press: 1–46.

Hassan, S. and Ali, A. (2009) *Not Myth But Reality. The Indigenous People of Bangladesh*, Dhaka: Pathak Shamabesh Books.

Hutchinson, S. (1978) *Chittagong Hill Tracts*, Delhi: Vivek Publishing Company.

Keck, M.E. and Sikkink, K. (1998) *Activists beyond Borders. Advocacy Networks in International Politics*, Ithaca, NY, London: Cornell University Press.

Lachenmann, G. (2010) "Globalisation in the making: Translocal gendered spaces in Muslim society", in U. Freitag and A. von Oppen (eds) *Translocality. The Study of Globalising Processes from a Southern Perspective*, Leiden, Boston: Koninklijke Brill, pp. 335–67.

Lewin, T.H. (1884) *Wild Races of the Eastern Frontier of India*, Delhi: Mittal Publications.

Löffler, L.G. (1968) "Basic democracies in den Chittagong Hill Tracts, Ostpakistan", *Sociologus. Zeitschrift für empirische Soziologie und Sozialpsychologie*, 18: 152–71.

Long, N. (2001) *Development Sociology. Actor Perspectives*, London: Routledge.

—— and Long, A. (1992) *Battlefields of Knowledge: The Interlocking Theory and Practice in Social Research and Development*, London: Routledge.
Marcus, G.E. (1998) *Ethnography through Thick and Thin*, Princeton, NJ: Princeton University Press.
Merry, S.E. (2006) "Transnational human rights and local activism: Mapping the middle", *American Anthropologist*, 108(1): 38–51.
Mey, W. (1984) "Implications of national development planning for tribal concepts of economy and politics: A contribution to a critique of concepts of development", in M. Shah Quereshi (ed) *Tribal Cultures in Bangladesh*, Rajshahi: Institute of Bangladesh Studies, pp. 325–44.
Mohsin, A. (1997) *The Politics of Nationalism. The Case of the Chittagong Hill Tracts, Bangladesh*, Dhaka: University Press Ltd.
—— (2003) *The Chittagong Hill Tracts, Bangladesh: On the Difficult Road to Peace*, Boulder, CO: Lynne Rienner Publishers.
Mosse, D. (2009) "Dalit Christian activism in contemporary Tamil Nadu", in D. Gellner (ed) *Ethnic Activism and Civil Society in South Asia. Governance, Conflict, and Civic Action*, Vol. 2, New Delhi, Thousand Oaks, CA, London: Sage, pp. 173–214.
—— and Lewis, D. (2006) "Theoretical approaches to brokerage and translation in development", in D. Lewis and D. Mosse (eds) *Development Brokers and Translators. The Ethnography of Aid and Agencies*, Bloomfield, CT: Kumarian, pp. 1–26.
Muehlebach, A. (2001) "'Making place' at the United Nations: Indigenous cultural politics at the U.N. Working Group on Indigenous Populations", *Cultural Anthropology*, 16(3): 415–48.
Neubert, D. (1995) *Entwicklungspolitische Hoffnungen und gesellschaftliche Wirklichkeit. Eine vergleichende Länderfallstudie von Nicht-Regierungsorganisationen in Kenia und Ruanda*, Berlin: Campus Verlag.
Oldham, P. and Frank, M.A. (2008) "'We the peoples . . . ' The United Nations Declaration on the Rights of Indigenous People", *Anthropology Today*, 24(2): 5–9.
Pfaff-Czarnecka, J. (2005) "Das Lokale als Ressource im entgrenzten Wettbewerb: Das Verhandeln kollektiver Repäsentationen in Nepal-Himalaya", *Zeitschrift für Soziologie*, Sonderheft "Weltgesellschaft": 479–99.
—— (2007) "Challenging Goliath: People, dams, and the paradoxes of transnational critical movements", in I. Hiroshi and K. Nawa (eds) *Political and Social Transformations in North India and Nepal*, Delhi: Manohar: 399–433.
—— (2010) "'Minorities-in-minorities' in South Asian Societies: Between politics of diversity and politics of difference", in S. Kumar Das (ed) *Minorities in South Asia and in Europe*, Kolkata: Samya, pp. 100–31.
—— and Rajasingham-Senanayake, D. (1999) "Introduction", in J. Pfaff-Czarnecka, A. Nandy, D. Rajasingham-Senanayake and E.T. Gomez (eds) *Ethnic Futures. The State and Identity Politics in Asia*, New Delhi, Thousand Oaks, CA London, Sage: pp. 9–40.
—— and Toffin, G. (2011) "Introduction: Belonging and multiple attachments in contemporary Himalayan societies", in J. Pfaff-Czarnecka and G. Toffin (eds) *The Politics of Belonging in the Himalayas*, New Delhi, Thousand Oaks, CA, London: Sage: xi–xxxviii.
Schlee, G. and Werner, K. (1996) "Inklusion und Exklusion: Die Dynamik von Grenzziehungen im Spannungsfeld von Markt, Staat und Ethnizität", in G. Schlee and K. Werner (eds) *Inklusion und Exklusion*, Köln: Rüdiger Köppke Verlag, pp. 9–36.
Schütz, A. and Luckmann, T. (2003 [1978]) *Strukturen der Lebenswelt*, Konstanz: UVK Verlagsgesellschaft.

Spiegel, A. (2008) "Women's organisations and social transformation in Malaysia: Between social work and legal reforms", in G. Lachenmann and P. Dannecker (eds) *Negotiating Development in Muslim Societies*, Lanham, MD: Lexington Books, pp. 67–92.

Stewart, J. (2004) "When local troubles become transnational: The transformation of a Guatemalan indigenous rights movement", *Mobilization: An International Journal*, 9(3): 259–78.

Strauss, A. (1978) *Negotiations: Varieties, Contexts, Processes, and Social Cries*, San Francisco: Jossey-Bass.

Tarrow, S. (2005) *The New Transnational Activism*, Cambridge: Cambridge University Press.

Tsing, A. (2007) "Indigenous voice", in M. de la Cadena and O. Starn (eds) *Indigenous Experience Today*, Oxford: Berg Publishers, pp. 33–68.

van Schendel, W. (1992a) "The invention of the 'Jummas'. State formation and ethnicity in southeast Bangladesh", *Modern Asian Studies*, 26(1): 95–128.

—— (ed) (1992b) *Francis Buchanan in Southeast Bengal (1798). His Journey to Chittagong, the Chittagong Hill Tracts, Noakhali and Comilla*, Dhaka: University Press Limited.

—— (2002) "A politics of nudity: Photographs of the 'Naked Mru' of Bangladesh", *Modern Asian Studies*, 36(2): 341–74.

—— (2009) *The History of Bangladesh*, Cambridge: Cambridge University Press.

White, S.C. (1999) "NGOs, civil society, and the state in Bangladesh: The politics of representing the poor", *Development and Change*, 30: 307–26.

Wimmer, A. (1995) "Interethnische Konflikte. Ein Beitrag zur Integration aktueller Forschungsansätze", *Kölner Zeitschrift für Soziologie und Sozialpsychologie*, 3/1995: 464–93.

—— (2008) "Elementary strategies of ethnic boundary making", *Ethnic and Racial Studies*, 31(6): 1025–55.

—— and Glick Schiller, N. (2003) "Methodological nationalism, the social sciences and the study of migration: An essay in historical epistemology", *International Migration Review*, 37(3): 576–610.

Part III
Juxtapositions of Historiography after the Hegemony of the National

8 The Global, the Transnational and the Subaltern
The Limits of History beyond the National Paradigm

Angelika Epple

Ever since history became an academic discipline, writing national history has been the most honorable task of a historian's career. However, for today's historians, writing national history has lost the high reputation it held for roughly 150 years. Of course, there are still ambitious projects such as series editions of European national histories. However, they do not see themselves as traditional national history, but either as histories that analyze the making of nations or as histories that place the history of a certain nation within an international (Herbert 2010) or even transnational setting (Trentmann 2008; Grant *et al.* 2007; Tyrell 2007a). They are mitigated versions of strong national history. Traditional national history has had its day. Why?

As globalization processes continue, it becomes difficult if not impossible to legitimize a presumably given entity—such as a singular nation-state—with fixed borders. Indeed, one of the main criticisms of the nation-centered approach to history has been that it rarely worried about its own limits and exclusions. Interactions, transfers, mutual influence and shared developments were ignored. A lack of reflexivity on its own limits does not just lead to an exclusion of transnational dynamics. It also hides exclusions *within* the very nations or societies analyzed. Nation-centered history also tends to focus on a limited understanding of policy and society. Often, it elaborates on a limited group of actors and excludes many topics such as everyday life, ordinary people and gender history.

To make a long story short, national history seems to be too limited to add to our understanding of today's questions in a globalizing world. Even though the significance and role of the nation-state in a globalizing world cannot, and should not, be underestimated, the unity of territoriality, culture and national identity has proved to be a fiction.[1] Today, it is broadly accepted that space is not a closed container of historical development. Instead, it is a relational and contextual category, created by and through social interactions and social practices (Massey 2006; Löw 2001). This short reflection on the concept of space illustrates that only an analysis of theoretical concepts can help us understand history beyond the national paradigm. At the end of the day, it is theoretical concepts that shape the way historians write their (hi)stories. A revised concept of space does not just focus attention on interactions instead of geographically defined territories, it simultaneously delivers new sources, new questions and thus new methodologies. The criticism of the national paradigm along with both its theory and methodology could be summarized in just one single phrase: National history excludes too much.

How did the discipline react to this criticism? I see at least three major reactions:

- Extending national history into world history;
- Transforming national history into transnational history (Bungert and Wendt 2010; Gassert 2010; Núñez 2010; Rüger 2010; Conrad 2009; Jarausch 2006) and the history of entanglements (Schiel 2009; Werner and Zimmermann 2006; Randeria and Conrad 2002; Randeria 2000), an approach some call *global history* or even *new global history* (Sachsenmaier 2010; Mazlish 2006; O'Brien 2006) in contrast to *world history*;
- Undermining national history through subaltern and postcolonial history.[2]

Of course, these terms are not fixed, their application is confusing and their meanings often overlap. Generally speaking, however, world history tries to include the history of the whole world. It is influenced and mostly driven by a variation of modernization theory. Transnational and entangled history also include more than just one specific nation, but not necessarily the whole world. They reject the idea of fixed entities such as the nation-state, transcending the boundaries of the entities they analyze by stressing the interactions between them. Their basic assumption is that people have a shared history, though not the same history (Eckert 2009: 229; Conrad and Randeria 2002; Randeria 2002). Often they point to global asymmetries—one reason that this approach is also subsumed under the label of *global history*. Subaltern and postcolonial history, in contrast, reflect more on excluding processes (subaltern) and processes of asymmetric interferences (postcolonial). Without neglecting the differences between the two, I shall treat them as one reaction. They both share the main concern of uncovering forgotten or suppressed histories, in other words, histories beyond the borders of dominant narratives.

In the following, I shall sketch these three approaches and their internal differences before discussing the pros and cons of using each. I shall focus particularly on the issue of exclusion and inclusion, which is crucially important in the writing of history because it sets the "limits" that have to be understood in this process" (Guha 2002). In my final remarks, I shall start by arguing that the rejection of the world history approach leads to the conviction that the term *globalization*, if it is to be used at all, should only appear in the plural (Therborn 2000). Then I shall show that only a combination of the latter two approaches—of transnational/entangled/global history *and* subaltern/postcolonial studies—helps us to gain a better understanding of the globalizing world. Globalizations are both the effects and the bases for global–local entanglements. From there, I shall argue that the *microhistory approach* delivers a promising methodology that allows for a combination of global questions and local studies, a multiplicity of perspectives and a thorough contextualization of meanings. Microhistory also includes a reflection of its range of validity, which is, in other words, an explicit reflection on the limits of history. Such limits become all the more important when history goes beyond the national paradigm.

WORLD HISTORY AS A FAILED ATTEMPT TO INCLUDE THE WHOLE WORLD

"World History" has been written from the very beginning of historiography in Europe. You only have to think of Herodotus and his history of the *oikumene* or of the chronicles during the Middle Ages (Otto of Freising 1912) to realize immediately that world history always had high aspirations: to include the whole world of the time. In the age of European exploration, this world grew tremendously. World history widened its scope to include more and more peoples and cultures. Interestingly, the expectations and also the function of historiography within European societies remained more or less the same: providing instructive information for rulers, acquainting readers with the hitherto unknown and collecting important events for Christian readers. During the 18th century, however, the expectations of historiography in Europe changed dramatically. History was no longer to be just a presentation of examples. Instead historiography should *explain* why the world had become as it was. David Hume expressed this new challenge paradigmatically in his "Inquiry concerning human understanding" in 1748 (1826: 25). However, Hume had difficulties in handling this task in his *English History*. In his epistemology, every event was caused by a former event, but how could he then deliver a convincing explanation of the very first event and therefore the beginning of English history?[3] If this was already unmanageable when writing the history of an island, it would be an impossible task for world history. Without negating the differences between the British enlightened history of David Hume and the German *Universalgeschichte*, one could say that world history during the Enlightenment did its best to find causes for progress in history. August Ludwig Schlözer, for instance, expressed his understanding of world history in his two volume *World History for Children* as follows: Learning world history is "to search for the causes why one people has remained stupid, strong, and black, whereas the other has become wise, fussy, and white" (1806:

127). For Schlözer, as for most of his colleagues at the time, the history of humanity was a development toward the better. Human progress included the transformation from stupidity to wisdom, which he equated with the transformation of black into white races. Schlözer's text is a good example of what Jürgen Osterhammel has called the "inclusive Eurocentrism" (1998: 380) of Enlightenment intellectuals that was so widespread in 18th century Europe.

Around 1800, the writing of world history experienced another major shift in Hegel's works on history. Hegel inherited the term *world history* from Enlightenment philosophers, but he elaborated on it. World history came to be synonymous with *Reason* in history. World history, constructed transcendentally into a providential design, took on a higher quality of moral sanctity, writes Ranajit Guha in his book *History at the Limit of World-History* (2002: 2). The state for Hegel, continues Guha, as a concrete manifestation of the ethical whole, became a key link in the chain of supersessions of *Weltgeist* ("world spirit"). This is not the place to evaluate the role of the (nation) state in Hegel. A posthumously published article by Heinz Dieter Kittsteiner offers a new reading of Hegel's philosophy of history, the crucial role of the state and Hegel's Eurocentrism. Kittsteiner is of the opinion that the course of the Hegelian *Weltgeist* went from East to West, and, following Hegel's dialectic, will go back again. Hegel's Eurocentrism would then turn out to be a period in world history and not its hidden goal (Kittsteiner 2010: 62). Whatever Hegel's diagnosis for the future, it is important to point out clearly the effects that it had on modern historiography. Due to the overrated role of the state, world history became the prehistory of European nation-states and the civilization that made them happen. World history encountered pitfalls similar to those confronting national history at the end of the 19th century. While being more inclusive than ever before, it simultaneously became quite limited: It left out whole continents and cultures, ordinary people, most women and everyday life (Wolf 1982). In contrast to earlier exclusions, they were no longer left out as a result of being literally unknown. In compliance with the explanatory claim of historiography, they were excluded for a reason: World history dealt only with history, and all the excluded were transformed into *people without history*.

It is important to highlight that this exclusion works in a completely different way from the *inclusive Eurocentrism* of an August Ludwig Schlözer, who, of course, had also underlined European supremacy. From now on, Europe became the center from which modernity (or capitalism) originated, and from which it then spread out *over time*. Non-Europeans were banished to the "waiting room of history" (Chakrabarty 2000: 7–8). Some, like North Americans, were close to leaving the waiting room; others, like Africans, were never to leave. They had—presumably—no positive impact on the course of world history (Kittsteiner 2010: 65). The epoch of *exclusive Eurocentrism* in historiography had begun (Osterhammel 1998: 380).

Over the next 200 years, this tradition of world history influenced Western historians, even when most of them simultaneously refuted Hegelian philosophy. Leopold von Ranke, for instance, being a historist,[4] was a prominent opponent of Hegel's idealism. Ranke developed his concept of world history in discussions with—and in opposition to—his fellow professors at the Friedrich Wilhelms University of Berlin, one of whom was none other than Georg Wilhelm Friedrich Hegel himself. Following Ranke, world history did not begin with the emergence of states, but with interactions between previously isolated people. This sounds as if Ranke had invented the transnational approach. Actually, however, Ranke is quite often misperceived, not only for his underestimated world history approach or his assumedly naive historical objectivism, but also for his broadly celebrated introduction of scientific standards into historiography that turned out to be characterized by hegemonic masculinity and Eurocentrism (Smith 2009, 1998, 1995).

There are good reasons to take a closer look here: Ranke did not agree with the speculative idea of history as a teleological process, but was convinced that the (European, scholarly-trained, male, white) historian could trace the course of history by analyzing the past. He was one of the most influential scholars in the establishment of academic historiography. His whole work was guided by the belief that every epoch has its own intrinsic value that makes it worth examining and describing. Nevertheless, he added to this the opinion that only certain people had an impact on the course of each epoch, and as a result, that only certain people were worth investigating. Most people, in contrast, were people without history and thus a subject of study for anthropologists and not historians. At the time, Ranke's fundamental conviction was not at all exceptional, but simply common sense for European academics.

In short, a historiography of exclusion paved the way for 19th century imperialism. This changed during the first decades of the 20th century. Of course, the division of labor between history and anthropology still influenced the writing of world history, but after World War I it became clear that historiography had to change as well. Here is not the place to mention the many historians who have done world history since then. We shall also skip the revolutionary effects on methodology and historical thinking of the early French *Annales* School represented by Marc Bloch and Lucien Fèbvre (who were deeply influenced by the German universal historian Karl Lamprecht) and concentrate on the major changes in writing world history in the second half of the century. As early as the 1950s, Walter Markov, a communist resistance fighter during national socialism, built on Karl Lamprecht's non-Eurocentric approach to universal history when he became director of the Institute of Cultural and Universal History in Leipzig that had been founded by Lamprecht in 1909 (Brahm 2010: 112–18; Middell 2005: 846).

Marxism, to a different degree, also influenced prominent world historians. Fernand Braudel for instance, a significant member of the second *Annales* School generation, which was imbued with the ideas of Marx, also set the foundations for a new approach to world history (Wieviorka 2005). The understanding of the dynamics of capitalism was at the very center of his impressive oeuvre (Braudel 1985). Instead of small political entities as single actors, he concentrated on a region that had shaped the whole world in the 16th century. His approach to history allowed previously inconceivable inclusions. His masterpiece, *The Mediterranean and the Mediterranean World in the Age of Philip II* (1976a) deals not only with what he calls "traditional history" but also with structures of the *longue durée* that were almost "immobile," such as the influence of climate, landscape, mentalities and collective fates. In contrast to Neo-Rankeans and historians, who favored political individuals, Braudel also concentrated on economic conditions, processes and structures (1976b). As to the difference between world history and global history, Braudel—like Markov—seems to have been a forerunner in favor of the latter. His main interest was in analyzing interactions without constructing new fixed entities. Maybe he was able to avoid certain pitfalls because he dealt with early modern times. Thus, the seductive idea of the nation-state as a historical category did not seem to appeal to him. His influential concepts traveled not only throughout Europe but also across the Atlantic to the US, where they, of course, experienced major transformations.

During the 1960s and 1970s, the demand for courses covering world history grew tremendously at US universities. The hitherto general courses on Western Civilization, however, seemed to be too ethnocentric (Manning 2007; Bayly *et al.* 2006). One widespread response at the time was courses in world history. Quite often, they just extended the history of Western Civilization to international history, and thus tried to go beyond the North American and European nation-states by also including Asian and Latin American nation-states. Africa at that time still did not seem to be of any interest (Eckert 2003). Another, more ambitious attempt picked up Braudel's concept. The sociologist Immanuel Wallerstein combined Braudel's understanding of history with an approach borrowed from dependency theory. In his three volume history of the modern world system, he elaborated on the emergence and effects of asymmetric global interactions caused by capitalism (Wallerstein 1974–89). Wallerstein tried to show that world history is not about a growing inclusion of developing countries into Western modernity; world history is actually about the making of hierarchies by exclusion. Following Wallerstein, the creation of wealthy centers, midrange semiperipheries and poor peripheries cannot be avoided in capitalism; it is the nature of capitalism to produce a global division of labor and other asymmetries.

Like Markov and Braudel, Wallerstein also broadened the range of historiography without repeating an inclusive or exclusive Eurocentrism as practiced for such a long time in historiography. With the idea of an integrative world system, however, Wallerstein insisted—and this is one of many ways in which his work differs from that of Braudel—on one single mechanism to replace the master narrative of modernization as a development toward the better. Moreover, he did not even mention one of the major problems of historiography in general: the problem of perspective. Wallerstein located the first world system and the birth of capitalism in Europe. However, Janet Abu-Lughod, for instance, empirically illustrates the hidden Eurocentric perspective in the history of the world system by showing capitalistic entanglements in other world regions (1989), and other scholars also questioned his point of view.[5] Nonetheless, Wallerstein influenced many subsequent discussions within history, sociology and other disciplines. Despite all criticism, his world system has become an important reference point when doing world history (see Comstock, Chapter 9 of this volume). His main idea was that before 1492, there had been a world system in Europe but not one covering the whole world, and that this subsequently (after 1492) spread over the whole world due to entanglements. This was a first step toward decoupling world history and the history of the whole world. But it was only in the 1990s that the concept of world history was supplemented by an approach that, at first, left any kind of centrism behind it and elaborated on the idea of interactions between changing entities: transnational history.

Let me briefly summarize so far. Writing world history has a long tradition. The concept of *world history* has a history of its own. This makes it difficult to give strict definitions and demarcation lines to related concepts. Bearing in mind that there are other usages of the term, I would suggest the following characterization: The world history approach tries to include the history of the whole world. From the Enlightenment through German Idealism up until the capitalist critical positions of the history of the world system, the world history approach has four major unsolved problems: It sticks to a teleological understanding of history, it is ethnocentric, it does not examine local processes and ordinary people and it fails to consider the heuristic problems arising from the historian's standpoint. In my opinion, the attempt to capture the history of the whole world has failed.

TRANSNATIONAL, ENTANGLED AND (NEW) GLOBAL HISTORY AS ATTEMPTS TO OVERCOME ETHNOCENTRIC EXCLUSIONS

In the late 1980s, the nation-centered approach to history lost its explanatory power. Soon a new concept emerged and rapidly became a buzzword among historians: *transnational history* (Bayly et al. 2006: 1441; Thelen 1999; *American Historical Review* 1991). It first changed the way historians looked at nation-states and comparable entities, characterizing them as "invented traditions" (Anderson 1985) rather than a "container of society"

(Beck 2000: 63). Transnational history even went on to question the concept of *world history*. The main issue was transcending the boundaries of the nation-state without neglecting its historical importance. Transnational history preferred previously neglected subjects, such as the movements of people, ideas, technologies and institutions (Tyrell 2007b), as well as diaspora, border crossings, flows and circulation.[6] Instead of the supposed container of a nation-state, transnational history went back to dealing with contact zones as Fernand Braudel had already done in his work on the Mediterranean. Paul Gilroy, for example, wrote an influential book on *The Black Atlantic* (1993) as a counterculture of modernity. The Indian Ocean and the Pacific also became the subjects of important studies (Fernandez-Armesto 2002; Gilroy 1993).

It is important, indeed, to distinguish clearly between international and transnational history. International history analyzes the interactions between nation-states as sole agents—mostly with an emphasis on diplomatic and economic relations (Hopkins 2006: 4). Transnational history instead transcends politically defined and geographically fixed territories. If it deals with nation-states at all, it analyzes the process of making them. Transnational history started with a strong emphasis on overcoming the ethnocentrism accompanying nation-centered history.

Noting that after the *trans* prefix, *nation* is still at the very center of *transnational history,* many historians specializing in earlier epochs rejected the term. This points to enduring and controversial issues. Is transnational history defined by its content, or is it rather a perspective with which to look at and analyze history (Patel 2005)? Furthermore, what is the scope of transnational history? Different scholars have given different answers to these questions. Most agree with Sven Beckert's characterization that transnational history focuses on connections that are not necessarily global in scope. For him transnational history proves to be a perspective (Bayly *et al.* 2006: 1446)that we could add, sheds light on contents invisible in any nation-centered approach. Christopher Bayly also insists on the heuristic definition, but includes the question of scope. Following Bayly, "'transnational history' stands in the same relationship to 'international history' as 'global history' does to 'world history'" (Bayly *et al.* 2006: 1442). Global history in this understanding should replace world history. The adjective *global,* however, raises a problem that is not immediately apparent in *transnational:* the problem of defining the global (Cooper 2007). Let me elaborate on this briefly.

Bruce Mazlish, who has published broadly on the concepts of global and new global history, also feels uncomfortable with the concept of *world history.* Like Bayly, he wants to replace the term *world* by the term *global.* What does, according to Mazlish, *global* mean in contrast? In his words, *global* "points in the direction of space; its sense permits the notion of standing outside our planet and seeing 'Spaceship Earth.' . . . This new perspective is one of the keys to new global history, where, indeed, a new space/time orientation is observable" (2006: 18). For Mazlish, global history is about including the whole world. In contrast to world history, however, global history should prevent ethnocentrism by taking a neutral and literally universal standpoint. Mazlish's metaphor makes it easy to understand why the meaning of *global* and the question of perspective cause such problems. As we all know, nobody—not even a global historian—can stand outside our planet and observe this spaceship *sine ira et studio*. It is important to underline that there is no theoretical position from which a global historian could speak for all people and individuals on Earth. To get to the point: The global in this view is more a geographical definition (without bothering about the spatial turn) than a historical category of analysis. Furthermore, Mazlish's claim for a global historian outside our planet relies on a concept of scientific objectivity that goes back to Ranke's concept of history mentioned above. This concept went on to be exported throughout the colonized world. Since then, it has dominated academic history writing worldwide. I shall back up this consideration later by discussing Chakrabarty's criticism of Western historical thinking (2006).

The illusionary assumption of a neutral and omniscient reader did not escape profound criticism. For instance, in Jürgen Osterhammel's latest book on the transformation of the world in the 19th century, he underlines that only a conscious play with the relativity of perspectives may convincingly help to overcome Eurocentrism (Osterhammel 2010: 19). Likewise, Sven Beckert's understanding of global history as transnational history with a global scope seems to offer some promise (Bayly *et al.* 2006). If *global* points to scope, it is not necessarily connected to presumably given spaces such as the whole world, but to a special perspective. Actually, the adjective *transnational* also has the problem of a spatial definition. However, it is considerably less risky to define the transnational within geographic terms (and without reflecting on the spatial turn). The key term in any transnational approach, says Isabel Hofmeyr, is "its central concern with movements, flows, and circulation, not simply as a theme or motif but as an analytic set of methods which defines the endeavor itself" (Bayly *et al.* 2006: 1444).

Nevertheless, transnational history in practice did not always realize that interactions between entities lead to a new understanding of space in general. I believe this is the main reason that another term closely connected to the transnational approach also came into play: *entangled history* (Conrad and Randeria 2002).[7] Without repeating the scholarly subtleties, the term *entangled history* liberates transnational history from its national background. It highlights the fact that interactions can take place between any entities. From there, I believe the term *entangled history* expresses even more clearly mutual influences, responses and effects. In my concluding remarks, I shall push this thought a bit further still and argue that the concept of entangled history also helps to dissolve the dichotomy of macro and micro levels of analysis.[8]

I would like to summarize that in this perspective so far, the focus turns toward interactions between entities and thus transcends the boundaries between them. Of course, this also has an impact on how we define the objects of our analyses. Entities such as nation-states are no longer perceived as fixed but as fluid. Their importance, however, is not to be denied. The emphasis is not on the loss of significance of nation-states, but on their connectedness to each other and their mutual influences on different levels. Thus, this approach opens mental spaces that allow a new way of thinking about all dichotomies. The *other* and the *own*, for instance, become interwoven but not dissolved. Both the new understanding of historical entities and the stress on interactions make ethnocentrism difficult.[9]

In a nutshell, transnational, entangled and global history analyze shared histories by focusing on interactions. Abandoning fixed entities should also help to overcome ethnocentrism, as with such a perspective all entities turn out to be of hybrid origin. If practiced with a global scope, this approach seems to be all inclusive. But is it?

SUBALTERN AND POSTCOLONIAL HISTORY AS AN ATTEMPT TO EXPLORE THE LIMITS OF HISTORY

A completely different solution for dealing with nation-centered history was taken by the Subaltern Studies Group in the 1980s, which wanted to not only rewrite Indian history but also question the categories of historiography imposed by Western scholars within the colonial system (Kaltmeier *et al.* 2011). Under the leadership of the aforementioned Ranajit Guha, the group combined the critique of Eurocentrism with Gramsci's concept of the subaltern and of hegemony. Moreover, the role of intellectuals in creating this very hegemony remained an important point of reference. Most relevant articles by the Subaltern Studies Group members have been published in the journal of the same name that first appeared in 1982. At the beginning, their main aim was to democratize historiography and include as many groups into history as possible. Peasants and people of the lower castes such as Dalits became subjects of research (Guha 1983). With Gayatri Chakravorty Spivak, who was the first female member of the editorial board, the project changed profoundly. Her influential essay "Can the subaltern speak?" refused the conditions of possibility that the subaltern as such could contribute to a hegemonic discourse (Spivak 1988). On the one hand, Spivak was influenced profoundly by the understanding of productive power and governmentality developed in the works of Michel Foucault (Dreyfus and Rabinow 1983). On the other hand, she fundamentally questioned the critical position from which theorists like Michel Foucault and Gilles Deleuze spoke and made the limits of their historical analyses a subject of discussion. My reading of her arguments leads to a paradoxical conclusion: Subaltern subjects neither have positions to be heard nor do they even exist—not even as a subaltern consciousness as Guha had hoped in the early 1980s. Spivak underlines instead, "One must nevertheless insist that the colonialized subaltern *subject* is irretrievably heterogeneous" (1988: 284).

Spivak's argument is also a barb in the flesh of the transnational approach. Transnational history points to the interactions between entities that transform these very entities at any given time. Applying the transnational approach to subaltern subjects causes (at least) two major problems. First, we need to identify these subaltern subjects and thus run the risk of denying their heterogeneity, and, second, by reconstructing their voices through the historian's dependence on proof, we raise the question of who defines what counts as a proof.

To answer this question, we have to go back to the history of our discipline. Western historiography modeled after the German 19th century historian Leopold von Ranke introduced a scholarly methodology that gave the historian an extraordinary role. He became the only person who could ascertain professionally whether a narration of bygone events was true or ill-conceived. How is that? Due to his scholarly methodology, the historian now gave evidence through his documentary studies, he gathered evidence through his critique of the sources, and he had to prove the truth of his narration by referring exclusively to written sources and by degrading contemporary oral traditions (Epple 2010b). This shift in giving evidence had far-reaching consequences: The way historians proved the truth became the most important marker for highlighting the difference between popular and professional historians. According to Ranke, the explicit aim of the professional historian was to fight political partiality, and in this struggle "objectivity" seemed to be the best weapon. Scientific methodology should guarantee the erasure of the historian's subjective personality, his individual interests and most importantly, his political convictions. These would no longer influence the "objective" proofs of his narration. What Hume had begun a hundred years earlier was completed by Ranke: Historical impartiality became the main concern of professional history writing. Whereas Hume stressed causal explanation as the historian's instrument, Ranke established written sources as the very center of historiography. Popular historical narrations were degraded and excluded from national canons of historiography. These exclusionary and degrading factors of Western historiography were exported to India and other societies in the 19th century when colonial governments introduced their models of universities (Shils and Robert 2004).

This new kind of history was only possible due to a "crucial shift in the institutional site for the production of history" (Chakrabarty 2006: 106). The university became the only place for doing valid and genuine history. Masayuki Sato, a contributor to a volume on Western historical thinking, points out this development for China, and Dipesh Chakrabarty backs up Sato's findings for India. Professional historiography conquered history writing across the whole world. This expansion simultaneously narrowed the field of historiography. Popular authors and, even more importantly, popular subjects beyond political or economic history, along with women historians in general, were excluded from academic history writing for many years. This was not only true for China and India but also for Europe. It is only recently that historians have started to go back to these excluded traditions, to analyze how this exclusion worked and also to show its deeply gendered basis.[10]

The introduction of the Western version of history writing to non-Western societies such as India generated an "asymmetric ignorance." "Europe," says Chakrabarty, "remains the sovereign, theoretical subject of all histories, including the ones we call 'Indian'" (1992: 337). Europe is always a "silent referent." This leads to a basic asymmetry in historiography: Whereas a European historian might ignore non-European history, a historian of another world region cannot return this gesture.

In a review essay on the aforementioned volume about Western historical thinking, Chakrabarty illustrates the paradoxical situation of asymmetric ignorance with a historical example: The European academic discipline of history gained a hegemonic position in 19th century India and presumably also in other non-European societies. Before the encounter with the Western version of history writing, Chakrabarty explains, all societies had of course their own traditions of thinking and of narrating past events. Chakrabarty wonders, "Why did we end up with broadly the same global culture of professional historians all over the world?" (2006: 104). His rhetorical question is easy to answer: We did so because these excluded traditions did not influence academic history writing. Chakrabarty hopes that traces of an Indian tradition before the introduction of the scientific style might be found in marginalized popular narratives. He concludes by referring to the volume's editor, Jörn Rüsen: "Historical matters," writes Rüsen, "come back with a vengeance through mass media" (2006: 109).

It is definitely true that in Western societies, the global mass media are currently challenging the dominance gained by academic history two hundred years ago. Indeed, it is no coincidence that the question of historical truth and objectivity has been put back on the agenda with heated controversies throughout the academic discipline (*American Historical Review* 2009; Chakrabarty 2007). The assumed historical impartiality introduced by Ranke as the main marker of professional historians did not just turn out to be a Eurocentric perspective of Protestant, white, middle-class men. Impartiality lost its high reputation when it became obvious that the construction of history influences the making of identities, creates groups such as subalterns and shapes our world as a whole. As Elazar Barkan concludes in a forum in the *American Historical Review* on "Truth and Reconciliation," "Therefore it [the construction of history] often has to be treated as an explicit, direct political activity, operating within specific scientific methodological and rhetorical rules" (Barkan 2009).

If historiography is treated as a direct political activity, does our academic discipline then fall behind Ranke's or even behind Hume's standards for doing history professionally? Does history only legitimize certain political positions in the way that the Whig interpretation of history did? Is this the aim of subaltern or postcolonial history? Definitely not. But the example of Elazar Barkan, professor of International and Public Affairs at Columbia University, shows that the criticism of methodology has already influenced central disciplinary discussions.[11] As to the academic discipline of history, subaltern studies and postcolonial theory have made many important objections: their criticism of Western historical concepts that put some people in the "waiting room of history," their criticism of the power of concepts and the plea that subalterns are not a homogeneous subject, their considerations on Western historical thinking—these all make historians aware of the fact that they should not regard written proof as the only valid sources for professional histories. This convincing criticism, however, also applies to the Subaltern Studies Group itself, which tends to apply the same professional methodology and to homogenize the Western discourse. Nira Wickramasinghe supports this remark with the argument that the Subaltern Studies Group (when working historically) mostly referred to written documents and as a consequence overestimated the "essentiality" of colonial government (2011). Neither is there such a thing as *the* Western historical thinking, nor is the hegemonic discourse omnipotent.

I would like to briefly summarize my considerations on the subaltern and postcolonial approach. Most importantly, subaltern history points to the limits of history, which is, in other words, the exclusions drawn by historiography. At the same time, it underlines the productive power of these exclusions. Like gender history, subaltern and postcolonial history also show that a criticism of nation-centered and ethnocentric history is not only about excluded subjects. It is the historical thinking itself, the concepts historians use, their academic methodology and their way of proving the truth and of narrating the past that are at stake.

CONCLUSION: GLOBAL–LOCAL ENTANGLEMENTS—A MICROHISTORY APPROACH TO GLOBAL HISTORY

By suggesting a microhistory approach to global history, I wish to combine the two latter approaches, that is, to suggest a combination of entangled and subaltern history. Before doing so, let me first sum up this fragmentary overview of the three most interesting disciplinary reactions to the end of the national paradigm.

The first reaction was no reaction in the strict sense, because world history was already there several hundred years before the question of nation-states and national history arose. In any case, world history—as defined in this chapter—seems to have the same problems as the nation-centered approach to history: It relies on a teleological and Eurocentric understanding of history. World history cannot convincingly explain the standpoint from which the historian is speaking, and, as a result, does not reflect explicitly on its exclusions. Within the second group of reactions—the transnational, the entangled and the global history approach—entangled history seems to be the most promising. All three refuse teleology in history. They assume that there is such a thing as a shared history and that history consists of interactions between entities. Furthermore, they underline that these interactions transform the entities themselves. This leads to the conviction that entities are not fixed but fluid, that they cannot only be defined geographically and that theoretically all world regions should be included in historiography (though not in every historical study). Depending on the chosen definition, there are also some slight differences between these approaches. Transnational history is still tied to the nation-centered approach—which is useful in some cases, but makes it difficult to apply the term to historical epochs without nation-states. Moreover, transnational history implies that the nation-state is always of significance whereas the notion of entangled history instead allows us to focus easily on other entities. It stresses that history is not only about the interactions of nation-states, but about reciprocal influences of any given entity. Finally, global history—if contrasted with world history—does not refer to a geographically all-inclusive history but to a certain perspective in which there is an awareness that global questions matter most. The global history approach, however, most often tends to neglect the importance of local affairs, singular actors, ordinary people and everyday practices.

My discussion of subaltern and postcolonial theory has shown that transnational, entangled and global history should also reflect on their limits. Eurocentrism does not just exclude certain subjects, but also these subjects' own vocabulary and own concepts of historical thinking. This requires us to go back to the times when different local traditions all over the world were being excluded from scholarly historiography. Privileging written sources leads to a repetition of the exclusion of subaltern voices. The division of labor between history, anthropology and ethnology introduced by the historical discipline in Europe during the 19th century came to an end in the 1980s when both microhistory and the history-from-below approach came to the fore. The Subaltern Studies Group and postcolonial theory carry the history-from-below arguments to a global level and show the crucial importance of connecting global processes to local affairs. Apart from the criticism of subaltern and postcolonial approaches, they point to the trivial fact that interactions studied by transnational, entangled and global history are interactions within a system of power relations. This recognition should not lead, however, to an overestimation of colonial rule. If global history is linked to local affairs, if it shows how local affairs, ordinary people and singular actors have an impact on global structures, then it focuses on global–local entanglements and reestablishes the history-from-below approach on a new basis. In "A brief history of Subaltern Studies," Partha Chatterjee stresses not only the similarities between Subaltern Studies and the history-from-below approach but also the differences. He insists that "history from below" never "persuasively challenged the existence, stability or indeed the historical legitimacy of capitalist modernity itself" (Chatterjee 2006: 98). This might be true for the history-from-below approach as popularized by British Marxist historians such as E.-P. Thompson and Eric Hobsbawm. However, the history-from-below approach I would like to put forward here is not influenced by the Marxist theory of capitalism or similar teleological and Eurocentric ideologies. Instead, it is derived from the methodological approach of microhistory (Putnam 2006; Ginzburg 1993, 1992; Ginzburg and Poni 1985).

Microhistory or history-from-below—when contrasted with global history—means starting the analysis with an actor-centered approach on a local level. Global purposes and local actors seem to be contradictory only at first glance. A closer look at the relation between the global and the local reveals that both are in fact tied inseparably together. I believe we can only understand the global while studying the local. This is particularly important, and brings me back to my opening remarks concerning the concept of space. Let me very briefly elaborate on this.

The national paradigm came under fire when a relational concept of space questioned the unity of territoriality, culture and identity (Berking 2006b; Massey 2006; Löw 2001). However, this new concept of space was applied mainly to the traditional understanding of the nation as a closed container. The new concept of space led to the aforementioned three disciplinary reactions to the end of the national paradigm. But the concept at the time created a paradoxical situation: All three reactions provoked a dichotomy between the global and the local in which the first was connected to fluidity and changes, whereas the latter, in contrast, was again tied to a geographically defined small-scale space. The talk of "placeless, borderless and unbounded space of flows," as underlined by Helmuth Berking (2006a: 6), or also of an abstract and anonymous world society, as Martin Albrow would have it (1996), might suggest that space is a socially constructed category. Eventually, the limits of national history will be dissolved and space will be "deterritorialized." A closer look reveals, however, that the local reintroduces the notion of a fixed container. The local becomes the last refuge of traditionally defined space. The global space of flows becomes the opposite of a geographically determined space of place.

As part of these concluding remarks, I would like to cast doubt on this binary opposition of the local and the global. If we understand space as a relative category or, as Arjun Appadurai has put it, as a contextually defined space (Appadurai 1996: 178), we then also have to reformulate our understanding of both the global and the local. The local is no longer the last refuge for authenticity, autochthony or traditional identity. The local stands in relation to other localities, and it is defined by and through these relations. In their recently published anthology, Ulrike Freitag and Achim von Oppen have pointed out convincingly that the concept of locality should be broadened by the concept of *translocality* (Freitag and von Oppen 2010). Derived from entangled history, translocality focuses on the multiple relations between different localities. Theoretically speaking, translocalities also imply multiple perspectives, due to the fact that translocalities might differ for different observers.

I would like to push their thoughts even further: Translocality can also grant us a better understanding of the global after the spatial turn. Translocality works as a transition between the local and the global. If we study the local by studying translocal relations with a microhistorical approach, we get to global history through the sum of all translocalities. While this sum is actually always in motion, the global itself becomes dynamic and historically changeable. The global then turns out to be an entity in constant flux that cannot be studied as a whole by one single scholar. On the one hand, this understanding of global–local entanglements dissolves the binary dichotomy that has been established between the local and the global. On the other hand, it ties in with Doreen Massey's observation that places are not "victims" of globalizing processes; on the contrary, it is the places/localities that make the global (Massey 2006).

In conclusion, the study of global–local entanglements is inspired by the Subaltern Studies Group, by the history-from-below discussions and the methodology of microhistory. It centers on (individual) actors. It is important to underline, however, that it should neither concentrate on the social history of the working class[12] nor limit its fields of research to investigating the history of subalterns or everyday life. "Below" should designate only the micro level in contrast to global structures, insofar as global history-from-below borrows methodological tools from microhistory (Ginzburg 1993) and combines these with a new understanding of the global as the sum of translocal relations and as an entity in constant flux.[13]

NOTES

1. For an overview of the 1990s debate on the significance and role of the nation-state in a globalizing world, see McGrew (1998) and Berking (2006b).
2. Interestingly, the subaltern and the postcolonial studies approach did not influence the discipline of history as a whole. It has been far more important for the study of literature and cultural studies. For an overview of the latest literature on postcolonial history, see Lindner *et al.* (2011).
3. In another article, I have elaborated more profoundly on the relationship between epistemology and history writing. See Epple (2010a).
4. *Historist* is a German word that is difficult to translate into English. It designates a historian influenced by "Historism," a special attitude to history dominant in Germany and other European countries during the 19th and 20th centuries. Ranke was not a historicist in the way that Popper used the word *historicism*. See Berger (1997). Dipesh Chakrabarty, for instance, uses the term

historicism without clarifying how this differs from Popper's understanding—a source of several misunderstandings. See Chakrabarty (2000: 6–16).
5. Wolfgang Knöbl presents a concise summary of the debates between Immanuel Wallerstein and historians such as Janet L. Abu-Lughod or Andre G. Frank (Knöbl 2007: 118–28). Frank, however, despite liberating the world system from its Eurocentric bases, finally backs up Wallerstein by assuming the existence of such a world system.
6. For a good overview on this debate see Patel (2008).
7. A related concept is *histoire croisée*—a combination of the history of transfer and the history of comparisons. For further reading see Werner and Zimmermann (2002).
8. A characteristic that could also be ascribed to transnational history; see Bayly *et al.* (2006: 1451).
9. Even the terms *ethnicity* or *ethnic identity* become questionable because they rely on a fixed definition of the respective ethnicity. See Çaglar *et al.* (2006).
10. For European historiography, see also O'Dowd and Porciani (2004), Davis (1980), Melman (1993), and Epple and Schaser (2009).
11. Barkan (1994) already dealt with postcolonial theory in the 1990s. If transnational and postcolonial history have an impact on scientific concepts and on methodology—and, as I have tried to show, they do—then they should be measured by them (Siegrist 2005).
12. The history-from-below approach was developed as a result of the French *Annales* School in the 1960s. It is closely connected to E.P. Thompson's book *The Making of the English Working Class*, which first appeared in 1963.
13. Some results have already been presented or are forthcoming; see, for instance, Putnam (2006).

REFERENCES

Abu-Lughod, J.L. (1989) *Before European Hegemony: The World System A.D. 1250–1350*, Oxford: Oxford University Press.
Albrow, M. (1996) *The Global Age: State and Society beyond Modernity*, Cambridge: Polity Press.
American Historical Review (1991) "Forum", *American Historical Review*, 96: 1031–72.
——— (2009) "AHR Forum: Truth and reconciliation in history", *American Historical Review*, 114: 899–977.
Anderson, B. (1985) *Imagined Communities: Reflections on the Origin and Spread of Nationalism*, London: Verso.
Appadurai, A. (1996) *Modernity at Large: Cultural Dimensions of Globalization*, Minneapolis, London: University of Minnesota Press.
Barkan, E. (1994) "Post-anti-colonial histories: Representing the other in imperial Britain", *Journal of British Studies*, 33: 180–204.
——— (2009) "Introduction: Historians and historical reconciliation", *American Historical Review*, 114: 899–913.
Bayly, C.A., Beckert, S., Connelly, M., Hofmeyr, I., Kozol, W. and Seed, P. (2006) "AHR conversation: On transnational history", *American Historical Review*, 111: 1441–64.
Beck, U. (2000) *What Is Globalization?*, Cambridge: Blackwell Publishers.
Berger, S. (1997) *The Search for Normality: National Identity and Historical Consciousness in Germany since 1800*, Providence, RI: Berghahn.

Berking, H. (ed) (2006a) *Die Macht des Lokalen in einer Welt ohne Grenzen*, Frankfurt, New York: Campus.

—— (2006b) "Raumtheoretische Paradoxien im Globalisierungsdiskurs", in H. Berking (ed) *Die Macht des Lokalen in einer Welt ohne Grenzen*, Frankfurt, New York: Campus.

Brahm, F. (2010) *Wissenschaft und Dekolonisation: Paradigmenwechsel und institutioneller Wandel in der akademischen Beschäftigung mit Afrika in Deutschland und Frankreich 1930–1970*, Stuttgart: Franz Steiner Verlag.

Braudel, F. (1976a) *The Mediterranean and the Mediterranean World in the Age of Philip II*, 2 Vols, New York: Harper & Row.

—— (1976b) "Preface", in F. Braudel, *The Mediterranean and the Mediterranean World in the Age of Philip II*, Vol. 1, New York: Harper & Row.

—— (1985) *La Dynamique du Capitalisme*, Paris: Les Editions Arthaud.

Bungert, H. and Wendt, S. (2010) "Transnationalizing American Studies: Historians' perspectives", in B. Christ, C. Kloeckner, E. Schäfer-Wünsche and S. Butter (eds) *American Studies/Shifting Gears*, Heidelberg: Universitätsverlag Winter.

Çağlar, A., Glick-Schiller, N. and Guldbransen, T.C. (2006) "Jenseits der 'ethnischen Gruppe' als Objekt des Wissens: Lokalität, Globalität und Inkorporationsmuster von Migranten", in H. Berking (ed) *Die Macht des Lokalen in einer Welt ohne Grenzen*, Frankfurt, New York: Campus.

Chakrabarty, D. (1992) "Provincializing Europe: Postcoloniality and the critique of history", *Cultural Studies*, 6: 337–57.

—— (2000) *Provincializing Europe: Postcolonial Thought and Historical Difference*, Princeton, NJ: Princeton University Press.

—— (2006) "A global and multicultural 'discipline' of history?", *History and Theory*, 45: 101–9.

—— (2007) "History and the politics of recognition", in K. Jenkins, S. Morgan and A. Munslow (eds) *Manifestos for History*, Abingdon: Routledge.

Chatterjee, P. (2006) "A brief history of Subaltern Studies", in G. Budde, S. Conrad and O. Janz (eds) *Transnationale Geschichte: Themen, Tendenzen und Theorien*, Göttingen: Vandenhoeck & Ruprecht.

Conrad, S. (2009) "Double marginalization: A plea for a transnational perspective on German history", in H.G. Haupt and J. Kocka (eds) *Comparative and Transnational History: Central European Approaches and New Perspectives*, New York: Berghahn Books.

—— and Randeria, S. (2002) "Einleitung: Geteilte Geschichten—Europa in einer postkolonialen Welt", in S. Randeria and S. Conrad (eds) *Jenseits des Eurozentrismus: Postkoloniale Perspektiven in den Geschichts- und Kulturwissenschaften*, Frankfurt: Campus.

Cooper, F. (2007) "Was nützt der Begriff der Globalisierung? Aus der Perspektive eines Afrika-Historikers", in S. Conrad, A. Eckert and U. Freitag (eds) *Globalgeschichte: Theorien, Ansätze, Themen*, Frankfurt, New York: Campus.

Davis, N.Z. (1980) "Gender and genre: Women as historical writers 1400–1820", in P.H. Labalme (ed) *Beyond Their Sex: Learned Women of the European Past*, New York: New York University Press.

Dreyfus, H.L. and Rabinow, P. (eds) (1983) *Michel Foucault: Beyond Structuralism and Hermeneutics*, Chicago: University of Chicago Press.

Eckert, A. (2003) "Fitting Africa into world history: A historiographical exploration", in E. Fuchs and B. Stuchtey (eds) *Writing World History 1800–2000*, Oxford: Oxford University Press.

—— (2009) "Germany and Africa in the late nineteenth and twentieth centuries: An entangled history?", in H.G. Haupt and J. Kocka (eds) *Comparative and Transnational History. Central European Approaches and New Perspectives*, New York: Berghahn Books.

Epple, A. (2010a) "A strained relationship: Epistemology and historiography in 18th and 19th century Germany and Britain", in S. Berger and C. Lorenz (eds) *Writing National Historiographies*, Basingstoke: Palgrave Macmillan.
—— (2010b) "Questioning the canon: Popular historiography by women in Britain and Germany (1750–1850)", in S. Paletschek (ed) *Popular Historiographies in the 19th and 20th Century*, Oxford: Berghahn.
—— and Schaser, A. (eds) (2009) *Gendering Historiography: Beyond National Canons*, Frankfurt, New York: Campus.
Fernandez-Armesto, F. (2002) "The Indian Ocean in world history", in A. Disney and E. Booth (eds) *Vasco da Gama and the Linking of Europe and Asia*, Oxford: Oxford University Press.
Freitag, U. and von Oppen, A. (2010) "Introduction. 'Translocality': An approach to connection and transfer in regional studies", in U. Freitag and A. von Oppen (eds) *Translocality: The Study of Globalising Processes from a Southern Perspective*, Leiden, Boston: Brill.
Gassert, P. (February 16, 2010) "Transnationale Geschichte, Version: 1.0", *Docupedia-Zeitgeschichte*. Online: http://docupedia.de/zg/Transnationale_Geschichte?oldid=75537 (accessed May 11, 2011).
Gilroy, P. (1993) *The Black Atlantic: Modernity and Double Consciousness*, Cambridge, MA: Harvard University Press.
Ginzburg, C. (1992) *The Cheese and the Worms. The Cosmos of a Sixteenth-Century Miller*, Baltimore: Johns Hopkins University Press.
—— (1993) "Microhistory: Two or three things that I know about it", *Critical Inquiry*, 20: 10–35.
—— and Poni, C. (1985) "Was ist Mikrogeschichte?", *Geschichtswerkstatt*, 6: 48–52.
Grant, K., Levine, P. and Trentmann, F. (eds) (2007) *Beyond Sovereignty. Britain, Empire and Transnationalism c. 1880–1950*, Basingstoke: Palgrave.
Guha, R. (1983) *Elementary Aspects of Peasant Insurgency in Colonial India*, Delhi: Oxford University Press.
—— (2002) *History at the Limit of World-History*, New York: Columbia University Press.
Herbert, U. (2010) "Vorwort", in F.-J. Brüggemeier *Geschichte Großbritanniens im 20. Jahrhundert*, Munich: C.H. Beck.
Herodotus (1972) *The Histories*, ed. A.R. Burn, London: Penguin Classics.
Hopkins, A.G. (2006) "Introduction: Interactions between the universal and the local", in A.G. Hopkins (ed) *Global History: Interactions Between the Universal and the Local*, New York: Palgrave Macmillan.
Hume, D. (1826) "An enquiry concerning human understanding", in D. Hume (ed) *The Philosophical Works of David Hume*, Vol. IV, Edinburgh: Black and Tait.
Jarausch, K.H. (January 20, 2006) "Reflections on transnational history", *Humanities and Social Sciences—H Net Online*. Online: http://h-net.msu.edu/cgi-bin/logbrowse.pl?trx=vx&list=h-german&month=0601&week=c&msg=LPkNHirCm1xgSZQKHOGRXQ&user=&pw= (accessed May 11, 2011).
Kaltmeier, O., Lindner, U. and Mailaparambil, B.J. (2011) "Reflecting on concepts of coloniality/postcoloniality in Latin American, South Asian and African historiography", *Comparativ. Zeitschrift für Globalgeschichte und vergleichende Gesellschaftsforschung*, 21: 14–31.
Kittsteiner, H.D. (2010) "Hegels Eurozentrismus in globaler Perspektive", in W. Hardtwig and P. Müller (eds) *Die Vergangenheit der Weltgeschichte: Universalhistorisches Denken in Berlin 1800–1933*, Göttingen: Vandenhoeck & Ruprecht.
Knöbl, W. (2007) *Die Kontingenz der Moderne: Wege in Europa, Asien und Amerika*, Frankfurt: Campus.

Lindner, U., Möhring, M., Stein, M. and Stroh, S. (eds) (2011) *Hybrid Cultures—Nervous States: Britain and Germany in a (Post)Colonial World*, Amsterdam: Rodopi.
Löw, M. (2001) *Raumsoziologie*, Frankfurt: Campus.
McGrew, A.G. (1998) "The globalization debate: Putting the advanced capitalist state in its place", *Global Society*, 12: 299–321.
Manning, P. (2003) *Navigating World History. Historians Create a Global Past*, New York: Palgrave Macmillan.
—— (2007) "Nordamerikanische Ansätze zur Globalgeschichte", in B. Schäbler (ed) *Area Studies und die Welt: Weltregionen und neue Globalgeschichte*, Wien: Mandelbaum Verlag.
Massey, D. (2006) "Keine Entlastung für das Lokale", in H. Berking (ed) *Die Macht des Lokalen in einer Welt ohne Grenzen*, Frankfurt, New York: Campus.
Mazlish, B. (2006) *The New Global History*, New York: Routledge.
Melman, B. (1993) "Gender, history and memory: The invention of women's past in the nineteenth and early twentieth centuries", *History and Memory*, 5: 5–41.
Middell, M. (2005) *Weltgeschichtsschreibung im Zeitalter der Verfachlichung und Professionalisierung. Das Leipziger Institut für Kultur- und Universalgeschichte 1890–1990*, 3 Vols, Leipzig: Akademische Verlagsanstalt.
Núñez, X.-M. (2010) "Nations and territorial identities in Europe: Transnational reflections", *European History Quarterly*, 40: 669–84.
O'Brien, P.K. (2006) "Historiographical traditions and modern imperatives for the restoration of global history", *Journal of Global History*, 1: 3–39.
O'Dowd, M. and Porciani, I. (eds) (2004) *History Women* (special issue of *Storia della Storiografia*, 46), Milano: Jaca Book.
Osterhammel, J. (1998) *Die Entzauberung Asiens: Europa und die asiatischen Reiche im 18. Jahrhundert*, Munich: C.H. Beck.
—— (2010) *Die Verwandlung der Welt. Eine Geschichte des 19. Jahrhunderts*, Munich: C.H. Beck.
Otto of Freising (1912) "Chronica sive Historia de duabus civitatibus", in A. Hofmeister (ed) *Monumenta Germaniae Historica. Scriptores rerum Germanicarum in usum scholarum separatim editi 45*, Hannover: Hahn.
Patel, K.K. (February 2, 2005) "Transnationale Geschichte—ein neues Paradigma?", *H-Soz-u-Kult*. Online: http://hsozkult.geschichte.hu-berlin.de/forum/id=573&type=diskussionen (accessed June 27, 2011).
—— (2008) "Überlegungen zu einer transnationalen Geschichte", in J. Osterhammel (ed) *Weltgeschichte: Basistexte*, Stuttgart: Franz Steiner Verlag.
Putnam, L. (2006) "To study the fragments/whole: Microhistory and the Atlantic world", *Journal of Social History*, 39: 615–30.
Randeria, S. (2000) "Geteilte Geschichte und verwobene Moderne", in J. Rüsen, H. Leitgeb and N. Jegelka (eds) *Zukunftsentwürfe: Ideen für eine Kultur der Veränderung*, Frankfurt, New York: Campus.
—— (2002) "Entangled histories of uneven modernities: Civil society, caste solidarities and the post-colonial state in India", in Y. Elkana, I. Krastev, E. Macamo and S. Randeria (eds) *Unraveling Ties: From Social Cohesion to New Practices of Connectedness*, Frankfurt, New York: Campus.
—— and Conrad, S. (eds) (2002) *Jenseits des Eurozentrismus: Postkoloniale Perspektiven in den Geschichts- und Kulturwissenschaften*, Frankfurt: Campus.
Rüger, J. (2010) "OXO or: The challenges of transnational history", *European History Quarterly*, 40: 656–68.
Sachsenmaier, D. (February 11, 2010) "Global History, Version: 1.0", *Docupedia-Zeitgeschichte*. Online: http://docupedia.de/zg/Global_History?oldid=75519 (accessed May 11, 2011).

Schiel, J. (2009) "Crossing paths between East and West: The use of counterfactual thinking for the concept of 'Entangled Histories'", *Historical Social Research*, 34: 161–83.
Schlözer, A.L. (1806) *Vorbereitung zur Weltgeschichte für Kinder*, Erster Theil, 6th ed., Göttingen: Vandenhoeck & Ruprecht.
Shils, E. and Robert, J. (2004) "The diffusion of European models outside Europe", in W. Ruegg (ed) *Geschichte der Universität in Europa*, Vol. III, Munich: C.H. Beck.
Siegrist, H. (February 16, 2005) "Transnationale Geschichte als Herausforderung der wissenschaftlichen Historiografie", *Geschichte.Transnational*. Online: http://geschichte-transnational.clio-online.net/forum/id=575&type=diskussionen (accessed December 9, 2010).
Smith, B.G. (1995) "Gender and the practices of scientific history: The seminar and archival research in the nineteenth century", *American Historical Review*, 100: 1150–76.
—— (1998) *The Gender of History: Men, Women, and Historical Practice*, Cambridge, MA: Harvard University Press.
—— (2009) "Gendering historiography in the global age: A U.S. perspective", in A. Epple and A. Schaser (eds) *Gendering Historiography: Beyond National Canons*, Frankfurt: Campus.
Spivak, G.C. (1988) "Can the subaltern speak?", in C. Nelson and L. Grossberg (eds) *Marxism and the Interpretation of Culture*, Urbana: University of Illinois Press.
Thelen, D. (1999) "The nation and beyond: Transnational perspectives on United States history", *Journal of American History*, 86: 965–75.
Therborn, G. (2000) "Globalizations: Dimensions, historical waves, regional effects, normative governances", *International Sociology*, 15: 151–79.
Thompson, E.P. (1963) *The Making of the English Working Class*, New York: Pantheon Books.
Trentmann, F. (2008) *Free Trade Nation. Commerce, Consumption, and Civil Society in Modern Britain*, Oxford, New York: Oxford University Press.
Tyrell, I. (2007a) *Transnational Nation: United States History in Global Perspective since 1789*, Basingstoke: Palgrave Macmillan.
—— (2007b) "What is transnational history?", excerpt from a paper presented at Ecole des Hautes Etudes en Sciences Sociales, Paris. Online: http://iantyrrell.wordpress.com/what-is-transnational-history (accessed May 12, 2011).
Wallerstein, I. (1974–89) *The Modern World System*, 3 Vols, New York: Academic Press.
Werner, M. and Zimmermann, B. (2002) "Vergleich, Transfer, Verflechtung: Der Ansatz der histoire croisée und die Herausforderung des Transnationalen", *Geschichte und Gesellschaft*, 28: 607–36.
—— (2006) "Beyond comparison: 'Histoire Croisée' and the challenge of reflexivity", *History & Theory*, 45: 30–50.
Wickramasinghe, N. (2011) "Colonial governmentality: Critical notes", *Comparativ. Zeitschrift für Globalgeschichte und vergleichende Gesellschaftsforschung*, 21: 32–40.
Wieviorka, M. (2005) "From Marx and Braudel to Wallerstein", *Contemporary Sociology*, 34: 1–7.
Wolf, E.R. (1982) *Europe and the People without History*, Berkeley: University of California Press.

9 Incorporating Comparisons in the Rift
Making Use of Cross-Place Events and Histories in Moments of World Historical Change

Sandra Curtis Comstock

This chapter discusses the four comparative strategies historical sociologists use to explain social variation and changing geopolitical arrangements across time and space. It describes the strengths and limitations of three conventional methods of comparison, namely, the hermeneutic, experimental and encompassing approaches.[1] It then lays out an alternative, incorporating comparative approach. Incorporating comparison recognizes that general world contradictions and particular inter-local dynamics both play pivotal roles in reconfiguring the world's geopolitical landscapes. It helps uncover the significance of geo-cultural and geo-political differences as key elements making strong innovations in everyday practices and institutions possible. It is often when people begin to combine dissimilar tactics or misapply solutions from one context to a new and distinctive one that they unintentionally disrupt long-standing patterns and open space for radically new actions and thinking to take hold. Joining and reorganizing the reach and application of practices across disparate places and groups is one of the principal ways that widespread, unprecedented changes happen. One of the most compelling aspects of incorporating comparison is that it does not treat places, nations, nation-states or nation-state systems as fixed, self-perpetuating entities, but rather as dynamic, historically changing and mutually constituting configurations.[2]

The first sections of the chapter present a critical examination of how hermeneutic, experimental and encompassing approaches compare in terms of their goals and ways of using comparison to evaluate the significance of different causes of social change and variation over time and space. It shows how hermeneutic comparisons highlight the causal primacy of local historical particulars, whereas experimental and encompassing comparisons emphasize the causal primacy of repeating patterns found in multiple places and times. This particularizing/generalizing divide limits our ability to understand how new connections and interactions between heterogeneous places can reciprocally alter local practices and serve as catalysts that initiate broader changes in cross-place boundaries, relations and patterns. As the following section explains, this tendency to prioritize either the particular or general also contributes to different forms of methodological nationalism or stateism in which nations, nation-states, colonial states or wider nation-state systems are treated as fixed and constant units of analysis and generators of change over time (McMichael 1990: 385). The next section shows how the incorporating comparative method overcomes these limitations by historicizing the shifting connections, meanings and overlaps among polities and groups over time (McMichael 1990). The incorporating approach accomplishes this by integrating historical knowledge of changes in one set of places into the analysis of changes in other places.[3] It historicizes cross-cultural and spatial relations by integrating the histories of key places. In this way it illuminates how interplay among different histories contributes to new local understandings, distinctions and practices, often with global implications.

The goal of incorporating comparisons is to identify the changing conduits of influence linking groups and localities to one another. Entertaining the notion of changing sources of cross-place influence lends incorporating comparisons special insight into how major geopolitical reconfigurations are initiated and cemented. I conclude the chapter by offering some suggestions regarding how the incorporating method can be strengthened by adopting greater hermeneutic attention to the meanings social actors assign to events and how such meanings influence actions in the context of broad disruptions to business as usual.

HERMENEUTIC COMPARISONS: DISTINCTIVE LOCAL HISTORIES, PARTICULAR CAUSAL RELATIONS

Hermeneutic methods of comparison juxtapose the histories of different places to highlight how groups deploy shared historical concepts or strategies to uniquely interpret, act on and order local events and practices. The goal of comparison is to refine theoretical concepts that help us understand how cultures uniquely make meaning, develop paradigms of action and order social relations in different places. Hermeneutic comparisons judge a causal explanation or theoretical concept as adequate when it is capable of giving an in-depth account of the unique historical twists and turns occurring in each individual case. An explanation is also adequate when it respects local ways of interpreting and acting in the world (McLemore 1984; Steinmetz 2004; Somers 1996).

This way of judging the adequacy of causal claims is at the heart of the methodological reason that hermeneutically oriented comparisons treat societies compared as discrete entities. Hermeneutic approaches evaluate the adequacy of particular causal explanations by exploring the relationship between typical discourses, conditions and patterns of action in a defined cultural context and actors' uses of them in interpreting and acting on events under specific historical circumstances. To be significant, hermeneutic analyses must show how actors combine generalities and specifics to navigate an historical situation. Hermeneutic approaches require evidence of how groups define their options and rally others to pursue new paths and projects (McLemore 1984; Griffin 1993). Because hermeneutically inclined scholars are overwhelmingly interested in adequately explaining the particularities of each society's historical twists and turns, they tend to treat broader world cultural contexts as just that: an environment that shapes and impinges on the local, but which need not be historically accounted for in terms of how local histories themselves transform the broader world context (Giddens 1973: 265). As a result hermeneutic comparisons consist of contrastive stories in which local histories do not appear to substantially interfere with or directly influence one another or the encompassing context in which they are embedded. The hermeneutic method uses comparison to determine what is generally true about a common historical practice or epoch and how local particulars shape the way practices uniquely work and combine on the ground (Green 1994: 5).

A case illustrating the virtues and drawbacks of the hermeneutic approach is George Steinmetz's comparison of German colonial Samoa, Qingdao and South Western Africa in his book *The Devil's Handwriting* (2007). Steinmetz provides a compelling account of how colonial elites' differing uses of ethnographic representations, class competition and ways of identifying with their respective colonized subjects uniquely combined to shape each case. He shows how each combination distinctly influenced how bureaucrats formulated the question of how to treat different "native populations." To do so, Steinmetz first establishes how in the general historical moment of European colonization, typical European discourses on non-European people of the period and the state of class competition in Germany provided a common backdrop that colonial officials drew on as they pursued their state-making projects. Yet he also shows how elites were informed and constrained differently by these general conditions, depending on particular local events and circumstances faced on the ground.

The advantages of focusing on colonial leaders' distinctive uses of ethnographic representations, problems of late colonization, and class competition in constructing their colonial states is clearest in Steinmetz's historically flexible analysis of what made Southwest Africa distinct from Samoa and Qingdao. Specifically, in the Samoa and Qingdao contexts Steinmetz argues that colonial elite competition revolved around which political policies to pursue with native populations. In contrast, Steinmetz argues that negative ethnographic representations of the West African Herero and sharp inter-elite class competition encouraged colonial leaders to frame state projects around a different question: the question of whether they should treat the Herero as a political or a military problem (Steinmetz 2003: 85).

This fidelity to empirical circumstances and context-sensitive interpretation is one of the great advantages of the hermeneutic approach. Prioritization of historical nuance and accuracy over causal regularities and generalizations allows Steinmetz the flexibility to argue that the array of options bounded by his initial concept of political "native policies" did not adequately capture why and how the colonial massacre of the Herero took place. It also facilitates an appreciation of how a prevailingly negative ethnographic assessment of the Herero, and the Herero's own decision to stringently resist colonials, generated an alternative frame for colonial action that tragically involved the Herero's annihilation. As a result, Steinmetz's theoretical categories still hold and are in fact strengthened by their finesse in explaining fundamental categorical differences among the cases.

However, this individuation of the historical analysis within the Samoan, Qingdao and West African contexts also has a significant cost. Namely, Steinmetz does not entertain with the same degree of flexible finesse the question of the extent to which experiences with native policy in one colony or region informed those of other colonies. The explanatory power of Steinmetz's argument would be enriched with explicit discussion of the influence between colonies and whether the timing or movement of people and tactics between places shifted broader German colonial discourses or actions. It seems especially legitimate to consider these influences given the intriguing connections Steinmetz mentions between figures like Solf in Samoa and Heyking and Franke in China, as well as those between Chinese laborers, colonial officials and Samoans in the Samoan context (Steinmetz 2003: 45).

For instance, in the case of Samoa, it would be fruitful to understand how shifting discourses about Samoans and Chinese laborers developed in Samoa and Chinese subjects in China combined to influence the twists and turns of Samoan representations and imperial policies. To what degree did native policies in Samoa and Samoans' roles in interpreting and maneuvering within these policies influence how Germans contrasted Samoans with the Chinese or Melanesian laborers they brought to work in Samoa (Steinmetz 2007: 328–9, 338; Moses 1973; Firth 1977)? How did knowledge of German colonial experiences with Chinese subjects in China influence German colonial thinking in Samoa? Chinese laborers, the particular ethnic discourses ascribed to them and their lower status *vis-à-vis* Samoans clearly facilitated the political and material viability of treating the Samoans otherwise. Yet we have little sense of the comparative and material politics of these contrastive uses of ethnicity in fashioning state policies toward Samoan and Chinese subjects.

In the case of West Africa, it seems logical that overall German imperial ethnic discourses and the horizon of colonial possibilities would likely have been altered by experiences with the Herero. What happened to imperial comparative ethnographic discourses as colonists situated elsewhere made sense of the news of the Herero massacre? To what extent did news of the Herero massacre and discussions of its meaning alter imperial projects? Steinmetz's account does not unravel these important aspects of German empire building and ethnographic discourse. Perhaps the reason such connections are not more deeply explored has to do with macro-historical comparison's tendency to assume that cross-place circulation of ideas, people and historical experiences ought to produce synthesis and continuity, rather than novel forms of difference and distinction (Sahlins 1985; Mongia 2007).

In sum, hermeneutic comparisons use the history of places with common historical experiences or roots (often a national- or state-based one) to bring into relief the differences and textures of historical processes in other places. This ingeniously highlights the unique internal dynamics shaping local processes of ongoing differentiation. It also helps us understand how shared historical elements exercise a common influence on social change. This works well in moments of relative world historical stability in which the boundaries between locales and practices within them are regularly reproduced. However, the predisposition to limit analysis to general "global" processes and particular "local" ones can make hermeneutic strategies of comparison inadequate to the task of detecting when, how and why specific local histories begin to intersect and intimately influence one another in dramatically new ways (Fabian 2002: 38–51).

EXPERIMENTAL COMPARISONS: SEPARATE HISTORIES, REPLICABLE CAUSAL RELATIONS

In contrast to hermeneutic comparisons, the goal of path-dependent experimental comparisons is to construct general explanations identifying the common conditions and events responsible for change in place after place compared. One advantage of general explanations is that they help identify analogous patterns of change among places. Another advantage is in the ways they attend closely to how deviations in the timing and sequence of changes within local histories can influence outcomes.

Experimental historical comparisons weigh the significance and validity of different causes of change by measuring the extent to which they consistently combine to produce similar historical changes in all places considered. This helps the investigator narrow the number and kinds of events, actions and conditions entertained as plausibly significant in driving the historical trajectory that follows. However, because the frequency with which events occur uniformly in place after place is the measure of causal importance, some of the most obvious reasons for historical turning points and unprecedented path-changing shifts may be left out.[4] Specifically, it is often novel interactions between unique historical particulars (unfolding in separate or overlapping territorial or cultural scopes) that most often radically reorganize world spanning relations and practices (Sahlins 1981; Friedmann 2006).

A study illustrating the strengths and drawbacks of the experimental approach, James Mahoney's *Legacies of Liberalism* (Mahoney 2001), argues that the character of 19th century liberal reforms carried out in Guatemala, El Salvador, Costa Rica, Nicaragua and Honduras established institutions and patterns of societal conflict that would determine each country's political fate far into the next century. Prioritizing regularities in the natural experiment mode helps Mahoney identify how dictators' initial strategies of pursuing liberal reform in the 19th century contributed to patterned bouts of state–society tension and struggle across the 20th century. Moreover, for the period leading up to each state's turn toward liberal reform, Mahoney uses the concept of reactive regionally derived sequences of change to move away from the experimental dictate that states be treated as equivalent isolates (Mahoney 2000: 509). This allows him to appreciate how liberal reform choices were shaped by intersecting, cross-border histories involving interstate military forays and bouts of borrowing military and political tactics among Central American dictators and elites.

To give an example, Mahoney's analysis of the periods leading up to liberal reforms in Central America suggests that Guatemalan ambitions and proximity to El Salvador encouraged tense cross-border elite rivalries that encouraged both Salvadoran and Guatemalan leaders to develop militarized states backing radical liberal reform projects (Mahoney 2001: 85–6). Likewise, Mahoney argues that Honduras' experiences of constant interference from Guatemala and El Salvador kept Honduran elites from stabilizing national power. This, he argues, weakened support for liberalization and delayed Honduran elites' reform efforts. Meanwhile Costa Rican leaders' relative lack of interaction with Guatemala and El Salvador allowed them to pursue liberal reforms earlier and with a land-holding population supportive of reformist liberalization (Mahoney 2001: 99). Moreover, Mahoney notes that the later timing of Honduran reforms presented Honduran leaders with a level of interference from US capitalists and marines that did not exist in the region in the moment when Costa Ricans were pursuing their reforms (Mahoney 2001: 172). Thus, Mahoney's initial account suggests how cross-regional events and interactions and shifts in more general world-historical environment shaped reform efforts.

Unfortunately, this reactive cross-place analysis is restricted to the abnormal "break period" inaugurated by independence and ceases with each state's earliest turn toward liberal reform. Thereafter, analysis takes a classic experimental tack toward analyzing each state's historical trajectory as if it had no influence on those of its counterparts. Overemphasis on the general in constructing a simplified model of how liberal reforms take place and their consequences leads Mahoney to minimize the compelling causal importance of the unique, nonequivalent cross-border interactions covered in his earlier nuanced discussion of regional differences in the timing of the liberal turn. In his pared-down model, he selects as causally significant only conditions and actions construed as unfolding in equivalent fashion in nation after nation. *Modeling* the move of each dictator to liberalism, Mahoney presents each leader's initial choices as if each faced a relatively open field of parallel, non-mutually-interfering choices, constrained early on only by internal elite cleavages, general levels of economic modernization, and general world historical conditions. Moreover, from the moment in which each dictator initiates reforms, or US intervention decisively aborts a state's course, Mahoney presents each nation's path as internally driven by individualized state–society interactions strongly shaped by founding dictators' reform choices or failures (Williams 1994).[5]

This pattern of cordoning off break points is typical in experimental path-dependent analysis. Strong breaks between past practices and ways of organizing social life and new ones confound explanations of change that rely on old divisions, interests and alliances to explain change. They equally confound explanations that begin from the vantage point of the polities and practices that emerged after the change in question (Mahoney 2000: 511, 515–26). The usual solution is to treat abrupt changes as the result of an abstracted exogenous shock. This allows experimentally inclined investigations to begin formal comparisons after the break period such that the histories and places compared less inconveniently overlap or idiosyncratically influence one another. But this approach shies away from explaining the precise historical processes and contingencies by which spatial and cultural terrains were reconfigured from time A to time B.

In sum, comparing the histories of Central American countries to pinpoint and "test" how frequently equivalent combinations of conditions and events produce comparable effects in different places identifies common themes and broad historical turns in time and space. Unfortunately, it discourages identification of the crucial empirical historical events linking place histories and choices to one another and connecting one epoch to the next. Seeking out general parallels within cases elides how places with linked problems and histories can predispose some groups to creatively compare and innovate *across borders* and in response to one another. Instead, in the experimental mode continuities between cases appear as if they were produced primarily as a result of internal "national" experiences or externally derived shocks and infringements on the local.

The problem with dividing up countries' experiences in this way in Mahoney's case is that the borders between Central American countries have historically been vastly more porous than the experimental comparative method can acknowledge. Looking for common patterns occurring within each national context obscures how groups and leaders belonging to one state frequently learned from, influenced or constrained the options others might devise. Interstate go-betweens traveling or referring to extra-national problems and solutions are often pivotal in defining the character and direction of big cross-place changes. It is their penchant for continually drawing analogies between foreign experiences and their own primary context that produces novelty. In such instances, the timing and sequence of changes in one place are often derived from the changing perceptions and analogies go-betweens devise as they apply, jerry-rig and misapply other people's solutions to their own local problems (Fabian 2002; Sahlins 1981).

The experimental approach's limitations underscore the need to develop better methods for identifying and evaluating the causal role played by unique cross-place events and actions in which knowledge of events and strategies elsewhere inform local decisions and options. Only through such a method will we begin to theorize how, when and why certain cross-place interactions gain the power to provoke people in different localities to "combine and redefine [their practices and understandings] in ways that form something new and unpredictable" (O'Hearn 2001: 3). The biggest disadvantage of fixating on place against place regularities is that pivotal events and turning points are relegated to the realm of mysterious exogenous shocks and viewed as incapable of being explained "on the basis of prior historical conditions" (Mahoney 2000: 508). In fact, pivotal events and turning points can be explained historically. They can be explained in terms of how people in times of crisis become interested in others' historical experiences and problems and generate new solutions through this reflexive use of the foreign.[6] Moreover, the shifts in perspectives and strategies produced through cross-place comparisons are also strongly shaped by asymmetric relations of power and uneven interactions between localities.[7] Preoccupied with repeating place-contained causes, experimental comparisons have no conceptual apparatus to account for such dynamics.

ENCOMPASSING COMPARISONS—A COMMON OVERARCHING HISTORY, SIMILAR CAUSAL RELATIONS

In contrast to experimental and hermeneutic comparisons, the encompassing comparisons approach often seeks out and compares nonequivalent, asymmetric localities. Nonequivalent local histories are selected on the basis of their distinctive relation to an encompassing world process (McMichael 1990: 391; Hopkins 1978; Tilly 1984: 61, 125; Wallerstein 1979: 6). The goal of such comparison is to discern which connections to an encompassing world process best explain the differences and continuities in the historical trajectories of different places (Tilly 1984: 123).

The hypothesis that differentiated local histories are all shaped by a common external historical process justifies encompassing comparisons' search for regular correlations between changes in a world historical process and mirrored patterns of change in local histories (Tilly 2005: 226). Like their experimental cousins, encompassing comparisons prioritize abstracted generalizations over the discovery of unique historical particulars.[8] For encompassing comparisons, causes worthy of the name are those regular features, events, actions or processes that produce predictable outcomes. The idiosyncratic events and interpretations valued by the hermeneutic approach are of lesser interest. The problem with this definition is that it complicates explaining how and why social dynamics dramatically change from one epoch to the next, as well as what exactly causes such change. Without a way of identifying pivotal particularities that explain historical reversals of fortune we veer toward teleological explanation.[9] Where we neglect pinpointing the intricacies of how new practices are generated and selected, the practices chosen often appear predetermined, inevitable and less contingent than they really are.

The strengths and drawbacks of this approach are evidenced in Charles Tilly's *Coercion, Capital, and European States* (1990) in which he seeks to explain early variation and the ultimate convergence of European state forms across time and space. Tilly's focus on regularities in cross-place processes helpfully identifies the moment in which distinct but interdependent war-making, coercion-intensive states and capital-intensive cities begin to unevenly appear in different parts of Europe at the end of AD 900. Having identified this variegated pattern, Tilly turns toward discerning how two general motivations drove the pattern's emergence and shifts:

1) Militaristic elites' interest in expanding their capacities to coercively dominate surrounding territories.
2) Capitalist elites' interest in increasing cross-local exchange, accumulation and exploitation.

The exercise of identifying enduring logics of action and their propensity to generate repeating event sequences allows Tilly to discover and substantiate his claim that, when faced with resistance from cities, militaristic elites initially cobbled together a third, "national" state form that was at once extremely coercive and capital intensive. It also helps him to discern how repeating processes of war, conquest and competitive emulation led to the diffusion of the territorial national state form across Europe. As Michael Mann notes, ideal typical similarities in the histories of European national states and their historical relations go a long way in explaining the rise and diffusion of the territorial European state through the 1700s (Mann 1990: 1260–1).

However, the search for enduring regularities between the periods before and after the waning years of the 18th century becomes much less effective precisely because it elides how quite new kinds of cross-continental fiscal crises, social movements and mass mobilizing industrial warfare generated distinctive problems, demands and points of leverage with which state makers had to contend (Mann 1990: 1261; 1993: 224–52). As the work of Giovanni Arrighi, Beverly Silver and Eric Slater suggests, connecting the histories of two such distinctive periods requires moderating the search for regularities. It requires an effort to identify the unique problems people confronted as contradictions in inter-state forms of competition threatened their continued reproduction (Arrighi 1994; Silver and Slater 1999). It also requires attention to the novelty of the solutions devised and to how such situations aided in moving existing states out of entrenched stalemates and into dramatically new arrangements. It further involves explaining how the unprecedented cross-class, mass mobilizing nation-state was incrementally invented and amended piecemeal as actors of the time compared, applied and revised elements and strategies across contexts and crises.

For example, the incorporating analysis of Silver and Slater suggests that these unprecedented institutional solutions were arrived at through contingent cross-place events made possible by the mounting fiscal crises of the late 1700s:

> A commercial depression combined with financial speculation (across much of the world) led to growing social polarization and a withering of middle-class support for the political status quo. With the breakdown of intra-elite unity and the alienation of the 'middle classes,' the space was opened for revolts from below by the excluded and exploited. (Silver and Slater 1999: 160)

Silver and Slater explain how this type of polarization fomented an elite–middle class American Revolution. They note how government fiscal crises in the US and France and world market speculation fomented related forms of elite and popular discontent in both places. However, Silver and Slater also note how fateful *differences* between the anti-colonial opportunities in America and the fiscal constraints, grain shortages and peasant revolts erupting in France produced distinctive social uprisings. They argue that the earlier example and consequences of the American Revolution combined with the specifics of the French crisis to produce a far more radical popular revolution in France. These events injected new ideas of cross-class belonging onto the world stage. Additionally, Silver and Slater show how the French Revolution set off a chain of back and forth events between France and Haiti that led to an even more radical slave-based Haitian Revolution. The example of Haiti threatened US elites to such an extent that Americans began to move to politically enfranchise plebian whites in unprecedented ways in the hope of avoiding a repeat of the Haitian Revolution on US soil (Silver and Slater 1999: 159–72; Clavin 2010).

From these unique cross-place events and the specifics of revolution in America, France and Haiti radically new state practices, strategies, functions, and meanings were invented. These transformed the manner in which history around the world unfolded. True, it was the general momentum and practices of war-making and commerce that generated the new fragilities and interests that made these revolutions possible and helped ignite them. But each revolutionary episode and set of interactions between one revolution and those that followed introduced vital and unprecedented tactics, dynamics and logics of action that transformed how state stewarded war-making and commerce worked. By emphasizing the regularly occurring interactions that encouraged the emergence and replications of the nation-state from 990 to 1990, Tilly's approach obscures how both the substance and the form of nation-states incrementally changed across the raucous age of financial crises and social revolution. Moreover, as the substance and form of the nation-state metamorphosed through the advent of the Haitian Revolution, so did other "third world" groups' reasons and motivations for aspiring to nation-statehood.

In sum, the encompassing concept of the force of collective cross-place dynamics takes us beyond hermeneutic and experimental approaches. It helps us account for how distinct places take connected but asymmetric paths across a given historical epoch. However, the prioritization of regularly repeating patterns of interaction in assessing and discerning the causes of world historical change becomes an obstacle in moments of dramatic world reconfiguration. Like locality-oriented experimental comparisons, the encompassing approach's focus on regular patterns offers little leverage for explaining how one set of regular patterns in one epoch is specifically related to a different set of arrangements in the next (Haydu 1998: 350–51). Identifying previous or subsequent regularities from one era to the next does not in itself help us to adequately explain such change. It does not aid investigators in identifying and explaining the unique interactions that jostle local histories out of one set of practices into new ones (Sewell 2005: 262–70).

COMPARISON AND METHODOLOGICAL NATIONALISM: A CRITIQUE OF CONVENTIONAL APPROACHES TO ACCOUNTING FOR DRAMATIC HISTORICAL CHANGE

As we have seen, conventional hermeneutic, experimental and encompassing comparisons analyze moments of historical reconfiguration in different localities alongside one another with different purposes in mind. Hermeneutic comparisons juxtapose different instances of local change with the prime goal of illuminating and explaining the historical particulars of each locality's transformation. Hermeneutic comparisons aim to distinguish local causes of change from the general causes deriving from the historical events or conditions that places may share (Green 1994: 5). Experimental comparisons analyze social change in different places with the goal of pinpointing the common social mechanisms responsible for what investigators presume are roughly equivalent transformations simply taking place in different times or places (Sewell 2005: 95). Encompassing approaches juxtapose changes occurring between dissimilar localities occupying different places in a world hierarchy. Their aim is to discover the overarching world-level mechanisms or dynamics producing nonequivalent but related shifts over time (Tilly 1984: 125).

Implicit in these methods' goals and criteria for analyzing social variation across space and time are assumptions about the scale and scope at which potentially historically significant facts should be sought out and accounted for. Earlier analysis noted that experimental and encompassing strategies share similar criteria for assessing the relative importance of particular events or causes of social variation. However, as I will show in the following section, when we consider assumptions about the scale and scope of causes, it is hermeneutic and experimental approaches that resemble one another most; they both emphasize locally occurring actions and events as the key causes of social variation across place. In contrast, encompassing approaches emphasize collectively derived, world-scale causes of variation. Yet, these differences are mostly a question of degree of focus on unique or shared aspects of change and local versus global sources of transformation. What they all share is a similar tendency to rather rigidly interpret causes as one of two types: either locally/individually originated or world-collectively generated. In interpreting causes in this dualistic way they all assume a certain consistency in the scopes and scales of activity through which change occurs—at least for the period they choose to investigate. Thus, while hermeneutic and experimental approaches emphasize the local and encompassing approaches emphasize the global all methods of comparison (by juxtaposing statically conceived units of analysis) presume an unwarranted constancy in local–global scopes, divisions and relations.

Thus, we find that both the hermeneutic and the experimental approaches divide and demarcate the world into separable entities—be they states, colonial states, cultural groups, empires, etc. These are usually taken for granted or viewed as enduring if evolving entities. More often than not, hermeneutic and experimental approaches use some type of nationally bound territory as the preferred unit of analysis. They typically presume that territorial polities are the consistent principal organizers of political and economic activities occurring within their borders, as well as the primary mediators of relations between populations within their borders and their broader "world environments" (Giddens 1973: 265; Martins 1974: 276; Smith 1979: 191; Chernilo 2006). This assumption encourages both hermeneutically and experimentally oriented scholars to pay minimal attention to historically contingent *interactive* cross-place sources of local and world change. To be sure hermeneutic and encompassing comparisons acknowledge the ways that generalized "world conditions" impinge on local dynamics. However, they rarely consider how the convergence or combining of events across a specific constellation of places can revolutionize the look and feel of local and world contexts.

In seeking to remediate the local or nation-centric bias of hermeneutic and experimental comparisons, the encompassing approach presumes that the state system and world economy are the consistent master organizers and mediators of "system-wide" political and economic activity (McMichael 1990: 386). Encompassing comparison starts from the premise that state and economic actors operating in particular localities are subject to the general norms or collective pressures of the majority of state or economic actors at the whole-system level. The encompassing method juxtaposes historical changes occurring within pre-assumed national boundaries against general changes in the encompassing system. It does so to determine the degree to which collective systemic changes correspond with more localized or national ones. Once again the world remains divided and demarcated into macro system and sub-systemic units. Only this time repetitive macro systemic patterns, recurring subsystem-to-subsystem interactions and repeating patterns internal to different types of subsystems define the three definite and unaltering scales at which causes of social change may occur. The problem with this strategy is that the potential significance of *unusual, unique and rapidly morphing* cross-border interactions cannot be properly appreciated.

Overall, hermeneutic, experimental and encompassing methods share a common assumption about the *consistency* in the sources of transformation and about the constancy of the scopes and scales where change occurs. None of these approaches fully historicizes and interrogates how changes in the meaning and scope of states, "world systems" or other connective arrangements transform the logics of action, perceptions and social projects of people moving across multiple contexts and vice-versa (Mongia 2007: 384). The assumption of the regularity of the scope at which social change and reproduction occur makes it especially difficult to notice the influence of *particular cross-place* interactions. It elides the importance of the shifting dynamics and ranges of influence that specific cross-place interactions exhibit. In this way, all three strategies of comparison impede perception of the special role that *changing* and *particular* cross-place relations play in altering how world patterns and social configurations vary through time.

INCORPORATING COMPARISONS—INTERSECTING HISTORIES AND CROSS-PLACE CAUSAL RELATIONS

In contrast, incorporating comparisons do not presume consistent sources or scopes of change during dramatic cross-world transformations in patterns of behavior. A primary goal of incorporating comparisons is to ferret out the particular cross-place interactions that alter the meanings, uses and scopes of different jurisdictions, identities, practices, or infrastructures. As Philip McMichael puts it:

> Incorporating comparison includes the theoretical proposition that international organization is continually evolving. The goal is not to develop invariant hypotheses via comparison of more or less uniform

'cases', but to give substance to a historical process (a whole) through comparison of its parts.... Whether considering nation-states or a singular world system, neither whole nor parts are permanent categories or units of analysis. Generalization is historically contingent because the units of comparison are historically specified. In short, comparison becomes the substance of the inquiry rather than its framework. (McMichael 1990: 386)

In other words, McMichael addresses the question of how the meanings and concepts defining our initial units of comparison historically change through time. His incorporating concept considers how social actors reciprocally reproduce and transform one another through time and across places. Historicizing and flexibly tracing how localities are constituted and altered through their changing interactions with one another is the primary concern of incorporating comparison. This strategy not only avoids nation-state or world-system centrism but also provides the researcher with tools especially adapted for tracing the origins of world reconfiguring change that conventional approaches do not. Moreover, the incorporating approach allows us to appreciate how growing drift in broad cross-place patterns and more contingent and specific inter-local interactions play distinctive but equally pivotal roles in transforming world historical relationships and norms of social delimitation.

Incorporating comparisons' goal is to discover the changing relations and mediums through which the histories of differing places and social actors become fatefully bound and mutually influence one another. It does so by identifying how widening contradictions produce general crises in which disparate localities' individual responses to crises interact with one another, and encourage unprecedented cross-fertilization of practices and ideas, which in turn generate innovations and initiate broader reconfigurations in outlooks and habits.

Much like the hermeneutic approach discussed earlier, incorporating approaches relate the histories of particular practices in specific localities in order to account for how and why those histories unfold differently on the ground. But they do so in order to identify the links *between* those histories and to shed light on when, how and why differences in these histories mutually influence and transform one another (Sewell 1967; Bloch 1953, 1967).

Incorporating comparisons also adopt the encompassing technique of comparing multiple local histories to pinpoint the moments and geographical starting points from which notable bouts of change begin to occur across multiple places. This practice aids in provisionally delimiting where the analyst might look for significant intersecting cross-place events. Where linked events and actions appear to instantiate innovations, certain questions arise that incorporating comparisons focus on: What events encouraged and allowed disparate groups to alter their patterns of behavior in response to one another? Which events helped link group actions from distinctive places and realms in new ways? How did they encourage groups to compare and react to the actions and understandings of other groups in new ways? How did these crisscrossing events and comparisons contribute to surprising innovations and deviations from previous practices?

An example of incorporating comparison can be found in Ellen Rosen's book *Making Sweatshops* (2002).[10] Her incorporating history of the US, Asian and Caribbean/Mexican garment industries demonstrates how the intersection of local histories and practices can crucially define the emergence of new cross-world relations, behaviors and expectations. Rosen shows how US and East Asian interactions in the 1950s reconfigured US clothing politics, helped generate new forms of pan-Asian apparel production and inaugurated a novel overarching regime of world clothing and textile trade. She also reveals how US- Latin American events and interactions in the 1980s initiated a distinctive form of pan-American apparel production that reconfigured US, Latin American and East Asian countries' clothing politics once again. In both cases, she details how particular complexes of events incrementally brought to life new productive and regulatory responses, fixes and compromises that would redefine production strategies and trade the world over.

Rosen's incorporating comparison builds upon the hermeneutic approach in that she illuminates the role that cultural and historical particularities played in shaping East Asian, US and Latin American historical trajectories and turning points. For example, she explains how unique postwar concerns over reconstructing a non-militarized Japan and over the growing Soviet influence in East Asia encouraged the US State Department to foment Asian apparel and textile exports to the US. She also shows how the Communist victory at *Dien Bien Phu* in 1954 just prior to an American congressional vote over whether to allow the American President untrammeled powers to negotiate trade pacts convinced reticent protectionist Southern congressmen to lend the President the power to open US apparel and textile trade with Asia. Rosen shows how this vote set off a reactive chain of events leading to the bilaterally determined Short Term Arrangement (*STA*) on cotton apparel and textile trade of 1961—an agreement that would shape Asian and US firms' and governments' courses of action for the next forty years. In short, Rosen's account attends to hermeneutic concerns for the local twists and turns in US and East Asian clothing politics. But, in contrast to the hermeneutic approach, Rosen's incorporating account does so by showing how unique historical events in the US and Asia interactively shaped local and broader geopolitical relations.

In addition, Rosen's incorporating approach also deploys the experimental technique of comparing the politics of forging new Latin American apparel export platforms in the 1980s with the politics producing East Asian platforms of the 1950s and 1960s. In some ways Rosen's investigatory strategy resembles Mahoney's attention to event sequence regularities and variances between the Asian and Latin American cases she compares.

Like Mahoney, Rosen makes analytical use of the similarities and differences in US–East Asian apparel developments in the 1950s and US–Mexican developments in the 1980s to pinpoint common patterns of events and circumstances preceding each development. That is, Rosen observes how in both cases economic devastation (WWII related in the first case and debt crises in the second) and rising communist threats provided economic opportunities and political cover for the State Department to similarly mold US-oriented markets and trade ties in both regions.

However, she does not treat these developments as equivalent, independent trials of the same natural experiment as Mahoney does. Rather, she relies on a method that accounts for continuities and differences on relational grounds in which she asks how the first episode shaped the second, and how later events in Latin America altered practices and tactics in East Asia (Haydu 1998: 356–9). Moreover, Rosen implies that similarities between these episodes had to do partly with US State Department officials' reflexive comparisons and uses of East Asian experiences in the 1950s to guide their actions in Latin America in the 1980s. Rosen also shows how the situation and strategies differed thanks to how the outcome of the earlier Asian experiment had changed US apparel and textile industry perspectives. That is, US firms suddenly faced explosive East Asian competition in the mid-1980s. This spurred American firms to support anti-communist State Department interventions in Latin American economies and lobby for trade rules helping them establish export processing facilities there. This second intervention of the American State in foreign apparel markets didn't just create alternate Americas-based export processing platforms. Creating a new type of US- Latin American apparel co-production changed system-wide dynamics in ways that would ultimately remake the character and rules of the world regime of which it was a part.

In taking this relational approach, Rosen's comparative strategy recalls Tilly's encompassing comparison. Like Tilly, she takes note of the general emergence of new Asian apparel export platforms in the 1950s and their relation to distinctive Latin American platforms emerging in the 1980s. Taking an encompassing tack, Rosen asks what overall system-wide dynamics and regular cross-place interactions help account for these similarities and differences.

However, Rosen moves beyond encompassing comparisons' exclusive focus on how general interactions between stable national US, Asian and Latin American industries and policies explain changes in each place. Interrogating the changing shape of the industries, interests, and policies under scrutiny, Rosen identifies a major break in how US apparel and textile firms conceptualized their clothing politics. Specifically, she is able to detect that from 1984 to 1992 US firms went from viewing their strategies in nationally defined protectionist terms to defining the protection of apparel assembled in Latin America as also in US national interest. These firms began to argue that increasing American imports of apparel co-produced across US-Latin

192 *Sandra Curtis Comstock*

American borders allowed US firms and workers to compete with their Asian counterparts. Following an incorporating logic, Rosen then seeks out the specific events and dynamics accounting for this substantive change in the meaning of US industry interests. To discover the reasons for these new US-Latin America connections, Rosen asks what events encouraged groups from both places to combine practices and forces in this way. This helps Rosen identify how (1) Latin American debt crises and communist insurgencies, (2) US and Latin American government initiatives to set up Latin American export processing zones to combat crisis and unrest, and (3) drastic, debt crisis-related declines in Latin American wages encouraged US firms' turn toward Latin America. This helps explain why, after years of nationally oriented activity, US firms began to consider the possibility that new US trade rules and Latin American conditions might help them dominate the Pan-American apparel export business in the manner East Asians had achieved across Asia. This helps Rosen identify how both general contradictions associated with Asian competition and US trade rules and unique cross-place events in the US and Latin America combined to alter US industry actions and their scope of operation.

A tactic that would further Rosen's incorporating strategies of checking and enriching our understanding of such cross-place connections would be to explicitly search out and analyze evidence of actors' direct engagements in comparative cross-place or cross-time problem-solving (Haydu 1998). A more thorough incorporating comparison of postwar clothing politics in the US, Asia and Latin America might ask how, for instance, US State Department officials, senators and congressional representatives specifically invoked and disagreed over the similarities and differences between the earlier East Asian episode and the unfolding Latin American situation. Researchers might look in the minutes of industry, labor, congressional or state meetings to answer these questions. They might generate interviews asking how and why key players' perceptions and distinctions comparing East Asian, US and Latin American clothing production schemes changed over time. They might ask how these perceptions framed and shaped debates and choices. Such an inquiry would attend closely to the specific historical experiences and places actors invoked as they devised new strategies. It would involve asking how the group of participants included in key policy making sessions and surrounding events shaped central players' choices in highlighting specific past experiences and constructing understandings of their own dilemmas.

Elaborating just how such attention to cross-cultural interpretations and comparisons might improve our strategies of discovering and validating the causal role of cross-place events and interactions is beyond the scope of this chapter.[11] Nonetheless, it should be clear how such attention would enhance our understanding of the changing circumstances and events linking specific Asian, US and Latin American historical experiences to one another through time. In general, using these strategies would allow incorporating comparisons to more precisely account for exactly why and how Asian export practices contributed to the sudden and unprecedented US–Latin

American apparel co-production innovations of the 1980s. Attending to reflexive and event-sensitive human uses of others' past experiences would also highlight the contingencies involved in the particular direction such Latin American innovations finally took. Such a hermeneutically informed analysis would also offer incorporating comparison another avenue for confirming causal hypotheses. That is, it would help us confirm the relative causal importance of local and far-removed events and circumstances by asking which ones actors actually invoked or reacted to as they imagined new strategies and policies. Moreover, it would help us appreciate how differences in competing groups' perceptions and uses of disparate events and circumstances moved collective perceptions, actions and solutions in one direction and not in other equally plausible ones.

CONCLUSION

In describing hermeneutic, experimental, encompassing and incorporating methods of comparison, I have identified some of the desirable goals that a more compelling historical comparative method should accomplish. The ideal comparative method should avoid prioritizing the general at the expense of the particular, or vice-versa, because both broad patterns and contingent and specific inter-local dynamics typically play pivotal roles in reconfiguring cross-place relations and paradigms of action. Incorporating comparisons have the potential to achieve this sort of balance.

Like the hermeneutic approach, incorporating comparisons help illuminate the role that cultural and historical particularities in different localities play in shaping local historical trajectories and world turning points. Moreover, like both experimental and encompassing analyses, incorporating comparisons satisfyingly explain why multiple places' historical trajectories suddenly take divergent or convergent tacks all at once. In addition, like encompassing comparisons, incorporating approaches alert us to the potential causal significance of historical events that fall outside the territorial confines of the place analyzed. Finally, incorporating comparisons are unique in attending to how novel cross-place connections or events interrupt older logics of action and help propagate the unprecedented behaviors, perceptions and tactics that can reconfigure prevailing practices at home and across the world.

The incorporating comparisons approach achieves this by searching for general shifts in flows of ideas, materials and people that amplify latent contradictions in and between localities. Such comparisons also accomplish this by pursuing indications of the kinds of spreading cross-world crises that typically encourage tendencies toward comparative cross-place problem-solving. They complete the task by seeking evidence of how specific, closely occurring crisis events (in diverse parts of the world) converge or agglomerate in ways that push differently situated groups to fuse distinctive problems and related dilemmas and invent unprecedented, socially revolutionary ideas and tactics (Friedmann 2006; Gootenberg 2008; Zimmerman

2010). Incorporating comparisons show how this interplay between generalizing and unique cross-place dynamics serve as a creative well-spring inspiring the invention of new practices and understandings and initiating the conditions most likely to facilitate a world historical switch point.

As suggested above, the incorporating comparisons method might also improve its arguments by drawing on a more hermeneutically oriented strategy of establishing the "meaning adequacy" of potential explanations (McLemore 1984: 294–5). In other words, it could significantly strengthen its explanations by seeking and evaluating evidence indicating just when, why and how disparate groups begin to compare, relate and make use of one another's experiences to interpret their own. Following this strategy, which I refer to elsewhere as "cross-place problem-solving," incorporating comparisons could better identify the contingencies generating new social interests and revolutionizing group projects and courses of action (Comstock 2011). Such sensitivity to particular cross-place interpretive interactions alongside other types of events provides special leverage for explaining the emergence of unprecedented practices. It moves beyond encompassing explanations of world change by helping us pinpoint and explain how specific cross-place events and interactions pivotally and contingently alter the human motives and interests driving geopolitical change.

In sum, the incorporating method of comparison flexibly traces cross-local historical relations giving rise to new social arrangements and groupings. In so doing, it challenges the apparent timelessness of social differences, similarities or connections. It also denaturalizes the prevailing assumptions driving much comparative historical research design: that processes of social change occurring within different localities or groups consistently unfold independently of one another. Incorporating comparison challenges these assumptions most strongly when working in a hermeneutic vein to establish how continuities and differences across place and time are linked to the human tendency to relate their own experiences to those of groups from other places and times. The incorporating comparisons approach thus makes its biggest contribution to comparative historical research when the comparisons document and theorize precisely when, why and how certain groups begin to intensely compare and draw upon foreign or unfamiliar experiences to better comprehend and act on their own.

NOTES

1. I use the concept *hermeneutic* as Steinmetz does in describing a hermeneutic circle in which a melding "of the horizons of the present and past, rather than a subordination of present and past to the observer [is achieved, and the researcher tries] . . . to find resources in our language to understand initially alien phenomena without applying distortive prejudices" (see Steinmetz 2004: 390; Sewell 2005: 225–70; McLemore 1984: 293–4).

I use the term *experimental* to indicate a model of comparison that depends on treating cases compared as "analogous to separate trials of an experiment. This means the trials must be both equivalent and independent. The principle of equivalence implies that each new trial . . . be a genuine replication of earlier trials, with all relevant variables held constant" (Sewell 2005: 95, 97).

I define *encompassing comparison* as comparisons that "select locations within [a large] structure or process and explain similarities or differences among those locations as consequences of their relationships to the whole" (McMichael 1990: 388; Tilly 1984: 123).
2. Major world historical change is defined as the rewriting of juridical rules delineating, dividing and linking polities and social groups to one another and the reworking of broad-ranging social practices and understandings in many parts of the world.
3. By *place* and *locality* I mean provisional physical spaces that cohere through shared physical infrastructures, institutions and/or cultural affinities and practices. I use the notion of place and locality because it is often the material groundedness of our lives, our experiences and access to specific physical resources that lend solidity to our cultural practices and perceptions and our cultural practices that lend intelligibility to the things that surround us and that we use. These are not fixed but provisionally significant, materially substantive spaces, relevant depending on the historical moment and context in which they are invoked and discussed (Sewell 2005: 137).
4. William Sewell points out that "experimental comparisons must presume (1) that all places compared begin with equivalent world-historical contexts, social classes, institutions, capacities, and endowments and (2) that the events and conditions unfolding in one place have no effect on those happening in another" (Sewell 2005: 96–7).
5. One need only consider the effects of the Nicaraguan Revolution on other insurgencies and on other states' perceptions and collaborative strategies for managing the threat of revolution (Williams 1994; Paige 1997).
6. In moments of rupture actors with distinct concepts, projects and expectations are likely to begin to relate to each other in new ways District parties may act according to their own presuppositions but each having their own cultural standpoint may not respond in line with their counterpart's expectations or concepts. This generates a situation where "recieved categories are potentially revalued and transformed" (Sahlins 1981: 35, 67–8).
7. In Mahoney's story, for instance, the significant resources that Salvadoran elites had at their disposal for pushing back against Guatemalan incursions and the minimal resources available to Hondurans to act similarly seems pivotal in explaining their distinctive paths. Yet these asymmetries and overlaps are not explored from a relationally dynamic perspective. Rather, they appear as static, historical, intrinsically derived antecedents, variable-like in conceptualization (see also Williams 1994).
8. Tilly's method of discovering law-like dynamics is to build "robust" ideal-typical models that account for the repeated diffusion of widespread social practices. He begins by analyzing numerous empirical event sequences associated with the diffusion of a practice from one place to the next. He arrives at "the most robust" ideal-typical sequences of diffusion by determining which types of conditions and actions most regularly recur with uniform results (Tilly 2005).
9. Wallerstein's description of his encompassing world system explanatory strategy as predicting the past from the present suggests just this kind of teleology (Wallerstein 1979: 3, 6–7).

10. In critiquing earlier studies, I have used examples of incorporating approaches to show how it enriches our understanding of how places and polities are not constituted *sui generis* but in relation to other polities' localities.
11. I am currently writing an article that references Jeffrey Haydu's work on reiterative problem-solving and takes Haydu's work a step further to examine sequences and episodes of cross-place problem-solving during pivotal world historical turning points.

REFERENCES

Arrighi, G. (1994) *The Long Twentieth Century: Money, Power, and the Origins of Our Times*, London, New York: Verso.

Bloch, M. (1953) *The Historian's Craft*, New York: Random House.

——— (1967) "A contribution towards a comparative history", in M. Bloch (ed) *Land and Work in Medieval Europe*, Berkeley: University of California Press, pp. 44–81.

Chernilo, D. (2006) "Social theory's methodological nationalism. Myth and reality", *European Journal of Social Theory*, 9: 5–22.

Clavin, M.J. (2010) *Toussaint Louverture and the American Civil War: The Promise and Peril of a Second Haitian Revolution*, Philadelphia: University of Pennsylvania Press.

Comstock, S.C. (2011) "Thinking about comparative methods from a world-historical perspective: The case for incorporating comparison and cross-place problem solving", in S. Beckert and E. Manela (eds) *Workshop on the History of North America in Global Perspective*, Cambridge, MA: The Charles Warren Center for Studies in American History, Harvard University.

Fabian, J. (2002) *Time and the Other: How Anthropology Makes Its Object*, New York: Columbia University Press.

Firth, S. (1977) "Governors versus settlers: The dispute over Chinese labour in German Samoa", *New Zealand Journal of History*, 11: 155–79.

Friedmann, H. (2006) "From colonialism to green capitalism", *Research in Rural Sociology and Development*, 11: 227–64.

Giddens, A. (1973) *The Class Structure of the Advanced Societies*, London: Hutchinson.

Gootenberg, P. (2008) *Andean Cocaine: The Making of a Global Drug*, Chapel Hill: University of North Carolina Press.

Green, N.L. (1994) "The comparative method and poststructural structuralism: New perspectives for migration studies", *Journal of American Ethnic History*, 13: 3–22.

Griffin, L.J. (1993) "Narrative, event-structure analysis, and causal interpretation in historical sociology", *American Journal of Sociology*, 98: 1094–1133.

Haydu, J. (1998) "Making use of the past: Time periods as cases to compare and as sequences of problem solving", *American Journal of Sociology*, 104: 339–71.

Hopkins, T. (1978) "World system analysis: Methodological issues", in B.H. Kaplan (ed) *Social Change in the Capitalist World Economy*, Thousand Oaks, CA: Sage.

McLemore, L. (1984) "Max Weber's defense of historical inquiry", *History and Theory*, 23: 277–95.

McMichael, P. (1990) "Incorporating comparison within a world-historical perspective: An alternative comparative method", *American Sociological Review*, 55: 385–97.

Mahoney, J. (2000) "Path dependence in historical sociology", *Theory and Society*, 29: 501–48.

───── (2001) *The Legacies of Liberalism*, Baltimore: Johns Hopkins University Press.
Mann, M. (1990) "Review: coercion, capital, and European states", *American Journal of Sociology*, 96: 1260–61.
───── (1993) *The Sources of Social Power: The Rise of Classes and Nation-States 1760–1914*, Vol. 2, Cambridge: Cambridge University Press.
Martins, H. (1974) "Time and theory in sociology", in J. Rex (ed) *Approaches to Sociology*, London: Routledge, Kegan Paul.
Mongia, R.V. (2007) "Historicizing state sovereignty: Inequality and the form of equivalence", *Comparative Studies in Society and History*, 49: 384–411.
Moses, J.A. (1973) "The coolie labour question and German colonial policy in Samoa 1900–1914", *Journal of Pacific History*, 8: 111–17.
O'Hearn, D. (2001) *The Atlantic Economy*, Manchester: Manchester University Press.
Paige, J.M. (1997) *Coffee and Power: Revolution and the Rise of Democracy in Central America*, Cambridge, MA: Harvard University Press.
Rosen, E.I. (2002) *Making Sweatshops: The Globalization of the Us Apparel Industry*, Berkeley: University of California Press.
Sahlins, M. (1981) *Historical Metaphors and Mythical Realities: Early History of the Sandwich Islands Kingdom*, Ann Arbor: University of Michigan Press.
───── (1985) *Islands of History*, Chicago: University of Chicago Press.
Sewell, W. (2005) *Logics of History: Social Theory and Social Transformation*, Chicago: University of Chicago Press.
Sewell Jr., W.H. (1967) "Marc Bloch and the logic of comparative history", *History and Theory*, 6: 208–18.
Silver, B. and Slater, E. (1999) "The social origins of world hegemonies" in *Chaos and Governance in the Modern World System*, Minneapolis: University of Minnesota Press.
Smith, A.D. (1979) *Nationalism in the Twentieth Century*, Oxford: Martin Robertson.
Somers, M. (1996) "Where is sociology after the historic turn? Knowledge cultures, narrativity, and historical epistemologies", in T.J. McDonald (ed) *The Historic Turn in the Human Sciences*, Ann Arbor: University of Michigan Press, pp. 53–90.
Steinmetz, G. (2003) "'The devil's handwriting': Precolonial discourse, ethnographic acuity, and cross-identification in German colonialism," *Comparative Studies in Society and History*, 45, 41–95.
───── (2004) "Odious comparisons: Incommensurability, the case study, and 'small n's' in sociology", *Sociological Theory*, 22: 371–400.
───── (2007) *The Devil's Handwriting*, Chicago: University of Chicago Press.
Tilly, C. (1984) *Big Structures, Large Processes, Huge Comparisons*, New York: Russell Sage Foundation.
───── (1990) *Coercion, Capital, and European States: AD 990–1990*, Studies in Social Discontinuity, Cambridge, MA: Blackwell Publishers.
───── (2005) *Identities, Boundaries, and Social Ties*, Boulder, CO: Paradigm Publishers.
Wallerstein, I. (1979) "The rise and future demise of the world capitalist system: Concepts for comparative analysis", in I. Wallerstein (ed) *The Capitalist World-Economy*, Cambridge: Cambridge University Press, pp. 1–36.
Williams, R.G. (1994) *States and Social Evolution: Coffee and the Rise of National Governments in Central America*, Chapel Hill: University of North Carolina Press.
Zimmerman, A. (2010) *Alabama in Africa: Booker T. Washington, the German Empire, and the Globalization of the New South*, Princeton, NJ: Princeton University Press.

10 Interrogating Critiques of Methodological Nationalism
Propositions for New Methodologies

Radhika Mongia

Reflecting on formulating a fresh agenda for comparative study, Harry Harootunian (2005) has argued that analyses in the humanities and interpretative social sciences are increasingly marked by a privileging of spatial categories with an accompanying decline in addressing questions of temporality. For Harootunian, the dominance of a range of static, space-specific categories—such as culture, civilization, modernity, nation, center and periphery, area and region, global and empire—have banished considerations of the temporal to produce a situation in which effect is routinely substituted for cause, the explanatory potential of the interpretive sciences is stymied and comparative analysis, working with spatial categories, has naturalized rather than analyzed capitalism's necessarily segmenting and uneven character. Harootunian elucidates how this troubling state of affairs has emerged in a wide range of scholarship. For instance, identifying modernity as a spatial category, restricted to Europe, has produced the logic of alternative modernities; understanding the globe as the requisite frame for any number of analyses has naturalized rather than explained the concept. The dominant tendency of area studies to inquire into the specificities of national and native cultures has served to essentialize culture and suture it to space; more recently, some postcolonial theory has replicated this very move and also essentialized culture as space-specific. Finally, by Harootunian's account, an overvaluation of the spatial categories of nation, region or area that underwrites much work on diaspora and migration conceives of border crossings and hybrid identities in primarily spatial terms, and the still prevalent logics of modernization and developmentalism misrecognize the unevenness *produced* by and *necessary* to capitalism as, instead, inhering in and deriving from specific spaces.

To address the situation, Harootunian makes an impassioned plea for the urgent need to attend to questions of temporality and develop integrated spatio-temporal analysis. Though, in my view, Harootunian might be overstating the dire condition prevailing in the humanities and interpretive social sciences as well as misapprehending some of the arguments advanced by scholarship on diaspora and post-colonialism, his call for more rigorous spatio-temporal analysis is, I believe, well placed and especially relevant to thinking beyond methodological nationalism.

Interrogating Critiques of Methodological Nationalism 199

In this chapter, I take up his call to temporalize spatial categories and offer three reformulations and realignments that enable a more nuanced spatio-temporal analysis to address some conundrums of methodological nationalism with respect to the study of migration. First, drawing on Rogers Brubaker's (1996) discussion of what he calls "developmentalist" and "eventful" formations of nationhood, I suggest that the "nationalization" of migration is best grasped as a medley of "eventful" formations of nationhood. Such a perspective, I argue, is most appropriate to apprehending the scattered, uneven temporality of the suture between nationness and migration. Second, to index a world different from one composed of and dominated by nation-states, I deploy the formulation of the empire-state. In drawing attention to *imperial* territorial, economic, state, social and subjective formations, the spatial notion of the empire-state goes some way in historicizing the national and in undoing the anachronistic logic that attends the nomenclature of the transnational. It also aids in ensuring that colonial formations are not remaindered out of our analyses of the making of the world or accorded the status of derivative formations as the sites of the diffusion of putative originals crafted elsewhere. Finally, just as the critique of methodological nationalism has entailed that rather than produce national histories, we historicize the national, I suggest that rather than produce transnational histories, we historicize the transnational. Whereas the former can take the form of simply cataloguing connections across the globe, the latter has the benefit of foregrounding how such connections are understood, regulated and experienced anew, as mediated by a *mutating* nation form.

Working with the reformulations and realignments I offer here could prove analytically helpful in a number of domains. In this chapter, however, I restrict my attention to an examination of methodological nationalism and the study of migration, emphasizing, in particular, the colonial dimensions of the nationalization of state control over migration. To this end, in the first section of this chapter, I begin by interrogating two important critiques of methodological nationalism with respect to migration, coming from the domains of cultural studies and of transnational migration studies. Despite their very significant contributions, these critiques retain what I call a methodological stateism that reifies and dehistoricizes state-space and, therefore, stop short of a thorough critique of methodological nationalism. A significant aspect of challenging the suspect verities that inform methodological nationalism is historicizing the nation-state. This is a vexed exercise. Attempts to outline core elements that define nations—such as a common language, culture, ethnicity, race or religion—have been unsuccessful and there is no consensus on theories regarding the origin and spread of nationalism. However, it is clear that the nation form has historically demonstrated an unusual mutability; that the nation-state, even as it has spawned new institutions, has also harnessed "a multiplicity of institutions dating from widely differing periods" into its fold (Balibar 1991: 87); and that nationalist myths are enormously successful in presenting such incorporations as, precisely, prenational forms, presaging, indeed compelling the advent of the nation-state. Against such teleological histories of the nation-state, that inform both nationalist myths and methodological nationalism, where a range of "qualitatively distinct events spread out over time, none of which implies any subsequent event" are interpellated and arranged as specifically prenational, Etienne Balibar suggests that we attend to how "*non-national* state apparatuses aiming at quite other (for example, dynastic) objectives have progressively produced the elements of the nation-state or . . . have been involuntarily 'nationalized' and have begun to nationalize society" (Balibar 1991: 88, original emphasis). Balibar's insight here serves as a warning to not impute national characteristics to all operations of the state and points to the dangers of attributing, retroactively, a national character to "non-national" forms. Instead, it invites one to track how, historically, non-national forms can be mobilized to assume a national character and also opens the possibility of inquiring into *contingent* historical conjunctures that produce "new" national state forms. Combining Balibar's approach with Rogers Brubaker's discussion of eventful formations of nationhood, I will argue that attending to contingent, spatio-temporally heterogeneous forms of nationalization are especially germane to undoing methodological nationalism in the field of migration studies.

Keeping such an anti-teleological approach in view, in the next section of this chapter, I turn to an examination of two important moments in state control of migration from the Indian subcontinent in the 19th and early 20th centuries. I provide a conjunctural, eventful analysis of how state control over migration would come to be understood in national terms to challenge the widespread view that assumes, rather than historicizes, the nationalization of state sovereignty authorizing such control. In other words, I focus on historicizing the relation between migration and the state so we do not risk congealing a certain ahistorical, and frequently Eurocentric, understanding of the state that is unable to grapple with what is peculiar about the historical suture between migration, the nation and the state. I conclude with a discussion of what is at stake in producing histories of the transnational as distinct from transnational histories.

METHODOLOGICAL STATEISM AND THE ANALYSIS OF MIGRATION: INTERROGATING CRITIQUES OF METHODOLOGICAL NATIONALISM

As with the human sciences more broadly, the analysis of migration has been framed (in terms, both, of providing an *orientation* for analysis and of serving to *enclose* and delimit the analysis) by a profound methodological nationalism. The framework of methodological nationalism works on a foundationalist and presentist logic, wherein the nation-state is divested of its historicity and peculiarity and invested, instead, with a dehistoricized and circular logic. In this way, the very notions—of nation, nationality and the nation-state—most in need of explanation are both the starting and the ending points of analysis. Thus, for instance, migration was customarily understood as the movement of people from one nation-state to another and analyses, working with the paradigm popularized by the Chicago School, were largely configured to inquire into how migrants are assimilated, or not, into a "host" society understood as a pre-existing national space. A corollary to the assimilationist paradigm, focused on assessing migration as a phenomenon of *im*migration, has been the lack of attention to understanding migration as, simultaneously and necessarily, also *emi*gration (Green and Weil 2007). In recent decades, the implicit and explicit methodological nationalism that has dominated the study of migration has received sustained critiques from at least two quarters. One critique, associated with the influential work of cultural studies, has vigorously questioned notions of a fixed, stable culture and cultural identity, in general, and notions of unchanging, discrete national culture, in particular (for example, Hall 1981, 1996; Gilroy 1991, 1993; Clifford 1992, 1997; Appadurai 1996). Breaking with analyses that understand culture and cultural identity as temporally invariant, pure, organic, space-specific formations that take shape within and are restricted to the "neat, symmetrical units" of the nation-state (Gilroy 1993: 29), such work has demonstrated the dynamism, circulation and syncretism that characterizes culture to undo claims to an authentic, pristine, immemorial national culture. As a result, cultural studies literature has importantly challenged the perspective—equally commonsensical and scholarly—that positions migrant, particularly minoritized and racialized communities, as posing a threat to an essentialized notion of a "national culture." Instead, this work has advocated the adoption of spatial analytical units other than the national (for example, the Atlantic world or the Indian Ocean world) for understanding culture, highlighted themes of mobility and travel—literal and metaphoric—as critical to the making of culture in the modern world and urged a reconceptualization of culture untethered from its spatial articulation with the national.

Whereas culture has been the primary object of analysis in the critique of methodological nationalism I have just outlined, another critique of methodological nationalism with respect to migration has emphasized how its insular, territorial logic obstructs our ability to grasp the dense networks and circuits of connections between people, discourses, commodities, artifacts, ideas and so on that extend beyond national state borders. A transnational approach, with lineages in a more traditional sociological paradigm and often drawing on ethnographic research, has been one of the most significant methodological innovations in addressing the limitations exposed by the second critique of methodological nationalism (for example, Basch, Glick Schiller and Szanton Blanc 1994; Glick Schiller 1999; Portes, Guarnizo and Landolt 1999; Pratt and Yeoh 2003; Levitt and Glick

Schiller 2004). Key to this approach is distinguishing between state space and social space, and reserving the term *transnational* "to capture all of the cross-border social relations of migrants" (Glick Schiller and Levitt 2006: 4). Rejecting the container model embodied in methodological nationalism, a transnational approach thus draws attention to an array of practices and processes—ranging from social, economic and political relations to the affective attachments and institutional engagements of migrants—that exceed the boundaries of the nation-state and are, instead, constitutive of the production of transnational social space.

Thus, the former critique demonstrates that the framework of methodological nationalism thoroughly misunderstands how culture works, even as it produces "the fatal junction between the concept of nationality with the concept of culture" (Gilroy 1993: 3) where, in particular, the "limits of nation coincide with the lines of 'race'" (Gilroy 1991: 60). The latter foregrounds how the national container model cannot apprehend, let alone analyze, a range of phenomena that characterize migration and, more specifically, the practices and experiences of migrants (see Glick Schiller 1999). Both these critiques are important interventions that have significantly shaped recent migration research. However, each evinces a residue of what we might call a *methodological stateism* that, in fact, does not push the critique of methodological nationalism far enough. By methodological stateism I wish to refer to three, often interrelated, perspectives:

- First, the position that does not historicize the state, for instance by viewing its contemporary formation as ordinary and immutable and thus not subject to constant, frequently radical, transformations. In this perspective, the state, thus, is simply there; it matters little what prefix—national, colonial, modern and so on—we affix to it.
- Second, my use of the term methodological stateism refers to what others have called state-centrism (Brenner 1999) and is not far from what is often subsumed under methodological nationalism: the assumption that the territorial boundaries that define (nation) states serve to provide a container for important social, economic, political and cultural relations. This aspect of methodological stateism, moreover, tends to naturalize presentist state-territorial boundaries—bracketing historical contractions and expansions—even as it fixes what is meant by, or entailed in, the notion of state borders.
- Third, by methodological stateism I refer to the unreflexive adoption of categories produced by the state as categories of analysis within the human sciences. Just as a critique of methodological nationalism has entailed that we be vigilant toward utilizing what Rogers Brubaker calls "categories of practice" as "categories of analysis" (1996: 15), a critique of methodological stateism requires that our categories of analysis do not uncritically duplicate the categories deployed by the state.

A methodological stateism is embedded, if unwittingly, in the two critiques of methodological nationalism launched, respectively, by cultural studies and transnational migration studies literature and, in fact, is pervasive in migration scholarship more broadly. With regard to cultural studies scholarship, analyses of the state have been largely absent, even when certain (national) state spaces are the central locus of concern. Though we have rich accounts of the (re)making of national cultures, methodological stateism enters by way of an assumption of a dehistoricized, invariant, usually coercive state that frames and orients the analysis but is not itself subjected to examination (for example, Lowe 1996).

In the transnational approach, the problems of a methodological stateism are more acute, if paradoxical. Given that its main objective is to inquire into processes and practices that cross the boundaries of the nation-state, the existence of the nation-state and the salience of particular, *already "nationalized,"* understandings of borders between states are central to every definition of transnationalism and transnational migration (see, for example, Glick Schiller 1999: 96). By distinguishing between state space and social space and focusing attention on the latter, what is lost is a historicization of how, when and why borders between fungible states come to be congealed or of what events and processes produce borders as containing fixed territories and populations understood in specifically national terms.[1] Methodological stateism works here, once again, by way of a dehistoricization that requires stable national state boundaries and demands that they be imbued with the kinds of significations and institutional structures that currently attach to international migration. While this approach is useful for understanding certain recent (trans)formations, it is not as helpful for historical inquiry since, in its reliance on the formulation of the "national," it introduces the problem of presentism in a particularly acute yet unacknowledged fashion. The problem is embedded in the very nomenclature: The formulation of the trans*national* obliges, if not shackles, us to assumptions of space, state and subjectivity *already* conceived in *national* terms.[2] Scholars of transnationalism are, of course, aware of the problems posed by this anachronism; their attempts to address it, however, have not been satisfying or consistent.[3] Moreover, the term transnational has now circulated to a range of analyses, from varying periods and places, as simply a synonym held to capture connections between different parts of the globe—a perspective that overwhelmingly characterizes, for instance, the approach (notwithstanding the impressive scope and scale) of the recent *Palgrave Dictionary of Transnational History* (Iriye and Saunier 2009). In this way, the "national" is further naturalized and dehistoricized by way of the indiscriminate use of the term "transnational" as a descriptor for these varied connections.

A chief reason for the confusing deployment of the national framework in migration scholarship relates to the fact that mass migrations have not been an important element of influential treatments of the historical development of nationalism and the nation form (for example, Anderson 1991; Gellner 1983; Chatterjee 1993; Smith 1986; Hobsbawm 1990). But instead of supplementing—or critiquing—this literature, by developing accounts of *how* migration comes to be nationalized, much migration scholarship has, essentially, taken this to be the case. Rather than *assume* that state organization of migration in national terms, or, indeed, state organization and monopoly over migration, was a teleology simply waiting to unfold, we must examine *how* certain events in certain historical conjunctures produced a tight confluence between migration, nationness and stateness as a contingent—if enduring—result. Rogers Brubaker's distinction between developmentalist and eventful perspectives in thinking about nationhood proves useful here. Whereas the developmentalist literature "traces long-term political, economic, and cultural changes that led, over centuries, to the gradual emergence of nations" (1996: 19), an eventful perspective thinks of "nationness as an event, as something that suddenly crystallizes rather than gradually develops, as a contingent, conjuncturally fluctuating, and precarious frame of vision and basis for individual and collective action, rather than a relatively stable product of deep developmental trends in economy, polity, or culture" (Brubaker 1996: 19).

The historical nationalization of migration is best grasped through an eventful perspective, in which certain migrations, at particular moments, come suddenly to provoke the framing of identity in national and nationalist terms, or to catalyze the introduction of nationality as an institutionalized category into migration law, or to produce unforeseen eruptions of fervent nationalist claims. Historically, the nationalization of migration has taken a piecemeal and uneven trajectory, pointing to the fact that processes of nationalization are "temporally heterogeneous" (Sewell Jr. 1996: 263); they do not all work in tandem nor all have the same intensity, and nationalization in one domain or in some state territorial spaces does not entail, or foretell, nationalization in others. Thus, for instance, the piecemeal nationalization of migration Adam McKeown (2008) describes and analyzes in terms of Chinese migration to the US in the late 19th century does not entail or foretell the nationalization of migration in terms of Indian migration to Canada in the early 20th century that I have described and analyzed (Mongia 1999, 2007). Temporal succession, in other words, is not equivalent to causation, duplication or diffusion, which are matters that require an investigation simultaneously empirical and theoretical. Given this temporal-spatial heterogeneity, while we might now speak of a thorough nationalization of migration on a global scale, the particularities of this nationalization do not all replicate each other and are instead unstable. Moreover, while I cannot develop and illustrate the point here, an eventful approach permits an analysis of the gendered and sexualized contours of nationalist and state discourse as they shape the nationalization of migration—an analysis that largely cannot be, and has not been, accommodated within developmentalist approaches.

Interrogating Critiques of Methodological Nationalism 205

AN EVENTFUL PERSPECTIVE ON NATIONALIZING MIGRATION AND THE STATE

If the existence and significations of state borders, understood in national terms, underlie theorizations of transnationalism, another important aspect of methodological stateism that characterizes scholarship on migration is the assumption that controlling migration across these putative borders is a long-standing and noncontentious element of state sovereignty. Scholars of migration have noted that different kinds of states, at different times, have sought to control the mobility of people, including what we call emigration and immigration, and that the axes for such control have varied widely (for example, Salter 2003; Green and Weil 2007; McKeown 2008). They have also noted that several states, such as the US, that have seen a flow of migrants for centuries, attempted to develop comprehensive federal immigration laws only toward the end of the 19th century (for example, Calavita 1994; McKeown 2008). Both past and current migration policies are increasingly scrutinized and debated. Scholars have also understood the extent and mechanisms of control, particularly on emigration, as yardsticks to classify state forms as, for instance, liberal or totalitarian.[4] In sum, several elements of state control over mobility have received attention. However, even as different aspects of state control over mobility have occupied migration scholars, they have tended, with rare exceptions (for example, Mongia 1999, 2007; Torpey 2000; McKeown 2008), to assume that such control is a defining, definitive, unchanging and unchangeable element of (state) sovereignty, typically attributing this feature to the 1648 Treaty of Westphalia (Zolberg 1999, 2006; Hollifield 2005, 2007; Portes and DeWind 2007).[5] In other words, the different policies, legislative actions and mechanisms of control—over almost four centuries—are understood as so many diverse "applications" of the "principles" or doctrines implied by the Treaty of Westphalia. As a result, the "nationalization" of sovereignty—in terms both of how pre-existing aspects of other state forms are remade in national terms and of how new, specifically national forms emerge—has not received sufficient attention. Not only do such appeals to a Westphalian ideal of the state and the inter-state system rely on an insufficient historicization of the state and state sovereignty in relation to migration, they also sidestep the issue of how—and if—the Westphalian ideal was globalized and if we might chart any relations between this ideal and colonialism.[6] More broadly, such a view is premised on the notion that the practices of governance and the institutions of the state have a fidelity to, can be deduced from and are reflective of a set of principles and actually abide by treaties. Rather than understand the state as a coherent, interpretatively stable set of principles (even if these are literally proclaimed in constitutions or are encoded in treaties) that it puts into practice, I focus on practices to examine how they understand, interpret, navigate and remake principles in *particular historical conjunctures*. Thus the state will emerge, in my analysis, as an unstable, historically changing entity, rather than an entity that adheres to principles and fulfills static definitional criteria. Such a perspective will enable us to avoid the pitfalls of a methodological nationalism that would not only have us believe that migration has always been controlled in national terms but also believe that state sovereignty embodies an inviolable right to exercise such control.

An analysis of migration from the Indian subcontinent demonstrates, firstly, that, in the first half of the 19th century, appeals to state sovereignty as embodying the authority to control "free" migration were anything but common sense and, secondly, that, in the early 20th century, attempts to suture migration, the nation and the state were cause for extensive debate and, once again, anything but common sense. In each instance, the shape of state control was justified via entirely *ad hoc* arguments that spoke to the specificities of the precise historical conjuncture that obtained. The context for the debate in the 19th century concerned the migration of Indians following the abolition of slavery in British colonies in 1834. While historians now routinely refer to this as indentured migration, what preoccupied the state, in the wake of abolition, was how to ensure that it was free. The uniqueness of the circumstances produced a lasting paradox: The state regulated "free" migration precisely in order to ensure that it was "free." However, this paradoxical and less than logical resolution, that took the concrete form of requiring potential emigrants to consent to a labor contract, emerged after an extensive and extended debate, beginning in 1835 and not resolved till 1842, between state, quasi-state and non-state participants that moved between England, India, Mauritius and the Caribbean. The orienting frame, spatial scale and economic imperatives of these debates were imperial and not (proto) national. In addition, the very fact of a debate reveals that there were no ready-made principles that could simply be applied to justify state control of migration. The latter issue, in fact, had not escaped authorities in England who had noted " that this practice [of controlling migration] has no foundation in any existing law".[7] Lacking recourse to a pre-existing principle, how was such control to be justified? An analysis of the debate reveals that the eventual justification for state control, crafted by some of the best legal minds of empire, was to argue that the peculiar situation of the abolition of slavery combined with colonialism and "the character of the natives" warranted an *exception* to general principles regarding free movement. Thus was instituted the practice of Indian indentured migration under a state-supervised contract that would continue for almost a century, only to be terminated in the 20th century. I point to this debate to highlight the following:

1) The imperial, though uneven and jagged, spatial scale across which it unfolded.
2) The considerable difficulties that confronted the early liberal state (British colonialism was largely a liberal project) when it sought to intervene in migration.

3) That the extensive debates made *no* recourse to the 1648 Treaty of Westphalia and presumed notions of sovereignty as providing the justificatory legal ground on which to base the actions of the state.

Perhaps this is not surprising, since Britain was not a signatory to the Treaty of Westphalia. But if the 19th century hegemon and its vast colonial ventures cannot be accommodated into Westphalian models, scholars will need to contend with an important set of historical and theoretical issues, rather than attempt to sidestep them. At any rate, appeals one might now make to the Westphalian ideal are a retroactive attribution, or a presentism, that serve to dehistoricize the modern state. However, and this is an important point, what the 19th century debates on colonial Indian migration and the resulting resolution *do* indicate is a profound refashioning of state sovereignty in relation to migration.

In order to further explicate genealogies of state sovereignty and migration control, particularly how it gains an explicitly *national* character, I will turn, momentarily, to the debates occasioned by the migration of "free" Indians in the early 20th century. Crucial to the 19th century state regulations I refer to above was what the documents called the "necessary ignorance" of the "class of persons" who might be duped into indenture. The regulations that were framed thus did not extend to those *not* deemed "necessarily ignorant" or in danger of being duped. Indeed, until the early 20th century, arms of the empire-state monitored *only* the movement of indentured Indian labor and did not interfere with the migration of those not participating in the indenture system. In fact, within the law, the terms "emigrate," "emigration," and "emigrant" referred *only* to indentured labor. Thus Act XXI of 1883, the definitive Indian emigration regulation till 1915, states: "'Emigrate' and 'Emigration' denote the departure by sea out of British India of a native of India under an agreement to labour for hire in some country beyond the limits of India other than the island of Ceylon or the Straits Settlements."[8] The term "to labour," moreover, had been interpreted as "manual labour," thus exempting, in particular, emigrants from the wealthier classes. Moreover, the act specified, expressly, the countries to which one could "emigrate." Thus, state control over "emigration" covered only the large-scale movement of indentured labor to specific destinations. Given the nature of the legislation, emigrants who did not contract to labor prior to embarking on their journeys, or those not engaged in "manual labour," or those whose destination was not among the specified destinations of "emigration" (including Ceylon and the Strait Settlements), were free to travel unhindered, especially between parts of the British Empire. In other words, the initial paradox of regulating "free" migration precisely in order to ensure that it was "free" would yield the further paradoxical situation of what we can call "more free, free migration." Further, though we are accustomed today to thinking of state regulation of migration as operating along lines of constraint and prohibition, what is significant about these early 19th century regulations is that they were put in place and functioned along lines of facilitation. In other words, the goal of the regulations was not to constrain the migration but rather to facilitate it, while guarding against charges that indenture was but slavery by another name.

State control over migration that explicitly draws on a logic of constraint and curtailment has a different history; it is a history that mobilizes a justificatory discourse of state sovereignty and security in terms more familiar to us today. As I have pointed out above, until the early 20th century state control over Indian migration covered only indentured migration. Within the history of Indian migration regulations, it is only with the migration of small groups of non-indentured Indians to the (white-) settler colonies of Australia and Canada, in the first decades of the 20th century, that we see the vigorous demands to extend state control to cover all types of movement. Conceiving the space of the settler colony as race-specific, the explicit aim of these demands was to restrict and prohibit the migration on racial grounds.

Canada's request, in 1906, for such prohibition would result in a protracted 10-year debate that would be resolved only in 1915. I provide here a minimal sketch of this complex debate (for details, see Mongia 1999) whose official participants included prime ministers in Canada, viceroys in India, secretaries of state for the Colonies in England, members of the House of Commons in Canada and any number of other administrators and legislators at each site, who struggled to devise a solution that would retain the legal equality of British subjects and institute their patent inequality. Also party to the debate were British Indian subjects who respectfully petitioned the state, British Indian revolutionaries—spread across the globe—who, in consort with other revolutionaries, threatened to overthrow it, as well as lay people and nationalists who organized meetings in Indian cities to discuss the paradoxes produced by imperial identity. The official debate quickly reached an impasse: No principles could be found to justify a prohibition on Indian migration, even as there was wide sympathy for the racist logic of the Canadian demand. The eventual solution to restrict Indian migration to Canada followed a proposal initially put forth by Wilfred Laurier, prime minister of Canada in 1908, to institute a system of passports, issued selectively, to emigrants in India. (This is akin to what we now understand as a visa.) The Government of (British) India had consistently objected to this proposal on the grounds that it opposed all prevailing policy and violated Act XXI of 1883. They had, however, not only supported but also suggested that Canada devise immigration policy so long as its racist motivations were suitably disguised, a suggestion that Canada, in the absence of other means, would enthusiastically pursue. Notably absent from these discussions was a discourse of state sovereignty, its corollary, a discourse of state security, or their articulation to a discourse of nationality. It would take the arrival, at Vancouver, of the ship the *Komagata Maru* carrying

Indian immigrants in the context of an impending world war that would provide the occasion for activating these discourses in any credible way.

The *Komagata Maru* arrived at Vancouver on May 23, 1914, with 376 passengers, mostly Sikhs. Unfortunately, I cannot provide here an account of the extraordinary web of events surrounding the *Komagata Maru* incident (see Johnston 1979; Mongia 1999), except to note that it was refused permission to dock in the Vancouver harbor and the passengers were kept on the ship for two months. The ship was eventually escorted out of the harbor by what then constituted half the Canadian navy and, on its return to India, the passengers were met by the police as seditionists, with 20 killed, 31 imprisoned, and 27 made fugitives. The ship's arrival at Vancouver had generated a furor in the Canadian House of Commons and impelled a rapid transformation in policy on the part of the Government of India. Unable to have recourse to an explicitly racial logic, framing the responses at both sites was the appearance of a discourse of state sovereignty and, more specifically, a discourse of *national* sovereignty. For instance, in the Canadian House of Commons, Frank Oliver voiced his objection to the immigrants thus:

> This is not a labour question; it is not a racial question; it is a question of national dominance and national existence.... This [the *Komagata Maru* incident] is an organized movement for the purpose of establishing as a principle the right that the people of India, and not the people of Canada, shall have the say as to who may be accepted as citizens of Canada.[9]

R.W. Gillian, in India, took a similar position. He argued that while the Government of India's reluctance to interfere with "free" migration rested on the principle that "a British subject [had] a right to go and reside in any part of Empire," this position could not, for Gillian, be "defended on its merits, since it denies in effect the right of our Colonies and even of other countries to settle their own affairs."[10] Viceroy Hardinge echoed this theme, proclaiming: "thoughtful people will agree that states and countries have an inherent right to decide whom they will or will not admit within their borders."[11] However, such appeals to the "inherent rights" of states were not without problems, particularly in a world dominated by empire. As Gillian pointed out, "If the right of Canada or Australia to manage their own affairs is admitted, what about India? If the right is denied to her, the result is immediately to emphasize her subjection in an extremely unfortunate manner."[12] According to Gillian, the justification for such state control over migration would best be managed through a mechanism that would "secure some kind of reciprocity"[13] which, as R.E. Enthovan, another official in India put it, would "above all things... have the *appearance* of giving equal treatment to British subjects residing in all parts of the Empire."[14] State sovereignty understood in national terms would prove to be this mechanism, interweaving an exclusionary racial logic with a purportedly neutral legal logic. In other words, events such as those I have described here would provoke the novel articulation of state sovereignty and nationality, resulting in the formulation of *national sovereignty*. This articulation would do the job of "securing some kind of reciprocity," "have the appearance of giving equal treatment" to all subjects of the Empire and legitimate a state monopoly over migration in the discourse of equivalent state sovereignty and security. Indeed, the official rules that required state authorization for all "free" migrants departing from British India appeared as Defence of India (Passport) Rules, which were a subsection of the Defence of India (Criminal Law Amendment) Act of 1915. This act—that was more about the defense of a White Canada, than about the defense of India—made embarking on a journey from any port in British India without a passport a criminal offence.[15]

The solution offered by Gillian and Enthovan in India that sutured sovereignty to migration control via the mechanism of nationality—simultaneously universal and particular—was an inspired and *ad hoc* solution—a solution, moreover, that had evaded all parties to the discussion for 10 years. Indeed, Viceroy Hardinge's appeal to "thoughtful people" and the "inherent rights" of states clarifies explicitly the historically contingent, eventful nature of the relation between national sovereignty and migration control. For the "inherent rights" to which Hardinge appealed had not made themselves apparent earlier to any party to the debate for a decade. From reading much current scholarship on migration one would think that state control of migration is an inviolable and persistent feature of state sovereignty that dates not merely to Westphalia but to some even prior mythic time.[16] In examining the formation of such control, however, one finds a rather different genealogy—one that points in the direction of the piecemeal development of state control over migration that eventually culminates in nation-state monopoly over migration. Colonial relations, moreover, were central to the emergence of such new formations that radically transformed understandings of the purview of sovereignty and thus were central to the formation of what is called sovereignty *doctrine*.

CONCLUSION

I have offered this brief analysis of debates in the history of state regulation of Indian migration in an attempt to address the methodological stateism embedded in two critiques of methodological nationalism I outlined at the outset. Whereas cultural studies scholarship has largely simply ignored the state, transnational studies has reified it. As a consequence, both dehistoricize it. In order to not fall into the trap of methodological nationalism, I

Interrogating Critiques of Methodological Nationalism 211

have avoided the terminology of the transnational and deployed, instead, the formulation of the empire-state. Second, in historicizing the relations between migration, the nation and the state, I aim to address the dehistoricized understanding of the state that, despite its best intentions, underwrites transnational migration studies. As with Benedict Anderson's famous definition of the nation that, as I have argued elsewhere (Mongia 2007), relies on a fixed definition of the state and of state sovereignty, definitions of transnationalism, transnational migration and transmigrants likewise depend on certain presentist notions of the state: an independent national state, with fixed boundaries, and forms of sovereignty that delimit territory as well as populations understood in national terms. The impulse toward defining transnationalism and its cognates exists in acute tension, sometimes within the same essay (for example, Glick Schiller 1999), to historicizing it. The latter impulse poses a grave challenge to the former, as it belies the fragility and contingency of the categories deployed in definitions. It is in the nature of definitions that we explain one term by way of reference to other terms. If these other terms do not have fixed meanings and refuse to stabilize, we have a serious problem on our hands. This is the situation with which we are confronted, where definitions of transnationalism and transnational migration require that we do not overly trouble the category of the state.

What is to be done? My view is that rather than replicate the problems that have dogged attempts to define nations, nationalisms, and nation-states in general terms, we refrain from providing general definitions of the transnational. For such definitional propositions have the effect of assuming precisely what needs explanation: the nation and its cognates. Such general definitions can prove ineffective in outlining, for instance, how transnational migrants differ from migrants who have lived lives across state borders that are either imperceptible and/or are not regulated, conceived or experienced in national terms. In this way, unless we historicize the state, a methodological nationalism surreptitiously enters our analysis through the back door. One of the paradoxes of the nation form, that it is simultaneously universal and particular, has meant that it cannot be grasped "in any but particular terms" (Anderson 1996: 2). Acknowledging this, students of the nation have sought to move away from attempting generalized formulations to focus on the particulars that give flesh to the universal. In like manner, we might turn to analyses that *explicitly* attempt to grasp transnationalism in particular terms that would show how it is temporally and spatially co-dependent, though heterogeneously so, with the nation form.[17] This would enable inquiries into how mutating processes of the transnational are differentially related to mutating processes of the national, producing in the process specific state and social spatial forms. Such an endeavor would entail that we shift our focus away from transnational histories to histories of the transnational.

NOTES

1. For a discussion of how migration regimes become a centralized, federal matter, with inter-state borders the chief locus of concern, see McKeown (2008).
2. Among others, Waldinger and Fitzgerald (2004: 1189) have pointed to the anachronism embedded in the term *transnationalism* and that social identities might well not be organized in national terms. On the latter point, see also Markovits (2000).
3. For instance, in responding to Waldinger and Fitzgerald's (2004) charge of the anachronism embedded in *transnationalism,* Glick Schiller and Levitt point to the literature within transnational migration studies that documents how migrants, to the US for instance, came to identify as "nationals" from their "nation-state of origin" as a result of the discrimination they faced (2006: 7). Left uninterrogated is why and *how* racial discrimination is resolved by way of and sutured to identity conceived in national terms: the issue explored by cultural studies scholars I have briefly addressed above. Also problematic is the formulation of "nation-states of origin" (2006: 7) that assumes, rather than explains, states conceived in national terms.
4. Currently, barring *emigration* is seen as an index of a totalitarian state; barring *immigration*, common in liberal and nonliberal polities, is simply seen as the legitimate purview of the state. Quite the reverse understanding of the liberal state—as one that did not prohibit *immigration*, but might well prohibit *emigration*—prevailed in the 19th century. In other words, the characteristics of what constitutes a liberal state shift and are historically specific and malleable.
5. This is the position vigorously assumed and advanced by Hollifield (2005, 2007), a position reiterated by Portes and DeWind, who make it into a foundational, definitional matter and write, "*By definition*, states seek to regulate what takes place within their borders and what comes from outside" (2007). In this view, not only are borders natural, naturalized and static, bypassing the specificities of "what," precisely, comes from "outside"; in addition, investigations into the specificities of state forms are also rendered irrelevant, replaced with a continuist, untroubled history that traverses centuries. Aristide Zolberg (1999, 2006) also takes this position, though, by my reading, his detailed work on US migration policy and on innovations such as "remote control" (the varied practices of attempting to shape emigration in other states) points in the direction of, precisely, changes in sovereignty.
6. I leave aside here the issue of how, much like Weber's ideal types, the Westphalian *ideal* does not have rigorous empirical coordinates, a matter that is relevant not only to how we understand this ideal's relation to colonized sites but also to formations in the heart of the metropole—or to colonizing sites.
7. Secretary to the Colonial Office, London, to Law Commissioners, India, May 25, 1836, quoted in Edward Lawford, solicitor to the East India Company, to David Hill, June 12, 1838. In East India Company (1838: 2).
8. "Question whether the term 'emigrant' applies to soldiers recruited in India under agreement with the colonial secretary for service in Africa," Home Department, *Sanitary/Plague Proceedings,* no. 114–117, February 1899.
9. "Official Report of a Debate in the Canadian House of Commons on Asiatic Immigration," Department of Commerce and Industry, *Emigration Proceedings A*, no. 1, October 1914.
10. Comments of R. W. Gillian, June 23, 1914, Department of Commerce and Industry, *Emigration Proceedings A,* no. 18–20 (confidential), September 1914.

11. Comments of Lord Hardinge, Viceroy of India, July 8, 1914, Department of Commerce and Industry, *Emigration Proceedings A*, no. 18–20 (confidential), September 1914.
12. Comments of R. W. Gillian, June 23, 1914, Department of Commerce and Industry, *Emigration Proceedings A*, no. 18–20 (confidential), September 1914.
13. Comments of R. W. Gillian, June 23, 1914, Department of Commerce and Industry, *Emigration Proceedings A*, no. 18–20 (confidential), September 1914.
14. Comments of R. E. Enthoven, June 13, 1914, Department of Commerce and Industry, *Emigration Proceedings A*, no. 18–20 (confidential), September 1914 (emphasis added). NAI
15. "Compulsory Passport Regulations," Department of Commerce and Industry, *Emigration Proceedings A*, no. 8–22, June 1917.
16. An exception here is John Torpey's (2000) work. However, Torpey too does not consider the colonial genealogies at stake. Moreover, he adopts a sequential, serial approach that recounts how different European states would come to monopolize migration control and sees such trends in the colonized world as an imposition of metropolitan norms. My argument here and elsewhere (see Mongia 2005 for a direct engagement with Torpey) suggests that the colonies were not sites for either the diffusion of or deviation from metropolitan norms. They were, rather, sites crucial to the *production of norms* (see Mongia 2007 for an extended discussion of the latter point).
17. The particularity of transnational formations is *implicit* in scholarship deploying a transnational framework. Though coming from different intellectual traditions, two examples wherein the transnational is elaborated via a focus on a particular nation-state (the US and Canada, respectively) are Grewal (2005) and Goldring and Krishnamurti (2007).

REFERENCES

Anderson, B. (1991 [1983]) *Imagined Communities: Reflections on the Origin and Spread of Nationalism*, London, New York: Verso.
—— (1996) "Introduction", in G. Balakrishnan (ed) *Mapping the Nation*, London: Verso.
Appadurai, A. (1996) *Modernity at Large: Cultural Dimensions of Globalization*, Minneapolis: University of Minnesota Press.
Balibar, E. (1991) "The nation form", in E. Balibar and I. Wallerstein (eds) *Race, Nation, Class: Ambiguous Identities*, New York: Verso.
Basch, L., Glick Schiller, N. and Szanton Blanc, C. (1994) *Nations Unbound: Transnational Projects, Postcolonial Predicaments, and Deterritorialized Nation-States*, Amsterdam: Gordon and Breach.
Brenner, N. (1999) "Beyond state-centrism? Space, territoriality, and geographical scale in globalization studies", *Theory and Society*, 28: 39–78.
Brubaker, R. (1996) *Nationalism Reframed: Nationhood and the National Question in the New Europe*, Cambridge: Cambridge University Press.
Calavita, K. (1994) "U.S. immigration and policy responses: The limits of legislation", in W.A. Cornelius (ed) *Controlling Immigration: A Global Perspective*, Stanford: Stanford University Press.
Chatterjee, P. (1993 [1986]) *Nationalist Thought and the Colonial World: A Derivative Discourse?*, Minneapolis: University of Minnesota Press.
Clifford, J. (1992) "Traveling cultures," in L. Grossberg, C. Nelson and P. Triechler (eds) *Cultural Studies*, New York: Routledge.

—— (1997) *Routes: Travel and Translation in the Late Twentieth Century*, Cambridge, MA: Harvard University Press.
Department of Commerce and Industry (September 1914) *Emigration Proceedings A*, nos. 18–20 (confidential), New Delhi: National Archives of India, without pagination.
Department of Commerce and Industry (October 1914) *Emigration Proceedings A*, no. 1, New Delhi: National Archives of India, without pagination.
Department of Commerce and Industry (June 1917) *Emigration Proceedings A*, nos. 8–22, New Delhi: National Archives of India, without pagination.
Department of Home (February 1899) *Sanitary/Plague Proceedings*, nos. 114–117, New Delhi: National Archives of India, without pagination.
East India Company (1838) *Papers Respecting the East-India Labourers' Bill*, London: J. L. Cox and Sons.
Gellner, E. (1983) *Nations and Nationalism*, Ithaca, NY: Cornell University Press.
Gilroy, P. (1991 [1987]) *"There Ain't No Black in the Union Jack": The Cultural Politics of Race and Nation*, Chicago: University of Chicago Press.
—— (1993) *The Black Atlantic: Modernity and Double Consciousness*, Cambridge, MA: Harvard University Press.
Glick Schiller, N. (1999) "Transmigrants and nation-states: Something old and something new in the U.S. immigrant experience", in C. Hirschman, P. Kasinitz and J. DeWind (eds) *The Handbook of International Migration: The American Experience*, New York: Russell Sage.
—— and Levitt, P. (2006) "Haven't we heard this somewhere before? A substantive view of transnational migration studies by way of a reply to Waldinger and Fitzgerald", Working Paper 06-01, Princeton, NJ: Center for Migration and Development, Princeton University. Online: http://cmd.princeton.edu/papers/wp0601.pdf (accessed March 10, 2008).
Green, N. and Weil, F. (eds) (2007) *Citizenship and Those Who Leave: The Politics of Emigration and Expatriation*, Urbana: University of Illinois Press.
Goldring, L. and Krishnamurti, S. (eds) (2007) *Organizing the Transnational: Labour, Politics, and Social Change*, Vancouver: University of British Columbia Press.
Grewal, I. (2005) *Transnational America: Feminisms, Diasporas, Neoliberalisms*, Durham, NC: Duke University Press.
Hall, S. (1981) "Notes on deconstructing the 'popular'", in R. Samuel (ed) *People's History and Socialist Theory*, London: Routledge, Kegan Paul.
—— (1996) "Cultural identity and diaspora", in P. Mongia (ed) *Contemporary Postcolonial Theory: A Reader*, London: Arnold.
Harootunian, H. (2005) "Some thoughts on comparability and the space-time problem", *boundary 2*, 32(2): 23–52.
Hobsbawm, E. (1990) *Nations and Nationalism since 1780: Programme, Myth, Reality*, Cambridge: Cambridge University Press.
Hollifield, J. (2005) "The emerging migration state", in I. Toshio and I. Masako (eds) *Motion in Place/Place in Motion* (JCAS Symposium Series, 22), Osaka: The Japan Center for Area Studies.
—— (2007) "The emerging migration state", in A. Portes and J. DeWind (eds) *Rethinking Migration: New Theoretical and Empirical Perspectives*, New York, Oxford: Berghahn Books.
Iriye, A. and Saunier, P.-Y. (eds) (2009) *The Palgrave Dictionary of Transnational History*, Basingstoke: Palgrave Macmillan.
Johnston, H. (1979) *The Voyage of the Komagata Maru: The Sikh Challenge to Canada's Colour Bar*, New Delhi: Oxford University Press.

Levitt, P. and Glick Schiller, N. (2004) "Transnational perspectives on migration: Conceptualizing simultaneity", *International Migration Review*, 38(3): 1002–40.

Lowe, L. (1996) *Immigrant Acts: On Asian American Cultural Politics*, Durham, NC: Duke University Press.

McKeown, A. (2008) *Melancholy Order: Asian Migration and the Globalization of Borders*, New York: Columbia University Press.

Markovits, C. (2000) *The Global World of Indian Merchants, 1750–1947: Traders of Sind from Bukhara to Panama*, Cambridge: Cambridge University Press.

Mongia, R. (1999) "Race, nationality, mobility: A history of the passport", *Public Culture*, 11(3): 527–56.

——— (2005) "Abolition and 'free' migration: On historicity and Eurocentricity in migration studies", in I. Toshio and I. Masako (eds) *Motion in Place/Place in Motion* (JCAS Symposium Series, 22), Osaka: The Japan Center for Area Studies.

——— (2007) "Historicizing state sovereignty: Inequality and the form of equivalence", *Comparative Studies in Society and History*, 49(2): 384–411.

Portes, A. and DeWind, J. (2007) "A cross-Atlantic dialogue: The progress of research and theory in the study of international migration," in A. Portes and J. DeWind (eds) *Rethinking Migration: New Theoretical and Empirical Perspectives*, New York, Oxford: Berghahn Books.

Portes, A., Guarnizo, L.E. and Landolt, P. (1999) "The study of transnationalism: Pitfalls and promise of an emergent research field", *Ethnic and Racial Studies*, 22(2): 217–37.

Pratt, G. and Yeoh, B. (2003) "Transnational (counter) topographies", *Gender, Place, and Culture*, 10(2): 159–66.

Salter, M.B. (2003) *Rights of Passage: The Passport in International Relations*, Boulder, CO: Lynne Rienner.

Sewell Jr., W.H. (1996) "Three temporalities: Toward an eventful sociology," in T. McDonald (ed) *The Historic Turn in the Human Sciences*, Ann Arbor: University of Michigan Press.

Smith, A.D. (1986) *The Ethnic Origins of Nations*, Oxford: Blackwell.

Torpey, J. (2000) *The Invention of the Passport: Surveillance, Citizenship and the State*, Cambridge: Cambridge University Press.

Waldinger, R. and Fitzgerald, D. (2004) "Transnationalism in question", *American Journal of Sociology*, 109(5): 1177–95.

Zolberg, A. (1999) "Matters of state: Theorizing immigration policy", in C. Hirschman, P. Kasinitz and J. DeWind (eds) *The Handbook of International Migration: The American Experience*, New York: Russell Sage.

——— (2006) *A Nation By Design: Immigration Policy in the Fashioning of America*, Cambridge, MA: Harvard University Press; New York: Russell Sage Foundation.

Part IV
Conclusions

11 Transnational Social Spaces
Between Methodological Nationalism and Cosmo-Globalism

Ludger Pries and Martin Seeliger

It is not only among sociologists that can reference to the so-called spatial turn (Warf and Arias 2008) be encountered. Taking a closer look at the adaptation of the ongoing debate about *the spatial* in the context of current academic debates about the phenomena of progressing internationalization, we find that (not only) social science has been set on the issue of *transnationalism*. Here, the reconfiguration of social processes and structures in relation to spatial orders takes an especially distinctive shape. Trying to evaluate the scientific achievements gained by transnational studies, we can identify a central innovation: in contrast to general studies on globalization, transnational research conceptualizes geographical and social space as not necessarily bound to the "container" of the nation-state. It seems clear that the critique of methodological nationalism (Wimmer and Glick Schiller 2002) can unquestionably be regarded as a crucial advance and argument against the dominant approaches and methodology of international studies. On the other hand, there also remains the danger of throwing out the baby with the bathwater, through underestimating the still very strong weight of nation-states and the national level of analysis or even dissolving the geographic-spatial bonding of the social into the air of deterritorialization, spaces of flows and global cosmopolitanism.

By proposing a differentiation between three streams of literature, each one establishing a specific perspective on the nation-state within the context of internationalization, the argument presented here pursues a goal of systematization. In our view, a more adequate approach has to explicitly reflect on concepts of space and to navigate between the Scylla of methodological nationalism and the Charybdis of globalism (Pries 2008). In the first section we give an overview about contemporary positions shaping the landscape of the study of cross-border phenomena. Subsequent to this, we present a particular understanding of space which we find useful for analyzing structures and processes of internationalization. Finally, to contribute to the systematization of the field, we combine the above-mentioned differentiation between the three types of international research with a perspective on three epistemological dimensions.

GLOBALIZATION, METHODOLOGICAL NATIONALISM AND ITS CRITIQUE

When looking at the developmental path humanity has proceeded on over the course of history, we find that the first roots of *homo sapiens* can be traced back to a nomadic existence beginning 400,000 years ago that makes up the largest portion of human history. The first stages of sedentary life, as the second longest period of the spatial organization of human society, began approximately 30,000 years ago. If we consider the comparatively short history of the nation-state, reaching back to the late 18th century, we can now stress this relativization somewhat further, pointing out the seemingly ridiculous value that living together in national societies would represent on a strictly temporal scale. As can be encountered in current discussions, the development of nation-states as (one of) the structural features of modernity is increasingly being challenged more and more.

Society and the Nation-State

In the course of the 20th century, the term *society* gained its scientific meaning as the unit of analysis for phenomena like social inequality, demographic change or societal integration, intrinsically tied to a certain understanding of the territory to which this specific spatial extension would refer. As has been shown by various scholars reflecting on this development (Anderson 1983), the dominant mode of conceptualizing the spatial was the nation-state. From a social science perspective, nation-states can be viewed as a continuum of four major aspects, which can be differentiated in an ideal-typical manner. First, the nation-state comprehends a certain fixed territory, governed by a sovereign state with the monopoly of legitimate power. A second shared reference point for citizens and inhabitants is a common or dominant language spoken within this territory. Moreover, nation-states are integrated by a shared understanding of a common history, often closely related to a certain (imagined) ethnic background(s). Finally, a particular national culture is constituted by a specific set of values, traditions and significant symbols.

At the same time, these developments can be viewed from the perspective of the current debate on globalization. Viewed from a historical perspective, the genesis of the nation-state as a concept of social order is rooted in two political agreements: the Peace of Augsburg of 1555 and the *Pax Westfalica* of 1648. Here, the principle of *cuius region eius religio* stated that the population of a certain geographical territory had to practice a fixed religious orientation, according to the rule of the political leader. This principle of societal order led to an *exclusive and mutual embeddedness of social and territorial space*, which is explicated below. Starting from the center of Europe, the concept of nation-states as a major principle of societal order spread all across the globe (Sassen 2006). As the climax of this

Westphalian Order, Hobsbawm (1996) describes the "short 20th century" as organized according to the guiding principle of culturally more or less homogenous societies, embedded in significantly nation-state-bound "containers." According to this idea, within a geographically coherent territory there is only "space" for one social space, and each social space requires exactly one geographic space. The approach of methodological nationalism states that "coexistence amongst people and processes of socialization became more and more tied, in reciprocal exclusiveness, to more or less clearly definable and known geographic spheres. A defined space extending over a geographic area (a 'territory' or 'locale') corresponded to one and only one socially compressed space (for example, a community or a national society). Conversely, every social space 'occupied' precisely one geographically specific space" (Pries 2001b: 15).

Especially since the second half of the 20th century a general agreement has been reached that ongoing processes of internationalization and globalization are of increasing importance. Giddens defines globalization as "a worldwide social relationship which links distinct localities in such a way that local happenings are shaped by events occurring miles away and vice versa" (1990: 64). But even before the debate over increasing international activities that led to the intense discussions of the 1980s and 1990s, at least three branches of scientists approaching cross-border-phenomena can be identified. While a first branch, world civilization theorists such as Toynbee (1934–1954) and Lewis and Wigen (1997), pursued the project of a world historical analysis, a second stream of literature dealt with the (post) colonial order of the international world system (Wallerstein 1979). A third body of writing, which can be combined under the term *world society theories*, has developed a more abstract perspective on comprehensive social relationships. These relationships are seen as being detached from their territorial bounds through the development of new technologies of communication and transportation (Luhman 1984; Gregory and Urry 1985).

While the spatial dimensions of shifting cross-border relationships have not been the central point of reference, spatial phenomena have gained significance in the course of the debate which has been ongoing since the last decade of the 20th century. Without going into greater detail, we can distinguish between two branches of scientific discussion. Whereas the first one takes a position (also reflected in the above quote by Anthony Giddens) that social relations encounter a massive expansion in the course of globalization, the second stream of literature pushes this point even further, leading to the view that geographical space is subsumed under the new range of social relations: "Globalisation—refers both to the compression of the world and the intensification of consciousness of the world as a whole" (Robertson 1992: 8). While the pioneering character of the research forbids heaping fundamental criticism on contemporary scholars, it has to be acknowledged that along with further research on phenomena of globalization, the need to differentiate between various forms of internationalization has become more apparent. In the following subsections we will propose an approach to systematize this discussion, first turning to a position crucial for understanding problematic basic assumptions that are, at least to some extent, implied in the vast majority of previous and contemporary social research on internationalization.

Epistemological Challenges—Methodological Nationalism and Beyond

In the course of their reflections on implications unfolding within the epistemological foundations of past and contemporary (social) science, Wimmer and Glick Schiller developed the critique of methodological nationalism "understood as the assumption that the nation/state/society is the natural social and political form of the modern world" (2002: 301). With a particular focus on migration research, the authors' main criticism points at the concept of the nation-state as the key unit of reference for social scientists' analyses. As they further state, the perspective of methodological nationalism treats the nation-state or national society as the taken-for-granted unit of reference for social research. At the same time, processes taking place *beyond* the national container are conceptualized in a way that could be described as "analytically detached" from the nation-state as a unit of reference. "The social sciences have become obsessed with describing processes within nation-state boundaries as contrasted with those outside, and have correspondingly lost sight of the connections between such nationally defined territories" (Wimmer and Glick Schiller 2002: 307).

To understand sociology's lack of awareness and/or willingness to develop a reflexive attitude toward its own, often implicit premises, one has to take into account the specific connection of the subject's genesis and development. Here, the context of the formation of modernity as a complex of enlightenment, with shifting patterns of lifestyles, norms and values, and political restructuring, holds crucial significance for bringing about the organization of social life within nationally segmented spaces. Along with this has come the development of specific national scientific cultures, with a significant number of opportunities to interconnect (via the internet, international conferences, etc.), with nationally oriented scholars.[1] As the core assumption, constituting the epistemological basis, the above-mentioned idea of a reciprocal exclusiveness of geographic and social spaces can be identified.[2] From this point of view, every social space occupies precisely one particular geographical space. If we take this point seriously then social configurations (Elias 2004) such as families, daily life within local communities, enterprises or soccer fan clubs are not supposed to be distributed over several geographic spaces, but located in just one coherent locale or territory. Accordingly, in one geographic space conceptualized as a "socially occupied territory" there is room for one *and only one* corresponding social space.[3] The close interconnectedness between the social realities of modern societies and their idealistic reflection within the social sciences now culminates in the paradigm of methodological nationalism as the dominant societal project during the course of the 18th to 20th centuries, still revealing a decisive impact in a world with increasingly shifting patterns of nation-state significance. Thus, as will be shown below, for the 21st century it seems far from adequate to treat nation-state/national society as a crucial unit of reference seems far from completely adequate unless embedded in a differentiated framework of relations between social and geographic spaces. In the next section, we will develop our own proposal to systematically conceptualize the constantly shifting, overlapping and often contradictory processes of internationalization.

Critiques of Methodological Nationalism

Two basic lines of critique of methodological nationalism can be distinguished: transnationalism and what can be called *cosmo-globalism*. Repeating the critique of methodological nationalism some scholars argue that the world more and more is increasingly becoming a global social unit where cosmopolitanism is the most appropriate approach for scientists and for citizens in general. Viewed from this perspective, developments that are usually mentioned as causing progressing globalization have increasingly led to a framework in which nation-states do not serve as unquestionable frames of reference for global inequalities. Taking up the traditional Kantian idea of world citizenship, in this sub-branch of internationalization theory the development of a new collective sense of identity emerging in the course of progressive globalization is emphasized (Beck 2004, 2008).

Despite numerous signs of the erosion of the nation-state-based paradigm, we can still identify many specific references to concrete localities in the case of social structures, as well as in daily phenomena such as locally bound families, working arrangements, languages, social networks and national or regional identities, all of which contribute to providing social order through subjective structures of belonging. Even in the case of world travellers (scientists, intellectuals or managers) (Calhoun 2003), it still sounds like an exaggeration to state that national (and other types of local-spatial) references are losing significance. While methodological nationalism as the (former) basis of sociological analysis can no longer meet the requirements of the increasing complexity of social organization, it seems crucial, also, not to go to the other extreme and let go of the nation-state as an important unit of sociological analysis, by proclaiming a new cosmopolitan world society. Transnationalism could be a strong research agenda *in between* the extremes of methodological nationalism and cosmo-globalism.

One strategy to overcome methodological nationalism is its focus on cities and on *rescaling* social relations and power structures within and between cities (see Glick Schiller, Chapter 2 of this volume). Sassen's pioneering work on this issue dates back to 1991. Marcus (1995) has proposed a methodology for tracing cross-border phenomena by following people, things, metaphors, stories, biographies and conflicts. In political science, a multi-level approach including local, national and supranational stages has been developed, mainly in European studies (Kohler-Koch and Eising 1999; recently Kohler-Koch and Larat 2009). There are promising current attempts to systematically integrate a perspective of international relations studies (Faist and Ette 2007; Quack and Djelic 2010). A general pleading and several proposals for combining the levels of analysis of the city, the nation-state and the international system have been present since the early 1990s. Even earlier there were proposals to combine the analysis of nonurban localities or locales, which are far away from mega-cities but are included in transnational social configurations (Kearney and Nagengast 1989). Another branch of transnational studies deals with analyzing the role of international businesses. The logics of transnational value chains and capital strategies are very complex, and include organizational culture, power relations and strategies, as well as national institutional settings of incentives and restrictions (far beyond social policy aspects) and also local (rural and urban) conditions and embeddedness (Pries and Dehnen 2009).

A crucial aspect of more recent transnational studies refers to aspects of power. Highlighting and questioning societal relations of dominance and inequality has been an important task in transnationalism research ever since (for example, Goldring 1997). The debate on transnational reproduction work can be named as an example of reflections about power relations, shaping the daily life-worlds of not only the households that demand (e.g. home help and the (mostly female) workers), but in a lot of cases also directly affecting the workers' families in the countries of origin (for example, Ehrenreich and Hochschild 2002; Lutz 2008). A stream of literature systematically sheds light on labor regulations within the context of internationally operating enterprises. Here, recent findings point to the fact that negotiations of European Works Councils in automobile companies show transnational features (Hertwig *et al.* 2009; Hauser-Ditz *et al.* 2010). Finally, during the last few years theoretical and empirical contributions to the increasingly popular debate about transnational inequalities have developed (Berger and Weiß 2008; Bayer *et al.* 2008). Although the spatial turn and multi-level concepts of transnational analysis have flourished during the last two decades, there are few explicit reflections on concepts of space. In the following section, a multidimensional and integrative approach to space will be presented.

THE CONCEPT OF SPACE IN SOCIAL SCIENCE

In (social) science as well as for actors in their daily life-worlds, space is used as a concept to subjectively perceive and structure the social and material environment. Not only does every society constitute specific conceptions of space according to their contemporary needs and beliefs, and in connection to their specific modes of (re)production, leisure and everyday practices, but the very same processes take place on an individual level, by actors subjectively conceptualizing the world that surrounds them. In an early and comprehensive description, Georg Simmel (1903) pointed out the social quality of geographic space (geo-space), distinguishing five basic qualities:

1) While on the one hand geo-space stands out by establishing a potential exclusiveness for some social relations, it maintains permeability for other social relations; for example, in a university building there should be no military training, professional car trading or religious missionaries, but there could be students falling in love.
2) At the same time, geo-space is also marked and structured by certain limitations and borders. Although constructed socially, geo-spaces are characterized by confines, demarcations and other constraints of social actions and relations.
3) Geo-space has the quality of fixing, freezing and localizing social relations that cannot exist outside. It is difficult to imagine a love relationship that exists exclusively in cyberspace—and even in such a case cyberspace would be "frozen" in geo-spaces like keyboards, screens, internet cables and so on.
4) Geo-space thus has an impact on the quality of social relations; it is easier to intensively pray in a church than in a party-room.
5) Finally, space comprises, enables and limits positive, functional or centripetal forces of spatial mobility relevant for individuals or social groups. A gated community surrounded by walls, electronic fences or even armed guards offers a certain stability of social relations for the inhabitants, and marks the exclusion of others.

Against the background of Simmels's broad and comprehensive understanding of space as a physical *and* social phenomenon, we can look at the various conceptions of space that have been historic proposed to find a range of different approaches. Two opposing paradigmatic perspectives can be distinguished throughout almost all scientific disciplines (Gosztonyi 1976): a substantial and a relational approach to space. The physical–mathematical concept of space as an absolute container that is infinite, homogeneous, empty and independent of the presence of any objects was a significant precondition for classical mechanics as developed by Isaac Newton. From this substantial perspective, space is seen as merely existing by itself as a container, which maintains its qualities without relation to other objects. Famously representing such a substantial concept of space are such figures as Galileo, Copernicus, Kepler, Newton and Ptolemy. On the other hand, Gottfried Wilhelm von Leibniz developed a theory opposing Newton's concept of space. Leibniz felt that space possesses no existential qualities of its own whatsoever, but is rather a relational configuration of material objects.

This opposition of substantial views (space as an absolute unit with its own characteristics and qualities) and relational concepts (space as a configuration of density, distances, clustering, distribution and so on of things) has continued to pervade all scientific reflections about space for centuries (Gregory and Urry 1985).

In physics, Einstein's theory of relativity and of a relational time–space concept went directly against Newton's model. Einstein criticized the absolutist container concept of space as a "reality as if it were superior to the material world" (Einstein 1960: xiii). Although it is now commonly accepted that Einstein was right, for the vast majority of everyday problems Newtonian mechanics and the corresponding substantial idea of space is sufficient (for example, the concept of gravity). Similar to physics, in social sciences a general theory of space has to include the interrelation of space, time and things. There is not the "space" here for extensive discussion on this topic, but it is worthwhile to summarize that substantial and relational approaches to space are common in almost all sciences. They should not be treated as an either-or but rather an as-well-as couple; both approaches can be useful for certain ends.

This also holds for social sciences and social spaces. For the matter of this chapter it might be sufficient to define *social space* as the triad of social practices, symbols and artifacts (where artifacts are understood as material things made or appropriated by actors). As outlined above, the position of methodological nationalism can be allocated in this context. If, firstly, one geographic space *contains one* (and only one!) social space and secondly, each social space requires one (and only one!) geo-space, then the underlying idea implies an understanding of space as passively framing social actions without being subject to social constructions and negotiations. Against such a substantial understanding of social spaces (ordered in concentric circles from the household outward to the local community, then to national societies and finally to the world system) a relational perspective can be found, for example, in the work of Bourdieu (1985), whose sociological writings deal with the relational positioning of individuals and classes within a multidimensional social space. Such a relational perspective defines *space* as a set of relations between social positions structuring actors' activities. A characteristic of such a relational concept of space lies in the idea that social relations are not framed within a specific territorial container or set of limitations, but rather social space itself is seen as a framework of positional relations of socially relevant elements constituting clusters and concentrations (of material and social resources, symbols and meanings, and social practices). In general terms, during the last two decades relational approaches have gained influence; meanwhile, substantial concepts of space have often been seen as out of fashion.

Our basic argument is that neither a substantial nor a relational approach is sufficient on its own, but that substantial and relational perspectives of space as well as social and geo-spaces *have to be combined*. An early reference to the necessity of such an integrative understanding of what can be called the "spatial spanning of the social" can be found in the work of Gregory and Urry, who argue against a misleading "division of work" between sociologists and geographers: According to them, spatial structure should be "seen not merely as an arena in which social life unfolds, but rather as a medium through which social relations are produced and reproduced" (Gregory and Urry 1985: 3).

Substantial and Relational Approaches to Space

Starting from a general understanding of space as a structured positional relation of elements (Pries 2001a), we take the differentiation between substantial and relational concepts of social and geographic spaces as a starting point in order to develop an integrative approach (Table 11.1). Social spaces or socio-spaces can be considered as human-life relations with three different dimensions.[4] Firstly, we understand *social practice* as the examination and interrelation of actors with other actors, with nature and with oneself which takes place in a situation that is taken for granted or "socio-naturally given." *Significant symbols* constitute the second component of social spaces. As complex and interrelated signs for and within a certain context, symbols are used to frame certain situations with their meanings, while at the same time being subject to constant (re-)construction and negotiation (Blumer 1969). Thirdly, social space derives from the existence and use of *artifacts*, understood as objectified results of human appropriation and action. The ideal-typical character of this threefold differentiation can be easily pointed out by referring to the example of the red card in a soccer game, which has to physically exist in the first place (artifact), be pulled by the referee (social practice), and be understood according to its specific punitive connotation (symbol). It seems noteworthy that the relation between geo-space and socio-space remains an analytical one: Since society and territory are bound together in a genuinely dialectical relationship, there can neither be social phenomena without a spatial dimension, nor spatial phenomena without a social dimension.[5] Nevertheless, differentiating socio- and geo-spaces analytically helps to clarify and explain the ongoing restructuring of the spatial patterns of the social as exemplified in Table 11.1.

Table 11.1 An Integrative Typology of Approaches to Socio-geo-spaces (source: authors)

Social Space \ Geographic Space	Substantial	Relational
Substantial	National society in national territory/ World society on the globe	Diaspora
Relational	Multicultural society/ Social diversity in one place	Transnational social spaces

Analytically substantial and relational socio- and geo-spaces helps to distinguish different types of socio-geo-spaces. In this way, the model of a national society in a nation-state territory reflects a substantial understanding of geo-space and of socio-space. There is a substantial social entity characterized as a homogenous socio-space embedded in one clearly identifiable geo-space.[6] In the case of a *diaspora*, there is the idea of a unifying substantial socio-space (for example, a common religion or shared ethno-cultural constituent) which is spread over different locales as a relational geo-space. A relational concept of socio-space is combined with a substantial understanding of geo-space that leads to the model of a multicultural society or to socio-cultural diversity in the same geo-space. Finally, linking relational socio- and geo-spaces allows transnational social spaces to appear as multilayered, constantly reconstructed social practices, symbols and artifacts existing in a relational network of pluri-local geo-spaces. This leads to a typology of internationalization processes, which will be presented in the next section.

IDEAL TYPES OF SOCIO-GEO-SPACES

As pointed out above, references to *globalization* often come along with a certain blurry character, making the expression seem like a nonspecific catch-all term, signifying a lot of different, often incongruent or even contradictory things. Therefore, we would like to propose a typology of different forms of internationalization to illustrate the complex and dynamic character of the most important combinations of socio-geo-spaces. Generally it can be stated that internationalization has to be conceptualized as a process which includes economic, social, political, cultural, technological and ecological dimensions. As such, internationalization is not only a multidimensional process in terms of the concrete subject of internationally emerging phenomena. Additionally, the shape of cross-border activities themselves can vary from, for example, international student-exchange programs between France and the Netherlands to globally perceived threats, such as current characterizations of climate change or Al-Qaida terrorism. As proposed in greater detail by Pries (2008), a typology of seven different forms of internationalization can serve as a contribution to a systematic perspective, opposing the current tendency to interchangeably use genuinely precise expressions like *globalization, internationalization* or *transnationalization*. Four of these ideal-types correlate to a substantial understanding and the other three are based on a relational understanding of space.

Four Internationalization Patterns Based on a Substantial Concept of Space

First—and distinct from the conception of internationalization that generally includes *all* cross-border phenomena—we would like to propose the term *inter-nationalization* (with hyphen) to refer to relations and interactions between nation-states and national societies. Inter-nationalization in obviously is based on a substantial model of space, as in methodological nationalism. Nation-states are the basic unit of reference and inter-nationalization refers to the intensification of relations between them.

Second, the term *supra-nationalization* describes the emergence of political governance structures—like the European Union (*EU*)—which operate above the level of nation-states and below the level of the entire globe. Supra-nationalization can be thought of as lifting the substantial concept of space from methodological nationalism and extending it toward the macro-regional level, where the same principles, such as an imagined community in a demarcated geographic space, are at play. Supra-nationalization in this sense leads to definable specific geographic areas of sovereignty (like the Schengen Area for the free mobility of people or the Eurozone).

Third, the term *globalization* refers to the worldwide span of cross-border transactions, communications, social practices and symbols, as well as to the worldwide perception and awareness of problems, risks, rights and incidences. Keeping in mind the fundamental claims made with regard to varying concepts of space, globalization does not overcome the substantial notion of space of methodological nationalism, but (mostly implicitly) extends it to the world level. While the processes described comprise phenomena located beyond the single nation-state container, the substantial concept that assigns one social space (for example, humankind, human rights, cosmopolitanism) to one specific geographic space (the globe as a whole) remains unchallenged.

Fourth, an—at first sight—contradictory pattern of reaction to increasing cross-border activities can be found in *re-nationalization*: a development that constitutes a certain kind of contra-tendency to the aforementioned process of inter-nationalization, supra-nationalization and globalization. Strengthening of existing national boundaries (for example, by nationalist or racist movements) or dividing formerly more or less homogeneous socio-geo-spaces (like Yugoslavia or the USSR) into various new socio-geo-spatial entities, or social forces claiming their own geographic space and territories can thus be understood as re-nationalization.

Three Internationalization Patterns Based on a Relational Concept of Space

In contrast to the aforementioned patterns, the following three ideal-types of internationalization are based on a relational understanding of space. The asynchronic notion of cross-border phenomena becomes apparent in the tendencies of the fifth case—*glocalization*. Here, the dialectics between a global and local level of social space becomes apparent. Global tendencies and processes are related to and interconnected with local concentrations of power, technology, knowledge, money and other resources and occurrences.

And conversely, trends and challenges at a global geo-space level (like global warming) can be traced back to very specific local social practices (driving in cities with six- or eight-cylinder cars), symbols (commercial lighting in Tokyo, air conditioning in poor countries) and artifacts (energy-consuming skyscrapers in New York, assets for coal mining and oil production).

A sixth type of internationalization comes into play through the existence of a shared social space that spreads over different geo-spaces and boundaries of civilizations or nations. The shared socio-space is integrated or constituted mainly by reference to a common "motherland," as in the case of the relationship between Jewish communities all around the globe and the state of Israel. We call this type of internationalization *diaspora-internationalization*.

Finally, with the (seventh) concept—*transnationalization*—we turn to possibly the most enigmatic bundle of processes discussed in the literature of the past twenty years. Basically, the discussion of transnational phenomena draws on the quantitatively and qualitatively growing importance of pluri-local and transnational social relations, networks and practices. Accordingly, transnationalization indicates the emergence of pluri-local socio-spaces that extend above and between the traditional container spaces of the concentric circles of local, regional, national, supra-national and global phenomena. Transnationalization is thus based on a relational socio-geo-space and not on a container space with its mutual and exclusive embeddedness of social space and geographic space. We can therefore define *transnational social spaces* as pluri-local frames of reference that structure everyday practices, social positions, biographical employment projects and human identities, while simultaneously existing above and beyond the social contexts of national societies.

Based on these ideal-types of internationalization, transnational phenomena in the narrow sense can be seperated with regard to their varying degrees of duration, density and institutionalization into transnational social relations, transnational social fields and networks and transnational social spaces. Transnational social spaces then are pluri-local nation-states spanning social configurations composed of genuine social practices, significant symbols and artifacts with relatively high density and stability in comparison to "simple" social relations (for example, social encounters based on touristic travel) and fields (for example, cross-border work relations in an international company). The multidimensional context in which the three components (social practices, significant symbols and artifacts) gain their specific meaning is pointed out by Basch *et al.* (1994), who describe the process of the semantic construction of artifacts within a transnational social space between Haiti and the United States:

> If someone sends a barbecue grill home to Port-au-Prince, the grill does not stand in and of itself as an item of material culture reflecting and producing hybrid cultural constructions. The grill is a statement about social success in the United States and an effort to build and advance social position in Haiti. (Basch *et al.* 1994: 28).

As in the case of transnational social spaces, transnational relations and transnational fields need to be looked at with regard to their social and geographical references. In the next section, we will summarize the findings and concepts introduced so far, presenting them within the outlines of a systematic research agenda that focuses on cross-border phenomena.

CROSS-NATIONAL, WORLD SYSTEM AND TRANSNATIONALIZATION RESEARCH

As shown above and as already noted by Sassen (2001: 189) the analysis of cross-border phenomena "requires multi-sited research rather than simply comparative studies." But does this mean that international comparison is no longer important? Should and could transnationalism research be included simply in world system or global studies? Is a cosmopolitan perspective on cross-border phenomena sufficient? As in the case of the relation between socio-spaces and geo-spaces and between substantial and relational approaches, the basic argument here is that it is not an either/or but that the different traditions of international studies all have strengths and weaknesses. Their specific differences can be appreciated by taking a closer look at the units of analysis, the units of reference and the units of measurement in each of the cases (see Table 11.2). First, the theoretical–analytical entity, about which a scientific statement is made, can be coined as the specific *unit of analysis*. Furthermore, the *unit of measurement* can be understood as the unit to which the collection of empirical data or theoretical reasoning is related. The specific *unit of reference* finally signifies the particular socio-spatial-temporal entity to which scientific research and statements are referring.

Within the literature introduced above, one can find at least three general orientations (Kohn 1987). A first branch of literature aims at the comparison of specific national settings in the tradition of *cross-national or international comparison*. Studies from comparative political economy or social policy analysis especially, such as Hall and Soskice (2001) or Esping-Andersen (2002), view the specifics of a national settings in orderto finally position the specifics in systematic relation to each other. In conceptualizing such research, three central problems can be noted:

- First, the famous objection of John Goldthorpe (1997) comes into play that the small number of cases forbids the application of the variables necessary to model the complex functional logic.
- A second problem arising in the context of cross-national comparisons is the cultural influence on the research perspective, which derives from the specific situation and origin of the scholar(s) establishing it.
- Finally, there is a paradox which in literature often is described under the label of the Galton problem.

When doing international comparison, (national) "societies" and "cultures" are presupposed as taken-for-granted coherent units and particular objects that can be distinguished one from another. Only under this condition of separate, discrete and independent entities can these units be compared according to their similarities and differences. But in societal reality, these entities of comparison—institutional arrangements, societies or cultures—have to be considered as mutually influencing and forging. India and the UK (Mexico and Spain, Germany and China, Japan and the USA) cannot be compared as completely independent units of analysis, because they have forged each other in multiple ways (by colonialism and imperialism, by cultural exchange and learning, by partial transfer of institutions and so on). Therefore, a particular phenomenon to be compared (like citizenship concepts, education system and vocational training, production systems, labor regulation) could be understood either as originating from the isolated development path of the countries compared or as a result of processes of learning, diffusion or domination.

A second stream of literature can be identified as world systems approaches, such as the work of Wallerstein (1979). Here, the focus is on the interdependence of macro-regional relations of dominance, based on economic and political power, inscribed in the modern capitalist world system. This world system is structured in centric and peripheral areas that are functionally intertwined. A similar approach can be found in the writings of Manuel Castells (1996, 1998). At least two points of critique need to be addressed in this context: In analytically homogenizing national conditions when referring to the relation of specific countries in the context of a world system, this kind of research gets—once again—caught in the trap of methodological nationalism. The vast differences between East and West Germany, persisting even more than 20 years after reunification, illustrate this more than adequately. A second critique traditionally directed toward world systems theory refers to its functionalist and often economist bias. As the world is considered an integrated clockwork, all regions and locales are assumed to fit in one and just one functional and hierarchical position. On the contrary symbolic interactionism (in our view: plausibly) holds that the meaning of socially relevant factors is negotiated in the process of interaction itself—there is no "objective position" from which to divide and structure the world.

Meanwhile, cross-national comparison sticks to the basic assumptions of methodological nationalism, and world systems analysis can be related to the assumptions of cosmo-globalism. Transnationalism can be characterized as a third and distinctive branch of international research. Transnational studies deal with social cross-border phenomena, standing out through their pluri-local spanning without having a clear center around one particular focal point (as in the case of diasporas, but existing in a more decentered manner). While a lot of research of this type deals with migration topics, it is also applied to phenomena such as transnational social movements, companies, environmental risks or pop culture.

As can be derived from Table 11.2, cross-national comparison, world system research and transnational studies mainly differ with relation to their corresponding *units of reference*. Meanwhile, the units of analysis and the units of measurement are substantially the same (although there are some elective affinities between types of international research and preferred units of analysis and measurement). In the case of transnational studies, the units of reference (for example, transnational migrants' socio-spaces between locales in different countries of the EU or between locales in Germany, in Turkey, in Iran and Iraq) cannot be considered as taken for granted. *Apparently* in the case of cross-national comparison and of world systems research, the corresponding units of reference are given "by nature": the nation-state/national society and the world as a whole.

On closer inspection and based on the critiques of methodological nationalism and of cosmo-globalism, in each of the three types of international research an explicit reflection on the most adequate units of reference is needed. And again, for analyzing certain socially relevant phenomena, often a mix of these three streams of international studies is useful. Therefore, transnational studies should not be blamed for not integrating all of the aspects normally focused in world systems or global-value-chain research. The strengths of cross-national comparison lie in its focus on national institutional settings (of values and culture, legal norms and polities, actor constellations and conflict-solving mechanisms and so on) and the ability to control systematically for the influence of this kind of institutional embeddedness. The strengths of world system research are based on a holistic view of history, economy, power relations and value-chains. Transnational studies are definitely strong in looking at social relations above and beyond the classic formal units of reference (national societies and the world system).

What can be learned from the threefold perspective established in this chapter is that the three streams of literature each provide a particular

Table 11.2 Three Types of International Research (source: authors)

	Cross-National Comparison	World Systems Research	Transnational Studies
Units of Reference	Nation states/ National societies	World system, entire globe	Border-crossing pluri-local socio-spaces
Dominant Units of Analysis	Social classes, values, institutions, identity	Center-periphery structures of social classes, values, etc.	Biographies, families, organizations, institutions, identity
Dominant Units of Measurement	Individuals, households, rituals, texts, practices	Flows of goods and information, organizations	Individuals, households, rituals, flows of goods, etc.

perspective on phenomena of modern society. It is noteworthy that the international constellation develops more and more intensified interrelations between social spaces within nationally bound territories. As also underlined by Quack (2006: 65), the comparison of seemingly unconnected development paths of nation-states neglects the role of transfers and interactions conducted within a cross-border constellation.

However, it would be fatal to reduce the nation-state to the idea of a "useful illusion," as put forward by Schroer (2006: 179). The numerous examples of explicitly nationally bound policies and polities, like welfare or subvention regimes, immigration laws or other legislative rules, show that nation-states as political actors within a specific geographical territory are relevant on more than just an illusionary or imagined basis. Therefore, a fundamental critique of methodological nationalism seems more than exaggerated. Against the background of persisting inequalities, which shape relationships among and between inhabitants of the "Western" nations and the countries of the "Global South" (Webster *et al.* 2008), approaches from the branch of world system research can serve as a crucial contribution to developing a reflexive position.

CONCLUSIONS

Subsequent to an overview about contemporary approaches to the study of international phenomena, we have highlighted the specific epistemological challenges between methodological nationalism and cosmo-globalism. It should be pointed out that the critique of methodological nationalism *alone* does not meet the requirements brought about by the agenda of international research. It has been argued that methodological nationalism cannot simply be overcome by cosmo-globalism swinging from one extreme to the other. This is due to the fact that the world is not simply becoming more and more globalized, but that *local, regional, national, supranational* and *global* relations are intertwined with *glocal, diaspora* and *transnational* interactions. A significant national shaping power persists, unfolding its impact for instance in the case of international power plays, in nationally implemented social policies or immigration laws. As long as these phenomena differ between various states (and there is no signal that these will merge into one homogeneous world system or converge in all relevant aspects), there will also be a necessity for cross-national comparisons, based on the conceptual perspective of an "enlightened methodological nationalism" that explicitly reflects on the nation-state-bound national society as one possible and under certain circumstances valuable unit of reference. After having established some general reflections on the concept of space within social sciences, the specific understanding of space should enable scholars to systematically understand the multi-sited spatial spanning of the social in the course of globalization. Finally, three types of international studies were distinguished, which complementarily constitute the scientific reference points of a research agenda, able to analyze phenomena of internationalization in their stunning variety.

Concerning the project of establishing, reflecting and improving transnational studies as a specific branch of research, four future tasks and challenges can be identified.

First, it seems crucial for development of transnational studies to further shape and specify appropriate units of analysis for transnational phenomena (where topics like social inequalities, power relations or collective actors are more prominent). It seems therefore appropriate to point out the need to focus not on transnational relations in general, but on transnational *societal units* as relatively dense and durable configurations of transnational social practices, symbols and artifacts. The distinction between units of analysis, units of reference and units of research can be regarded as a contribution on this issue.

A second prospect of transnational studies is the project of empirically based current developments of transnationalization, according to a narrow definition as presented in this chapter.

A third future task of transnational research can be found in the systematic considerations of internal structures and processes of transnational societal units, as well as the interrelation between transnational and non-transnational types of units of analysis. This is especially true in regard to reflections on the changing role of the nation-state.

Finally—to draw a bottom line on this text—the need to develop an adequate methodology and satisfactory methods for transnational research has not only to be identified but also substantiated.

NOTES

1. As for instance Offe (2005) has systematically shown in his work on Tocqeuville's, Weber's and Adorno's (forced) stays in the United States, such measures of cross-border engagement were not totally unusual before the second half of the 20th century. For today's configuration, it is important to note that internationalization of research, teaching and publicizing can—not only in sociology—be identified as one of the major focal points of leading academic representatives all around the globe. A vast and growing number of international host-professorships, institutionalized exchange programs such as ERASMUS and initiatives of the International Sociological Association to support networking among junior social scientists (www.isa-sociology.org/junior_sociologists_network.htm) go in the same direction.
2. For the major part of the "classics" of sociology and familiar subjects, Harvey (1990: 428) even diagnoses a bias, resulting in the systematic (and in some cases teleological) favoring of time over the systematic reflection of spatial phenomena: "Social theory of the sort constructed in the diverse traditions of Adam Smith, Marx, or Weber tends to privilege time over space in its formulations, reflecting and legitimizing those who view the world through the lenses of spaceless doctrines of progress and revolution."

3. In fact this is obviously not the case in reality; we can find evidence to underline the need to reconceptualize the relationship of geographical and social space, which will be further explained below.
4. Lefèbvre (1974) started from the idea of a socio-material continuum and distinguished between spatial practice, representation of space and spaces of representation as interconnected parts of this socio-material continuum. In accordance with the critique of Gregory and Urry (1985: 3) cited above we underline the (fruitfulness of the) analytical distinction of geographic/material space and social space.
5. The far-reaching character of the consequent application of this perspective can be illustrated with reference to the example of the traditional dichotomy between nature and culture, contemporarily serving as a reference point in a broad range of scientific sub-branches like gender studies (Butler 1993), human–animal studies (Arluke and Sanders 2009) or life sciences (Harraway 1991): Even if we plainly perceive nature as "the environment," we cannot help but subjectively conceptualize (frame) it under aspects that we learned in the course of socialization. Accordingly, the socially situated phenomenology of the Himalayas will not appear as a "thing in itself," but as the border region between India and Tibet, the home of the Yeti or a suitable territory to break Reinhold Messner's climbing records.
6. Concepts of world society and cosmo-globalism often are based on such substantial constructions as "global humanism" or "cosmopolitism of humankind"; for a critical discussion see Barnett and Weiss 2011; Pries 2011.

REFERENCES

Anderson, B. (1983) *Imagined Communities*, New York: Verso.
Arluke, A. and Sanders, C. (eds) (2009) *Between the Species: A Reader in Human-Animal Relationships*, Boston: Pearson Education.
Barnett, M. and Weiss, T.G. (2011) *Humanitarianism Contested*, London, New York: Routledge.
Bartlett, C.A. and Ghoshal, S. (1989) *Managing across Borders*, Boston: Harvard Business School Press.
Basch, L., Glick Schiller, N. and Szanton Blanc, C. (1994) *Nations Unbound. Transnational Projects, Postcolonial Predicaments, and Deterritorialized Nation-States*, Amsterdam: Gordon and Breach.
Bayer, M., Mordt, G., Terpe, S. and Winter, M. (eds) (2008) *Transnationale Ungleichheitsforschung. Eine neue Herausforderung für die Soziologie,* Frankfurt/Main, New York: Campus.
Beck, U. (2004) *Der kosmopolitische Blick*, Frankfurt/Main: Suhrkamp.
——— (2008) *Die Neuvermessung der Ungleichheit unter den Menschen*, Frankfurt/Main: Suhrkamp.
Berger, P. and Weiß, A. (eds) (2008) *Die Transnationalisierung sozialer Ungleichheit*, Wiesbaden: VS Verlag für Sozialwissenschaften.
Blumer, H. (1969) *Symbolic Interactionism*, New Jersey: Prentice-Hall.
Bourdieu, P. (1985) *Sozialer Raum und "Klassen"*, Frankfurt/Main: Suhrkamp.
Butler, J. (1993) *Bodies That Matter*, London, New York: Routledge.
Calhoun, C. (2003) "The class consciousness of frequent travellers", in D. Archibugi (ed) *Debating Cosmopolitics*, London, New York: Verso.
Castells, M. (1996) *The Rise of the Network Society*, Cambridge: Blackwell.
——— (1998) *The Information Age*, Cambridge: Blackwell.

Ehrenreich, B. and Hochschild, A. (eds) (2002) *Global Woman*, London: Granta Publications.
Einstein, A. (1960) "Vorwort", in M. Jammer (ed) *Das Problem des Raumes. Die Entwicklung der Raumtheorien*, Darmstadt: Wissenschaftliche Buchgesellschaft, pp. xii–xvii.
Elias, N. (2004) *Was ist Soziologie?*, München, Weinheim: Juventa.
Esping-Andersen, G. (2002) *Why We Need a New Welfare State*, New York: Oxford University Press.
Faist, T. and Ette, A. (2007): *The Europeanization of National Policies and Politics Of Immigration: Between Autonomy and the European Union*, Houndmills: Palgrave Macmillan.
Giddens, A. (1990) *The Consequences of Modernity*, Cambridge: Stanford University Press.
Goldring, L. (1997) "Power and status in transnational social spaces", in L. Pries (ed) *Soziale Welt* (Sonderband 12, "Transnationale Migration"), pp. 179–96.
Goldthorpe, J. (1997) "Current issues in comparative macro-sociology", *Comparative Social Research*, 16: 1–26.
Gosztonyi, A. (1976) *Der Raum: Geschichte seiner Probleme in Philosophie und Wissenschaft*, 2 Vols, Freiburg, München: Alber.
Gregory, D. and Urry, J. (eds) (1985) *Social Relations and Spatial Structures*, Basingstoke, London: Macmillan.
Hall, P.A. and Soskice, D. (2001) *Varieties of Capitalism*, Oxford: Oxford University Press.
Harraway, D. (1991) *Simians, Cyborgs and Women*, New York, London: Routledge.
Harvey, D. (1990) "Between space and time", *Annals of the Association of American Geographers*, 80: 418–34.
Hauser-Ditz, A., Hertwig, M., Pries, L. and Rampeltshammer, L. (2010) *Transnationale Mitbestimmung? Zur Praxis Europäischer Betriebsräte in der Automobilindustrie*, Frankfurt/Main, New York: Campus.
Hertwig, M., Pries, L. and Rampeltshammer, L. (eds) (2009) *European Works Councils in Complementary Perspectives*, Brussels: Etui.
Hobsbawm, E.H. (1996) *The Age of Extremes*, New York: Vintage Books.
Kohler-Koch, B. and Eising, R. (eds) (1999) *The Transformation of Governance in the European Union*, London, New York: Routledge.
Kearney, M. and Nagengast, C. (1989) *Anthropological Perspectives on Transnational Communities in Rural California*. Davis/California: Institute for Rural Studies, Working Group on Farm Labor and Rural Poverty (Working Paper 3).
Kohler-Koch, B. and Larat, F. (eds) (2009) *European Multi-Level Governance*, Cheltenham: Elgar.
Kohn, M. (1987) "Cross national research as an analytic strategy", *American Sociological Review*, 52: 713–31.
Lefèbvre, H. (1974) *Production de l'espace*, trans. D. Nicholson-Smith (1991) *The Production of Space*, Oxford, UK, Malden, MA: Blackwell Publishing.
Levitt, P. (2001) "Transnational migration", *Global Networks*, 1: 195–216.
Lewis, M.W. and Wigen, K.E. (1997) *The Myth of Continents*, Berkeley, Los Angeles, London: University of California Press.
Luhmann, N. (1984) *Soziale Systeme*, Frankfurt/Main: Suhrkamp.
Lutz, H. (ed) (2008) *Migration and Domestic Work*, London: Ashgate.
Marcus, G.E. (1995) "Ethnography in/of the world system", *Annual Review of Anthropology*, 24, 95–117.
Offe, C. (2005) *Reflections on America*, Cambridge: University Press.
Pries, L. (2001a) "The disruption of social and geographic space", *International Sociology*, 16: 55–74.

—— (ed) (2001b) *New Transnational Social Spaces*, London, New York: Routledge.

—— (2005) "Configurations of geographic and societal spaces", *Global Networks*, 5: 167–90.

—— (2008) *Die Transnationalisierung der sozialen Welt*, Frankfurt/Main: Suhrkamp.

—— (2011 forthcoming) "Ambiguities of global and transnational collective identities", *Global Networks*, 11(4).

—— and Dehnen, V. (2009) "Location tendencies of the international automotive industry", *International Journal of Automotive Technology and Management*, 9: 415–37.

Quack, S. (2006) "Die transnationalen Ursprünge des deutschen Kapitalismus", in V. Berghahn and S. Vitols (eds) *Gibt es einen deutschen Kapitalismus?*, Frankfurt/Main, New York: Campus.

—— and Djelic, M. (eds) (2010) *Transnational Communities*, Cambridge: University Press.

Robertson, R. (1992) *Globalization: Social Theory and Global Culture*, London: Sage.

Sassen, S. (1991) *The Global City: New York, London, Tokyo*, Princeton, NJ: Princeton University Press.

—— (2001) "Cracked casings. Notes towards an analytics for studying transnational processes", in L. Pries (ed) *New Transnational Social Spaces*, London, New York: Routledge.

—— (2006) *Territory, Authority, Rights*, Princeton, NJ: Princeton University Press.

Schroer, M. (2006) *Räume, Orte, Grenzen*, Frankfurt/Main: Suhrkamp.

Simmel, G. (1903) *Soziologie des Raumes*, reprinted in H.J. Dahme and O. Rammstedt (eds) (1983) *Simmel, Schriften zur Soziologie*, Frankfurt/Main: Suhrkamp.

Toynbee, A.J. (1934–1954) *A Study of History*, Vols. I–X, edited in two shortened and authorized volumes by D.C. Somervell (1947 and 1957), reprint 1987, London: Oxford University Press.

Wallerstein, I. (1979) *The Capitalist World-Economy*, Cambridge: Cambridge University Press.

Warf, B. and Arias, S. (2008) *The Spatial Turn*, London, New York: Routledge.

Webster, E., Lambert, R. and Beziudenhout, A. (2008) *Grounding Globalization*, Oxford: Blackwell.

Wimmer, A. and Glick Schiller, N. (2002) "Methodological nationalism and beyond", *Global Networks*, 2: 301–34.

12 Concluding Remarks
Reconsidering Contexts and Units of Analysis

Thomas Faist and Devrimsel D. Nergiz

The introduction has opened up a Pandora's Box of methodological challenges for cross-border studies. Concomitantly, the underlying aim of the various chapters has been to present various methodological alternatives in fields of study such as cross-border migration, cultural and material globalization, and cross-border histories. In this way, we have tried to take a step forward toward dealing with the criticism of methodological nationalism in theoretical as well as empirical terms.

It is now time to summarize the endeavor pursued in the previous chapters. We do so by addressing three select issues. The first section takes a closer look at the challenge of classification in cross-border studies. This implies a discussion of the relationship between contexts and units of analysis. The second section reflects on reasons beyond the increasing relevance of methodological debates in cross-border studies, focusing on how to deal with binaries such as local vs. global or national vs. transnational. The third and final section seeks to shed light on the implications of new terminological dichotomies raised in the preceding chapters for future research.

CLASSIFYING CROSS-BORDER STUDIES: FROM CLEAR-CUT TYPOLOGIES TO A MORE FLEXIBLE RELATIONSHIP BETWEEN UNITS OF ANALYSIS AND CONTEXTS

The contributions to this volume have addressed various ways in which cross-border studies contextualize research and define the units of analysis in question. Consequently, one way to classify cross-border studies is to see them as a *continuum* of various positions with regard to different ways of relating units of analysis and contexts to each other.

At one end of this continuum we have a position that relates units of analysis and contexts to each other in a clear-cut way. The second position—in the middle of our imagined continuum—advocates a historically contingent relationship between the units of analysis and contexts in question. Finally, the third optic—at the oppositional end of this continuum—views the correspondence between the units of analysis and contexts as contingent. This means that this optic avoids a concrete predefinition of the relationship between the "cases" and contexts in question at the early stage of the research process.

The first position, that units of analysis and contexts have to be clearly predefined from the onset of research, is put forward by Ludger Pries and Martin Seeliger (Chapter 11 of this volume). They distinguish three types of international studies: cross-border comparisons, world systems studies and the transnational approach. In their view, two of them—cross-national comparison and world systems studies—refer to an essentialist understanding of spatiality in order to design the contexts of research, while transnational studies are more likely to interpret space in a non-essentialist manner, treating it as a relational concept. This dualistic distinction of types of cross-border studies, characterized by a distinction between essentialist versus relational concepts of space, suggests that units of analysis and contexts relate to each other in a clear-cut manner. The advantage of Pries and Seeliger's typology of international studies is a distinct correspondence between the contexts and the "cases" studied. Indeed, they manifestly postulate how units of analysis and contexts should correspond to each other in each type of studies. For example, Pries and Seeliger argue that flows of capital can only be studied in the context of the world capitalist economy, but not in the context of cross-national comparison or transnational social spaces.

The second position of relating units of analysis to contexts—which appears in the middle of our continuum—is the incorporating comparison approach (McMichael 1990), advocated by Sandra Comstock in this volume (Chapter 9). This vision is characterized by a more flexible consideration of the relationship between the units of analysis and contexts because it defines them as historically specific and, thus, changeable. In doing so, she uses the example of Ellen Rosen's study (2002) on the history of the US, East Asian, Caribbean and Mexican garment industries. Building on Rosen's argument she exemplifies two mutually determining, cross-place interactions in apparel production. First, she relates how US and East Asian cooperation in the 1950s reconfigured America's clothing politics and co-influenced the emergence of new forms of pan-Asian apparel production. Second, she refers to how US and Latin American interactions later in the 1980s generated a distinctive form of pan-American apparel production. In particular, she points to how both variants of cross-border interactions influenced the emergence of novel regimes of world textile trade. For Comstock, both—units of analysis such as cross-border interactions in apparel production as well as relevant contexts such as world textile trade in Rosen's study—are transforming over time. Thus, reconstructing these transformations is necessary for an appropriate interpretation of the units of analysis and relevant contexts in question. From this point of view both units of analysis and contexts are not given or predefined, but are relational analytic categories. This position is compatible with two research approaches. First, this position joins up perfectly with multi-sited ethnography (David Gellner, Chapter 6 of this volume) where both units of analysis and contexts are understood as pluri-local and multi-sited and are not by definition strongly connected to each other. The relevance of multi-sited ethnography to cross-border research results from its capability to define "sites" (and thus also units of analysis) of an empirical field both as territorial and as concatenations of social and cultural practices by following peoples and artifacts. Second, it emphasizes Nina Glick Schiller's main argument (Chapter 2 in this volume) that focuses on ways in which transnational linkages of migrants influence the transnationality of cities. To predefine units of analysis and contexts of cross-border phenomena is not seen as necessary. Instead entry points to the research on the phenomena in question are sought.

The third position—at the opposite end of our continuum—includes studies that define relationships between units of analysis and contexts in an even more contingent manner. The strategy underlying this position is to abandon thinking of units of analysis as containers, and to take a closer look at the contexts as multiple and varying (Anja Weiß and Arnd-Michael Nohl in Chapter 4, Eva Gerharz in Chapter 7 and Zsuzsa Gille in Chapter 5, all in this volume). For example, Eva Gerharz builds on her analysis of indigenous activism from the *bottom up* using the results of her empirical research to understand a multifaceted activity within global as well as local contexts, without assuming these settings are mutually exclusive. Acknowledging this approach to units of analysis and contexts we characterize the relationship between them as flexible or even mobile. To use adjectives such as flexible or mobile attempts to avoid a static conceptualization of the relationship between cases and contexts. For example, Anja Weiß and Arnd-Michael Nohl (Chapter 4 in this volume) compare the relevance of different contexts, such as the national, the transnational and that of the nation-state system, in order to understand their impacts on the labor market access of highly skilled migrants. They posit that these three potentially relevant contexts influence the unit of analysis, such as the labor market access of highly skilled migrants, in different ways. Weiß and Nohl argue that scholars would not be able to consider these different impacts by predefining the relationship between cases and contexts. This understanding of the relationship between units of analysis and contexts can be characterized as mobile because cases and contexts relate to each other in a contingent manner. This is how the third position differs from the second: It does not build exclusively on the argument of historic specificity of contexts or of units of analysis, although this is an important point. Going further, it advocates an even more contingent approach to be more open and flexible while researching cross-border practices. Thus this view is a promising one, because it potentially enables researchers to shed light on those particular cross-border practices that otherwise would not be considered. For example, Zsuzsa Gille (Chapter 5 in this volume), using her research on the Hungarian paprika ban in 2004, suggests the reconstruction of global socio-material transformations not by presuming a "global context," but by following global–local networks involving material artifacts such as the poison aflatoxin, transnational companies and institutional actors, such as the EU bureaucracy.

In sum, without neglecting the relevance and importance of the first two positions included in our imagined continuum, we argue that the third way of approaching the relationship between units of analysis and contexts can be seen as the most flexible, but also as the most promising for future empirical research. Nonetheless, a fundamental question remains: Does the conceptualization of the relationship between units of analysis and contexts as flexible and mobile also imply a specific understanding of methodology in cross-border studies?

CAN METHODOLOGY BE USED AS A TOOL TO CONTEST CATEGORICAL BINARIES?

The previous chapters have not viewed methodology and methods as neutral tools that can be used without understanding their effects on field research. The authors argue that methods continuously produce new meanings and interpretations of cross-border phenomena. Various chapters in this volume understand methodology as an instrument to reflect on methodological nationalism and to interrogate concepts such as nation, space, ethnicity or mobility (see, for example, the contributions by Goldring and Landolt in Chapter 3, Gellner in Chapter 6 and Mongia in Chapter 10, all in this volume). Moreover, the authors of most contributions have used methodology as an instrument to contest binary thinking and other categories that have too often been implied in the concepts just mentioned, such as the distinctions between global and local or migrant and non-migrant, which have all too often been treated as self-evident (see also Levitt and Glick Schiller 2004). For example, Goldring and Landolt (Chapter 3 of this volume) reflect on categories they used in their empirical study on transnational activity of Latin American migrant organizations in Canada to question the often-used distinction between the context of departure and context of destination. Applying a transnational studies approach on migration by comparing different migrant groups, they exemplify how this distinction prevents a differentiated view on cross-border migration. The already-mentioned study by Eva Gerharz also implies a contestation of binary thinking by using novel methodological tools. Gerharz's application of methodology seeks to overcome the dichotomy between the global and the local. In doing so, she conceives of socio-spatial scales as interactive "sites" of complex social arenas.

This way of dealing with methodology makes cross-border studies more attractive because questioning binaries fosters more differentiated views on cross-border phenomena. Such a critique of established categorical binaries relates to criticisms of, for example, unequal power relations within a transnationalized capitalist economy (Glick Schiller, Chapter 2 of this volume), the multiple categorizations of subjects (Gerharz, Chapter 7 of this volume), and nested spatiality (Pries and Seeliger, Chapter 11 of this volume). All of them necessitate a methodological examination that transcends existing interpretations of cross-border processes and events.

WHAT CATEGORIES HAVE BEEN "EXCLUDED" FROM CROSS-BORDER STUDIES THAT USE NEW METHODOLOGICAL TOOLS?

Angelika Epple (Chapter 8) has advocated for historiographic perspectives that bring in excluded histories and the histories of the excluded, in particular, the postcolonial (Chakrabarty 2000) and the subaltern history (Chatterjee 2006) approaches. Transferring our focus to the excluded we need to address the implications of new categories replacing older ones. This step has been missing from the methodologies of cross-border studies collected in this book. In doing so, we again refer to the reflexive turn (Clifford and Marcus 1986) within social sciences that considers both theoretical and positional reflexivity as relevant to the research process. The reflexive turn suggests researchers pay attention to the categories they use in order to better understand how their own theoretical positions influences research outcomes.

On the one hand, all authors have emphasized how important it is to surmount container-centered thinking in cross-border research and have devised appropriate methodologies to reach this goal. On the other hand, the efforts seem to summon new binaries, such as transnational versus national, cosmopolitan versus national and "container" versus "non-container." Furthermore, the unintended by-product of the collected chapters is a positive connotation of cross-border relations and an implicitly negative projection of categories and units referring to national entities. To make it very clear, in no way do we advocate a negligence of the national. Quite the contrary, a cross-border approach helps to overcome the unquestioned dominance of the national as a quasi-natural point of reference for methodological tools, and expands the universe of contexts above, below and across the national. It also allows for vantage points other than the national, such as the transnational, global or cosmopolitan. Concomitantly, one needs to be well aware that the endeavor that has guided this book not only provides alternatives for how to overcome container-centered thinking but has also paved the way for new categorical binaries, such as container versus non-container or essentialism versus non-essentialism or methodological nationalism versus methodological transnationalism.

Overall, the chapters in this volume open the door for a discussion rather than end the debate. In this regard, ideas such as a flexible relationship between units of analysis and contexts mentioned earlier imply an open-ended search for alternatives to methodologically nationalist binaries and container-centered thinking. Needless to say, we are aware that our approach results in emerging and new dichotomies. Nonetheless, the added value to the discussion triggered by this book remains the questioning of methodological nationalism from an interdisciplinary perspective through new approaches, new assessments and new categorizations. We hope that we simultaneously help to generate and to question also new categorical dichotomies that have to be subject to further discussion.

REFERENCES

Chakrabarty, D. (2000) *Provincializing Europe: Postcolonial Thought and Historical Difference*, Princeton, NJ: Princeton University Press.

Chatterjee, P. (2006) "A brief history of subaltern studies", in G. Budde, S. Conrad and V. Janz (eds) *Transnationale Geschichte: Themen, Tendenzen und Theorien*, Göttingen: Vandenhoeck & Ruprecht, pp. 94–104.

Clifford, J. and Marcus, G.E. (eds) (1986) *Writing Culture. The Poetics and Politics of Ethnography*, Berkeley: University of California Press.

Levitt, P. and Glick Schiller, N. (2004) "Transnational perspectives on migration: Conceptualizing simultaneity", *International Migration Review*, 38(3): 1002–40.

McMichael, P. (1990) "Incorporating comparison within a world-historical perspective: An alternative comparative method", *American Sociological Review*, 55: 385–97.

Rosen, E.I. (2002) *Making Sweatshops: The Globalization of the US Apparel Industry*, Berkeley: University of California Press.

Wallerstein, I. (1976) "A world-system perspective on social sciences", *British Journal of Sociology*, 27(3): 343–52.

Contributors

Anna Amelina is a senior researcher at the Faculty of Sociology at Bielefeld University. Her research addresses subjects such as social inequality and migration, transnationalization of gender regimes and methodology of cross-border studies. Empirically she focuses on the genesis of social inequalities in the context of transnational migration between Germany and the Ukraine. Her latest publications include "Searching for an appropriate research strategy on transnational migration: The logic of multi-sited research and the advantage of the cultural interferences approach", *Forum: Qualitative Social Research*, 11(1), Art. 17 (2009); "Turkish migrant associations in Germany. Between integration pressure and transnational linkages", co-authored with Thomas Faist, *Revue Européenne des Migrations Internationales* (REMI), 24(2) (2008).

Sandra Curtis Comstock received her PhD in Development Sociology from Cornell University in 2008. Her research on the global garment industry has included Fulbright and SSRC funded fieldwork in Asia and Mexico. She is currently a postdoctoral fellow at the Charles Warren Center for Studies in American History at Harvard University, where she is completing a manuscript tentatively titled *The American Blue Jean: US Clothing Politics at Home and Abroad across the 20th Century*.

Angelika Epple is a Professor of Modern History at Bielefeld University. She has taught history at the University of Hamburg and at the Albert-Ludwigs-University of Freiburg. She works on the history of historiography, theory of history, gender history, and cultural and economic history of globalizations. Among her publications in English are "A strained relationship: Epistemology and historiography in 18th and 19th century Germany and Britain", in Stefan Berger and Chris Lorenz (eds) *Writing National Historiographies*, Basingstoke: Palgrave Macmillan (2010); "The 'Automat': A history of technological transfer and the process of global standardization in modern fast food around 1900", *Food & History*, 7(2) (2010); and *Gendering Historiography. Beyond National Canons*, co-edited with Angelika Schaser, Frankfurt, New York: Campus Verlag (2009). Her most important books in German include *Das Unternehmen Stollwerck. Eine Mikrogeschichte der Globalisierung*, Frankfurt, New York: Campus Verlag (2010); *Globale Waren*, edited with Dorothee Wierling, Essen: Klartext-Verlag (2007); and *Empfindsame Geschichtsschreibung. Eine Geschlechtergeschichte der Historiographie zwischen Aufklärung und Historismus*, Köln: Böhlau Verlag (2003).

Thomas Faist is a Professor for the Sociology of Transnationalization, Development and Migration at the Department of Sociology, Bielefeld University. His research focuses on migration, citizenship, social policy and transnationalization. Recent book publications include *Diasporas and Transnationalism: Concepts, Theories and Methods*, co-edited with Rainer Bauböck, Amsterdam: Amsterdam University Press (2010); *Beyond a Border: The Causes and Consequences of Contemporary Immigration*, co-authored with Peter Kivisto, Thousand Oaks, CA: Pine Forge Press (2009); *Dual Citizenship in a Globalizing World: From Unitary to Multiple Citizenship*, Houndmills: Palgrave Macmillan (2008) and *Citizenship: Discourse, Theory and Transnational Prospects*, co-authored with Peter Kivisto, Oxford: Blackwell (2007).

David N. Gellner is a Professor of Social Anthropology and a Fellow of All Souls College, University of Oxford. He has carried out research on religion, politics and ethnicity in Nepal since 1982. Since 2009 he has been principal investigator of a project on religious practices among the Nepali diaspora in the UK. His most recent ethnographic monograph is *Rebuilding Buddhism: The Theravada Movement in Twentieth-Century Nepal*, together with Sarah LeVine (Harvard, 2005). His most recent edited volumes, all published by Sage and all outcomes of the MIDEA project on democratization in South Asia (www.uni-bielefeld.de/midea), are *Local Democracy in South Asia* (with K. Hachhethu)(2008), *Ethnic Activism and Civil Society in South Asia* (2009), and *Varieties of Activist Experience: Civil Society in South Asia* (2010).

Eva Gerharz is a Junior Professor of Sociology of Development and Internationalization at the Ruhr University Bochum, Germany. Formerly, she was a senior researcher at the Department of Social Anthropology, Faculty of Sociology at the Bielefeld University, Germany, where she also obtained her doctoral degree in sociology in 2007. Her main research interests are development sociology, activism and identity politics, diaspora and development, globalization, and transnational and translocal dynamics in South Asia. She is the author of *The Politics of Reconstruction and Development in Sri Lanka*, London: Routledge (forthcoming) and *The Making of World Society: Perspectives from Transnational Research*, with Remus Anghel Gabriel, Gilberto Rescher and Monika Salzbrunn, Bielefeld: transcript (2008).

Contributors 247

Zsuzsa Gille is an Associate Professor of Sociology at the University of Illinois at Urbana-Champaign. She is author of *From the Cult of Waste to the Trash Heap of History: The Politics of Waste in Socialist and Postsocialist Hungary*, Bloomington: Indiana University Press (2007)—recipient of an honorable mention of the American Association for the Advancement of Slavic Studies Davis Prize; *Post-Communist Nostalgia*, co-edited with Maria Todorova, Oxford: Berghahn Press (2010); and *Global Ethnography: Forces, Connections and Imaginations in a Postmodern World*, co-authored with Michael Burawoy et al., Berkeley: University of California Press (2000). She was the special guest editor of *Slavic Review*'s thematic cluster on Nature, Culture, Power (2009). She has published on issues of qualitative methodology as it relates to globalization and new concepts of space, on environmental politics and on the sociology of food. She is currently researching the politics of food in post-socialist Hungary, and is collaborating with the University of Sheffield on its The Waste of the World project. Her next book in progress is *Pigs, Paprika, and Predestination: The European Union as Material Civilization*.

Nina Glick Schiller is a Professor of Social Anthropology and the Director of the Research Institute for Cosmopolitan Cultures, University of Manchester. Her books, exploring migration, cities, transnational processes, long distance nationalism, methodological nationalism and diasporic cosmopolitanism, include *Cosmopolitan Sociability: Locating Religious and Diasporic Networks*, co-edited with T. Darieva and S. Gruner-Domic, New York: Routledge (2011); *Migration, Development, and Transnationalization: A Critical Stance*, co-edited with T. Faist, Oxford: Berghahn Books (2010); *Locating Migration: Rescaling Cities and Migrants*, co-edited with A. Çağlar, Ithaca, NY: Cornell University Press (2010); *Georges Woke Up Laughing: Long Distance Nationalism and the Search for Home*, with G. Fouron, Durham, NC: Duke University Press Books (2001); and *Nations Unbound: Transnational Projects, Postcolonial Predicaments, and Deterritorialized Nation-States*, with L. Basch and C. Szanton Blanc, Abingdon, UK and New York: Routledge (1994).

Luin Goldring is an Associate Professor of Sociology at York University in Toronto. Her research investigates immigrants and precarious work, non-citizenship and precarious status, immigrant politics and community organizing, and transnational studies. She is involved in collaborative research projects with Patricia Landolt on Latin American and Caribbean immigrants and precarious work as well as Latin American community organizing in the Greater Toronto Area. Recent co-authored publications include "Caught in the work-citizenship matrix: The lasting effects of precarious legal status on work for Toronto immigrants", with P. Landolt, *Globalizations* (Special Issue on Migration and Citizenship, 2011); "Political cultures and transnational social fields: Chilean, Colombian and Canadian activists in Toronto", with P. Landolt, *Global Networks* (2010); and "Institutionalizing precarious immigration status in Canada", with C. Berinstein and J. Bernhard, *Citizenship Studies* (2009). She is co-editor with P. Landolt of *Producing and Negotiating Non-Citizenship: Precarious Legal Status in Canada* (forthcoming, Toronto: University of Toronto Press).

Patricia Landolt is an Associate Professor of Sociology at the University of Toronto, Scarborough. Her research examines the production and reproduction of systems of social exclusion and inequality associated with global migrations and develops a comparative analysis of political mobilization and incorporation, income security, precarious work and precarious legal status. Much of her work focuses on Latin American and Caribbean populations living in the city of Toronto. Recent co-authored publications include "Caught in the work-citizenship matrix: The lasting effects of precarious legal status on work for Toronto immigrants", with L. Goldring, *Globalizations* (Special Issue on Migration and Citizenship, 2011); "Agenda setting and immigrant politics: The case of Latin Americans in Toronto," with L. Goldring and J. Bernhard (American Behavioral Scientist, 2011); and *Working Rough, Living Poor: Employment and Income Insecurities Faced by Racialized Groups in Black Creek and Their Impact on Health*, with R. Wilson et al. (Access Alliance Multicultural Health and Community Services, 2011).

Radhika Mongia is an Associate Professor of Sociology, Women's Studies, and Social and Political Thought at York University, Toronto, where she has also served as the Director of the Graduate Program in Sociology. Among other venues, her essays have appeared in journals such as *Public Culture, Gender & History, Cultural Studies*, and *Comparative Studies in Society and History*. Her book *Genealogies of Globalization: Migration, Colonialism, and the State*, is forthcoming from Duke University Press and Permanent Black Press (in India).

Devrimsel Deniz Nergiz is a doctoral fellow at the Bielefeld Graduate School in History and Sociology (BGHS). Her PhD project focuses on migrant-origin politicians in German parliaments. Her main research interests include integration and migration in Europe, political participation and representation of migrants. Recent publications include "Gäste können nicht mitspielen: Mandatsträger mit Migrationshintergrund kommen zu Wort", in Marvin Oppong (ed) *Migranten in der deutschen Politik*, Wiesbaden: VS Verlag (2011); "German politicians with Turkey origin: Diversity in the parliaments of Germany", in Robert Danisch (ed) *Citizens of the World: Pluralism, Migration and the Practices of*

Citizenship, Amsterdam and New York: Rodopi (2011); and "Diversity in Parliaments of Germany: Turkey-origin Members of Parliament(s) in Germany", Chapter 10 in *Boundaries: Dichotomies of Keeping In and Keeping Out*, Julian Chapple (ed), Volume 122 of At the Interface series 'Diversity and Recognition', online access at http://www.inter-disciplinary.net/wpcontent/uploads/2010/05/pic5ever2050510.pdf

Arnd-Michael Nohl is a Professor for Education Science at the Helmut Schmidt University in Hamburg. He received his PhD at the Freie Universität Berlin in 2000. His doctorate thesis was published under the title *Migration und Differenzerfahrung. Junge Einheimische und Migranten im rekonstruktiven Milieuvergleich*, Opladen: Leske & Budrich (2001). From 2001 to 2004 he was a senior lecturer at the Institute of Education Science of the Otto-von-Guericke-University Magdeburg where he delivered his postdoctoral thesis *Bildung und Spontaneität*, Opladen: Budrich (2006). From 2004 to 2006 he was an Assistant Professor for Intercultural Education at the Freie Universität Berlin. Since 2006 he has been a Professor for Education Science, with an emphasis on philosophy of education, at the Helmut Schmidt University in Hamburg. His main areas of research are migration, qualitative methodology, learning and contemporary Turkish studies. His recent publications include *Pädagogik der Dinge*, Bad Heilbrunn: Julius Klinkhardt (2011) and *Interview und dokumentarische Methode*, Wiesbaden: VS Verlag (2009).

Ludger Pries holds a Chair for Sociology at the Ruhr University Bochum. He has conducted research in Brazil, Mexico, Spain and the US. He was a visiting fellow at the Universidade Federale de Minas Geráis (Belo Horizonte), Universidad Autónoma Metropolitana and El Colegio de Mexico (Mexico City), University of Pennsylvania (Philadelphia), Cornell University (Ithaca) and Columbia University (New York). His main fields of research interest are the sociology of organizations, work and labor regulation, and migration in international comparison, especially transnationalization, transnational migration and processes of social incorporation.

Martin Seeliger is a researcher at the Faculty of Social Science at the Ruhr University Bochum. He is currently working on a project on cross-border coordination in for-profit and nonprofit organizations between Mexico and Germany. Previously, he carried out research on labor regulation within and between the South African and German automotive industries. Further fields of scientific interest include gender and cultural studies as well as political sociology and research on social inequality.

Anja Weiß is an Assistant Professor for Macro-Sociology and Transnational Processes at the University of Duisburg-Essen. She received her PhD in 2001 from the Humboldt University in Berlin and was a senior researcher at the Collaborative Research Center, Reflexive Modernization, in Munich, and later in the department of Ulrich Beck at the Ludwig-Maximilians University, also in Munich. She has been a guest researcher at the Institute for Conflict Analysis and Resolution at George Mason University in Virginia. Her theoretical interests in social inequality translate into comparative empirical studies on highly skilled migrants, (institutional) racism, ethnic conflict and anti-racist struggle, and qualitative research design. She is currently developing a transnational model of social inequality. Her recent publications include *Transnationalisierung Sozialer Ungleichheit*, co-edited with Peter Berger, Wiesbaden: VS Verlag (2008) and "The racism of globalization", in D. Macedo and P. Gounari (eds) *The Globalization of Racism*, Boulder, CO and London: Paradigm Publishers (2006).

Index

A

abolition of slavery (British), 206
activism, 6, 12, 55, 59, 129–32, 134–5, 137–9, 141, 143, 145–7, 148, 241
Actor-Network-Theory / ANT, 11, 95–100, 106–7, 108
analytical category /-ies. *See* categories
anthropology, 2–3, 36, 111–3, 120, 121, 124, 159, 168
   cultural a., 11, 12, 111, 113, 118, 121
   social a., 1, 2, 11–2, 113
approach, 3–8, 10–5, 24, 28–31, 34–5, 41–2, 47, 49, 53, 55–7, 59, 70–73, 75, 84, 91, 115–6, 121, 131–2, 135, 139, 142, 143, 146, 148–9, 155–7, 159–62, 164, 167–9, 170–1, 176–7, 181–2, 184, 186–191, 196, 200, 202–4, 213, 218, 221–7, 232, 234, 241–4
   comparative /-ison a., 3, 10, 13, 14, 15, 23, 44, 48, 73, 176, 240
   encompassing comparison a., 13, 183
   ethnography /-ic a., 8, 11, 12, 71
   experimental (comparative) a., 44, 48, 57, 181, 183, 186–7
   global history a., 168
   hermeneutic a., 177–9, 184, 189–90, 193
   history a., 3, 6, 13, 44, 58, 156, 161, 168, 243
   history-from-below a. (*see* history-from-below)
   incorporating comparisons a., 3, 193, 240
   methodological a. (*see* methodological)
   microhistory /-ical a., 157, 167, 170
   nation-centered a., 155, 161, 162, 168 (see *also* history /-ies)
   network a., 5, 101
   relational a., 191, 225–6, 227, 231
   scale a. (*see* scale)
   translocality a. (*see* translocality /-ities)
   transnational a., 2, 159, 163, 165, 201–3, 240
   transnational space a., 134
   transnational studies a., 14, 242
   world polity a., 5
   world system a. (*see* world system)

B

Bangladesh(i), 6, 12, 122, 129–30, 134–7, 138, 141–4, 146–7
border, 23, 25–6, 29, 42, 49, 53, 68, 72, 76, 80, 82, 103, 106, 121–2, 134, 146, 155–61, 162, 182, 192, 187, 198, 201, 202, 203, 205, 209, 211, 212, 225, 236
   b.-crossing, 134, 147, 233 (*see also* cross-border)
   b.land, 122
   cross-b., xv, 1, 3–14, 23, 24–5, 146, 181–8, 219–21, 224, 228–32, 234, 235, 239–43
   cross-b. comparison, 240
   cross-b. history /-ies, xv, 1, 4, 6, 8, 9, 14, 15, 181, 239
   national b., 25, 68, 72, 80, 130, 147
   transb., 26, 121
boundary /-ies, 25, 42, 53, 55–6, 58, 91, 121, 123, 131, 133, 137,

252 *Index*

    143, 145–6, 147, 156, 162, 164, 177, 180, 202, 203, 211, 230
  b.-drawing, 144–5. (*see also* ethnic b.-drawing)
  b. of the nation-state / nation-state b., 91, 162, 202–3, 222
  categorical b., 14
  disciplinary b., 4
  ethnic b. (*see* ethnic)
  ethnic b.-making (*see* ethnic)
  national b., 42, 133, 147, 188, 229
  social b., 6, 58

C
Canada, 8, 10, 13, 43, 45, 46, 48, 49, 50, 55–6, 59, 60, 73, 76, 204, 208–10, 213, 242
Canadian migration policy. *See* migration
Caribbean, 190, 206, 240
case, 6, 11, 28, 29, 32, 44, 49, 51, 54–6, 57, 65–83, 91, 97, 101–7, 108, 111, 116, 119, 122, 129–31, 139–41, 147, 167–8, 177–9, 182, 189, 190–1, 195, 204, 223–5, 228, 229, 231, 233–4, 235–6, 240–1
  c. and contexts, 65, 67, 73, 79, 81, 240–1
  c. definition, 72, 80
  c. group, 11, 67, 78, 80–1
  c. study /-ies, 6, 60, 72, 97–8, 100, 101–2, 114, 240
  comparison of c., 73, 74
  contexts on/of/in the c., 67, 71, 73
  typologically situated c. groups, 67, 75, 78–81
  category /-ies, xv, 1, 41, 43, 44, 48–9, 50–1, 53, 54, 56–9, 67, 132, 134, 137, 144, 146, 160, 163, 169, 179, 189, 195, 202, 204, 211, 242, 243
  analytical c., 41–3, 46–7, 48, 52, 53, 56, 202, 240
  c. for/of comparison, 46
  c. of context / context c., 42, 67, 155
  c. of refugee / refugee c., 44, 48–50, 53, 57
  conceptual c., 44, 47, 56, 58
  ethnic c., 5, 144, 145
  social c., 48, 58
  unifying c., 132, 137, 145
causality, 67, 69
Chile(an), 43–9, 51–7

Christianity, 33, 142–3
cities, 6, 10, 23–32, 34–6, 70, 184, 208, 223–4, 230
  global c., 1, 27, 31, 34, 35
  industrial c., 26
  positionality /-ties of (the) c., 31, 34, 36
  transnationality of c., 26, 28, 30, 31, 34, 35, 241
citizenship, 122, 223, 232
Colombia(n), 44, 46, 47, 48–9, 52, 53, 55–7
colonialism, 96, 136, 198, 205–6, 232
colonial Indian migration. *See* migration
comparative, 10, 11, 23, 24, 28, 29, 31, 34, 42–4, 58, 67, 68, 73, 78, 136, 144, 176, 177, 179, 192–4, 220, 231
  c. analysis, 28, 49, 52, 77, 198
  c. migration research, 42, 57, 72
  c. research, 27, 41, 57, 72
  c. studies, 24, 31, 57, 198, 231
  experimental c. approach, 44, 48
  experimental c. method, 43, 50, 57, 182
  (internationally) c. research, 11, 27, 41, 57, 66, 67, 72, 76–7, 81
  macro-sociological c. research, 66 (*see also* macro)
  c. strategies, 67, 81, 176, 180, 191
comparative / comparison
  c. approach (*see* approach)
  c. method / method of c., 13, 31, 68, 176–7, 182, 187–8, 193–4
  country c., 11, 66–7, 72–3, 76–7, 78
  historical c. / history of c., 72, 171, 180, 193
  incorporating c., 13, 176–7, 188,90, 192–4
  incorporating c. approach, 3, 193, 240
  incorporating c. method, 13, 177, 194
  multi-level c. (research), 11, 65, 81
comparison, 14, 28, 31, 41, 46, 50, 57, 67–71, 73–8, 80–2, 123, 171, 176–195, 230, 231- 2, 234
  c. of cases, 73, 74
  case comparison, 73, 74, 75, 81
  categories for/of c., 46
  cross-border c., 240
  cross-national c., 14, 231–4

encompassing c., 176, 183–4, 186–8, 191, 193, 195
encompassing c. approach, 13, 183
experimental c., 13, 180, 183, 186–7, 195
hermeneutic c., 13, 176–8, 180, 183, 186
international c., 231–2
units of c., 189
conceptual categories. *See* categories
context, 4–5, 8–1, 14–5, 25, 30–1, 33, 42–5, 49–51, 57–9, 65–84, 111, 118, 121, 132, 134–5, 137–9, 140–1, 143, 145, 147–9, 176–9, 183, 185, 187–8, 195, 206, 209, 219, 222, 224, 226–7, 230–2, 239–44
cases and c., 65, 67, 73, 79, 81, 240–1
c. in/of/on/ the cases, 67, 71, 73
c. of departure, 10, 41–4, 46–8, 50, 57, 58, 242
c. of reception, 10, 42–4, 46–8, 50–2, 57, 59
global c., 8, 12, 44, 129, 242
national c. (*see* national)
social c. (*see* social)
cosmo-globalism, 219, 223, 232–4, 236
cosmopolitan, 1, 3, 5–6, 7–8, 15, 28, 30, 32, 145, 223, 231, 243
c. urbanism, 35
cosmopolitanism, 1, 30, 36, 219, 223, 229
cross
c.-border. *See* border
c.-border networks, 8, 146
c.-cultural, 177, 192
c.-ethnic, 134, 146
c.-local, 184, 194
c.-national comparison, 14, 231–4
c. place, 12–13, 176–7, 180–94, 196, 240
c.-place problem-solving, 192, 193, 194
culture, xv, 2, 6–7, 11, 15, 29, 44, 48, 54–6, 58, 113, 114, 123, 140, 144, 155, 157, 158, 169, 177, 198–9, 201–2, 204, 224, 230, 232–3, 236
global c., 166
local c., 123, 142
native c., 198
national c., 7, 29, 48, 53, 54–6, 58, 198, 201, 203, 220, 222, 232

political c., 44, 50, 52, 55–6, 58–9, 134, 143
sociology of c., 43, 53, 55
cultural, 2, 6–12, 15, 23–5, 27, 29–30, 32, 35, 42, 45–6, 54–6, 58, 68, 70, 84, 94, 95, 112, 114–5, 120, 129, 132, 142, 146, 148, 159, 176–7, 180, 182, 187, 190, 193, 195, 202, 204, 221, 228, 230, 231–2, 239
c. anthropology /-ist (*see* anthropology)
c. capital, 31, 33, 67, 72, 76, 83
c. context, 66, 178
c. diversity, 45, 70, 228
c. practices, 142, 148, 195, 241
c. processes, 24, 27, 114, 129
c. studies (*see* studies)
c. tool-kit, 54–5
c. transformations, 1, 6, 8, 11
cross-c., 177, 192
multic. (*see* multicultural)

D

development, xv, 1, 6, 26, 32, 34, 65, 71, 73, 95, 112, 121, 129, 134, 136, 139–44, 147, 148, 155, 158, 161, 165, 191, 198–9, 204, 210, 220–3, 229–32, 234–5
developmentalist, 199, 204
dialogue, 1, 54, 56, 59
activist d., 56
types of d., 56, 59
diaspora, 24, 162, 198, 227–8, 232, 234
d.-internationalization, 230
diasporic cosmopolitanism, 36
diffusionism, 122–3

E

empire-state, 13, 199, 207, 211
empirical studies. *See* studies
ethnic, 5–7, 12, 26, 29, 35, 41, 45, 55, 60, 65, 71, 76, 134, 136–7, 140, 143–4, 145–6, 179, 220
cross-e., 134, 146
e. boundaries, 29, 132, 133, 144, 145
e. boundary-drawing, 130, 137, 143, 149
e. boundary-making, 12, 134, 135, 143, 147
e. category /-ies, 5, 144, 145
e. differences, 132, 144, 146

254   Index

e. group /-ism, 15, 29, 65, 76, 111, 122, 129–30, 132, 143, 146
e. identity /-ties, 59, 113, 135, 144, 171
e. labor market segregation, 74
e. lens, 29, 71–2, 132
e. network, 32, 83
pan-e., 46, 53–4, 59
ethnicism, 112, 123. *See also* tribalism; methodological
ethnicity /-ies, 2, 9, 11, 42–3, 96, 129, 132, 137, 143–6, 171, 179, 199, 242
epistemology, 2, 41, 99, 157, 170
ethnography, 10, 12, 36, 94, 111, 113–21, 134
  global e., 8, 11–2, 71, 91, 93–5, 100, 101, 105–7, 108, 111, 113–5, 118, 121, 123
  Global E. 2.0, 91, 93, 95, 100, 101, 106
  multi-sited e., 3, 8, 15, 111–5, 119, 121, 241
eurocentrism, 158–60, 163, 164, 168
exclusion, 53, 80, 83, 108, 134, 144, 155–6, 158–61, 165–7, 168, 210, 225
experimental method. *See* method
explanatory sequence. *See* sequence
eventful, 13, 199, 200, 204, 205, 210
event sequence. *See* sequence

F

fieldwork, 52, 70–1, 77, 81, 94, 101, 111, 116–7, 119–21, 123, 124, 139
formations of nationhood, 199–200
  eventful f. (*see* eventful)
  developmentalist f. (*see* developmentalist)
functionalism, 113

G

gender, 9, 29, 46, 58, 114, 118, 119, 145, 166, 204, 236
  g. history, 155, 167
Germany, 10, 33, 65, 73, 75, 76, 77–8, 79–80, 82–3, 135, 138, 170, 178, 232–3
global, xv, 1, 3–8, 10–1, 15, 24, 26–8, 30–4, 36, 42, 50, 65, 69–70, 93–4, 96, 99, 101–2, 105–8, 111–2, 115–7, 122–3, 129–33, 135–41, 143–8, 155–7, 160, 162–4, 166, 168–70, 177, 180, 187, 198, 204–5, 219, 223, 228–30, 233–4, 236, 241–3
  cosmo-g. (*see* cosmo)
  g. and/or national, 122, 147, 239 (*see also* national and/or (the) g.)
  g. assemblages, 97, 98, 101, 108
  g. cities, 1, 27, 31, 34, 35
  g. context, 8, 12, 44, 129, 242
  g. discourse, 137, 140, 146
  g.-level, 99, 101, 102, 106, 107, 168
  g.-local / g. and local, 6, 12, 23, 99, 134, 169, 130, 134, 229, 242
  g.-local entanglements, 157, 168, 170
  G. Ethnography 2.0. *See* ethnography
  g. history (*see* history /-ies)
  global s. (*see* scale)
  g. transformation, xv, 6, 8, 9, 11, 12
globalization, 3–6, 8, 11–2, 14, 24–5, 42, 65, 71, 81, 91, 94–5, 97, 101–2, 105, 108, 111–3, 115, 117, 118–9, 124, 129, 157, 220–1, 223, 228–9, 234, 239
  g. studies / studies of/on g., 3, 4, 5, 11, 15, 91, 97, 101, 219
  methodologies of g., 4
grounded theory, 72, 100, 135
Guatemala(n), 43–4, 45, 46, 47, 48–9, 51, 55, 181, 195

H

history /-ies, xv, 2, 6–8, 12–15 25, 28, 46, 50, 55, 111, 115, 117, 122, 123, 136, 144, 155–71, 176–8, 180, 182–5, 188–90, 190, 200, 208, 210, 212, 220, 233, 240, 243
  cross-border h. (*see* border)
  entangled h., 3, 6, 12–3, 15, 156, 163, 168, 170
  environmental h., 95, 97
  gender h., 155, 167
  global h., 156–7, 160, 161–4, 167–70
  h. from below, 168–71
  h. of the transnational, 200, 211
  h. writing, xv, 1, 12–4, 163, 165–6, 170
  limits of h., 155, 157, 164, 167, 169
  local h., 13, 177–8, 180, 183, 186, 189–90
  microh., 13, 157, 167–70

national h., 6, 7, 49, 155–6, 158, 167, 169, 199
nation-centered h., 12, 155, 162, 164 (*see also* approach)
people without h., 158, 159
postcolonial h., 12, 13, 167, 156, 164, 170, 171
shared h., 13, 156, 164, 168, 177, 180
subaltern h., 12, 167, 243
transnational h., xv, 1, 156–7, 161–3, 165, 168, 171, 199–200, 203, 211
understanding of h, 160, 161, 168
waiting room of h., 158, 167
world h. / h. of the (whole) world, 12–3, 156, 157–63, 167–8
historical sociology, 43
holism, 111, 117, 123

I

identity /-ties, 5, 7, 25, 28–9, 42–4, 46, 48–9, 53–4, 58, 60, 69, 71, 108, 113, 130, 135, 140, 155, 166, 169, 188, 198, 201, 204, 208, 212, 223, 230, 233
  ethnic i. *See* ethnic
immigration. *See* migration
immigrant. *See* migrant
imperial spatial scale. *See* scale
India(n), 8, 13, 32, 119–20, 122, 136, 138, 146, 148–9, 162, 164–6, 200–1, 204, 206–10, 212–3, 232, 234
indigenous, 6, 12, 53, 96, 113, 129–47, 148, 241
interface, 131, 133–4, 137, 144, 147, 148
inter-local, 176, 189, 193
inter-state, 91, 185, 205, 212

K

knowledge, 9, 12, 14–5, 23, 26, 32–3, 68, 73, 74, 76, 82, 95–6, 106, 108, 118, 119, 123, 130, 131, 133–5, 137, 140, 141, 144, 146–7, 148, 177, 179, 183, 229
  k. production, 9, 14, 45

L

Latin America(n), 10, 41–3, 45, 46, 47, 51–2, 53–4, 57, 59, 60, 103–4, 160, 190–3, 240, 242

local(ly), 6–8, 11–15, 23, 28–31, 32–6, 42, 44, 49–50, 52, 58, 71, 76, 80, 93–4, 97, 99–101, 105–6, 107–8, 112–3, 116–8, 123, 129–35, 138–157, 161, 167–70, 176–8, 180, 182–4, 186–7, 189–90, 193, 221–4, 228, 229–30, 232–4, 239, 241–2
  crossl. (*see* cross-local)
  inter-l. (*see* inter)
  l. community /-ies, 116, 222, 226
  l.-global / l. and global, 28, 93, 101, 107, 129, 131, 187, 239
  l. history /-ies. (*see* history /-ies)
  l. scale (*see* scale)
  l. social, 8, 134, 138, 230
  pluri-l. (*see* pluri)
  transl. (*see* translocal)
locality /-ities, 7, 10, 24, 27, 30, 35, 36, 46, 94, 101, 117, 129, 133, 142, 143, 147, 169–70, 177, 183, 186, 188, 189, 193–4, 195, 196, 221, 223–4. See also translocality /-ities

M

macro-sociological research, 71–2, 75, 80. *See also* comparative
Mauritius, 206
meaning adequacy, 194
methodological, xv, 3, 4, 11–3, 15, 24, 41, 43, 45, 49, 57, 67, 72, 75, 91, 94–5, 100–1, 111–2, 115, 117, 120, 132–3, 137, 166, 177, 201, 239, 243
  m. approach, 7, 9, 121, 169
  m. challenges, 4, 239
  m. ethnicism, 112, 123
  m. materialism, 11, 91, 93
  m. nationalism, xv, 1–5, 7, 10–2, 15, 29, 41–4, 47, 49, 57–8, 65–9, 72–4, 77–8, 81 83, 91–3, 101, 104, 111–3, 122–4, 129–32, 135, 146, 177, 198–203, 206, 210–1, 219, 221–3, 226, 229, 232–4, 239, 242–4
  m. problem, xv, 13, 45, 83, 132
  m. questions, 3, 9, 66
  m. stateism, 177, 199, 202–3, 205, 210
  m. strategy /-ies, 14, 69, 130, 134, 147
  m. transnationalism, 243

m. tool, 9, 14, 133, 148, 170, 242, 243
method, xv, 11–4, 27, 30, 31, 35, 41, 45, 60, 73, 82, 101, 114, 115, 118, 119, 121, 123, 134–5, 140, 163, 177–8, 182, 183, 187–8, 191, 194, 195, 235, 242
  comparative /-ison m. / m. of comparison, 13, 31, 57, 68, 176–7, 182, 187–8, 193–4, 196
  documentary m., 67, 72–3, 74–5
  experimental comparative m., 43, 50, 57, 182 (see also comparative)
  incorporating c. method, 13, 177, 194
migrant, 7, 10–1, 23, 25–36, 41–7, 49–53, 55–6, 57–9, 60, 65, 68, 70–4, 76–7, 78, 80, 82–3, 94, 121, 149, 201–2, 205, 210–1, 212, 241–2
  highly skilled m., 11, 32, 33, 67, 69, 72, 78, 82, 241
  m. groups / groups of m., 10–1, 32, 46, 242
  m. population 29, 51–2 (see also population)
  m. spouses, 79–80
  people / persons of m. background, 25, 28–9, 32–6
  transnational m., 6, 23, 28, 211, 233
migration
  colonial Indian m., 207
  forced m., 44–6, 58
  free m., 206, 207, 209, 210
  indentured m., 206, 208
  m. control, 207, 210, 213
  m. scholarship, 58, 203–4
  m. studies, 2, 4, 9, 15, 28, 44, 81, 82, 200 (see also studies; transnational)
  nationalization of m., 199, 204
  transnational m. studies (see transnational)
multicultural, 32, 33, 114, 227, 228

N

nation, xv, 1, 2, 7, 12–3, 23, 69, 91, 112, 138, 144, 155–6, 161–2, 164, 167–8, 169, 176–7, 182, 187, 198–9, 201, 202, 204, 211, 222, 230, 234
  n. and (the) (nation-)state, 2, 4, 9, 200, 201, 206, 211

n.-building, 5, 112, 144
n.-centered, 1, 2, 12, 13, 155, 161–2, 164, 167–8, 187
n. state, 2–5, 7, 9–11, 13, 23–5, 29, 35, 41–2, 65–9, 71–2, 76–83, 91, 93–4, 105, 107–8, 113, 130–1, 134, 146, 155–6, 158, 160–2, 164, 168, 176–7, 185–6, 189, 199–203, 210, 212–3, 219–24, 228–30, 233–5, 241
national, xv, 3–5, 7, 10–3, 15, 24, 27, 29–30, 32–6, 42–3, 49, 53–4, 58–9, 65, 68, 72, 76, 83, 91–3, 95, 101, 103–5, 107–8, 113, 122, 130–4, 136–47, 148, 155, 159, 163, 165, 180–2, 188, 191, 199–203, 205–6, 209, 211, 219–20, 223–4, 230–4, 239, 241, 243
  cross-n. comparison, 14, 231–4
  n. and/or (the) global, 23, 30, 107, 129, 131, 133, 145, 230 (see global and n.)
  n. borders, 25, 68, 72, 80, 130, 147 (see also border; cross-border)
  n. boundaries (see boundary /-ies)
  n. context, 11, 47, 67, 68, 71, 75, 77–80, 83, 143, 146, 182 (see also cross-n.)
  n. container, 13, 42, 94, 202, 222
  n. culture (see culture)
  n. group, 15, 46, 49, 53, 60
  n. history /-ies (see history /-ies)
  n. origin, 46, 49, 52, 53, 104
  n. paradigm, 155–7, 167, 169
  n. society /-ies, 7, 130, 141, 220–3, 226–230, 233–4
  n. sovereignty, 209–10. (see also state sovereignty)
  n. terms, 200, 203–6, 209, 211, 212
nationalism See methodological n
nationality, 41–4, 46, 48, 49, 52–4, 58–9, 201, 202, 204, 208, 210
  concept of n., 23, 202
nationalization, 6, 8, 13, 199–200, 204, 205
  inter-n. /intern., 219, 221–2, 223, 228, 229–30, 235
  n. of migration. See migration
  re-n., 229
  supra-n., 229
  trans-n. (see transnationalization)
nationhood, 13, 14, 199, 200, 204

negotiation, 106, 129, 131–4, 137, 144, 147, 148–9, 223, 226, 227
neoliberalism, 25, 27
network, 5, 7, 13, 25–7, 32, 34–5, 42, 49–50, 58, 68, 83, 95–7, 101–3, 106–7, 112, 114–5, 122, 130–1, 133, 136–7, 144–6, 201, 228, 230, 235, 242
  Actor-Network-Theory (*see* actor)
  cross-border n., 8, 146
  institutional n., 7, 106
  social n., 5, 25, 35, 60, 82, 223
  ethnic n., 32, 83
  transnational network, 6, 33, 34, 35, 80, 131, 133, 230

P
participant observation, 35, 115, 118, 119, 121, 123, 135
place-making, 7, 8, 25, 29, 51, 52
pluri-local, 66, 228, 230, 232, 233, 241
political culture. *See* culture
population, 5, 29, 32, 33, 44, 45–6, 49, 51, 52, 57, 59, 60, 70–1, 121–2, 135, 139, 141, 178, 181, 187, 203, 211, 220
  given p., 41, 43, 44, 47, 50, 59
  indigenous p., 129–30, 136–8, 143, 144
  migration p. (*see* migration)
  p. of migration, 65 (*see also* migrant)
positionality, 9, 30. *See also* cities
positivist epistemology, 41
postcolonial studies. *See* studies
problem-solving, 192, 193, 194, 196
  cross-place p., 192, 193, 194
  reiterated p., 196

Q
qualitative research method. *See* method

R
race, 42, 102, 106, 158, 199, 202, 208
reflexive /-ity, 9, 14, 15, 155, 183, 191, 193, 202, 222, 234, 243
  positional r., 9, 243
  theoretic r., 9, 14, 15
reformulation, 41, 44, 57–8, 131
refugee, 41, 44, 45–48, 51–52, 56, 57, 59, 60
  r. category / category of r. (*see* category)

relational concept of s., 169, 226, 228, 229
re-nationalization. *See* nationalization

S
Salvador(an), El, 43–49, 51, 55, 60, 181, 195
scale, 3, 5, 8, 10–1, 23, 27–8, 34, 42, 66–7, 70–1, 76–7, 81–3-2, 93–100, 107–8, 112, 115–6, 118, 124, 129–30, 132–3, 134–5, 137, 141, 143, 146, 169, 187–8, 206–7, 220
  geographic(al) s., 7, 24, 58, 100, 107–8
  global s., 34, 94, 98, 99, 107, 133, 204
  local s., 8, 94
  national s., 3, 15, 108, 143
  s. approaches, 3
  scope(s) and scale(s), 187, 188, 203
  social s., 99, 101
  socio-spatial s., 6, 12, 133, 143, 242
sequence, 181, 184, 190, 195–6
  event s., 184, 190, 195
  s. of change, 180, 181, 183
space, xv, 2–5, 7–10, 15, 26–30, 42, 44, 66, 82, 94, 98, 105–8, 114, 129–30, 132–3, 136, 138–9, 146–7, 155, 162–4, 169, 176, 185, 187, 195, 198–9, 201–4, 208, 219–36, 240, 242
  concept(s) of s., 14, 155–6, 163, 169, 219, 225–9, 234, 240
  geographic s. / geo-space, 42, 43, 221–7, 228, 229–30, 231
  relational concept of s. (*see* relational)
  social s., 66, 92, 131, 133, 143, 202, 203, 219, 221–2, 226–7, 229–30, 234, 236
  socio-geo-s., 227–30
  s.-time / s. and time, 116, 124, 163, 187, 226 (*see also* time-s.)
  substantial concept of s. (*see* substantial)
  time-s. / time and s., 23, 28, 41–2, 50, 176, 182, 184, 226 (*see also* s.-time)
  translocal s., 129, 131, 133, 137, 141–2, 146, 147, 148
  transnational s. approach, 134
  transnational s. space (*see* transnational)

understanding of s., 14, 163, 219, 225–9, 234
spatial turn, 163, 170, 219, 224
spatio-temporal analysis, 198–9
sociability /-ies, 28, 29, 30
social, xv, 3–5, 7, 9, 11, 13–5, 23–36, 42–4, 48–53, 55–6, 58–60, 68–70, 72, 77, 81–3, 91–7, 99–102, 106–8, 111–4, 116–8, 129, 131, 134, 138, 142, 145, 147–8, 155, 170, 176–7, 180–2, 184–9, 194–5, 199, 202, 211–2, 219–35, 241–2
  local s. (*see* local)
  s. anthropology, 1, 2, 11–2, 113
  s. boundary /-ies (*see* boundary /-ies)
  s. category /-ies, 48, 58
  s. context, 2, 8, 10, 11, 66, 67, 72, 230
  s. field, 25, 50, 132 (*see also* transnational s. field)
  s. inequality /-ies, 69, 140, 144, 220, 235
  s. life, 2, 25, 41–2, 50, 96, 124, 182, 222, 227
  s. network, (*see* network)
  s. phenomena. 66, 68, 69, 76, 81, 227
  s. process, 24–6, 41, 59, 111, 129, 219
  s. relation, 2, 7, 27, 29, 42, 50, 78, 91, 97, 101, 106, 177, 202, 221, 223, 225, 230, 233
  s. science, 2–4, 9, 14–5, 23, 26, 42, 60, 66, 68–70, 91, 96, 101, 113, 118, 120, 122, 124, 129, 131, 198, 219–20, 222–4, 226, 234, 243
  s. space (*see* space)
  s. theory, 5, 26, 30, 83, 235
  transnational s. field (*see* transnational)
  transnational s. space (*see* transnational)
state, 2–5, 13, 25–27, 33, 35, 47–8, 52, 59, 66, 77, 79–80, 91, 93, 95–6, 99, 102, 108, 112, 117, 121–2, 132–3, 137–9, 141, 143–4, 146–7, 158–9, 177–82, 184–88, 192, 195, 198–200, 202–213, 230, 234
  nation-s. (*see* nation)
  s. borders, 42, 201, 202, 205, 211, 212

s. sovereignty, 200, 205–11, 220. See *also* national
studies, xv, 2, 6, 8–11, 14, 30, 44–5, 57, 82, 91–3, 98–100, 157, 162, 164–5, 167–70, 196, 198, 224, 231, 236, 240–1
  case s. (*see* case)
  cross-border s., xv, 1–5, 7, 9, 14, 239–40, 242–3 (*see also* cross-border; border)
  cultural s., 2, 3, 27, 170, 199, 201, 203, 210, 212
  empirical s., 3, 6–10, 14, 15, 94, 96
  globalization s. (*see* globalization)
  international studies, 14, 219, 231, 233, 234, 240
  migration s., 2, 4, 9, 15, 28, 44, 81, 82, 200
  postcolonial s., 66, 97, 157, 170
  transnational migration s., 41, 42, 44, 199, 203, 211, 212
  transnational s. (*see* transnational)
  transnational s. approach, 14, 242
  urban s., 24, 26, 31
substantial concept of space, 225, 226, 228, 229

T

teamwork, 120–1
thinking, 24, 132, 164, 166, 176, 179, 198, 204, 207, 241
  binary t., 131, 242
  bounded t. 3–4, 14, 15
  container(-centered) t., 8, 10, 243–4
  historical t., 159, 163, 165–8
  static t., 5, 7
translocal, 133, 134, 135, 137 144, 148, 170
  t. space(s). (*see* space)
  t. social spaces, 143
translocality /-ities, 13, 24, 129–30, 133, 134, 170. See *also* locality
  t. approach, 13, 133, 134
transnational, xv, 1, 3, 6–7, 10–1, 13, 15, 23–32, 35, 41, 43, 46, 49–51, 81–2, 94–5, 97, 101, 105–7, 117, 123, 129, 131–2, 138, 155, 162–4, 168, 199–200, 202–3, 211, 213, 219, 224, 230–2, 234–5, 239, 241–3
  t. approach (*see* approach)
  t. engagement, 10, 41–3, 45, 47, 49–50, 56–7
  t. history /-ies (*see* history /-ies)

t. migrant, 6, 23, 28, 211, 233
t. migration, xv, 1, 44
t. migration studies, 41, 42, 44, 199, 203, 211, 212 (*see also* migration; studies)
t. network (*see* network)
t. field, 7, 8, 31, 231
t. phenomena, 72, 230, 236
t. processes, 24, 26–9, 34
t. relations, 7, 231, 235
t. social field, 5, 10, 23, 25, 26, 28, 30–2, 35, 41, 42–3, 50–1, 59, 70–1, 82, 131, 230
t. social space (*see* space)
t. social space, 202, 219, 227, 228, 230–1, 240
t. societal units, 235
t. space, xv, 7–8, 58, 66, 134, 147, 187–8
t. space approach, 134
t. studies, 1, 7, 14, 42, 58, 93, 210, 219, 224, 232, 233, 235, 240
t. turn, 131
transnationalism, 23, 41–2, 45, 60, 81, 112, 113, 203, 205, 211, 212, 219, 223–4, 231, 232, 243
transnationality, 23–32, 34–6, 95, 241 (*see also* cities, t. of)
transnationalization, 4, 5, 15, 71, 80, 94, 228, 230, 235
tribalism, 12, 112
types of violence. *See* violence.
types of dialogues. *See* dialogues

typologically situated case groups. *See* case

U
unit(s), 57, 113 115, 117, 133, 188, 201, 222–3, 226
  bounded u., 3, 8
  u. of analysis, 1, 2, 3, 4, 5–7, 9, 11–4, 15, 25, 42, 44, 46–7, 52, 58–9, 67, 132, 134, 177, 187, 189, 220, 231–3, 235, 239–42, 244
  u. of comparison, 189
  u. of reference, 222–3, 229, 231, 233, 234, 235

V
vernacularization, 12, 130, 135, 138
violence, 47–49, 53, 58, 136, 143
  experiences of v., 49, 57–8
  types of v., 59

W
Westphalia, Treaty of, 205, 207
Westfalica, Pax, 220. *See also* Westphalia, Treaty
world systems, 13, 14, 123, 160–1, 171, 188, 189, 195, 221, 226, 231–4, 240
  w. s. analysis, 232
  w. s. approaches, 14, 232
  w. s. research, 233–4
  w. s. studies, 240
  w. s. theory, 13, 44, 93, 232